Musical Metropolis

Los Angeles and the Creation of a Music Culture, 1880–1940

Kenneth H. Marcus

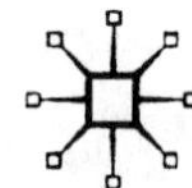

MUSICAL METROPOLIS

First published in 2004 by
PALGRAVE MACMILLAN™
175 Fifth Avenue, New York, N.Y. 10010 and
Houndmills, Basingstoke, Hampshire, England RG21 6XS
Companies and representatives throughout the world.

PALGRAVE MACMILLAN is the global academic imprint of the Palgrave Macmillan division of St. Martin's Press, LLC and of Palgrave Macmillan Ltd. Macmillan® is a registered trademark in the United States, United Kingdom and other countries. Palgrave is a registered trademark in the European Union and other countries.

ISBN 1–4039–6418–1 hardcover
ISBN 1–4039–6419–X paperback

Library of Congress Cataloging-in-Publication Data

Marcus, Kenneth H.
Musical Metropolis: Lost Angeles and the creation of a music culture, 1880–1940 / by Kenneth H. Marcus.
p. cm.
Includes bibliographical references (p.) and index.
ISBN 1–4039–6418–1 (alk. paper)—ISBN 1–4039–6419–X (pbk.: alk paper)
1. Music—California—Los Angeles—19th century—History and criticism. 2. Music—California–Los Angeles—20th century—History and criticism. 3. Music—Social aspects—California—Los Angeles. I. Title.

ML200.8.L7M37 2004
780'.9794'94—dc22 2004042843

A catalogue record for this book is available from the British Library.

Design by Newgen Imaging Systems (P) Ltd., Chennai, India.

First edition: December 2004

10 9 8 7 6 5 4 3 2 1

Printed in the United States of America.

To the memory of my mother
Laura Hearne Marcus
(1922–2003)

Contents

A CD containing musical selections discussed in this book can be found on the back cover.

List of Illustrations

List of Tables

List of Recordings

1. Rosa and Luisa Villa, "La Serenata" (1904)
2. Zoellner Quartet, Medley: "Dixie" and "Swanee River" (1915)
3. Kid Ory's Sunshine Orchestra, "Ory's Creole Trombone" (1922)
4. Margaret Messer Morris and Charles Wakefield Cadman, "At Dawning" (1922)
5. Charles Wakefield Cadman, piano solo, "Land of the Sky Blue Water" (1926)
6. Olga Steeb, Edward MacDowell's "Rigaudon, Op. 48/s" (1922)
7. Olga Steeb, Frederic Chopin's "Mazurka in B-flat, Op. 7" (1923)
8. Grauman's Symphony Orchestra, cond. by Ulderico Marcelli, Erno Rapée's "Echoes From the Iron Horse" (1925)
9. Aimée Semple McPherson, "I Ain't Gonna Grieve" (1926)
10. Don Clark Orchestra, with Bing Crosby and Al Rinker, "I've Got the Girl" (1926)
11. Los Angeles Philharmonic, cond. by Eugene Goossens, Antonin Dvorak's "Carnival Overture" (1928)
12. Percussion Ensemble, cond. by Nicolas Slonimsky, Edgard Varèse's "Ionisation" (1933)
13. RKO Studio Orchestra, cond. by Max Steiner, Vincent Youmans's "Carioca" from *Flying Down to Rio* (1933)
14. Lawrence Tibbett, Elinor Remick Warren's "Sweetgrass Range" (1935)
15. Johnny Green and male quartet, George Gershwin's "Bidin' My Time" (1937)
16. Arnold Schoenberg, Gershwin eulogy, Gershwin Memorial Broadcast (1937)
17. Bob Crosby and His Orchestra, "Panama" (1937)
18. WPA Los Angeles Federal Symphony, with Colored Chorus, cond. by William Grant Still, excerpts from "Lenox Avenue" (1938)
19. José Arias Troubadours, "El capotin" (1949)
20. José Arias Troubadours, "Cielito lindo" (1949)

Acknowledgments

Several institutions helped make this book possible. The Huntington Library granted two short-term fellowships in 2001 and 2002, the latter of which was as a John Randolph Haynes and Dora Haynes Foundation Fellow. The Historical Society of Southern California granted two Research Stipends through the Haynes Foundation, which enabled me to research archives at the Seaver Center for Western History Research, at Special Collections at the University of Southern California, and at the Huntington Library. The Faculty Research Committee at the University of La Verne provided a generous grant to cover the costs of photographs, copyright fees, and the production of the CD, as well as time off from teaching, for which I am very grateful.

I would like to thank four scholars in particular who gave me the benefit of their knowledge and wisdom. Gloria Lothrop's enthusiasm in Los Angeles studies is truly inspiring. She read through each chapter, sometimes multiple drafts, and her insightful suggestions greatly improved the manuscript and enriched this study beyond measure. Gloria first suggested I contact Lance Bowling, who is a tremendous source of knowledge about Los Angeles music and musicians. Lance read through and commented on all the chapters, and opened up his private archive of theater programs, photographs, and memorabilia, which revealed a wealth of detail without which this book would have been a lesser work. His wide experience in historical recordings made possible the production of the CD that accompanies the book.

John Koegel proved a highly valuable colleague. He was willing to read carefully through the drafts, writing meticulous notes on every page, and on numerous occasions even sending copies of related materials he had come across. I very much appreciate his sharing his great knowledge of music in the Southwest, and his helping me to avoid the traps that can befall a historian who steps into another field. Another musicologist, Bill Thomson, provided very useful suggestions after a thorough reading of the manuscript, corrected some errors, and for good measure revealed details of the Los Angeles jazz scene of the 1930s and '40s.

Several historians and musicologists read through one or more of these chapters, each sharing his or her particular area of expertise: Martin Ridge, Robert Dawidoff, Mike Engh, Bill Deverell, Laura Marcus, Hal Barron, Andrew Rolle, Mark Wild, Peter Blodgett, Catherine Parsons Smith, John and Lyn Pohlmann, Alan Marcus, and Dave Smith. I thank them all. The Los Angeles History Research Group provided much useful feedback on the book's first chapter, and the guidance of Mike Engh and Clark Davis made the group a delightful source of fellowship. I also presented ideas in this book at Robert Dawidoff's Thursday Forum at Claremont Graduate University; a Faculty Forum at the California State Polytechnic University, Pomona; and at a conference I organized on Community and Culture in Los Angeles at the University of La Verne. I further thank the students from my course, "Los Angeles: The Study of a City," for their input and suggestions.

Several individuals made unique contributions. My editor at Palgrave Macmillan, Brendan O'Malley, believed in this project and helped make it a reality. On the production side, both Donna Cherry and Theresa Lee proved highly beneficial in the final stretch.

I would like to thank those who shared their experiences with me, some of whom saw the events in these pages firsthand. They are Thomas Cassidy; David Raksin; José Arias Jr.; Glenarvon Behymer Jr.; Robert Kursinski; and Leni Boorstin.

For their efforts in facilitating archival materials or photographs, I thank Steve Lacoste at the Los Angeles Philharmonic Archives, Julio Rodriguez at the Music Center Archives, Dace Taube at Special Collections, University of Southern California, Phil Brigandi at the Ramona Pageant Association Archives, Dennis Bade at the Los Angeles Philharmonic Association, John Cahoon at the Seaver Center for Western History Research, Carol Merrill-Mirsky at the Hollywood Bowl Archives, Warren Sherk at the Margaret Herrick Library, Academy of Motion Picture Arts and Sciences, Kim Walters at the Southwest Museum Braun Research Library, and Marc Wanamaker at Bison Archives. I thank the staffs at the library of the University of La Verne, Honnold/Mudd Library, and the Huntington Library, especially Sue Hodson, Romaine Ahlstrom, Alan Jutzi, Cathy Cherbosque, Jean-Robert Durbin, and Erin Chase. I also thank Edward Mac from Mac Color Lab for the production of the illustrations.

My wife, Christine Ersig-Marcus, took time away from her own work and, as always, made very helpful comments on the chapters, and provided inspiration when I most needed it. She has been with this project from the beginning, and saw it through to the conclusion. The example she sets of parenting our little one, Davy, is a model of how a writer might go about tending to his or her subject: with love and devoted attention. While my mother did not live to see this work come to fruition, her influence is on every page. I dedicate this book to her.

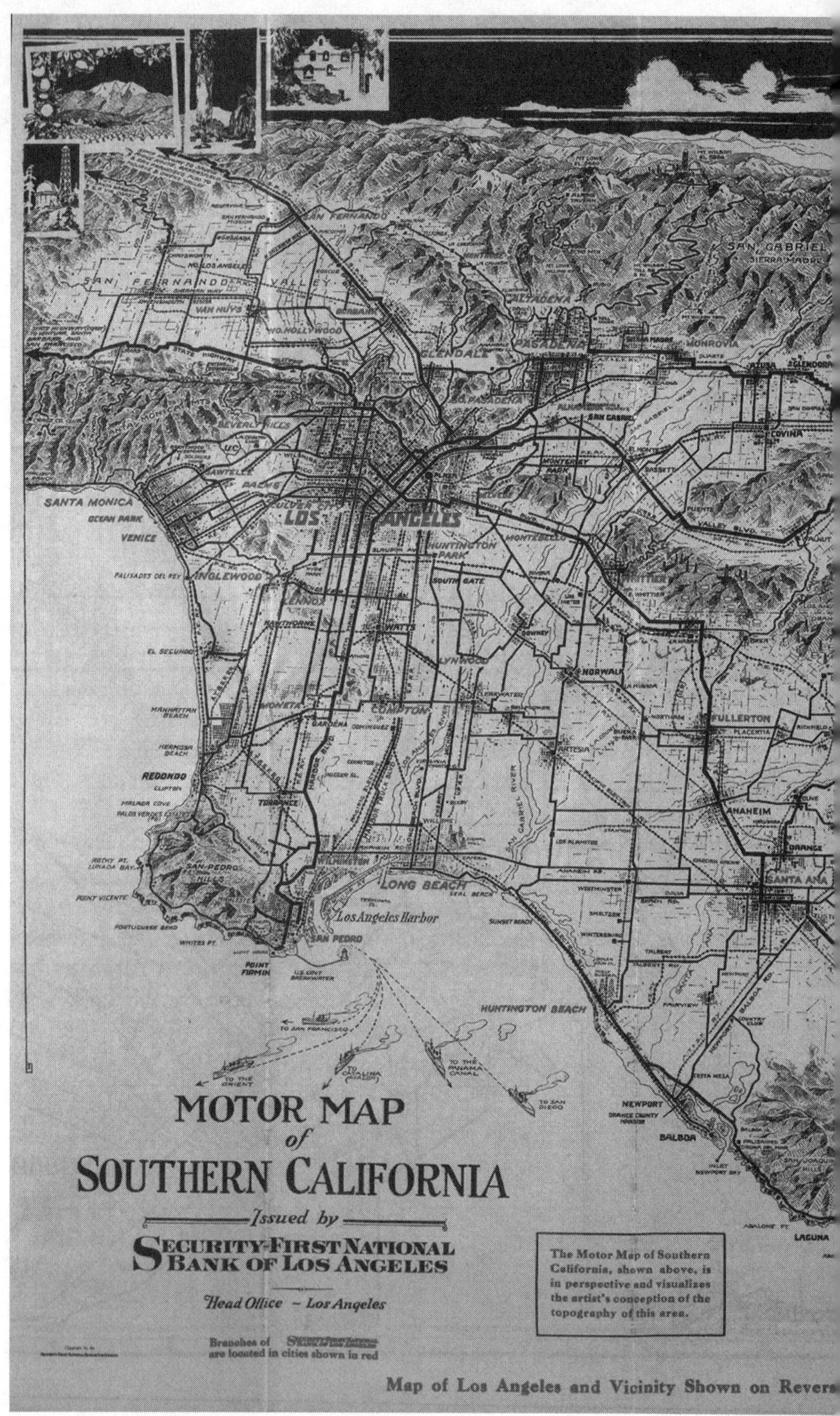

Southern California, ca. 1920

MOHAVE DESERT
BIG PINES RECREATION CAMP
SAN BERNARDINO MTS.
RIM OF THE WORLD 101 MILE DRIVE
ETIWANDA
HIGHLAND AVE
UPLAND
CUCAMONGA
RIALTO
SAN BERNARDINO
FONTANA
CLAREMONT
ONTARIO
COLTON AVE
BLOOMINGTON
COLTON
REDLANDS
MENTONE
LOMA LINDA
POMONA
SO. PAC. RY.
WINEVILLE
CHINO
HIGHGROVE
YUCAIPA VAL.
EL CASCO
RIVERSIDE
BEAUMONT
SAN BERNARDINO CO.
RIVERSIDE CO.
SHERMAN INSTITUTE
ARLINGTON
NORCO
MARCH FIELD
ALLESSANDRO
CORONA
VALVERDE
LAKEVIEW
SAN JACINTO
PERRIS
HEMET
WINCHESTER
SANTIAGO PK.
ELSINORE
LAKE ELSINORE
WILDOMAR
IRVINE
EL TORO
MURRIETA
MISSION SAN JUAN CAPISTRANO
TEMECULA
PACIFIC OCEAN

Introduction

When the Civic Bureau of Music and Art in Los Angeles published a brochure in 1929 titled *Culture and the Community*, its members waxed eloquent over the endless cultural amenities of the region.[1] The list was impressive, and ranged from painting and architecture to music and drama, leaving almost no field of the arts untouched. The message was clear: Los Angeles had become a major cultural metropolis. Writer Carey McWilliams criticized the brochure as mere fodder for tourists, stating that members of the Civic Bureau "will meet each incoming Southern Pacific train with stacks of 'Culture and the Community' to distribute along with 'Los Angeles: The White Spot of the Nation'."[2] Yet the Civic Bureau did have a point: The enormous diversity of achievements in expressive culture in Los Angeles over the past several decades was evidence that its residents had not been idle under the southern California sun.[3]

That Los Angeles had something to offer in the realm of the arts besides the film industry may have come as a surprise to some people, but not to the thousands of musicians and artists who worked in the many fields of cultural expression, nor to the far greater number of people who comprised the audiences. The existence of orchestras, choruses, pageant associations, dance ensembles, and similar groups seemed to cry out for recognition by fellow citizens in the Midwest and on the East Coast. Los Angeles may have seemed a cultural backwater to naysayers, but that was not the picture that city boosters wanted to project, nor was it the actuality, as the city's wide variety of cultural institutions would attest. As it grew into a major center of entertainment in the country, Los Angeles had also become a center for the performance of music.

The main argument of this book is that both diversity and decentralization characterized the music culture of Los Angeles between 1880 and 1940. "Music culture" entails a set of traditions and institutions that involved the production, performance, and teaching of music. This culture fully integrated classical and popular styles, a point I shall return to later. "Los Angeles" denotes the vast, metropolitan region within Los Angeles County. It eventually stretched from the San Fernando Valley in the northwest to Long Beach in the south, from Santa Monica in the west to Pomona in the east, an area that by the 1920s comprised some 4,083 square miles, or a space larger than the state of Connecticut.[4] Two transcontinental rail lines built during the nineteenth century led directly to a real estate boom and a dramatic increase in Los Angeles's population, from about 11,000 in 1880 to over 50,000 a decade later.[5] By World War II, Los Angeles had become a metropolis of international renown, with a population of 2.6 million people, one of the fastest-growing urban regions in the country.[6] This population explosion led to the growth of numerous cultural institutions, which included the creation of indoor and outdoor theaters, the formation of music education programs in schools and conservatories, and the rapid expansion of the recording, broadcasting, and film industries. Each of these institutions contributed to a thriving cultural life by the first half of the twentieth century, which seemed almost limitless in its prospects for growth.

We can consider the term "diversity" on several levels. Los Angeles's music culture had long been ethnically diverse. When a *pueblo* was founded on the site in 1781 by a group of Latinos, Native Americans, and African descendants from the Spanish colonial empire, the music of its inhabitants necessarily came from several different sources, such as the music of the Gabrieliño Indians, the Masses at the Spanish missions, and the *fandangos* and *jotas* from Spain and then Mexico. While the homes of large property-owners were common locations for musical performances, downtown theaters by the mid-nineteenth century catered to a large, Spanish-speaking population that benefited from touring companies, mainly from Mexico and Italy. Southern blacks who had migrated since the 1850s brought spirituals and a rich tradition of folk music, and the Chinese who worked on the railroads and settled in Los Angeles in the 1870s created theaters that provided music as well as drama. Japanese immigrants, too, who came to outnumber the Chinese by the turn of the century, brought with them a tradition of music and dance. Despite the enormous changes in the region's demographics during the second half of the nineteenth century, with a shift toward a predominantly Euro-American population, Mexican Americans, African Americans, and Asian Americans continued to have a role in the region's music culture.

Ethnicity also includes different shades of "whiteness." The ethnic groups of migrant Anglos to Los Angeles included Germans, English, Italians, and Jews, to name but a few. If we are to believe the results by the Americanization Committee of the Los Angeles District and California Federation of Women's Clubs, then by 1921 at least 27 different European countries were represented within the boundaries of the City of Los Angeles alone; in addition, there were Arabs, Chinese, Japanese, and Hindus.[7] Even allowing for exaggeration in estimates, there is little doubt that recent migrants brought with them many different cultural traditions and practices, and these traditions found expression in the city's music.[8]

Diversity also includes gender. Women were active in all levels of cultural endeavor, whether as performers, philanthropists, or audience members. They participated as teachers, as composers, and as organizers of concerts, and were adamant in seeking to improve the artistic offerings available to Angelenos. There was very much a sense of Los Angeles as a kind of new Eden or Zion, in part a result of the Progressive movement in America, which sought to improve the social, political, and economic structures of the country during a period of almost unprecedented immigration. With the population explosion in Los Angeles during the late nineteenth and early twentieth centuries, women became deeply involved in transforming the city's expressive culture.

The involvement of children and adolescents broadens our notion of diversity still further. When theater audiences became more diverse at the end of the nineteenth century in terms of both age and class, young people as well as women formed a significant proportion of those audiences, and they also took part in theatrical productions. Similarly, the purpose of music education programs was not merely to foster an appreciation of song and dance, but to enable children to take part in musical performances from kindergarten through high school. From the organization of youth concerts, to the growth of music schools and conservatories, to the widespread use of books and records on music appreciation, young people had numerous opportunities to study and perform music.

Finally, the notion of diversity includes what we could call "media diversity," the performance and production of music in recordings, on radio, and in film. These media proved increasingly important in Los Angeles as it grew into an epicenter of entertainment in America. While New York was the main recording hub during much of the early twentieth century, there were efforts in Los Angeles to record artists in a variety of fields that included indigenous, classical, and popular music. Much as in other regions of the country, early radio comprised a broad range of programming, and typically included an eclectic mix of both classical and popular styles, since few stations specialized in any particular type of music before 1940. This musical eclecticism further characterized the film scores produced by the region's eight largest film studios, each of which by the 1930s had a music department and a full orchestra.

As with diversity, decentralization was an important aspect to the music culture of Los Angeles. Orchestras, choral groups, and pageant associations existed throughout the Southland, and because the central city did not dominate music culture as in the East, a great diversification of music experience emerged in the communities of greater Los Angeles. In other words, what was playing downtown was not necessarily what was playing in Pomona. The geographic dispersal of the region's inhabitants, made possible by the automobile and the electric rail line, directly affected both the production and performance of music.

The development of a decentralized music culture in Los Angeles was fully in keeping with the city's own urban development. Developers and urban planners envisioned a city that represented a new kind of metropolis, one that in many ways differed from the cities in the Midwest and on the East Coast. Contrary to some descriptions of Los Angeles as merely a collection of suburbs, it became truly a "center city surrounded by many satellite sub-center cities and communities," according to the Los Angeles County Board of Supervisors in 1922.[9] Downtown provided the nucleus, which had expanded from a 12-block area with its center on Main Street between Temple and Fourth Streets, to a district of over 60 square blocks.[10] This nucleus then radiated out to communities that were relatively independent and self-contained. As a result, Angelenos "actively promoted the planned dispersion of people along with business, industry, and retail activities at the same time as they supported the development of a central business district equal to those in other major cities."[11]

The decentralized layout of the metropolis was one outcome of the movement of charter reform, which called for a diffusion of authority in city government since the late-nineteenth century. Los Angeles voters approved the Charter of 1889 that was a mandate for home rule by citizens, not legislators, and formed part of what political scientist Eric Schockman refers to as a "democratization of municipal affairs." Over the ensuing decades, seeking to avoid the political machines and endemic corruption that existed in Chicago, New York, and other American metropolises, progressive voters then approved the Charter of 1925, which called for further dispersion of political power by the city government. While the ultimate result of this charter did not necessarily lead to a better form of governance or the avoidance of corruption, the significant point here is that citizens both desired and sought to establish a different kind of model than they had known elsewhere: one that they believed to be more decentralized, and hence more democratic, in political and economic decision making.[12]

Just as the idea of creating a different type of model city has long inspired Angelenos, so have scholars in modern times searched for a new model to explain Los Angeles history. In a book review essay, historian Phil Ethington decried the hyperbole that accompanied much recent scholarship on Los Angeles.[13] The main problem with this scholarship, Ethington argued, is that it is based predominantly on post-World War II events, with considerable attempts to confer special status on Los Angeles yet with little effort to ground those analyses in archival study. Thus in their interest of establishing an "L.A. School" of urban studies, some scholars are prone to overlook the historical foundations of the city's cultural and civic development. Historian Bill Deverell has made a similar claim, calling on scholars to grapple with the history of the nineteenth and early twentieth centuries as a way of basing Los Angeles studies thoroughly on archival evidence.[14]

What might a study of the city's music have to do with an understanding of its history? I argue in this book that there is much in Los Angeles music that is unique or different, but that there is also much during this period that is in common with, or contiguous upon, inherited cultural traditions from the East Coast, the South, and the Midwest, as well as from Mexico and Europe. Many migrants came to Los Angeles to create a new life, as immigrants have long done, but they did not leave their past behind them. In studying cultural traditions in Los Angeles during and after the massive growth in its population, one thing becomes clear: There was at least as much continuity in that musical expression as there was the creation of new forms.

Thousands of migrants came to Los Angeles with a passionate interest in expressing themselves through music, and far more wanted to be witnesses to that cultural expression. Why? What was it about the city's music that attracted so many people over such a long period of time? What does the creation of a great variety of musical institutions tell us about the strong interest in community participation that existed in Los Angeles before World War II? While only a limited number of people were actually musicians, an almost endless number of people wanted to attend concerts, plays, pageants, and similar events. What does the enormous popularity in these events tell us about Los Angeles as a cultural center of the West?

There is something going on here besides mere entertainment, and I believe it can contribute to our understanding of the identity of Los Angeles itself. One subject with which any writer on southern California history must reckon is myth-making. Carey McWilliams, who attacked southern Californian myths with all the tools he could muster, asserted that in "the 'eighties it began to be said that Southern Californians 'irrigate, cultivate, and exaggerate.' "[15] One aspect of that exaggeration was the legend of the Californios, who represented to newly transplanted Anglos a romantic notion of the West. In those days, goes the myth, people lived a happy, simple life on the rancho, filled with music and merriment. Historian Glenn Gendzel has argued that recent migrants "invented founding myths for their communities in order to endow wondering, polyglot populations with unity, stability, and identity." Gendzel points out, however, that there is no "monolithic, racially defined white western narrative," but rather a narrative mosaic that inherited multiple cultural and ethnic influences.[16]

As a quintessentially western city that embodied that myth, yet which at the same time is utterly singular in western history, Los Angeles has had more than its share of creative imaginings. When city merchants organized the Fiesta de Los Angeles each year during the late 1890s, they were appropriating elements of an idealized Mexican past while seeking to establish hegemony over the region's history in their creation of a collective sense of civic unity. The Fiestas were immensely popular assemblies that eventually led to the creation of several pageants that played on similar themes. In upholding a booster view of the city's past, the borrowing of music from the ranchero was as much a part of creating that myth as was the procession of flowered cars that rode down the city's streets.

The presence of Hollywood has had much to do with the creation of myth. Even through the Depression, millions of Americans came together in a weekly ritual of movie theater attendance, expressing their communal appreciation for a medium that in essence represented a combination of drama and music. The musical themes that accompany Scarlett O'Hara's walk across Tara, or that follow King Kong as he scales the heights, or that rush to support Robin Hood as he slings arrows at the soldiers of the sheriff of Nottingham, are all essential aural elements of a visual tale. That thousands of Los Angeles musicians over the years benefited from Americans' love of myth-making is an essential part of the city's music culture. If Hollywood is a dream factory, then Los Angeles musicians played an essential role in the production of those dreams.

It is no myth, however, that a vital part of the city's culture and economy became (and remains) the entertainment industry, and music is vital to that industry. Whether in the theaters, or in recordings, radio, or film, musicians received gainful and often highly lucrative employment, and much of that music went out across the country and then the industrialized world in the form of film and records. Tourism was part of that industry, too, and drew a growing number of people to the region. There needed to be productions to attract tourists as well as inhabitants, just as there were many attractions of the physical environment that drew people to southern California. Cultural institutions such as vaudeville and movie theaters, the Hollywood Bowl, and music schools became a part of the built environment, and so became a part of the history of the region.

It is surprising, therefore, that no historian to my knowledge has studied music in Los Angeles in any depth. Of all the fields I will discuss here, only film music has received much attention by scholars. Yet even in this field there is a problem that is revealing: Most scholarship on film music seems to exist apart from the study of Los Angeles, almost as if Hollywood, to borrow a phrase, were an "island on the land."[17] To some extent that is true, but it was also vital to the music culture of Los Angeles, and so needs to be studied in relation to the city's history. Perhaps it is the nature of the subject of music itself that has led to its avoidance among historians, that scholars feel they lack the technical expertise to discuss with any precision the music that was so much a part of the region's history. Popular music, such as jazz, has received some attention, yet a discussion of classical or art music has rarely appeared in the literature. While not trained as a musicologist, I have long studied and performed music, and I have tried to combine the disciplines of music and history so that the study may be of value to historians as well as musicologists. If there is merit to this endeavor, it owes much to the benefit and counsel of specialists in the field, and the value of their work should be clear in the footnotes.

There are three musicologists in particular who have contributed much to the study of music in Los Angeles, and they have all sought to place that music in its historical context. Robert Stevenson pioneered the field in his research on both Euro-American and Latino music traditions, mainly during the eighteenth and nineteenth centuries. During the 1980s he founded a journal, the *Inter-American Music Review*, which provided a forum for many of his articles and for younger scholars to make tentative efforts in a little-known field.[18] His descriptions of orchestral institutions in the Southwest, for example, such as the Los Angeles Philharmonic and the San Diego Symphony, reveal both the large number of highly trained musicians in southern California by the early twentieth century and the degree to which philanthropists wanted to create cultural institutions of renown.[19] His research was carefully grounded on archival evidence, and he provided a model for future scholars who followed.

Catherine Parsons Smith has written numerous articles and co-authored two books on the field of art music in Los Angeles, especially the contributions of women and African Americans. She illustrated the lives of two composers in particular: Mary Carr Moore, who wrote operas, chamber music, and choral music as well as taught music theory, and William Grant Still, who moved to Los Angeles in 1930 and joined the "Los Angeles Renaissance" that was the West Coast version of the Harlem Renaissance of the 1920s.[20] Like Moore, Still had a passionate interest in opera, and he wrote both orchestral and choral music as well as at least one film score, for Frank Capra's 1945 film, *Lost Horizon*. In addition to her work on Moore and Still, Smith has written on subjects as diverse as the founding of the Hollywood Bowl, the People's Orchestra that formed in 1913, and pageantry.[21] Like Stevenson, she scoured Los Angeles libraries and archives for her research, and amassed a deep and enviable knowledge of the city's musical development.

The third scholar is John Koegel, who specializes in Mexican American music of the Southwest during the nineteenth century. Koegel's doctoral dissertation was the first in-depth analysis of the Charles F. Lummis recordings of Mexican American musicians, and he continued this research with two more articles on the recordings and their value to musicologists, historians, and anthropologists alike.[22] His analysis of the career of Mexican guitarist and teacher Miguel Arévalo revealed the extent to which Latino musicians in Los Angeles worked together with Anglo musicians, and Koegel explored the vibrant theatrical life of Los Angeles, when the community was still predominantly Spanish-speaking.[23] Like Stevenson and Smith, Koegel based his conclusions on careful analysis of both historical and musical documents, and he has proven to be a valuable guide in understanding trends of Los Angeles music scholarship.

The work of these musicologists has contributed enormously to this study, as has the work of a quite different scholar of American expressive culture, Lawrence Levine. Levine remains one of the few historians to deal seriously with the subject of music. In one book, based on the William E. Massey Sr. Lectures in the History of American Civilization that he gave at Harvard University in 1986, he developed the concept of what he called a "sacralization of culture." Levine proposed that during the nineteenth and early twentieth centuries, aspects of the country's expressive culture that had been popular had become "sacralized" or revered by the country's citizens in a process of forming a hierarchy of class separation. Thus, plays by Shakespeare, operas by Verdi, and symphonies by Beethoven were placed on pedestals as "high" art in a process of cultural deification.

This development, Levine argues, left a permanent mark on our understanding of "high" and "low" art. A combination of music critics, art patrons, and upper-class society mavens directly affected how Americans viewed their own culture. As a result, Americans lost "a rich shared public culture that once characterized the United States," and in its place, "institutions of high culture attempted to create and exercise cultural authority."[24] While Levine based his thesis primarily on the examples of Boston, New York, and Chicago, it is applicable to the West, with some modifications. As Levine is quick to argue, the rigid hierarchies of "highbrow" and "lowbrow" are not sufficient to describe the enormous variety of the country's culture. He cites sociologist Paul DiMaggio, who delineates "historically evolved systems of classification" to help explain why boundaries between different forms of culture, whether "high" or "low," have been in almost constant flux.[25] Thus while not avoiding these terms, Levine suggests, we need to adopt a more flexible model in seeking to describe forms of expressive culture.

Levine's argument, however, goes deeper than this. It was not only the perception of forms of expressive culture that changed, but the behavior of audiences. The taming or disciplining of audiences was essential to this process of sacralization, such as by printing expectations of behavior in concert programs, or lecturing audiences outright on how they should act in concert halls, museums, or landscaped parks. It was no longer acceptable for people to shout, talk indiscriminately, or otherwise act in a way that would disturb others from enjoying forms of high art. When Frederick Law Olmsted sought to change the public's use of open space in New York's Central Park, he referred to the "ruffianism and disorder" of the city's population that the Park Commission had to overcome.[26] While his son, Frederick Law Olmsted Jr., was less successful in ushering in a similar approach to open spaces in Los Angeles, Olmsted Sr.'s point was clear. Only with mutually accepted modes of discipline could the modern notion of a shared public space be truly achieved.

Levine's thesis has proven of great interest to other scholars in a range of fields, from musicology, to film and American cultural studies. One musicologist who answered Levine's call to pursue similar lines of research was Joseph Horowitz, who applied the sacralization thesis in his study of Wagnerism in America. "Only with Lawrence Levine's *Highbrow/Lowbrow: The Emergence of Cultural Hierarchy in America*," Horowitz claims, "have our historians begun to appreciate what kind of music American orchestras and opera companies were making before 1900."[27] While he criticized Levine's exaggeration of control that elites had in opera houses and similar institutions, Horowitz further applied the sacralization thesis in his discussion of how the modern American public had access to high art. He particularly emphasized the "culture gods" during the twentieth century, such as Italian conductor Arturo Toscanini, who served as symbols of elite or highbrow culture during a time when the United States was struggling to establish its own cultural identity.[28] Horowitz asserted that the *popularization* of "sacralized classical music" occurred when middle-class inhabitants of eastern and midwestern cities increasingly attended classical music concerts, and could hear the works of the "great masters" in recordings and radio.[29]

I argue that a similar process was at work in Los Angeles, but with some important differences that distinguished the city's unique music culture. While citizens established elite cultural institutions such as symphony orchestras and opera troupes as in other major cities, much as Levine has suggested, a parallel process of what we could call a "desacralization of culture" occurred at the same time. People across ethnic, class, and gender lines had access to forms of high culture since the late-nineteenth century, in indoor and outdoor theaters, in schools, in pageantry and plays, and from the media of recording, radio, and film. The great variety of cultural institutions in Los Angeles created a kind of musical synergy in which, I suggest, there was substantial interaction between musicians and artists who worked in the fields of high and low art, and they sought to transcend these categories in order to reach a wider public. This desacralization of culture, or its popularization, was critical to the production, performance, and teaching of music in Los Angeles.

The first chapter of this book discusses theater music during the late-nineteenth century, the "boom years" in terms of population growth and economic development, when theaters were the main venues for musical entertainment. There was much popular music available to theater-goers, such as vaudeville and operetta, which traveling companies and local musicians performed. Audiences also had access to opera and symphonic works during a time when men and women musicians founded the city's first symphony orchestras. In the second chapter I consider the role of music education in public schools and conservatories. By the turn of the century, almost five hundred music teachers had relocated to Los Angeles, many of whom were women, and the city became a center of music education in the West. There were several ways in which children and young adults could learn about music, such as by attending and participating in youth concerts, and these music programs appealed to children across race and class. Integral to this movement was the involvement of progressive reformers who saw music as a means of social integration and Americanization in the city's schools and on its playgrounds.

The third and fourth chapters analyze the uses of outdoor theater, which proved very popular in the temperate climate of southern California. One reason for the appeal of the Hollywood Bowl was precisely its environment: the romantic atmosphere of listening to music under the stars. The Bowl also provided a forum for various ethnic groups to perform, from African American choirs to Native American ceremonial dancers, and thus represented one of the leading cultural institutions that brought together diverse segments of Los Angeles's population. Outdoor theater also thrived with pageantry, which united the disciplines of music, dance, and drama, and encouraged community participation in the arts as a means of transforming the very notion of modern theater. Two pageants in particular, the Mission Play and the Ramona Pageant, claimed historical authenticity in showing the interaction between Californios, Anglos, and Indians during a time when many Angelenos were searching for historical roots. The Mexican Players, a dramatic troupe that formed in the 1930s, also blended music with dance in their portrayals of Latino culture and history.

The fifth, sixth, and seventh chapters deal with music in the media of recording, radio, and film, respectively. The cylinder collection of Charles Lummis comprises some of the first recordings of Indian and Latino performers in the West, which Lummis used to publicize the culture of the Southwest and gain members for the newly formed Southwest Society. Impresario and tenor Andrae Nordskog made several pioneering recordings in jazz, dance, and art music before Los Angeles became a national center for recording with the growth of the swing movement in the 1930s. The growth of two musicians unions, one for whites, the other for blacks, was notable in a city that was renowned for being anti-union. Radio stations enabled artists to greatly expand their audience base, and the broadcasts of the Los Angeles Philharmonic were part of a national trend: Radio audiences prior to World War II regularly tuned in to classical music. In the medium of film, the blending of classical and popular music was especially common. Highly-trained musicians were essential in staffing and running the music departments of the Hollywood studios, and composers created the symphonic score that defined most American film music from the 1930s through the 1950s. Cartoons provided further opportunities to popularize classical music, at times juxtaposed with jazz and folk songs, in a blending of music with humor.

The music culture of Los Angeles was both diverse and highly decentralized, because it reflected the region's social and physical environment. A study of music in Los Angeles is thus a study of identity, and basic to that identity is its reputation as an epicenter of entertainment in America. Because music became an important part of the entertainment industry, an understanding of how Los Angeles's music culture developed seems essential to understanding the city's development as a modern metropolis. While I do not propose to have set forth all the answers, I do hope to have opened a few doors.

1

Theater Music During the Boom Years

Theaters were at the center of musical life in late-nineteenth century Los Angeles. They were numerous; concert halls were few. Theater records, such as programs of plays and concerts, suggest that Los Angeles had an abundance of music and drama long before it had become the nation's epicenter of entertainment. Two things are evident from these early records and the corresponding reviews in local newspapers. First, theater owners sought to satisfy the tastes of a diverse public by offering a wide variety of works, from vaudeville and burlesque to plays and operettas. Second, large numbers of people, rather than an elite few, had opportunities to hear art music, mainly in the form of symphonies and opera. Nineteenth-century America had a flourishing musical life in its urban centers, and Los Angeles was no exception.

The arts, such as music and drama, proved to a growing public that Los Angeles was now "civilized." A sure enticement to residents on the East Coast and the Midwest was not merely good hotels, restaurants, running water and bathrooms, but also different kinds of entertainment. The city had no museum, which prompted one inhabitant to duly note that "[i]t has been stated that Los Angeles is the only city of its size not supporting a museum. A well appointed musee [*sic*] of instruction and art would be most welcome, but better none at all than one of the ten-cent-just-step-inside order."[1] But there were theaters. By the 1880s and 1890s, several major venues could vie with those in San Francisco and San Diego, not only in the quality of performances but also in terms of the interiors of the theaters themselves. A comment by one patron at the time was apt; with the opening of a new theater, the city had become "quite metropolitan, to be sure."[2]

The ease of rail transport enabled performers to come out West. A branch of the Southern Pacific arrived in Los Angeles in 1876, making the city one of the main terminals on the West Coast.[3] With the building of a second transcontinental railroad by the Santa Fe railroad company in 1885, a rate-war ensued that benefited farmers and brought thousands of migrants to Los Angeles.[4] City promoters and companies sought with remarkable success to

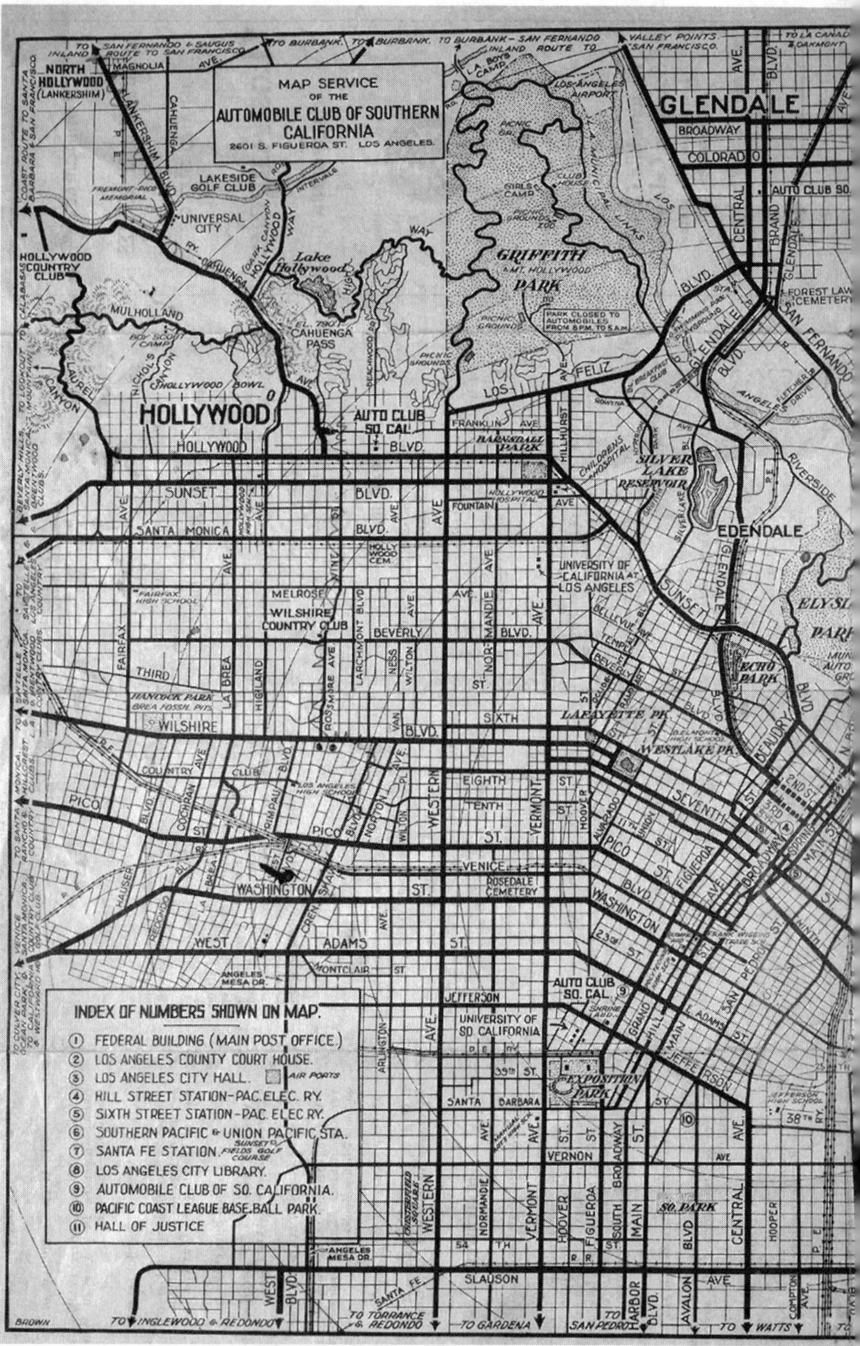

Figure 1.1 Los Angeles, ca. 1920

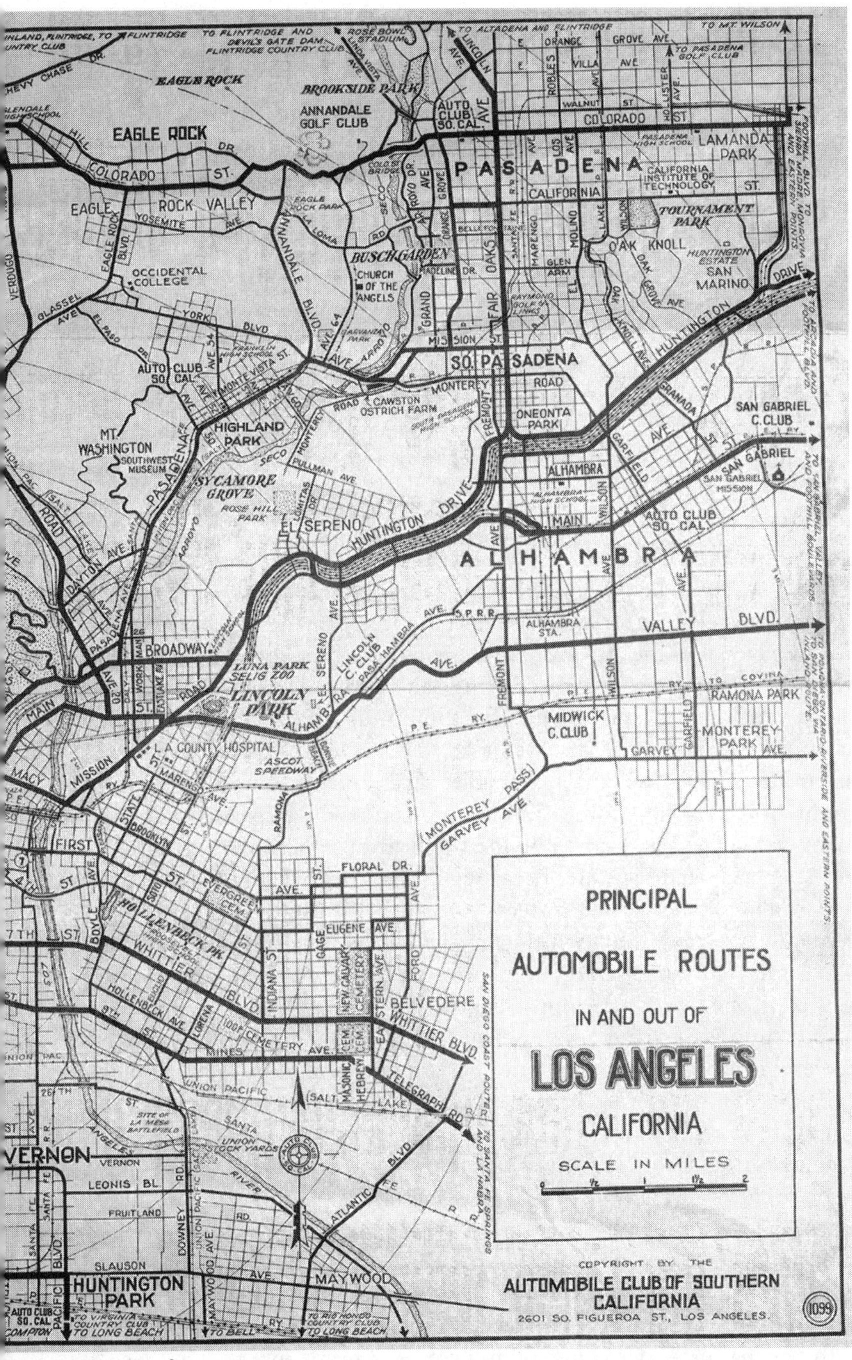
PRINCIPAL
AUTOMOBILE ROUTES
IN AND OUT OF
LOS ANGELES
CALIFORNIA
SCALE IN MILES
COPYRIGHT BY THE
AUTOMOBILE CLUB OF SOUTHERN CALIFORNIA
2601 SO. FIGUEROA ST., LOS ANGELES.
1099
PASADENA
ALHAMBRA
EAGLE ROCK
HIGHLAND PARK
SO. PASADENA
HUNTINGTON PARK
VERNON
MAYWOOD
BELVEDERE
LINCOLN PARK
SAN MARINO
LAMANDA PARK
SAN GABRIEL
EL SERENO
HUNTINGTON DRIVE
VALLEY BLVD.

lure people to what had been a remote area, which boosters now celebrated as the land of blue skies and endless orange groves. The management of the Southern Pacific railway had an abiding interest in bringing people to the region and took out a full page advertisement on the front cover of the programs of a local theater. Each advertisement featured a different view from a railroad car window, often with the caption: "Scene on the Southern California Railway, the Tourists' Favorite Line."[5]

These developments were not inevitable. Los Angeles had long vied with San Diego as the economic center of southern California. East Coast bankers, in fact, favored San Diego for the western railway terminal, mainly due to its fine harbor. The Civil War intervened, however, and by the 1870s businessmen focused increasingly on Los Angeles as a prime location. Ironically, merchants in San Francisco helped the cause of Los Angeles because they saw the city as a lesser threat. Unlike San Diego, Los Angeles had no harbor, so it would be much weaker in competing with San Francisco importers and exporters.[6]

To ease Los Angeles away from its previous lawless image, a paid, professional police force formed in 1879, and a year later, Main Street became the first street of the city to be paved. Telephones and electric lights were in operation by 1882, and electric streetcars replaced horse-drawn lines by 1890.[7] As newcomers arrived and the city grew, more and more businesses developed in the downtown area along Second, Spring, and Main Streets. Los Angeles experienced a major real estate boom, and thousands of people sought to buy new lots in the rush to get rich. Historian Glenn Dumke asserted that the optimism in the region "was unquenchable. Business found itself stimulated by the reduction in freight rates due to the Santa Fe's arrival, and buying enthusiasm was kept at high pitch by the publication of simmering statistics in the newspapers." Further, news items regularly reported "the formation of new land companies, irrigation enterprises, and real estate firms of which there were an estimated 2,300 within the city limits."[8] While the real estate boom had largely subsided by 1888, the growth in the city's population and businesses continued with amazing strength.

A regular supply of water was essential to this continued development. Los Angeles had two main sources: the Los Angeles and San Gabriel Rivers. The unreliability of these rivers, however, had prompted efforts as early as 1859 to pipe in more water, and a physician from Kentucky, Oliver M. Wozencraft, sought to make the Colorado River the main source. As "California's first important prophet of water," he proposed using the river to irrigate the desert Southwest. That dream would take almost a half-century to realize and cost millions of dollars and much manpower to fulfill.[9] The subsequent digging of wells and the construction of reservoirs enabled developers to create subdivisions that led directly to the decentralized, physical layout of Los Angeles.[10]

With the availability of electricity and water, and an increasingly viable system of transportation, Los Angeles experienced extraordinary growth during the decade of the 1880s. It grew from a population of 11,183 inhabitants in 1880 to over 50,000 by the end of the decade.[11] From a simple pueblo, with dirt streets, adobe or wooden houses, and small, brick buildings, it grew to a community of paved streets with a bustling city center. The immigrant population approached up to two hundred thousand during the 1880s alone.[12] As a haven for tourists, Los Angeles rivaled San Francisco, which was no longer the only city of renown in the West.

The Theaters

Several theaters existed in Los Angeles even before the boom years of the 1880s. These venues catered directly to the city's Latino inhabitants, far more than was the case in San Francisco. One of the first theaters, Sánchez Hall, was built in the early 1840s near Los Angeles Plaza. According to one visitor, it was "painted out in the most comical style with priests, bishops, saints, horses and other animals—the effect is really astonishing."[13] Another early venue was Stearns's Hall, which the real estate developer and cattle baron Don Abel Stearns built on Los Angeles Street in 1858 and formed part of his adobe residence, "El Palacio." Two groups who appeared there were the six-member California Minstrels, who performed comedy with violin accompaniment, and the Isidoro Máiquez Company from Mexico, which featured music in its plays.[14]

The founding of three more theaters marked a growing interest in the arts. Not long after the opening of Stearns's Hall, a local merchant, John Temple, built his own theater, which formed part of a multipurpose edifice that mainly consisted of the city hall, courthouse, and city market. Located on the second floor of the building, the theater was both small and poorly ventilated, but it did have armchairs and raised benches. By contrast, a strong rival to the Temple Theater was the Merced Theater, or Teatro Mercéd, built adjacent to Pico House in December 1870. It could seat 400 people, was 90 feet long and about 37 feet wide, and had four boxes near the stage, with curtains of red plush and gold fringe. The theater's acoustics were unimpressive, however, and even after a new owner, J. H. Wood, took the theater over in 1876, it closed two years later.[15] Somewhat more inviting was the Turnverein Hall ("Gymnastics Club Hall"), which the city's German immigrants opened in September 1872.[16] It consisted of a two-story, wooden-framed structure in what was increasingly becoming a thriving downtown area, on Spring Street between Third and Fourth Streets. The venue was 50 feet long and 26 feet wide and, while smaller than the Merced, its seating capacity also was 400 people. With better acoustics than its predecessors, the hall immediately became the city's main site for music performances by such nationally-known artists as violinist Ole Bull and opera diva Madame Inez Fabbri.

Still, Angelenos were not satisfied. In 1881, the editor for the *Los Angeles Times* compiled a list of "What the *Times* Would Like to See." Heading that list was "a first-class theater." The following year, a local drama critic noted that "Los Angeles would support a good troupe if there was a suitable theatre in

Figure 1.2 Main Street and Second, with Grand Opera House on right, ca. 1889

Figure 1.3 Hazard's Pavilion exterior view

this city."[17] Similarly, one resident of Los Angeles, Clara Brown, wrote as late as 1883 that "Temple theatre is not a structure to be proud of, and the theater . . . nothing more nor less than Turnverein Hall, is so inferior that good troupes do not often visit the city. Los Angeles claims a population of more than 20,000 now . . . and it seems as if such an aspiring place ought to build and support a first-class place of amusement."[18] Within a year she would see her wish become a reality.

The creation of three new venues changed the music culture of Los Angeles: the Grand Opera House, Hazard's Pavilion, and the Los Angeles Theatre. With the opening of the Grand Opera House on May 24, 1884, Angelenos at last had a theater of which they could be proud.[19] This huge venue was replete with modern conveniences such as electric lighting—an enormous advantage over gas, which could quickly make a room hot and stuffy. There were also a number of safety features that impressed patrons, including the installation of fire hydrants. According to one description, "the facilities for rapid exit consist of forty two feet of doorways. In addition there are twenty-five windows, one tier on the ground floor, and one on the balcony floor." The impresario Lynden Behymer later wrote that the Grand Opera House was "the one theater in Los Angeles whose acoustics are perfect; and there is not a seat in the house from which one does not have a full view of the stage." Moreover, the rows of the theater were "placed far enough apart so they may be passed between with comfort."[20] For good measure, owner Ozro W. Childs later added a gallery, a hall near the entrance, and new seats downstairs to attract more customers.[21]

Hazard's Pavilion was another important venue, located downtown at the northeast corner of Fifth and Olive Streets. Mayor Henry T. Hazard and an associate, George H. Pike, built the wooden hall in 1886 to serve a variety of purposes.[22] Its seating capacity of 4,000 made it larger by far than the Grand Opera House in San Francisco (2,020 seats), and Hazard's Pavilion soon became the preferred site for religious revivals, speaking engagements, boxing matches, and other popular events that attracted immense crowds. Despite the impressive size of the venue (120 × 166 feet), however, its acoustics were unremarkable. The Temple Baptist Church purchased the site in 1905 and razed the structure to build the Temple Auditorium the following year. Its owners later renamed it the Philharmonic Auditorium, once it became the home of the Los Angeles Philharmonic Orchestra.[23]

By contrast, the Los Angeles Theatre, which opened on December 17, 1888, represented a landmark in elegance.[24] It was smaller than Hazard's Pavilion, but far more luxurious in terms of the sheer quality of the interior. A contemporary writer stated that on either side of the stage, which was 40 × 60 feet, spectators could find "circular proscenium boxes most artistically arranged. The boxes are in bronze, white and soft red colors, terminating in

Figure 1.4 Los Angeles Theatre, interior and exterior views

a canopy top and draped in front in silver, blue, scarlet and copper plush, lending a delicious effect that is only heightened by the rich surroundings."[25] Nor were the amenities of patrons forgotten: on the back of each box was "an alcove with a dressing-room attached; adjoining them on either side is a large Patti [*sic*] box holding sixteen persons—arranged especially for theater parties. The walls of the boxes gleam and glisten in plastic relief work in bronze, silver and copper, that adds greatly to the rich effect."[26] Significantly, the theater had electric lighting, like the nearby Grand Opera House, as well as very comfortable seating. All of the chairs were upholstered "in scarlet plush," with gold plates indicating the number of each seat. In the dress circle arranged in a semi-circle were twelve boxes, each seating four persons, and bronze columns supported the balcony overhead. No expense was spared, and the designers, who had also constructed the city's Grand Opera House, the Pasadena Opera House, and the Alcazar Theater in San Francisco, had planned the hall to provide virtually every convenience possible at the time.

Why build these theaters? The growing size of the Los Angeles population, coupled with the relative affluence of many of its citizens, meant that there was an increasing demand for fine entertainment in beautiful surroundings. Professional theaters brought a sense of cultural pride, and from very modest beginnings the city could eventually boast of several fine venues that could rival others in California. While San Francisco had far more theaters, Los Angeles could compete favorably with San Diego, which had four theaters by the 1890s.[27] Angelenos' almost insatiable desire to attend shows was excellent news for both touring and local troupes, who provided the city's inhabitants with a continuous stream of music and drama.

Vaudeville and Burlesque

Vaudeville was one of the most popular forms of public entertainment in America from the 1870s to the 1920s. It actually combined several different genres, from comedy to minstrelsy, and another term for it was simply the *variety show*, for during each program a series of different acts would appear.[28] Its roots were in fifteenth-century France, and much as in the popular festivals of early modern Europe, vaudeville performers turned the world upside down: The lowbrow could mock the highbrow through songs, dances, and comic wit.[29] Vaudeville soon spread across the European continent, and by the first half of the nineteenth century performers brought it across the Atlantic. Vaudeville came to California shortly after the Gold Rush; one of the earliest records of such entertainment in California was of a French troupe that appeared in San Francisco at the Jenny Lind Theater in 1850.[30]

Vaudeville actually represented a form of socialization, for it enabled immigrants to learn about, and to participate in, their adopted society. Many of the performers were Irish, Italian, German, or Jewish, and while they may have anglicized their names, their humor was frequently ethnic or racial in content, particularly in the early period of the genre.[31] This humor gave rise to stereotypical, stock characters, such as the Irish drunk and the Italian lover. Vaudeville was above all interactive. Audiences' responses immediately determined the success of a joke, song, or act, often from a cross-section of the population. While the audience until the 1880s seems to have been overwhelmingly male, women gradually attended more performances when theater owners sought to orient vaudeville towards families. The impresario Tony Pastor was one of the first to try this approach in 1881 in New York and provided entertainment to which "children could bring their parents." Others, such as Benjamin F. Keith and Edward F. Albee, followed the same formula with great success. As songs became less racy and the jokes less offensive, more and more people came to see the shows, which meant greater profits for the theater owners.[32]

Not all types of theatrical entertainment, however, catered to a family audience. Burlesque, since the seventeenth century in England, had usually involved parody and exaggerated imitation, particularly of dignified or serious dramatic works. By the 1860s in America it had evolved into a lewd satire of "high" culture, with women in various stages of undress.[33] At one show, for which tickets cost $1 per couple, customers could watch minstrelsy, followed by "Vocal and Instrumental Music By our local Amateurs," and finally a comic burlesque opera.[34] Another troupe of 65 performers, Rice's Burlesque Company, presented *Evangeline* in 1888 at the Grand Opera House. An advertisement proclaimed that the performers were "more original than the originals themselves ever were."[35] While some traveling companies brought their own musicians, more often than not the theaters had their own house orchestras to play during performances or between acts.

The British star, Lydia Thompson, a highly acclaimed burlesque performer of the era, made a tour of North America in 1888—twenty years after its first American tour, when her troupe, the "British Blondes," created a sensation in New York.[36] Her enormous troupe of 60 female and male performers seems to have impressed American patrons no end. One critic called her respectfully "the She of burlesque—the silk-tighted divinity who-must-be-obeyed"; another referred to her as "still the world's reigning attraction on the burlesque stage."[37]

To the delight of Angelenos, Thompson's company performed the burlesques, *Penelope*, by the team of H. P. Stephens and Edward Solomon, and a new work, *Columbus*. *Penelope*, a satire of Homer's *Odyssey*, was clearly the favorite. One critic reported that it "filled the Grand opera house almost to overflowing last night. . . . The burlesque is very pretty indeed and the comedy element provocative of much laughter."[38] Certainly the women's costumes, which revealed much of the female form through tights and skirts, were part of the company's main attraction. The writer did not state how much of the male form had been revealed as well.

Despite such major troupes that made their way across the country, the quality of theatrical performances in the early years was probably uneven.

An example of one traveling group, fancifully titled "Prof. Herrmann's Trans-Atlantique Vaudevilles," provided audiences with that tried and true format of comedy, singing, and dancing. A critic noted that the orchestra "seems to have gotten restive during the vacation. In accompanying [the soloist] Miss Vance's songs they became utterly unmanageable and individually and severally they began a mad race to keep ahead of her until the finish. It is needless to say that they succeeded in their cacophonous intent, although the vocalist was almost winded when she reached the post."[39]

The first theater of Los Angeles devoted solely to vaudeville was the Orpheum, the new name of the Grand Opera House after 1895. Billed as "Los Angeles' Society Vaudeville Theater," a series of acts held forth every night on the stage. The *Los Angeles Times* reported that since the Orpheum's opening on January 2, it played "to an audience that packed [the house], not only every seat from the footlights to the gallery stairs, but standing-room was selling at a premium, and the crowds continue to flock in that quarter."[40] One evening's performance included a number of different acts: Price & Lloyd, a male and female team, who sang songs; George Evans and Haverly, an acting duo; the Big Four, with "knock-about feats" that were "excruciatingly funny and are worth going miles to see"; the McCarthy and Reynolds dancing team; Thomas and Welch as dancing artists, and the aerial artist and acrobat Caicedo.[41] This was variety entertainment in the true sense of the term.

Minstrel acts also made their appearance, several of them African American, often with their own orchestras or music ensembles. Launching the New Year in 1895, a group called "W. A. Mahara's Mammoth Colored Operatic Minstrels," comprised "the best Comedians, Dancers and Singers. The pick of the colored profession."[42] The group consisted of 85 members, one of the largest groups to perform in Los Angeles at that time. Several music groups formed part of the company: the Black Bird Band, the Pickaninny Drum Corps, and the Challenge Band of Drum Majors. Tickets were as high as $1, which was unusual for vaudeville acts. Other prices were 75 cents, 50 cents, and 25 cents. To advertise their appearance, the group even organized a street parade at noon on opening day. Similarly, Hiram "Hi" Henry's "Big Minstrel Revolution" made its appearance at the Los Angeles Theatre in January 1900, complete with basses, baritones, tenors, and even a male alto (or countertenor). The evening included an "Amusing Descriptive Overture by Our Unrivaled Concert Orchestra" during the interlude, as well as a "Militaire cornet solo by Hi Henry and his Military Band."[43]

Another minstrel group, the Creole Burlesque Company, featured a show enticingly titled "Tropical Revelries."[44] A reviewer noted that the group "was of the conventional minstrel kind," and that "[s]ome of the female members of the company are rather *passé* and lack the verve and snap to make a stage appearance attractive." One of the best features of the program, however, was the "challenge dancing contest" that closed the show. "It was full of genuine darkey 'go' that has music and tune in every foot patter," the reviewer exclaimed. "The antics of a colored brother on a sanded floor have a charm that wins the applause of even the blasé theater-goer, and this particular part of the programme was equal to anything of the sort seen here for a long time."[45]

Lynden Behymer, who booked vaudeville acts during his budding career as an impresario, felt compelled to defend the genre's existence. He and his wife Menetta moved to Los Angeles in 1886 from South Dakota, and both began working in the theaters by selling tickets.[46] Perhaps attempting to lend a certain dignity to vaudeville's often seedy reputation, Behymer stated that "the vocal and instrumental music admirers will learn something new, the atheletic [*sic*] members of the audience will revel in the feats of strength and agility, while the literary people present will enjoy intelligent jokes and refined monologue . . . " He further noted that vaudeville would not destroy more serious forms of art, such as drama, for it "is to the frequent visitor to the theatre, the same as a summer vacation, and the sort of a bill that anyone will enjoy after a siege of grand opera or a series of performances of tragedy or melo-drama."[47] The *Los Angeles Times* critic agreed, stating that "this class of entertainment is gradually attracting to it some of the best talent of the amusement world."[48] If the management wanted to fill the house, it presented what the public wanted to hear: song, dance, and comedy.

Operettas

A staple of light music of the era, the operetta, also enjoyed immense popularity in Los Angeles, as it did in the rest of the country. Like vaudeville and burlesque, the operetta was European in origin, and arose during the 1850s out of *opéra comique* in France.[49] American companies performed most of the operettas that appeared in Los Angeles, and one troupe that came to the city many times was "The Bostonians," which received special praise for the quality of its performances. Of its production of *Fatinitza*, with music by Franz von Suppé, the theater critic for the *Los Angeles Times* noted "[t]he rendition . . . was up to the high standard established by the Bostonians, and gave very evident satisfaction to the large audience. There is a neatness, a precision and a finish to the work of this organization that afford eloquent proof of long practice and careful rehearsals."[50] By contrast, when the Calhoun Comic Opera Company brought the same work to the Los Angeles Theatre, the response was far short of that given the Bostonians, although at least one of the characters "kept the audience in a gale of merriment."[51]

Works by the American composer Reginald De Koven were particularly in demand. His *Robin Hood*, written with the librettist Harry B. Smith, came to the Los Angeles Theatre on several occasions. When presented in the city for the first time in 1891, it won tremendous acclaim.[52] "The opening of the Bostonians last evening," stated one critic, "was honored by the attendance of as large an audience as could be crowded into the auditorium of the theater, and the rather risky practice of crowding in a quantity of extra chairs was resorted to in order to oblige patrons of the house, who would otherwise have had to stand or go away." The reviewer continued: "It is fair to say at the outset that the anticipations of the audience were most pleasantly realized, and that the performance proved here, as elsewhere, an artistic success." With the sheriff as "the principal funny man" and Friar Tuck engaging in "low comedy," *Robin Hood* evidently kept the audience roaring.[53]

The music, which The Bostonians' own orchestra performed, was equally delightful. The songs were "bright and sparkling throughout, abounding especially in imitations of the old madrigals and glees, which give a characteristic stamp to the time and country indicated in the piece." But not all was perfect: "The work abounds in dialogue to an unusual extent, but . . . no one seems to take the slightest pains to give it with point. This is particularly the case with the ladies, and this tameness injured situations that might otherwise have been worked into good dramatic effect."[54] The operetta nonetheless proved so popular that the company dropped its planned performance of another work, Thomas's *Mignon*, later in the week and replaced it with two further performances of *Robin Hood*.[55]

As if to confirm that the event was no mere fluke, the same company repeated its triumph two years later. One critic affirmed that "The Bostonians opened in *Robin Hood* last evening at the Los Angeles Theatre to one of the largest audiences ever within its walls. Every seat in the house was sold long before the doors opened, but the attraction had sufficient drawing power to make standing room appear to be something of a favor to those who could not find seats."[56] The show was an immense success: "Never was an opera presented to a more enthusiastic [group] of theater-goers, and it is safe to say [that] never was one more perfectly rendered in every detail to a local audience than was *Robin Hood* last night." Since the company was familiar to many in the audience, they greeted each principal performer with enthusiastic applause, and called for a series of encores. "The whole performance," the critic concluded, "is so thoroughly artistic, the dressings are so rich, and the air of refinement and good taste is so pronounced throughout that the Bostonians are deserving of all the handsome things the most facile writer can say."[57] This kind of entertainment found a ready audience, and the public duly showed its appreciation.

The debut of a comic opera in three acts by De Koven, *The Knickerbockers*, met with equal success.[58] "Another rousing house greeted the charming company of singers and players at the Los Angeles Theatre last night," wrote the *Los Angeles Times* reviewer, "the 'standing room only' placard being out at an early hour. Despite the adverse things said of *The Knickerbockers* by the San Francisco press, it was found to be bright, musical and as a comedy one of the cleverest things ever presented here in the way of a light opera." The reviewer also lauded the orchestra: "One of the delights of the performances now being given at the Los Angeles [Theatre] is the splendid work of the orchestra, under the baton of Samuel L. Studley. No such exquisite orchestral support has ever been given here to a company of singers since Theodore Thomas came to us several years ago with Mrs. Thurber's ambitious National Opera

Company. Mr. Studley is a master, and no little share of the Bostonians' great success is due to his splendid handling of the instrumentalists."[59] What delighted the reviewer and the patrons the most is that the company was *professional*, not only in terms of the players but also in terms of the orchestra that accompanied them. These were not ill-trained amateur acts that sought to provide some diversion for the desperate theater-goer. Groups such as The Bostonians came to Los Angeles because of the ample demand for such acts, and Angelenos repeatedly rewarded such efforts through the willingness for large numbers of people to lay down their money for quality entertainment.

Yet was it just entertainment? Or were theater-goers making a statement in their ritual of attendance, that the presence of theaters reflected a new-found urban confidence? Los Angeles was no longer a marginal outpost of the country, but had become a fixture on the theater circuit. The Grand Opera House was precisely that—a location for grand opera as well as vaudeville and operetta. These theaters suggest something distinctly new: Los Angeles deserved to be recognized as a burgeoning city that could more than hold its own against many of its eastern counterparts.

Angelenos also enjoyed "novelty acts," which were common on the stages of nineteenth-century America. One German group consisted entirely of dwarves, who called themselves "The Liliputians," and they staged a comic opera called *Candy*.[60] Performed at the Grand Opera House, it consisted of four acts, which included four ballets, a burlesque, and comedy throughout. A reviewer noted that "those charming midgets" managed "to draw an audience which . . . tested the capacity of that popular theater." The reviewer seemed to revel in the peculiar fascination with such acts: "The little folks are the most novel attraction now before the public," he stated, "and when one sits through an evening with them he does not wonder that they have been the recipients of the vociferous plaudits of every audience to which they have played, and the lavish encomiums of the press of every city in which they have appeared." The dwarves were not merely a novelty, but appear to have been able to sing, dance, and perform comedy on a par with other visiting troupes: "The ballet and spectacular features of the performance are very fine, embracing the dancing candies; the march of the Amazons, a glittering spectacle; the dance of the sailors, and the flower waltz, which was gorgeously beautiful."[61]

Local talent, while by no means as flourishing as traveling acts, had some opportunities to present their abilities. In a rare example of homegrown performers who received top billing, the Los Angeles Operatic Society performed two works by Gilbert and Sullivan: *Patience* and *The Mikado*.[62] Mr. C. M. Pyke led the orchestra, and advertisements proclaimed "popular summer prices" at 75, 50, and 25 cents.[63] The large audiences seem to have been appreciative, and one critic even gave the ultimate compliment, that performances by the Society "have become far superior to those of the average professional company."[64] As in San Diego, which had the "San Diego Amateur Opera Society," Los Angeles had a similar group, which called itself the "Society Amateur

Opera Club" and produced a variety of vocal and instrumental works. During one evening, a local, prominent musician, Professor Adolph Willhartitz, conducted the ensemble, beginning with the third act of *Aida* by Giuseppe Verdi and ending with *Marriage by Lantern*, an operetta by Jacques Offenbach.[65]

Not all local performers were created equal. A group billed literally as "local talent" produced a work titled *La Mascotte* by Edmond Audran, one of the most prominent European composers during the 1880s and 1890s.[66] A reviewer testified that comic opera "has always been popular with the Angeleños, but no better demonstration of this fact could possibly have been given than the reception which was tendered Audran's *La Mascotte* at this house last night on the occasion of its production by a company of local amateurs." The reviewer tried to be as encouraging as possible, saying that "Although the upper portion of the house was not overcrowded, almost every available inch of space downstairs was preempted by an ultra fashionable audience which, though not particularly enthusiastic, was unquestionably an appreciative one."[67] Venues such as the Los Angeles Theatre thus enabled local musicians and performers to display their talents on the stage. The comment in one issue of the Los Angeles Theatre program, *The Mirror*, however, suggests less than enthusiastic praise for local talent: "We are informed that amateur opera will be an important factor in the entertainment of the Los Angeles public this season. Gee whiz! our seal is doomed."[68]

Plays and "Serious Music"

In Los Angeles theaters, house orchestras regularly performed a blend of both serious and popular music for play-goers. One of the earliest examples was at the Los Angeles Theatre, whose orchestra of nine musicians (two violins, viola, bass, flute, clarinet, cornet, trombone, and drums) performed nightly, and the playbills list many of the pieces they played at intermission.[69] For a play called *Double Uncle Tom's Cabin Company*, the orchestra directed by Harley Hamilton performed several works, including the *Près de Toi* waltz by Emile Waldteufel.[70] Similarly, for a comedy called *My Friend from India*, the orchestra played several pieces between acts, such as Mendelssohn's *Grand Priest* march and a medley of arias from Verdi's opera, *Ernani*.[71] For a comedy drama titled *The Wolves of New York*, the house orchestra under the leadership of a new conductor, Signor Dionisio Romandy, performed overtures to Offenbach's *Monsieur Choufleuri* and Michael Balfe's *The Bohemian Girl*.[72] This diversity of both art music and more popular selections was commonplace at the theaters.

Further examples abound. One company put on the comedic farce *Miss Dixie*, and the orchestra performed various pieces, among them a march by the conductor Romandy himself, *To the Front*.[73] In another production, *The New South*, the orchestra performed Suppé's *Pique Dame* Overture, and for a play titled *The Butterflies*, it gave a rendition of Auber's *Fra Diavolo*

Overture, among other works.[74] A set program was common; in one week, the orchestra played the same four selections between acts of the four plays featured during that week, including Auber's *Le Maçon* Overture.[75] Pieces by these composers were immensely popular at the time.

Figure 1.5 National Opera Company

Even music genres that we tend to consider as "serious," such as operas or symphonies, often attracted a wide audience. A partial reason was that they did not necessarily fall into "highbrow" or elitist categories during this era. The roots of opera go back to the early seventeenth century in Italy as a courtly form of entertainment before moving into public theaters, first in Italy and then throughout Europe. By the nineteenth century, opera had become one of the most common forms of serious entertainment, both in Europe and in America. "Italian opera," notes one musicologist, "was not always the exclusive domain of the middle and elite classes, for it often attracted a general cross section of society, especially when performed at popular prices."[76] As early as 1865, a Mexican troupe had performed one act of Verdi's *Attila* in Los Angeles.[77] Yet performances of opera in southern California were special occasions. Many of the opera companies traveled from Europe and agreed only reluctantly to make the trek out to the West Coast during their American tours. Given the financial risks involved, theater managers presented operas destined to appeal to as wide a public as possible.

One of the most impressive troupes to appear in Los Angeles was the National Opera Company, founded by Jeanne Thurber in New York and led by conductor Theodore Thomas. Its purpose was to make European operas more "American" by using American artists and singing in English. The troupe consisted of over two hundred singers, dancers, and musicians, and its arrival in May 1887, made possible by a guarantee of $20,000 by a local wine merchant, received unprecedented response by Angelenos. Performing in the recently-opened Hazard's Pavilion to bring in the largest audiences possible, the troupe gave seven performances, including Gounod's *Faust*, Verdi's *Aida*, and Wagner's *Lohengrin*, to a total audience of between 24,500 to 28,000 people. Unlike in San Francisco, where the company recorded a loss, it actually made a profit in Los Angeles by charging $1 to $4 per seat. Although many concert-goers probably went to more than one performance, the total number of tickets sold was from 22,000 to 25,000, in a city whose total population was about 50,000 people.[78]

Local managers had several successes in the field of "high" art. The co-manager of the Los Angeles Theatre, Charles Modini-Wood, brought Bizet's *Carmen* to the city in 1895; the Marie Tavary Grand Opera Company, starring Thea Dorre, performed it.[79] A reviewer affirmed that the opera "drew a full house . . . and was a brilliant success," mainly because Thea Dorre "captivated her audience . . . [and] possesses a voice which it is a treat to hear."[80] The company performed Gounod's *Faust* the same week, and the choruses which accompanied the stars received special mention. "It is a common thing in traveling companies to find that although the stars may be all that is desirable, the choruses are weak," noted one critic. "In this case, however, it is surprisingly different," for the company "has won its way so completely into public favor [due to] the strength of its choruses."[81]

Modini-Wood topped this effort by organizing the first performance in the United States of Giacomo Puccini's *La Bohème* in 1897. He achieved this remarkable event by visiting the troupe, the Del Conte Italian Opera Company of Milan, during its appearance in Mexico. Because he could speak Italian, he managed to persuade the performers, who apparently could speak no English, to stop off at Los Angeles on their way north to San Francisco. The first of three performances took place at the Los Angeles Theatre on October 14, 1897, to an audience of 532 "mostly native Italians and Mexicans." The company got an enthusiastic response but made little money, with only $327.70 in box-office receipts, suggesting that far more seats in the 25 cent range, rather than one dollar, were sold.[82] Nonetheless, it was a beginning. The impresario Lynden Behymer, who later falsely claimed having brought *La Bohème* first to Los Angeles, did arrange for an American company, the Maurice Grau Metropolitan Opera Company, to give the opera at Hazard's Pavilion on November 9, 1900.[83] It is difficult to imagine opera companies crossing thousands of miles to perform for a public perhaps unaccustomed to the genre. The soprano Emma Juch, however, commented on her own reception: "Oh, I'm in love with [the Los Angeles] audience. . . . Just think, they have been there since 7:30 [P.M.], and we won't let them go home until 2 o'clock in the morning . . . I don't believe there is another audience in the world that could be held in their seats three hours waiting for the curtain to go up."[84]

In a marked change from the past, a single company arrived in town for several months and presented at the Los Angeles Theatre a series of some of the leading operas of the era. During the spring and summer of 1899, the Italian Grand Opera Company performed more than ten major operas, such as Gounod's *Faust*, Verdi's *Un ballo in maschera* Bizet's *Carmen*, Bellini's *Norma*, and Leoncavallo's *I pagliacci*.[85] For good measure, the company gave a comic opera, *Crispino e la comare*, written in 1850 by the brothers Luigi and Federico Ricci. The occasion marked the first time a company presented this comic opera in Los Angeles.[86]

American opera was no stranger to Los Angeles during this period, and here, too, there were blends of light and serious music. Henry Waller composed the music for *The Ogalallas*, which was billed as "A New American Opera," with a libretto by Young E. Allison.[87] Based on the Ogalala Sioux Indian tribe, this work appears to have attempted the opposite of preceding examples: It crossed over the line from light opera to more serious fare. A reviewer commented "that *The Ogalallas* is far nearer being grand opera than it is the lightsome thing which passes as opera comique." One reason was that the main character, an Indian named War Cloud, had "such an air of haughty pride and reserve, as to make the lugging in of sufficient comedy to make Allison and Waller's creation pass as light opera appear incongruous." The Indian, performed by H. MacDonald, garnered top marks: "There walked upon the stage of the Los Angeles Theater last night a noble red man right out of the pages of one of J. Fennimore Cooper's novels. . . . No one who saw *The Ogalallas* last night will question the thought that the central figure in it is this typical Indian warrior." Unfortunately, the company, The Bostonians, was better versed in light opera, and the opera was "far and away beyond the

Figure 1.6 Adolph Willhartitz

capacity of many of the voices which sang in it last night."[88] Despite the occasional failure, performances of opera improved the cultural image of Los Angeles abroad, which doubtless induced other companies to appear in the city.

Fledgling symphony orchestras began to make their appearance in Los Angeles during the Gilded Age. One of the first examples was the Philharmonic Society, which consisted of 40 musicians and a chorus of 120 members, brought together in 1888 by conductor Professor Adolph Willhartitz.[89] Willhartitz was dedicated to improving the cultural life of Los Angeles, and his concerts regularly featured both art music and operetta. Although the ensemble lasted only a few years, it did succeed in performing Haydn's oratorio, *The Creation*, in 1889.[90] Professor A. J. Stamm, an organist at St. Vibiana's Cathedral, took up the idea further, and formed the Philharmonic Orchestra in 1892. An immigrant from Germany, Stamm had

Figure 1.7 Harley Hamilton

first appeared in a brass band in Pasadena in 1883, and he assembled 35 professional musicians for an annual season of four concerts. When the orchestra proudly opened its second season at the Grand Opera House, it performed an eclectic blend of 12 works that included a piano concerto by Mendelssohn, excerpts from operas by Rossini, Wagner, Kretschmer, and Thomas, and pieces by De Koven and Strauss.[91] Its end-of-season concert, billed as the "Fourth Grand Concert," took place at the Los Angeles Theatre.[92] Another orchestra of 60 musicians gave a "Grand Orchestral Concert" under the direction of George Felton. In using the concept of the Theme Night, the orchestra also booked the Los Angeles Theatre for an "Opera Night" and a "Popular Concert."[93] These orchestras had to appeal to as wide an audience as possible, and they paved the way for two orchestras which were to follow: the Los Angeles Symphony Orchestra and the Woman's Symphony Orchestra.[94]

The Los Angeles Symphony Orchestra represented one of the city's major cultural institutions. Through the extraordinary dedication of its members, it

Figure 1.8 Lynden Behymer

managed to last over two decades (1897–1920), a testament both to Angelenos' growing interest in a permanent orchestra and to the musicians' tenacity in developing that interest.[95] Conductor Harley Hamilton brought together about 25 musicians, who either worked in the theater orchestras or taught privately. The orchestra began as a cooperative venture, with all members sharing profits equally. The manager was Lynden Behymer, and while neither he nor Hamilton were paid, the first season brought the other members $1.35 each. Behymer covered any incidental expenses, and Hamilton even mortgaged his home in order to assure the continued success of the venture. The saving grace came from a patron, Mrs. Emily Newton, who guaranteed the payment of all future deficits. By 1906 a total of about 60 musicians formed the orchestra, each receiving $6 per concert and $1 per rehearsal. Seasons consisted of six concerts, almost all of which took place in the local theaters, with season tickets from $3 to $5, and single seats from 50 cents to $1.[96]

Yet the oldest permanent group of instrumentalists in Los Angeles did not consist of male musicians at all but of women. The same team of Harvey Hamilton and Lynden Behymer founded the Woman's Symphony Orchestra in 1893, inviting both music teachers and amateurs to join. The orchestra at first consisted of 25 musicians: thirteen violins, two violas, two cellos, four cornets, and one each of bass, flute, clarinet, and trombone. The first "public rehearsal" took place in the fall of 1893, followed by the orchestra's first concert in April the following year at the Grand Opera House.[97] In subsequent years it gave from one to three concerts annually, and Hamilton served as conductor for the next 20 years, while Behymer managed the ensemble for 21 years. Although critics initially commented on the thinness of the sound, more musicians joined as the organization grew a following, and the orchestra continued to perform into the 1930s, by which time about 30 women's orchestras existed in the country.[98]

The examples of these orchestras suggest that there were exceptions to the notion of sacralized culture. The formation of symphony orchestras shows a clear effort to perform the "masterworks of the classic composers," yet the programs reveal less of a distinction between elite and popular genres than we might at first assume.[99] The Philharmonic Orchestra included works from opera and operetta in its programs, because of the popularity of these genres. Both men and women formed orchestras, calling on the talents of professional musicians and amateurs alike. The use of theaters for these organizations might seem unusual, given the theaters' reputation for mass entertainment. Because concert halls scarcely existed, however, patrons truly interested in classical music had to be content with the few choices they had. Among the only other venues for an orchestra or ensemble to give such concerts were in churches.[100] Musicians in these local orchestras earned a living either in the orchestras of theaters or they taught privately, and audiences of both kinds of music, popular and serious, could benefit.[101]

Audiences and Advertisements

Because information about the audiences attending concerts at the theaters rarely appears in newspaper reviews, the advertisements that filled the pages of theater programs provide our only clues. Advertisements helped pay for the programs and increased theater profits.[102] Local businesses consistently placed such advertisements, which underlined a clear relationship between commerce and music. Both the Los Angeles Theatre and Grand Opera House were located downtown in the heart of a thriving business district, and those businesses near the theaters could profit from the increase in pedestrian traffic.

Food services hoped to benefit from theater-goers, and they regularly placed ads in the programs. "Luxurious Ices, Dainty Creams and Sparkling Beverages" boasted Christopher's soda shop, located conveniently close to the theater. "Best Bread and Cakes in the City" claimed Potter's bakery. One establishment, the Opera Restaurant at No. 15 South Main Street, emphasized that the locale was "New, Neat and Clean! . . . This well-known and popular Restaurant, by the present proprietors, has been thoroughly remodeled and renovated. Everything is now First Class."[103]

Many advertisements sought to appeal to women. The Boston Shoe Store, at the corner of Main and Second Streets, offered "Ladies, Misses, Childrens Fine Footwear at reasonable prices."[104] "Opera Bonnets Made to order," declared an ad by Anette [*sic*] Rowe's Millinery Store at 141 So. Broadway.[105] Mrs. Graham's Cosmetics offered "Hairdressing, Shampooing, Facial Treatment, Electrolysis," as well as "MANICURING for Ladies and Gentlemen."[106] Mrs. F. E. Phillips competed with her Ladies Toilet Parlors, offering "Mme Rupert's Celebrated Cosmetics. Face Tonics, the finest in the world. Hair Dressing, Manicuring, Face massage."[107] Another business owner, Mrs. E. L. Roberts, described herself as a "Fashionable Hair Dresser," and the shop's most expensive service was a shampoo and hair dressing for 50 cents.[108]

Theater programs were ideal for advertisements offering lessons in music or dance, which were often oriented toward women. Mothers seeking piano lessons for their children could contact "Carlyle Petersilea's Music School," located in the Y.M.C.A. Building on 209 South Broadway.[109] They needed to look no further if they wanted to "Buy or Rent a Piano from Kohler & Chase," while one of the same company's ads in the program of a different theater declared that it represented the "Largest Importers on the Pacific Coast."[110] Those interested in a dance school could meet with Mr. and Mrs. E. W. Payne, "Professors of Dancing," at the Academy at Illinois Hall, whose ad included the notice: "We have had added to our Academy, which is 60 × 90, a Dining Parlor, Kitchen, Smoking Room and Refreshment Room, making it complete for receptions."[111]

Several ads offered luxury items or services. Customers could secure an "Imperial Face Massage" for 75 cents, which was the price of the highest ticket at the theaters. Or they could have their "Garments Cleaned, Dyed . . . and Renovated," and that could include one's collection of ostrich plumes.[112] The City Steam Carpet Cleaning Works stated that it could clean "Furniture, Parlor Sets, Easy Chairs, Lounges, Etc."[113] Particularly wealthy customers could purchase "Oriental Rubies, Sapphires, Opals, Turquoise and Other Fine Stones Mounted to Order in First Class Style."[114] Members of the audience might even use the Tally-Ho Stables, offering the "Finest Line of Carriages and Livery in the City," although a possible competitor was the I.X.L. Stables at 826 S. Main Street, which even listed its telephone number—something rare for businesses at this time.[115] All of these businesses advertised luxury items, and customers could expect to pay top dollar for their services.

These advertisements indicate several things. First, audiences had wide opportunities to spend their money nearby, whether on food and drinks, hair dressing or manicuring, or jewels and clothing. Second, many of the advertisements offered services or products that appealed primarily to women, such as hair dressing and shoes, and the ads had illustrations of women enjoying them. Third, a number of the businesses offered luxury goods and services, suggesting that members of the audience were relatively well-to-do. Advertisers would probably not seek to target these audiences over an extended period of time if they did not feel they were reaching the appropriate consumers. The theaters were good for local commerce, and local commerce was good for the theaters.

Conclusion

The theaters of Los Angeles hosted a considerable variety of entertainment. From vaudeville to operettas to plays, the public could count on a rich spectrum of music and drama from which to choose. On a consistent basis, house orchestras performed excerpts from classical music, operas, and operettas, as well as arrangements of popular songs. By the 1880s Los Angeles had theaters similar in quality, although not in quantity, to those of its rival city to the north, even though San Francisco had a far greater population, immense wealth, and more disposable income. Because of the efforts by theater managers to entice more women and children to their shows, Los Angeles audiences became increasingly diverse.[116]

Bringing acts and musicians to the Southland, however, was a challenging enterprise. Lynden Behymer, who eventually became one of the leading impresarios in the Southwest, noted that the Los Angeles manager had to contend with numerous other problems, among them "[c]ostly transportation and time of travel," and the fact that the "[m]ajority of home seekers here are from Middle West communities, who have not had privileges of opera, drama, symphony, concerts, [thus] taking slowly to advanced concert offerings."[117] Even once the performers arrived, the public, while generally appreciative, did not always know how to behave. The disciplining of audiences was a common aspect of nineteenth-century expressive culture, as Lawrence Levine has persuasively argued.[118] Reviewing a series of plays, one critic had particularly harsh words for the audience: "If some supreme power could be put forth to keep a Los Angeles audience seated until the players have finished their lines, the players, as well as a goodly portion of the audience itself, would look upon such an evidence of power as a great boon. Ladies and gentleman, please keep your seats until the curtain goes down!"[119]

It was possible, however, to overcome these problems and provide music to a public insatiable for entertainment, both "highbrow" and "lowbrow," and frequently a mixture of both. This eclectic blend of musical styles was a common feature of Los Angeles's cultural life during the boom years. Musicians who performed in the house orchestras also performed much of the city's serious music, such as symphonies and concertos, and the theaters where this music took place were not the "segregated temples devoted to 'high' or 'classical' art" that had become common on the East Coast and in the Midwest.[120] Rather, they served as symbols of something else, a shared public space in which men, women, and children by the end of the nineteenth century could hear a rich variety of music. We now turn to ways in which children could fully participate in Los Angeles's music culture.

2

“Making Friends with Music”: Music Education in the Classroom and Concert Hall

Neighborhood Music Settlement

When Progressive reformer Pearle Odell founded the Neighborhood Music Settlement on Mozart Street in East Los Angeles in 1914, she was building on a tradition of music education in the city that stretched back into the nineteenth century.[1] The settlement house served low-income children who had few other opportunities for studying music. Similar-minded teachers and administrators in the city's public schools saw music as a critical part of the education of any child, regardless of economic status or ethnicity. The development of music education programs in late-nineteenth and early-twentieth-century Los Angeles was mainly the result of three closely intertwined factors: the rapid expansion of educational institutions from kindergarten through college; the Progressive movement that called for fundamental economic, political, and social reforms; and the drive toward Americanization that sought to integrate children from diverse backgrounds into American society.[2] The purpose of this chapter is to demonstrate how music instruction in both the classroom and concert hall was available to a broad cross-section of children.

We can define “music education” to include a variety of ways of learning about music: in public school classes, in music conservatories, in private instruction, and by attending youth concerts. While private instruction was at first not easy to come by—only five music teachers officially advertised their services in the city directory in 1882—by the turn of the century there were over 165 teachers listed. The number of unlisted instructors doubtless drove the total far higher.[3] Many of these teachers were women. The federal census in 1890 showed that of the 203 musicians and music teachers then living in Los Angeles, over half of them, or 53 percent, were female. Ten years later, the total number of musicians had risen to 607, and women comprised 64 percent of that number.[4] Long before the film industry began attracting droves of talented composers, arrangers, and performers, Los Angeles had a growing cadre of men and women who were dedicated to the teaching of music.

The boom of the 1880s also witnessed an educational boom of institutions of higher learning. Many elementary and high school teachers received their training from these institutions, which attracted faculty out west and provided employment for local musicians to staff the music departments. One of the first major colleges to be founded at this time was the University of Southern California in 1880, a Methodist institution that owed its creation to three individuals: the Protestant Ozro W. Childs, a horticulturist and later owner of the Childs's Opera House; John G. Downey, a Catholic immigrant from Ireland and a former California governor; and Isaias W. Hellman, a German-Jewish banker and community philanthropist.[5] Other colleges joined this boom, most of them established by various denominations. Congregationalists founded Pomona College in 1887, and Presbyterians opened Occidental College in 1888. Two other private colleges both opened in 1891: Quakers founded Whittier College, and the German Brethren established Lordsburg College, renamed La Verne College in 1917.[6] One of the few nondenominational colleges to be founded during the boom was the State Normal School in 1882, which became the southern branch of the University of California in 1919.[7] These colleges shared a vital role in educating prospective music teachers and thus fostering the advancement of music education. By the turn of the century, Los Angeles had become an important center for education in the West.

The teaching of music to children and adolescents had a basic purpose. Teachers recognized that most children who received some instruction in music did not seek to become professional musicians. Rather, such training became part of the general education that parents and enlightened school administrators (not always a given in educational circles) considered vital for both socialization and Americanization. With almost half of all Los Angeles County schoolchildren foreign-born or the children of foreign-born by 1920—20,728 out of 50,445 students—music provided one way of uniting them around a common theme: the arts.[8]

Music Education in the Public Schools

One of the first types of schools in which music had an important role was the kindergarten. Based on the ideas of the German philosopher and educator Friedrich Froebel, who founded his first school in Jena in 1816, kindergartens were introduced in America in Watertown, Wisconsin in 1855.[9] According to Elizabeth Peabody of Boston, who studied Froebel's schools in Hamburg, "the school is designed specifically for children from the age of three to six, who are gently led over the threshold of learning by the seductive charm of flowers, music, games, pictures and curious objects."[10] An article in the *California Teacher* described the first kindergarten in California, founded in San Francisco in September 1863: "Froebel's idea, with such modifications as change of country and nation necessitate, has thus far been carried out with a success that renders it certain that playing set to music, and made to mean something, is nature's method of tuition for little children."[11]

The proliferation of kindergartens in Los Angeles owed much to the tireless efforts of progressive reformer Caroline Seymour Severance. Bringing the enthusiasm of the New England Woman's Club and New England Froebel Union, she moved to Los Angeles with her husband Theodoric in 1875, and helped persuade reluctant Angelenos that kindergartens could provide social services such as school lunch programs and day-care, and could also offer moral sustenance.[12] The first kindergarten in Los Angeles opened in December 1876 at 134 South Hill Street for children from four to seven years in age. Adjacent to it was a training school for kindergarten teachers, until the State Normal School in Los Angeles created a similar department for that purpose some twenty years later. The first decade was difficult, marked by a scarcity of funds and the loss of one of their best teachers, one of Froebel's own students, Emma Marwedel, who left for San Francisco. Undeterred, Severance and other reform-minded women founded the Los Angeles Free Kindergarten Association in 1884. With strong support by Severance's Friday Morning Club, the Los Angeles Woman's Club, bond sales, and a new city charter in 1889, the establishment and funding of kindergartens throughout the County became a reality by the end of the century.[13]

In keeping with Froebel's original intentions, many of these schools taught children simple lessons in melody and rhythm. Because music was ideal for both communication and socialization, the beginning of education for a large number of the city's toddlers also meant an introduction to music. Kindergartens at first were solely private, but in keeping with a movement to make them part of the public school system in other states such as Vermont, Indiana, and Connecticut, a similar effort was underway in California during the 1880s. In 1891 Los Angeles became the first city in the state to succeed in establishing public kindergartens.[14] The program was an immense success, and earned Los Angeles the reputation by the International Kindergarten Union in 1925 as the "greatest kindergarten city of the world." By 1932, 41,486 children attended 1,112 kindergartens in the public schools of Los Angeles County, compared to 6,096 children in 115 schools in San Francisco County, and 3,078 children in 70 kindergartens in San Diego County.[15]

As with kindergartens, music instruction became a formal part of the curriculum in Los Angeles's elementary and high schools. A common text for children during the 1880s was *Mason's Normal Singer*, written by Boston music educator, choir director, and administrator Lowell Mason.[16] With the appointment in 1892 of the first principal of music in elementary schools, Juliet Powell Rice, there was a broader commitment by the Los Angeles school board toward the formal teaching of music.[17] Within five years the board created a new position, "Supervisor of Music in Los Angeles Public Schools." One supervisor was Kathryn Emilie Stone, who introduced phonograph records in the teaching of music appreciation in the classrooms. She published a manual, *Outline for Music Appreciation for Elementary Schools*, which was a pioneering effort that was revised in 1922 to become *Music Appreciation Taught By Means of the Phonograph.*[18]

This use of recording technology in music education formed part of a national trend. A common resource was the Victor Record Collection, and the Victor Talking Machine Company created an educational department for the purpose of distributing the collection throughout the country's elementary and high schools. Frances Elliot Clark, head of Victor's educational department in 1921, stated that through music education, the United States could become "the greatest music nation in the world." She affirmed that the "[i]nstilling of the fundamental principles of music in the child at an early age is just as important as the teaching of other subjects." Clark further supported the forming of school orchestras as a critical part of music education programs.[19]

Listening to music in the classroom is one thing; having access to instruments is another matter. For parents of modest means, buying an instrument could be prohibitively expensive. One option was to rent, or purchase on installment, at one of the leading music stores, such as the Southern California Music Company or Bartlett's Music Store.[20] Yet there was another option: the public schools. In 1911, music teacher Jennie L. Jones founded the Elementary Orchestra Department in the Los Angeles Public Schools with the mission of enabling schoolchildren to play on quality instruments. For two dollars, students received instruments on loan from the department for five months, with the option to purchase the instrument after that time. The department possessed 130 violins from 1/4 to full size, 15 cellos of various sizes, 30 flutes, 91 clarinets, 104 cornets, 38 trombones, and 3 mellophones, with a combined value at the time of over $14,000. Two decades after she had started the department, Jones could proudly state that there were 231 elementary schools in Los Angeles with orchestras, and over 4,000 boys and girls between the ages of six and twelve performed in these orchestras.[21] This democratization of orchestral music enabled budding musicians to develop a skill that previously had been the privilege of the well-to-do. One of the most famous beneficiaries of this system was Alfred Wallenstein, conductor of the Los Angeles Philharmonic from 1943 to 1956 and one of the first American-born musicians to become director of a major American symphony orchestra. Wallenstein had first learned the cello in the public schools of Los Angeles.[22]

Similar programs in distributing instruments to children took place in other parts of the country. Theodore Winkler, Supervisor of School Music in Sheboygan, Wisconsin, noted in 1921 that he first observed a system of teaching instrumental music in Lincoln, Nebraska, which gave students "hands-on" experience with actual instruments. When Winkler introduced the program in Wisconsin, over 200 pupils signed up (about 15 percent of the student body) to learn the violin. He hoped to expand the program to include piano, then the other string instruments, followed by woodwinds and brass.[23] As in Los Angeles, many of the students would have been unable to afford private lessons or instruments, and the stimulus, enthusiasm, and competition among the students assured him that teaching violin to classes, rather than individually, had distinct merits.

What must have appealed to parents in Wisconsin as well as in other states was the cost. The total expense in the first year for 200 students, to both parents and the city, was $1,750 for instruction and instruments, or $8.75 per student, which was far less than what private instruction would have cost. Similar programs began appearing throughout the Midwest: in Minneapolis, Minnesota, Grand Rapids, Michigan, and Evansville, Indiana. Winkler cited Glen H. Woods, who introduced such a program in Oakland, California, and who could well have been speaking for most of these institutions in declaring, "Let the public schools become the junior conservatories of our country."[24]

The expansion of music education in Los Angeles public schools continued even into the Depression. By 1933 there were 58 music teachers in 23 junior high schools and 123 music teachers in 33 high schools in the city of Los Angeles. In other cities throughout southern California, at least 110 music teachers taught at 51 junior high schools, and 173 music teachers taught at 93 high schools, or an average of almost 2 music teachers per school.[25] These teachers not only introduced young people to the value of music, but played in community and civic orchestras themselves. They thus contributed both inside and outside the classroom to the music culture of Los Angeles.

A Music Manual

With the proliferation of music education programs, the idea arose of establishing a more uniformed approach to music instruction. At the height of the Depression in October 1935, a state-wide committee of the California-Western School Music Conference, then under the presidency of Mary E. Ireland, met to establish a comprehensive plan for music education in the state's elementary schools. It does not appear to have been a result of the New Deal, which the administration of President Franklin Roosevelt had instituted to try to solve the country's economic woes. Rather, this plan resulted from the urging of the far-sighted State Superintendent of Public Instruction, Walter Dexter. He asserted that music "is fundamental in the education of every child . . . [and] merits supports and encouragement in the school program equal to that given any other subject or area of experience." Its purpose was to create capable amateurs and "not primarily to discover musical genius" but rather to fulfill "an intellectual and an emotional need." Dexter emphasized that a proper program of music education provided students with "a means of artistic expression through which they may voice their aspirations and ideals not only for their own development but also for the contribution they may make thereby to the steady, onward progress of civilization."[26] Music, in the eyes of such educators, was to serve an integral role in the development of character rather than merely as an elective for schoolchildren. This notion of the "civilizing" aspect of music, to use primarily European art music as a form of Americanization, remained a leitmotif in the support for music instruction for decades to come.

The result of this conference was the publication in 1939 of *Music Education in the Elementary School.* This groundbreaking, 152-page manual consisted of practical suggestions to establish a coordinated program of music education for children in kindergarten through high school. Music teachers from across the state, from elementary school through college, served on committees to discuss a specific theme before writing one of the seven chapters. The committees were regionally-based, with chapters two and three the products of teachers from southern California; chapters four, five, and six from music educators in northern California; and the final chapter, on music education in rural schools, a product of teachers from both regions.

The first chapter, "Point of View in Music Education," explains the place of music in the curriculum: to develop "an integrated personality" in the child through music. Quoting from music educator Lilla Belle Pitts, the chapter's authors firmly believed that music "is the experience of the race objectified in permanent form for the enhancement of life and for the elevation of human thought."[27] The teaching of music could thus contribute to the primary goals of all education for children: the development of critical thinking, self-control, emotional stability, and the establishment of healthy social relationships. In keeping with a national trend, they noted that a balance of both vocal and instrumental music was important, and that *active participation* by all children, as opposed to merely listening to different types of music, was essential. In this way, through hands-on experience and a gradual understanding of the basics, even those not musically gifted could benefit from a learning of songs and rhythmic patterns.

The second chapter, "The Development of Vocal Music," discussed the basic goal of most music activity in schools: the singing of songs.[28] Students should begin with rote memorization of simple tunes in kindergarten, accompanied by rhythmic activities to emphasize the beat. They should always sing with the head voice (as opposed to that produced by abdominal control by trained singers) until their voices begin to change in their teenage years. Clear enunciation and accurate pronunciation (the joys of any English teacher) come from an emphasis on beautiful singing, correct phrasing, and proper breathing. To promote active participation by the students, the committee also emphasized the sheer pleasure of music through creative activity, dancing, and dramatization.

The plentiful suggestions of recordings was a hallmark of the manual. Building on an idea that Los Angeles educator Kathryn Emilie Stone had pioneered almost two decades earlier, the committee strongly advocated the use of recordings as illustration. Each chapter offers specific songs or pieces from the Victor Record Collection that ranged from simple tunes, such as "Tip-toe March" or "Theme for Skipping," to classical music or operatic selections, such as the "Triumphal March" from Verdi's *Aida* or the "Toreader Song" from Bizet's *Carmen*. Naming specific titles and giving the appropriate record identification numbers greatly lessened the chance for errors by instructors, not all of whom may have received extensive musical training.[29] As the children progressed through the grades, the recording selections became more challenging or musically complex, such as two pieces suggested for fourth grade students: "Funeral March of a Marionette" by Charles Gounod and "Solveig's Cradle Song" from the *Peer Gynt Suite* by Edvard Grieg. Clear melodies and unambiguous rhythms remained characteristic of all the musical selections.

The third chapter was significant, especially as it was the product of teachers from southern California. With the title of "Music as an Integrative Experience in the Major Learnings," it presented how students could both understand the state's musical heritage and participate in that heritage.[30] One approach was a study of early California and Mexico in which children could build small adobe houses, such as the Casa de Adobe near the Southwest Museum in Los Angeles. They then could learn the songs that inhabitants may well have heard at the time, such as "El cántico del alba," or "Dios te salve María," a Spanish song to the Virgin Mary. The children could also hear dance music of the early Californians, such as the *jota*, and re-enact scenes from the cultural life of the people. Because both instrumental and vocal music were truly integral to the life of the early Californians, this kind of cultural study fit well with a study of the era's history.[31] Students could further explore the history of other regions through their music, such as ancient Greece and Egypt, and one section was devoted to the music of China, complete with a list of recordings and instruments to use.[32] The remaining chapters continued to emphasize this multiethnic approach to music education, and the accompanying photographs showed how children combined the disciplines of drama and music.

This manual affirmed several trends of music education that had developed in California by the 1930s. First, it emphasized a thorough learning of music. Teachers were expected to devote at least 100 minutes per week to music lessons (increased to 150 minutes for the intermediate and upper elementary grades), with the goal that by the eighth grade students could sing in three- and four-part harmony, understand basic harmonic chords and rhythmic notation, sing individually, and appreciate both classical and folk styles. This was not merely a program of rote memorization, but one that aimed for genuine musical understanding.

Second, the manual affirmed the notion of music education as an interethnic endeavor. By integrating the diversity of California's ethnic heritage, as well as the music from other countries, children could learn how to take part in that heritage, even at a time when most schools were racially segregated. While one could argue that these educators were dealing in stereotypes—the "mission Indian" comes to mind—their integrated approach to learning music denied an exclusively European art music approach, which might inherently assume the superiority of "whiteness."

Finally, it showed a commitment to the teaching of music as an integral part of every child's education. The decision to bring together leading music instructors from across the state to develop a manual came from the highest state office in education, that of the Superintendent, who recognized the value that music could have in the teaching of children. During a time when one might expect music programs to be cut or greatly reduced, instructors had the Superintendent's support to devote several years to the formation of a viable music program that schools across the state could implement. That the manual was reprinted in 1944 suggests that its use was widespread.[33] The ultimate goal of the program was to create life-long learners of music within the diversity of the state's cultural heritage, and it provided a basis for music education in Los Angeles public schools that lasted well after World War II.[34]

The First Music Schools

Programs in the public schools formed only part of this commitment to music education in Los Angeles. As the population of the region blossomed, so did the number of music conservatories. By 1916, at least 16 different schools were operating in the County, and by 1930 that number rose to at least 20.[35] They ranged from the more traditional, such as the Los Angeles Conservatory of Music, to the more eclectic, such as the California School of Artistic Whistling.[36] Music teachers opened the first schools in or near downtown before founding similar institutions in outlying cities, from Long Beach to Pasadena. With so many schools in operation, individualized music instruction was accessible to a wide diversity of students, across ethnic and class lines.

One of the first renowned music teachers in Los Angeles was a guitarist from Guadalajara, Mexico. Born in 1843, Miguel Arévalo studied at a music academy in Guadalajara, the *Sociedad Filarmónica Jalisciense*, which attracted instrumentalists, composers, and opera singers from around Mexico.[37] Seeking a career abroad as both a guitarist and composer, he journeyed first to San Francisco, then relocated in 1871 to the warmer climate of Los Angeles. In the same year he advertised a Musical Institute he founded with J. D. Knell, an organist and choir director at several Catholic churches.[38] While little is known about Knell, Arévalo became one of the leading music teachers in Los Angeles until his death in 1900.

Professor Arévalo taught a large number of students in both guitar and piano. One guitar student, Luis Toribio Romero, immigrated to Los Angeles from Spain during the 1870s. After studying with Arévalo he founded music studios in San Jose, San Francisco, and Boston, and composed several works which are now in the Music Division of the Library of Congress. Two other students were pianists María Pruneda and Ysabel del Valle. After a concert debut in Los Angeles in 1876, María Pruneda became one of the first music teachers at the recently founded University of Southern California in 1880,

Figure 2.1 Miguel Arévalo, ca. 1872

where she was listed as one of the two music instructors in a total faculty of fourteen.[39]

The *Los Angeles Times* critic praised a benefit concert Pruneda gave at Turnverein Hall on January 12, 1882. She played Liszt's piano adaptation of Verdi's *Rigoletto*, among other works, and proved herself to be "an excellent performer on the piano, and was received with loud applause."[40] Ysabel del Valle gave concerts in Los Angeles and at her home in Rancho Camulos, the ranch that reputedly served as the model for Helen Hunt Jackson's novel, *Ramona*. Del Valle also gave concerts with Arévalo himself on several occasions, and in 1904 and 1905 she recorded Mexican folksongs with members of her family for Los Angeles writer and booster, Charles Lummis.[41]

Throughout his career, Arévalo tried to establish a link between Anglo and Latino audiences and musicians. Active as a soloist and accompanist, he appeared frequently at two of the main venues of Los Angeles during the 1870s and 1880s, the Merced Theater and Turnverein Hall.[42] He gave concerts throughout southern California as well as on the East Coast, where he played guitar arrangements of works by Spanish, Italian, and Mexican composers, including his own compositions.[43] He also joined the *Sociedad Hispano-Americana de Beneficiencia Mútua*, a mutual aid society that helped support local musicians—20 years before the founding of the Musicians' Mutual Protective Association of Los Angeles.[44] One indication of his renown was a benefit concert on May 13, 1889 to express appreciation for Arévalo's many musical accomplishments. Featuring 24 students and colleagues, including fellow composer, conductor, and teacher A. J. Stamm, the concert took place at Turnverein Hall. Among the luminaries present were Mayor Henry T. Hazard and the founder of the Grand Opera House, Ozro W. Childs, who thanked him for "his invariable courtesy and readiness to at all times co-operate to the success of charitable enterprises."[45]

Continuing Arévalo's tradition in pedagogy, one of the longest-lasting music schools in the region was the Los Angeles Conservatory of Music. In 1883, music store owner Louis J. Valentine and his wife Emily chose a location near the theater district, 406 South Main Street, to give professional music instruction in violin, voice, piano, and music theory. Emily Valentine, a pianist, also taught vocal music for at least two years at the State Normal School, from 1883 to 1885.[46] They joined a national trend that began after the Civil War, when the first conservatories in America appeared. Both the Oberlin Conservatory in Ohio and the New England Conservatory in Providence, Rhode Island (before the school's move to Boston) were founded in 1865, and conservatories in Cincinnati and Chicago were established two years later.[47] Music teachers opened similar institutions in New York, St. Louis, and San Francisco over the next two decades. One hallmark of the Los Angeles Conservatory of Music is that it was a family-run institution that included the Valentines' three children, Charles, Earl, and Emily.[48]

After ten years of successfully running the school, Valentine's wife and daughter broadened the school's goals. Following Louis Valentine's death they revised the name to the Los Angeles Conservatory of Music and Arts and moved to 730 South Grand Avenue. Students gave public recitals at the Conservatory's concert hall, and as audiences grew, the recitals took place in Symphony Hall in the Blanchard Building, which businessman and sometime impresario Frederick Blanchard owned.[49] By the 1930s the conservatory moved to 1324 South Figueroa Street, where Emily Valentine's daughter, Adeltha E. Carter, oversaw a faculty of 18 teachers in instrumental and vocal music and music theory. The school continued operations in its original form until 1961, when it merged with the Chouinard Art Institute to form the California Institute of the Arts, or "CalArts," now located in Valencia in northern Los Angeles County.[50]

One conservatory in Los Angeles that patterned itself solidly after the European model was the Von Stein Academy of Music, which the pianist Heinrich von Stein founded in 1907. Born in 1877 in Passaic, New Jersey of German immigrant parents, von Stein studied both medicine and music in

Berlin and took his music degree there at the Royal Academy of Music in 1897.[51] After studying with three of the leading pianists in Europe, Eugen d'Albert, Ferruccio Busoni, and Theodor Leschetizky, he gave concerts throughout Europe and America, and arrived in Los Angeles in 1905. Impressed by both the climate and the musical opportunities of the region, he opened a school in his own home dedicated to piano instruction. As demand for his services increased, he hired more faculty and moved to a larger location on Grand Avenue. Finally, in 1910 he leased a four-story building at the corner of Tenth and Hill Streets to accommodate the astounding number of some eight hundred students.[52]

Like the Los Angeles Conservatory of Music and Arts, the Von Stein Academy was a family-run operation. Von Stein's wife Sarah, his sister Juliet, and her husband Charles McCreary were all officers, directors, or teachers. At its new location, the school had 16 instructors, who taught over 14 instruments, including piano, violin, voice, and saxophone.[53] They all had either an American or European training, most had toured widely, and four teachers were European immigrants. One of the stars of the school was violinist

Figure 2.2 Heinrich von Stein, ca. 1911

Wenzel Kopta, born in Prague in 1850, who came to the United States at the age of 17 and subsequently performed under Theodore Thomas with the New York Philharmonic. Pianist Edoardo Lebegott, from Milan, Italy, studied at the Verdi Conservatory of Music in Milan, and conducted grand opera in 1903 in Rio de Janeiro and in Mexico City. He emigrated to San Francisco in 1910, then came to Los Angeles about one year later. Soprano Adelina Tromben-Lebegott, born in Vicenza in northern Italy in 1881, was a coloratura soprano in Milan and toured in Spain, Russia, and North and South America before marrying Edoardo Lebegott and moving to Los Angeles.[54]

Despite the European emphasis, there were some American-trained teachers. Pianist William Taylor Spangler, born in Chile, studied at the University of the Pacific in San Jose, California, and toured throughout South America in 1907 before relocating to southern California shortly afterwards. Soprano Elsie W. Kirkpatrick seems to have been the only instructor actually born in California, in San Jose. She studied vocal music in San Francisco, then taught voice for 20 years in both northern and southern California. After moving to Los Angeles, she performed as soprano soloist at the First Unitarian Church and at Temple B'nai B'rith in addition to her teaching duties. The sole instructor who grew up in Los Angeles (although born in Kentucky) was pianist Oscar Rasbach, while three other instructors hailed from New York, Illinois, and Massachusetts.[55]

There was a clear hierarchy to the school, which comprised two departments, Amateur and Academic. The Amateur Department offered a basic music education and probably consisted of the majority of students. There were two 12-week terms each year, with half-hour lessons given twice per week. Children at the elementary level for most instruments paid $24 per term, those at the middle and upper grades $36 per term. Voice instruction was more expensive: $36 per term at the elementary and middle grades and $50 at the upper level, with cello instruction even higher. Curiously, piano instruction was somewhat cheaper, possibly because of the intense competition among instructors in the city, with $18 at the elementary grade per term, $24 at the middle grade, and $36 at the upper grade.[56]

The theoretical model for this approach had been developed in the nineteenth century by two German instructors, Sigismund Lebert and Ludwig Stark. Together they published a manual in 1858, titled *Grosse theoretische-praktische Klavierschule* (literally, "Grand Theoretical-Practical Piano School"), which had phenomenal popularity in Germany and went through at least 11 editions before being published in the United States.[57] The method, which von Stein had learned at the Royal Academy of Music in Berlin, stipulated that only a mastery of the material of each level, and the passing of examinations, could enable students to advance to the next level. This kind of rigid hierarchical approach may not have made for happy students, but it appealed to those teachers who wanted to apply a "scientific" method of piano instruction.[58]

The real heart of the Von Stein Academy was the Academic Department. Only students who sought truly advanced instruction, with the goal of a professional music career, could enter into this hallowed domain, and lessons understandably cost more. Piano students at the elementary level could expect to pay $60 per term, while those at the upper level paid $100. For this princely sum students received 48 private lessons each term, as well as classes in harmony and duet, ensemble, and choral singing. Those fortunate to reach the "Artist" level, which was available solely in piano, violin, and voice, could expect to pay on average $200 per term. Lest the uncertain parent consider these charges excessive, the prospectus notes that "the prices quoted are at least 30 percent lower than those charged for like services and studying advantages in first class Eastern and European schools." Moreover, three scholarships were given every six months to those students "who prove themselves, in point of industry, as the most ambitious in our school."[59]

Who were these students, and what did they study? Teachers at the Academy were keenly aware of the decentralized nature of Los Angeles and sought to be accessible to students "from all parts of this city, and especially for patrons from suburban cities."[60] Students from such cities as Pasadena, Azusa, and Inglewood had relatively easy access to the school by streetcar, and so did not have to live near downtown to get a good music education. Photographs of the Class of 1907 and of a student recital indicate a predominantly female, Euro-American student body, ranging in age from perhaps seven to twenty-five years. Out of nine students who had received scholarships, six were female. It is possible that many were of German heritage, because German children by 1908 were one of the largest ethnic groups in the city's schools.[61] At least one student, however, was African American: the pianist and composer William Wilkins, who later opened his own school in Los Angeles, the Wilkins School of Music.[62]

Demands were rigorous, and the school achieved recognition far beyond the borders of Los Angeles. Students studied a thoroughly European repertory of Beethoven, Mozart, Chopin, Bach, and Schumann. They gave recitals—from memory—every Saturday at the Academy, and also once per month at the auditorium of a prominent musical society, the Gamut Club, on 1044 South Hope Street. These concerts were community social events, and evidently could attract between 800 to 1,000 people. Few schools in Los Angeles could attain this level of professionalism. As one prospectus commented on the public student recitals alone, "what higher test of efficiency can any musical institution *anywhere* in this wide world subject itself to?"[63] The San Francisco-based journal *Pacific Coast Musical Review* agreed, calling von Stein "one of the most successful musical educators in the country." It referred to a teaching method that von Stein developed, called the "Rector System," as "one of the finest methods of getting results that has ever come to our attention." The Von Stein Academy, the journal concluded, "is as fine a musical educational institution as can be found anywhere."[64]

One competitor arose in the 1920s: the Olga Steeb Piano School. Although no known recordings of Heinrich von Stein survived, Olga Steeb made several recordings with Thomas Edison in 1922 and 1923 that reveal an excellent piano technique (hear Tracks no. 6 and 7). A Los Angeles native, she studied with local teacher Thilo Becker and toured Europe and the United States as a piano soloist until returning to Los Angeles with the outbreak of World War I. She headed the piano departments at both the University of Redlands (from 1915 to 1919) and the University of Southern California (from 1919 to 1923) before opening her own school on 3839 Wilshire Boulevard near Hancock Park, where composer Mary Carr Moore taught theory and composition. The school continued until shortly after Steeb's death in 1941. Institutions such as the Von Stein Academy and the Olga Steeb Piano School helped establish a strong tradition of musical pedagogy in early twentieth-century Los Angeles.[65]

Progressivism in Music Education

The Neighborhood Music Settlement was a very different kind of institution. Social worker Pearle Irene Odell founded the school in 1914 in the East Los Angeles community of Lincoln Heights, which at the time consisted mostly of German, Irish, and Italian immigrants. Born in 1883 in South Dakota, Odell studied social work in New York and worked at the Philadelphia Settlement School before moving to Los Angeles.[66] Witnessing the plight of immigrant children who had few opportunities to learn English, let alone music, she dedicated herself over a period of almost 50 years to uphold the Settlement's original ideals of "music for all." To this end she brought together a dedicated group of musicians drawn to her mission of giving low-income children lessons on piano, violin, viola, cello, trumpet, and guitar, as well as voice and music theory. Each room was designated for the teaching of a specific instrument, and lessons usually took place weekday afternoons and during the summer. Students who could pay were charged 50 cents per lesson, while top students, as with the Von Stein Academy, received scholarships.

The Settlement soon moved to a two-story house on Boyle Street in nearby Boyle Heights, which since World War I was predominantly Jewish and Russian, with some Armenian, Japanese, and Latino residents.[67] The school's goals remained the same: to provide children with excellent music training at little or no cost, as well as to help them learn English and develop other skills and thus Americanize them.[68] It was a product of the Progressive era, which encouraged volunteers to develop an active social consciousness to aid the poor, particularly immigrant children. Based on the settlement model for cultural assimilation then popular in Midwestern and East Coast cities, such as the Settlement House in Chicago and Third Street Settlement in New York, these institutions became legendary centers of their communities. The social workers who ran the settlement houses helped immigrants to become

Americanized and to find much-needed support from caring individuals. What set the Neighborhood Settlement House apart was its steadfast emphasis on the value of immigrants to learn music.

Because of its unique mission, the school attracted notice. In the cultural guide that the Civic Bureau of Music and Art in Los Angeles published, *Culture and the Community*, the authors noted with admiration that "[s]ix thousand three hundred lessons were given in 1925 including instruction in all departments of music."[69] The civic boosters who published the guide were clearly delighted with the school, since they gave other, far more prestigious music schools only a brief mention. A distinguishing feature is that several of the faculty of the Neighborhood Music Settlement were members of the Los Angeles Philharmonic. Some taught for economic reasons, because of the Philharmonic's then 12-week season, and musicians needed to work off-season. Others taught for ethical reasons and sought to help interested students who could not afford professional music instruction elsewhere. The school was even the subject of a film, *They Shall Have Music*, released in 1939 and starring violinist Jascha Heifetz.[70]

The Neighborhood Music Settlement survived primarily on subscriptions and annual memberships.[71] During the Depression years the school escaped the fate of most music schools of the region by incorporating as a nonprofit institution in 1936. True to Odell's commitment, the volunteer Board of Directors vowed to remain loyal to their Progressive roots, and continued to see the school's primary mission as a "solid Americanization in teaching of music to the under-privileged."[72] In 1947 the Settlement moved up the street to a two-story, 13-room Victorian mansion, where it is currently located near the corner of Boyle and Fourth Streets. Like the Third Street Settlement in New York, the school has survived the hardships that closed similar schools. When the demographics of the surrounding community changed from Euro-American to primarily Mexican American after World War II, the Neighborhood Music Settlement continued its original goals of music instruction for all, regardless of age, ethnicity, or income. It is the sole music school in Los Angeles founded during the early twentieth century to survive into the twenty-first century.[73]

Similarly, opportunities existed for African American children to learn music at private academies during the Progressive era. Because of increasing migration from the South, the black population in Los Angeles grew rapidly, from 1,258 in 1890 to 7,599 in 1910 to comprise 2.4 percent of the city's total population.[74] At least five different black communities formed in Los Angeles by the 1920s, with the largest community along Central Avenue. Musicians held positions of prominence, and their number grew to 22 in 1910, 73 in 1920, 226 in 1930, and 260 in 1940. These musicians formed about 30 percent of the black professional class in 1910, and still represented almost a quarter of African American professionals in 1940.[75] Many were able to earn a living by teaching, in part because a thriving black middle class was able to afford music lessons for its children. Despite the expansion of housing restrictions

Figure 2.3 Neighborhood Music School

after 1910, blacks in Los Angeles had a higher level of homeownership and were also comparably better off than blacks in other American cities. At least until the Depression, "the persistence and growth of a Black middle class beyond the scale of other cities continued."[76]

The same Progressive spirit that drove Pearle Odell also inspired music teacher William Wilkins to establish his Wilkins School of Music, one of the most renowned African American music schools in Los Angeles. In 1912 Wilkins opened the school on Central Avenue at 14th Street and hired a total of six teachers, who taught 250 pupils in the Piano Academy as well as a "kindergarten department" of 40 children.[77] Not all students were black; some were reportedly white or Japanese. Like Odell, Wilkins was not a native Angeleno; he moved with his family from Little Rock, Arkansas to Long

Beach, where his father opened a tin shop on Ninth Street. The elder Wilkins played in a fife and drum corps, and taught his son to play by ear on piano, piccolo, and cornet. William attended Polytechnic High School in Los Angeles, a predominantly white school, where he was able to study piano while earning a degree in electrical engineering through the American Correspondence School. Upon graduation he became one of the first blacks to work for the Edison Electrical Light and Power Company as a line inspector, though he continued his piano studies with Professor von Stein at the Von Stein Academy.[78] After four years, Von Stein was so impressed with Wilkins' progress that he hired him to teach piano at the Academy.[79]

Wilkins's reputation among the local community was legendary. One former pupil, Samuel Browne, described Wilkins as "an imposing figure with long hair, in his cowboy hat, long coat, big bow tie . . . gloves, walking stick with golden knob and glasses with a long ribbon attached!"[80] His commanding appearance seems to have made him either much loved, or distrusted, by community members, but he achieved results. Browne, who later studied music at the University of Southern California and became a renowned music teacher in the Los Angeles public schools, recalled that Wilkins "pushed, cajoled, stormed, raged, and molded students and they loved him! He had charisma and was respected. . . . Conservatives did not appreciate him as he was so dramatic and wonderful, but he made his mark." Browne added that Wilkins "drove us, and congratulated us, and gave us every type of appreciation that one person could give to another. He became a surrogate father to all of us."[81]

Figure 2.4 William Wilkins (third row, far left) with class, ca. 1932

As with the Von Stein Academy, concerts by students at the Wilkins School were important community events. To demonstrate his pupils' accomplishments he held public recitals every Sunday at his home on Central Avenue by moving three of his six pianos onto the front lawn. Parents of pupils, friends, and associates set up chairs outside, where even passengers on the trolley that ran in front of the house could benefit from these occasions. Wilkins directed the activities or accompanied the students on piano. To further motivate students, he also organized annual recitals, such as the 15th Annual Recital that took place on Tuesday evening, July 10, 1928 at the St. Paul Baptist Church at the corner of 21st and Naomi Streets. After over a decade of such recitals, the event also included a commencement ceremony for which Wilkins gave out certificates of merit and promotion as well as diplomas for those who completed the program. Tickets cost 25 cents and 35 cents.[82]

In addition to these concerts, he sought to motivate students in other ways. He organized a Talent Night for children every first Sunday of the month at the Independent Church (also called the People's Independent Church of Christ) during the 1920s and 1930s.[83] He gave an annual concert for at least 16 years at Blanchard Hall, which according to Samuel Browne "was always a very big occasion for the black community."[84] Wilkins broadened his influence further by establishing five branches of his school in southern California, and students and teachers from these schools all participated in the Annual Recital on Central Avenue. These schools lasted long after the Wilkins School had closed after some 20 years in operation.[85]

The Gray Conservatory of Music resembled the Wilkins School in some respects. Founded in 1931 and located at 1106 E. 38th Street near Central Avenue, it too was interracial, with white and black students and teachers. At a time when the Progressive movement had waned nationally, the Gray Conservatory upheld the ideals of both Odell and Wilkins in its approach to interethnic education. Twenty-five teachers offered instruction in all instruments, voice, and music theory, as well as dancing and even languages. Its founder, John Gray, was a very different type of teacher from Wilkins. Whereas Wilkins was flamboyant, Gray was reserved; while Wilkins had a limited music education, Gray held degrees in music. Born in Norfolk, Virginia of a Canadian mother and an American father, he moved to Los Angeles in 1909 and, like Wilkins, graduated from Polytechnic High School in Los Angeles. His father was his first piano teacher, and Gray continued his studies at both the University of Southern California and at the Los Angeles State Normal School. To support himself he held various odd jobs during the day and studied music at night school to improve his knowledge of piano, harmony, counterpoint, and composition. He went to France to serve in World War I as sergeant in the Medical Corps, then studied at the Ecole Normale de Musique in Paris, France, which the famous French pianist and pedagogue Alfred Cortot had founded after the war. Gray obtained his teacher's diploma in piano in 1929 before returning to Los Angeles as one of the most educated black music teachers in the city.[86]

With these credentials Gray was able to hire well-qualified teachers and performers. One of his best teachers was Katie Miller, who studied at the New England Conservatory of Music, Oberlin Conservatory, and Northwestern University School of Music. Trained as a concert pianist, she taught in Illinois and Arkansas before coming to Los Angeles in the 1930s. Opportunities for musicians were limited during the Depression, particularly for African American women, and the school provided an immediate outlet for her talents. As both a teacher and performer, she gave concerts on both the East and West Coasts and taught privately as well as at Gray's Conservatory. While no records survive on the methods of instruction or content of the courses at Gray's school, the presence of teachers like Miller and Gray suggests strongly that instruction had a European art music emphasis.[87]

Similar to Wilkins, Gray maintained close connections to the Central Avenue community in several ways. He was the first organist at St. Philips Episcopal Church and gave performances at other houses of worship, such as the Second Baptist Church.[88] To establish a means of representing black musicians, as Arévalo did with Hispanic musicians, he formed the Musicians' Association in Los Angeles, which later became part of the National Association of Negro Musicians.[89] Above all he urged parents to support their children's endeavors. As one student recalled, Gray continually told parents at recitals, "We have to get behind the kids and push."[90] Through a combination of teaching and performing, Gray and his colleagues at the conservatory reached a multiracial student body and contributed to the community ethos on which the school was founded.

These three schools were significant in several ways. Instruction in art music was available to a diversity of students, across ethnic and class lines. The Progressive spirit of social improvement led to the creation of these schools, and their founders remained committed to their cause even after the progressive movement had ended. The schools were cultural models in their communities. The Neighborhood Music Settlement, the sole music school to survive intact into the present era, became a major cultural institution in Boyle Heights to reach students of modest means. The two predominantly black conservatories arose during a time of intense African American interest to instill cultural pride to counteract segregation and discrimination, and both Wilkins and Gray thus personified the "New Negro" in the Los Angeles Renaissance. All three music schools offered professional instruction while making the arts as accessible to young people as possible.

Youth Concerts

A final form of music education in Los Angeles consisted of youth concerts. Schoolchildren had ample opportunity to attend such concerts by the early twentieth century, which several different local music institutions made possible. The ultimate hope was that if students could hear classical music "live," they might continue to enjoy and attend concerts into their adult years. Similar to the efforts of conductor Walter Damrosch of the New York Philharmonic, who was one of the pioneers in youth concerts on the East Coast, several figures in Los Angeles spearheaded the organization of concerts specifically for children. Among them were impresario Lynden Behymer, conductor Walter Henry Rothwell, and educators Bess Daniel and William Hartshorn.

One of the first such coordinated efforts arose with the Los Angeles Symphony Orchestra. Students could buy a standard ticket for 25 cents, or get a student discount for any other seat in the house. The editor of the *Musical Review*, Alfred Metzger, wrote in 1906: "A great many students come to rehearsals, which are free to all subscribers and ticket holders. This is an excellent feature of the concerts, for it really assists directly in planting the germ of musical culture, giving the students an opportunity to become acquainted with the classical works." The board of directors further established a guarantee fund to keep the enterprise going, due to relatively low ticket prices. Active members contributed about $25 every three years, which did not include the price of a ticket. As Metzger concluded, the ultimate purpose of the fund was "educating the youth of Los Angeles in the art of listening to music."[91]

Building on this precedent, a leading series of concerts readily available to young people was the Philharmonic Series, which Lynden Behymer and his wife Menetta organized in the early 1910s. The purpose was to bring musical artists to schools and colleges so that students as well as the general public could hear art music by professional performers. These occasions proved to be so successful that the Behymers expanded the program in 1914. Public high schools in Pasadena, Long Beach, Hollywood, San Diego, Santa Barbara, Sacramento, and Fresno, as well as the colleges in Claremont, San Jose, and Marysville together created a series of four events for a season subscription price of one dollar. Called the Behymer Philharmonic Series, the 1915 season included appearances by composers Charles Wakefield Cadman and Amy Beach, who played their works on piano. Between 1,000 to 1,200 students attended the concerts each year, which also took place in other West Coast cities of 5,000 inhabitants or more.[92]

One ensemble, the Zoellner Quartet, was perfect for these occasions, since it was truly a family affair. It consisted of the father, Joseph Zoellner Sr., who had been first violinist of the Theodore Thomas Orchestra, and his three children, Joseph Jr., Antoinette, and Amandus. Born in Brooklyn, New York, the Zoellners eventually moved to Los Angeles, where members of the ensemble taught at the University of Redlands and Pomona College. Although its repertoire was primarily European, the quartet also performed American music, such as "Dixie" and "Swanee River," which it recorded in 1915, the same year it appeared in the Philharmonic Series (hear Track no. 2).[93]

A further means of educating students through performance was to allow them to participate in concerts themselves. In a concert series called the Behymer Matinees, begun in the 1920s, some of the best music students in

Los Angeles County had the experience of performing before the public. As Menetta Behymer recalled, "The many excellent music schools each vied to have their star pupils given a chance to appear on these programs." The audience consisted not only of parents and friends but also teachers, students, senior citizens, and "music-lovers who were never seen at our regular [Philharmonic] concerts in the Auditorium." The concerts took place at a small auditorium at the Barker Brothers store, located at Seventh and Flower Streets, every Wednesday afternoon at 2:30 P.M. Several musicians who went on to successful music careers got their start with the Behymer Matinees, among them pianist Eugene List, mezzo-soprano Nan Merriman, tenor Brian Sullivan, and soprano Anne Bollinger, the latter two of whom joined the Metropolitan Opera in New York.[94]

With these educational concert series providing the foundation, the youth concerts of the Los Angeles Philharmonic superceded everything that had come before. With its founding in 1919, Los Angeles finally had a truly permanent orchestra. The support of an independently wealthy music lover in Los Angeles, the amateur violinist and classical music enthusiast William Andrews Clark Jr., brought to an end the numbing need that previous orchestras had regularly experienced: to raise funds each season.[95] Clark's munificent efforts paralleled those of the founder of the Boston Symphony Orchestra, Henry Lee Higginson. Many Angelenos have expressed their steadfast appreciation since then, not least among them the musicians union itself.[96] Fortunately, Clark had a strong interest in making the orchestra of 90 musicians as available to the public as he could, and in its first season, the Los Angeles Philharmonic performed 12 different symphonic programs, 14 "Pops" programs, and 9 special concerts, including a series of appearances at elementary and high schools.[97]

The first conductor of the Los Angeles Philharmonic, Walter Henry Rothwell, proved to be ideal in the field of music education, because he was a pioneer in youth concerts. In 1907, when he was a conductor of the St. Paul Symphony Orchestra in Minneapolis, Rothwell organized and led one of the first concert series in America specifically for children.[98] What conductor Theodore Thomas had set out to do for adults almost 40 years earlier, Rothwell sought to accomplish with young people. These concerts, like music courses in the public schools, rested on the premise that exposure to art music could improve the aesthetic sensitivity of children, or in other words, "civilize" them. By showing them a world beyond the limits of popular music, educators sought to broaden both the musical and educational development of their pupils. As Los Angeles music educator William Hartshorn argued in his 1940 book, *The Mentor: Making Friends With Music*, one of the fundamental purposes of music appreciation should be to "promote a freedom of response, both intellectual and emotional, to the esthetic content of music."[99] Youth concerts provided one means of achieving that goal.

As with the youth concerts he founded with the St. Paul Symphony Orchestra, Rothwell organized and conducted five matinee concerts for

Figure 2.5 Walter Henry Rothwell

children and teachers at Trinity Auditorium and ten matinee concerts at Los Angeles high schools during the inaugural 1919–20 season. The first such concert took place on November 13, 1919, at a Thursday matinee for Los Angeles elementary schools at Trinity Auditorium, for which the orchestra played works by Elgar, Massenet, Tchaikovsky, Godard, and Chabrier. Students were segregated by age only, with concerts specifically for elementary school children and those at the intermediate level, and the only cost per child was a dime. Nothing on this scale had ever occurred in Los Angeles before.[100]

Similar concerts took place at Los Angeles high schools in the 1920s. Due to the decentralized layout of Los Angeles, the orchestra traveled to several different schools, and reached a diversity of students in terms of both ethnicity and class. During the months of November and December the orchestra performed at schools on the average of once per week: at Los Angeles Polytechnic High School, Los Angeles High School, Lincoln High School, and Manual Arts High School. At least two of these schools, Polytechnic High School and Manual Arts High School, served both Anglo and African American students.[101] The programs for the first two concerts were identical, with works by Elgar, Tchaikovsky, Massenet, Saint-Saëns, and Wagner, as were the programs for the second group of concerts, with music by Wagner, Tchaikovsky, Grieg, Massenet, and Chabrier.[102]

These concerts proved to be exciting for both students and conductor alike. Following a performance at Polytechnic High School, Rothwell stated that "I never enjoyed conducting more than today. Such enthusiasm and attention one might only expect from a grown-up audience. The moment I rapped for the attention of the men in the Orchestra there was absolute silence among the girls and boys. Imagine having to repeat the Prelude from [Wagner's] *Lohengrin* at the urgent request of these youngsters."[103] To strengthen the bond with Los Angeles teachers, two concerts were also given for the California Teachers' Association, both at Trinity Auditorium. The next year, the orchestra performed twice at Hollywood High School, and appeared again at Los Angeles High School, Polytechnic High School, and Manual Arts High School. The Los Angeles Philharmonic was, from the outset, dedicated to music education in the public schools.

These educational concerts continued in subsequent years. During the 1921–22 season, the orchestra gave eight concerts for elementary, intermediate and high school children at the Philharmonic Auditorium (the new name of Temple Auditorium) between November and April.[104] Even the University of Southern California benefited from this largesse, with three concerts on campus at Bovard Auditorium.[105] The orchestra was not restricted to Los Angeles County: Subsequent educational concerts took place at elementary, intermediate, and high schools in Anaheim, San Diego, Fullerton, and Santa Barbara.

Pasadena schoolchildren particularly benefited from the Los Angeles Philharmonic's touring schedule. Pasadena residents had long supported music associations and concert series, notably the Coleman Chamber Concerts that pianist Alice Coleman Batchelder started in 1903, and the city also had its own conservatory.[106] Pasadena public schools maintained music programs at all age levels, and school leaders worked with the Philharmonic management to bring the orchestra frequently to the city. In the 1921–22 season alone, the orchestra performed four times at the Pasadena High School Auditorium under the sponsorship of the Pasadena Music and Art Association.[107] Programs from later years indicate that on average three to four concerts took place annually in Pasadena for the city's schoolchildren.[108]

Who arranged these concerts? The Women's Committee of the Los Angeles Philharmonic was primarily responsible for contacting schools and setting up dates for the concerts. Bess Daniel was the commentator for the youth concerts for six years (1923 to 1929), followed by brief tenures of Educational Directors John Henry Lyons and Henry Purmort Eames, later a professor of "music culture and aesthetics" at Scripps College. The figure who then became virtually synonymous with educational concerts in Los Angeles was William Hartshorn, a music teacher at Beverly Hills High School, who became supervisor of music for the Los Angeles Public Schools during the 1930s. He worked closely with the Symphony Association to maintain the quality and educational value of the concerts over the next 30 years.

Figure 2.6 Philharmonic Auditorium

Hartshorn revealed his commitment to music education in a book, *The Mentor: Making Friends With Music*, which he co-wrote in 1940 with Helen Leavitt, the Director of Music at the Wheelock School in Boston. They emphasized a well-rounded approach to music appreciation to promote "the students' understanding of the music, rather than merely . . . the presentation of facts about it or drill in recognizing its . . . technical aspects."[109] Especially noteworthy in the book were its "Suggestions for Procedure," those aspects of the music that the teacher should highlight for discussion, both before and after playing the music. Because both authors also taught at the university level (he at the University of Southern California, she at Boston University), it seems that the text was designed for students at both the high school and college levels.

Hartshorn and Leavitt began the book by presenting different types of American music, from Indian folk music to works by composers Edward

Figure 2.7 Philharmonic Auditorium, interior view

MacDowell, John Alden Carpenter, and George Gershwin, among others. Only then did they discuss major European composers, primarily from the nineteenth century, such as Paul Dukas, Alexander Borodin, Robert Schumann, Richard Wagner, and Frederick Delius. The authors gave a brief description of the composer's life and the type of music (dance, symphony, opera) before analyzing specific musical themes. If a work was programmatic music, they described the scene the composer was attempting to illustrate. In this way, if students could visualize the music, then they might be able to develop a stronger association with it. Like the authors of *Music Education in the Elementary School*, both Hartshorn and Leavitt believed that music appreciation should become a *creative* activity. In the case of Borodin's String Quartet No. 2, the authors encouraged students to divide into two groups, then sing the theme in the form of a canon.[110] Students could thus learn about melody, harmony, and rhythm through active participation. Despite a European emphasis, the authors also stressed works by American composers, and so presented an integrated form of music education that recognized the country's own musical roots.

Among his many other accomplishments, Hartshorn strengthened the public school system's ties to the Los Angeles Philharmonic. During the Depression years, when budget cuts threatened such programs, the orchestra's outreach efforts to schools continued in a reduced form. The orchestra gave three "Young People's Concerts" at Philharmonic Auditorium annually, and appeared twice each season in Pasadena for youth concerts at the Civic Auditorium. Hartshorn helped arrange the concerts, prepared teachers for instructing students, and at times even wrote the program notes. In the 1937–38 season, there were four Young People's Concerts at Philharmonic Auditorium, featuring both traditional and modern works, such as by Beethoven, Mozart, Wagner, Stravinsky, Sibelius, and Scriabin.[111] The difference with previous seasons is that one of the most distinguished conductors to lead the orchestra in its history, Otto Klemperer, conducted several of these youth concerts. During his six year tenure as director (1933–39), he helped promote one of the original goals of the orchestra: to provide schoolchildren of all ages and backgrounds the opportunity to hear art music. Such youth concerts continued well into the 1960s under the title "Symphonies For Youth" and benefited hundreds of thousands of schoolchildren.[112]

Conclusion

The longstanding efforts of women and men in the field of music education contributed immeasurably to the music culture of Los Angeles. Good teachers not only produced good students, but reinforced the importance of music in the general education of countless schoolchildren. Just as it is difficult to imagine an entertainment industry in Los Angeles without professional musicians, it is equally difficult to imagine a self-sustaining music culture in Los Angeles without dedicated teachers. Across decentralized Los Angeles, music instruction was accessible to a diversity of students: rich and poor, Anglo, Black, Hispanic, and Asian.

It is all the more surprising that these music programs took place during a time of dramatic conflict in education, particularly during the 1920s. The Americanization movement engendered powerful ideological battles on both the right and left of the debate, and while little anger surfaced concerning the teaching of music, such education played an important role in the Americanization of immigrant children.[113] Discussion of the state's cultural heritage had much to do with how Californians imagined themselves. If children learned that the music of the Southwest, for example, consisted of melodies from the Californios as well as from African American spirituals, then they might absorb, consciously or unconsciously, a specific regional identity. During a time of real estate restrictions throughout much of Los Angeles County and segregation in most public schools, this diverse heritage may have seemed at odds with what they saw in everyday life. Yet the teaching of music, such as through the *Music Education in the Elementary School* or *The Mentor: Making Friends With Music*, encouraged a more tolerant stance in dealing with ethnic and class differences, while at the same time claiming that music education programs were a sign of progress and cultural achievement.

One contributing factor to the expansion of music education programs was a far greater access to musical instruments. Both the enormous popularity of town bands and the rapid growth of instrument-making companies in America during the nineteenth century had already made brass instruments almost ubiquitous in American towns and cities.[114] Similarly, instruments such as violins and pianos became more available to Los Angeles children of middle-class and even working-class families through such programs as Jennie L. Jones's Elementary Orchestra Department and the installment plans of the Southern California Music Company, thereby enabling parents to afford instruments on a restricted budget. Nor were these kinds of programs by any means limited to Los Angeles. What began during the Progressive era continued even into the Depression; by 1939, *Fortune* magazine could report that on a national scale, "more children were learning to play the piano than at anytime in history."[115]

Youth concerts, too, played a critical role in music education. Music teachers, orchestra administrators, and impresarios joined forces to arrange programs for students to hear professional musicians either in concert or during rehearsals. This format became standard practice in American cities with top orchestras such as New York, Chicago, and San Francisco, and youth concerts were common not only in concert halls but also at outdoor venues, such as the Hollywood Bowl and its counterpart in New York, Lewisohn Stadium. Listening to music thus became more of an event, because youth concerts helped to make the music that students studied in class "come alive."

Far from "sacralizing" this music, these teachers and administrators were trying to do precisely the opposite—to make that music more accessible to children across the boundaries of gender, ethnicity, and class.[116] Where people may have been divided by ethnicity or economic status, in the music classroom or concert hall they could be united in the common appreciation of music, hence its value in Americanization programs. The "great equalizer" in American society was not merely education itself but also the arts, which people from diverse backgrounds could hold in common, whether they came from the wealthy Westside of Los Angeles, or Pasadena, or Boyle Heights, or Central Avenue. The desacralization of music, or its democratization, was the purpose of these music programs, and thousands of children took part in that desacralization over the ensuing decades.

A certain zeal characterized the efforts of music teachers in Los Angeles County through the first half of the twentieth century. They believed Los Angeles to be a kind of Eden, and their mission—to educate schoolchildren and young adults in the field of music—was ultimately possible because a large cadre of well-trained musicians in the region saw the teaching of music as a form of calling. No one became rich from these programs. The constant efforts of Progressive reformers, the rapid expansion of educational institutions, and the Americanization movement all inspired teachers to make music an integral part of many children's lives. The creation of a wide variety of music education programs thus helped Los Angeles become a musical metropolis.

3

"Symphonies Under the Stars": The Romance of the Hollywood Bowl

The founding of the Hollywood Bowl dramatically altered the musical landscape of Los Angeles.[1] Under the stars each summer, tens of thousands of people heard symphonies, concertos, and arias from opera, as well as other music that reflected the city's diversity. Equally striking was the degree to which men, women, and children took part in activities at the Bowl, in what began as an experiment in community support for the arts. The Bowl represented far more than merely a local venue for concerts during the summer; it became a leading forum in southern California for performances, and it attracted the attention of music lovers around the country and abroad. The purpose of this chapter is to explain why the Bowl achieved such significance in Los Angeles's music culture.

Outdoor concerts were by no means new in America. Bandstands had long been common in American towns and cities, where brass ensembles regularly performed for passers-by during the warm summer months. Bandleader Patrick Gilmore organized at least two outdoor "Peace Jubilees" in Boston, which reportedly attracted thousands of people. On a more modest scale, conductor Theodore Thomas created a summer series of orchestral concerts in Central Park Garden in New York in 1865 that lasted for eight years, and conductor of the New York Symphony Orchestra, Walter Damrosch, recalled "long summer engagements," two concerts per day, in Philadelphia and in Chicago during the 1890s. During World War I, a concert at the Lewisohn Stadium in New York to raise funds for the war led to a series of open-air concerts at the stadium that continued long afterward.[2]

The idea of founding an outdoor theater in Los Angeles began to take shape after the phenomenal success of an outdoor performance of Shakespeare. In 1916, a group of actors and musicians presented *Julius Caesar* in nearby Beachwood Canyon, which like the Hollywood Bowl was a natural amphitheater. An audience of over 20,000 saw it, with reportedly 20,000 more trying to get in.[3] Three years later, several businessmen, art patrons, artists, and a doctor formed a community arts organization, the Theatre Arts Alliance, and they set out to find a similar venue in the hills above Hollywood. The Alliance's young secretary, H. Ellis Reed, scouted the rugged hills with his father for possible sites, and they soon happened across a dell that seemed perfect.[4]

The dell was long historically significant to the region. Located at the end of Bolton Canyon near Cahuenga Pass, the name derived from the Gabrieleño *cahuenga*, or "place of the mountain," and it had been a favored site for meetings and gatherings by local Indian tribes. During the eighteenth century, Cahuenga Pass was the throughway for the "King's Highway," or El Camino Real, the road that connected the California missions. It later became a supply route during the Gold Rush, and was the main northern route out of the city before the arrival of the Southern Pacific Railroad in 1876. The area also gained importance with the Battle of Cahuenga in 1845 between Mexican troops and the Californios, which ultimately led to the Californios' appointment of governor Pío Pico. For fortune-seekers, the dell retained an element of mystery as the site of a fabled (and still undiscovered) treasure of gold, silver, and jewels.[5]

What mattered most to the Theatre Arts Alliance were the location's acoustics. The dell had superb, natural acoustics—a great rarity indeed. If a person spoke in the middle of the dell, that person's voice could be heard on the hilltop a quarter of a mile away. Several musicians came to see—and hear—for themselves. Lynden Behymer and his daughter drove the famous German-American singer Ernestine Schumann-Heink to the area to test the acoustics, and she was amazed.[6] The violinist Leopold Godowsky Jr., a member of the newly-formed Los Angeles Philharmonic, performed a test with his Guarnerius violin.[7] On another occasion, the conductor of the San Francisco Symphony, Alfred Hertz, visited the site and greatly admired the quality of sound. It became apparent that the dell offered extraordinary possibilities for open-air concerts.

A second reason for choosing the site was its convenient location. Only a half-mile from downtown Hollywood, the Bowl was within easy walking distance of most homes in the area, and people long afterwards commented on the joy of walking up to the Bowl. Seven miles northwest of downtown Los Angeles, the Bowl was within reach for those Angelenos with cars and for commuters and tourists on the Red Car railway system.[8] Here was a pleasant and convenient site where people could sit comfortably outside and listen to music. Men could smoke; children could frolic in the trees around the dell. The location was enchanting and close enough for many people to participate in the grand experience of outdoor concerts.

The climate was ideal for such concerts. Summers in southern California are almost devoid of rainfall. In the Bowl's entire history, only a few concerts have been canceled due to inclement weather. Many people migrated to the region precisely for the weather and Mediterranean atmosphere, and city boosters regularly referred to southern California as "the New Italy, the New Spain, the New Athens . . . the New World Garden, the New Eden."[9] Inhabitants of the Midwest and the East, fed up with the harsh climate, sought southern California as a refuge. The Bowl seemed to typify the romantic, Mediterranean atmosphere of the area, and so served as a refuge within a refuge.

At the time of the Bowl's founding, Los Angeles was becoming a burgeoning metropolis. With a population increase from about 50,000 in 1890 to over 170,000 by 1900, and then to over 580,000 by 1920, it was the fastest-growing city in the United States.[10] Los Angeles surpassed its longtime rival, San Francisco, in population, and doubled in size from 1920 to 1924, becoming the fourth largest urban center in the country.[11] The construction of an aqueduct, the discovery of oil, and the development of a successful movie colony all brought substantial improvements to the region's economy.[12] Southern California beckoned what many Americans sought: good jobs, beautiful weather, and an abundance of space.[13]

Hollywood was part of this urban excitement, and local business people portrayed it as a "city of the future," although it was only a district of Los Angeles. It grew from a population of about 5,000 in 1910 to almost 50,000 ten years later. Within the decentralized geographic layout of Los Angeles, it presented an alternative to the crowded, older downtown district. Many business people during the 1920s believed that Hollywood would become the main commercial hub in the County. By the end of the decade, Hollywood Boulevard grew into a "skyscraper mile that formed the second largest business district in Los Angeles and one of the largest outlying centers in the United States."[14]

This image of a dynamic business center contrasted starkly with the negative perception of Hollywood as the main location for the movie colony. Those not in the movie industry tended to view movie people, whom they nicknamed pejoratively as "movies," as crass and even sleazy.[15] Actors, directors, and producers had little to do with the Hollywood business elite, and created their own community of artists. They came to southern California precisely to be independent of restrictions, real or imagined, imposed on them in New York, Chicago, or other urban centers. By the end of the 1920s, however, the movie colony had become a part of that business elite, and the film industry attracted musicians, composers, and arrangers who further stimulated the music culture in Los Angeles.

The economic dynamism of the boosters of Hollywood led to an advantageous environment for arts patronage and for the experimental venture that the Bowl represented. The founding of the Los Angeles Philharmonic in 1919 proved beneficial for both the Bowl and the orchestra. Until the 1920s, to attend an orchestral concert usually meant to go to a theater or concert hall. Not everyone interested in classical music, however, wanted to sit inside, particularly during the summer. How could one solve this quandary? The Hollywood Bowl provided the perfect solution.

Founders

With strong community support behind them, several men and women led the effort to make the dream of an outdoor concert venue a reality. They came from very different backgrounds, but were united in the belief that art music should be made available to as many people as possible. Two community activists, Dr. T. Perceval Gerson and Frederick W. Blanchard, fervently supported the idea of an arts center. Gerson was a physician as well as a devoted progressive reformer, much like his close friend, John Randolph Haynes.[16] He kept up a wide correspondence with famous liberal thinkers of the day, including Upton Sinclair, Lincoln Steffens, and Clarence Darrow, and among his myriad responsibilities was a member of the American Civil Liberties Union, a patron of the Committee for Planned Parenthood, and publisher of the *Los Angeles Municipal Newspaper*.[17] The idea of a community forum for music intrigued Gerson, and he immediately became the vice-president of the Theatre Arts Alliance, serving in various administrative positions until the end of his life.[18]

Frederick W. Blanchard was another early advocate of the arts in Los Angeles. A migrant from New England, he founded and operated a music store, arranged Chautauqua festivals, and in his spare time composed music. With music promoter James T. Fitzgerald he opened Blanchard-Fitzgerald Hall around 1894, an 800-seat venue for concerts and lectures. Convinced that music performances should be accessible to as many people as possible, he initiated a concert series with the slogan "popular prices will prevail," which the Hollywood Bowl later adopted. He also opened a music studio for local artists and musicians in 1901.[19] Like Gerson, Blanchard became a founding member of the Theatre Arts Alliance, and over the next several decades steadfastly upheld the notion of making concerts at the Bowl both affordable and of the highest quality possible.[20]

An influential figure in the Bowl's history from the very beginning was Charles E. Toberman. The real estate developer was in a better position than most to arrange a land deal essential to assuring the Bowl's early success. His own dream was to create a venue that might be like that in Oberammergau, Germany, which had an outdoor theater with a long history of community support.[21] Over the next 30 years, he helped arrange the purchase of land, the payment of the mortgage, and to protect the area from further development. He owned much land along the rim of the Bowl, which he donated so that no construction might mar the vista. When other developers were building Mulholland Drive nearby, Toberman renegotiated the route so that traffic "would not be seen or heard from the Bowl."[22] His interest, however, was not entirely altruistic. As a developer he stood to gain from whatever increases in real estate values resulted from being near the Bowl.

Pianist Artie Mason Carter soon joined this enthusiastic group.[23] She grew up in Missouri and studied the piano at American conservatories, and later accompanied her physician-husband to Vienna. There she studied under the renowned Polish pianist Theodor Leschetizky, whose pupils numbered such famous pianists as Ignacy Paderewski, Ossip Gabrilowitsch, and Artur Schnabel. Following their stay in Europe the Carters arrived in Hollywood, where Dr. Carter began his practice, and his wife soon became involved in community

Figure 3.1 Founders in dish (l. to r.): Charles Toberman, Harriet Grey, Mr. Sibertson, Artie Mason Carter, Frederick Blanchard, unidentified, Ellis Reed

cultural events, especially those of choral groups. She rose to prominence as leader of the Hollywood Community Sing, a group founded in 1917 during the patriotic fervor of World War I, which grew to over one thousand members.[24]

Carter showed remarkable talents in both organization and inspiring enthusiasm. A case in point was her relation to the city's leading arts patron, William Andrews Clark Jr. She met Clark during her work with the Hollywood Community Chorus, when she performed with the Los Angeles Philharmonic during an Easter service at the Bowl in 1921.[25] Carter suggested to him that the Bowl could become the summer venue for the orchestra, and Clark leapt on the idea. The result was the Bowl's first concert series, "Symphonies Under the Stars." Organizing numerous public fund drives, she generated overwhelming community support for the Bowl's mission. "Words utterly fail to do justice to the dynamic enthusiasm and leadership that Mrs. Carter brought to her inspired work for Hollywood Bowl," Dr. Gerson maintained. "It stands as a monument more enduring than bronze or stone."[26]

The two major financial contributors at this early stage were Christine Wetherill Stevenson and Marie Rankin Clarke. They joined a long list of women who patronized the arts in America during the nineteenth and twentieth centuries.[27] Stevenson hailed from Philadelphia, where her husband had made a fortune in munitions during World War I.[28] With this money and her own personal wealth, Mrs. Stevenson sought to establish a permanent home for the seven arts of acting, music, dancing, painting, literature, sculpture, and architecture. A fervent believer in theosophy, with its tenet of the universal brotherhood of humankind, she chose to come to southern California because of its reputation for artistic freedom. Accompanying her were artists and musicians from the East Coast to participate in her dream, a pageant play by Edwin Arnold, the *Light of Asia*, a dramatic re-enactment of the life of Buddha. While the Theatre Arts Alliance was less than delighted about her religious ideas, it did appreciate her wealth, and she served briefly as the Alliance's first president. She directly influenced how the Alliance invested its funds, and Gerson referred to her as "the real economic power in our group."[29] Marie Rankin Clarke, married to oil millionaire Chauncey Clarke, joined Stevenson in giving $21,000 toward the purchase of almost 60 acres of land. Members of the Theatre Arts Alliance contributed an additional $5,500.[30] This combination of community activism and philanthropy made the Bowl a reality.

The Democratization of Music

The Hollywood Bowl served a distinct purpose in the performance of art music. Its supporters believed that people would happily come to listen to concerts if they were accessible to everyone. Above all, ticket prices had to be low, and borrowing Blanchard's slogan of "popular prices will prevail," the lowest price for years remained 25 cents. Four concerts took place each week of the summer season, from July through the end of August, for a total on average of 32 programs. It is estimated that over 150,000 people came to these concerts during the first season alone, and more than 250,000 attended during the third season in 1924.[31] These concerts represented a "democratization of music" in the Southland.

At the time, the idea of democratizing music received wide support. Many leaders of the Progressive movement in the early twentieth century strove to improve the morals and virtues of the masses through social reform, and some saw music as a means of achieving that goal. The founder of Hull House in Chicago, Jane Addams, stated that "[w]e are only beginning to understand what might be done through the festival, the street procession, the band of marching musicians, orchestral music in public squares or parks, with the magic power they all possess to formulate the sense of companionship and solidarity."[32] Progressive women with a similar social consciousness strongly supported the Bowl's mission, including E. J. "Grandma" Wakeman, Mrs. Leiland Atherton Irish, and Harriet Clay Penman, as well as composers Gertrude Ross and Carrie Jacobs Bond, all of whom took part in fundraising drives for the Bowl. What better way to appeal to people's sense of civic virtue than through music? During a period when Los Angeles voters were demanding political reform, eventually resulting in the Charter of 1925 that changed city government, others called for cultural and social reform.[33] By bringing classical music to the public as a substitute for the city's "disreputable pleasures" of gambling, drinking, and worse, perhaps those same listeners would join in the spirit of improvement, of bettering the self—and the soul—through musical sustenance.[34]

The hope of uplifting the city's morals through music thus assumed almost a religious calling. Writer Perley Poore Sheehan noted in the opening pages of a Hollywood Bowl program of 1925:

> It is like a sort of new Nativity. Here is a Prototype. Here has been born a Guide and a Comforter—a Savior to the nations. It is a prophecy of that day when not communities merely but the powers shall do as we do here: confer together not of scourgings [*sic*] but of gifts; when the sons and daughters of these shall mingle joyfully, in harmony; and once more the starry night will resound—as it well may here and now: ". . . and on earth peace, goodwill toward men."[35]

Even writers not from the area, such as the *New York Times* critic Olin Downes, sensed this zeal in attending concerts at the Bowl. He traveled to southern California to see for himself, coming away astounded by its impact on listeners. Downes remarked that the concerts "have a flavor different from any other concert known to me. The setting must be seen to be realized: the beauty of the hills; the noble lines of a natural amphitheater which slopes and narrows down to the orchestral platform; the almost tropical sky, with its great stars . . ." But the beauty of the site, he continued, was only one part of the experience: "The orchestra places at the disposal of an immense public—probably, on the whole, the largest public that gathers for any series of orchestral concerts in the world—the entire orchestral repertory; not only this, the concerts dispense almost entirely with the soloist element; they favor the cause of creative art and encourage native composers, many of whom will be given special hearings this season; they cost a quarter of a dollar a seat and end the season with a profit."[36]

As a New Yorker, he then paid the Bowl the supreme compliment. "These concerts are self-supporting through the enormous number of tickets which can be sold and the immense audience accommodated for each concert, and they maintain a quality of program of which the average would not be amiss with a subscription orchestral concert audience in New York in the Winter season." Downes concluded with a ringing affirmation of one of the primary goals of the community activists, that listening to art music in this environment was a form of music education: "[I]t is no wonder that thousands upon thousands attend the four concerts given on as many evenings each week and that these people listen in a quiet and under a spell not known to audiences of concert halls, and that they learn . . . without lectures or technical guide-books or analyses, to love and to worship music."[37]

Children also took part in concerts. In the Bowl's first season, a "Concert for Young People" on a Sunday afternoon consisted of short works by Mozart, Mendelssohn, Beethoven, Dvorak, Debussy, and Kreisler.[38] On weekday afternoons, the Bowl management organized "school concerts" and gave out thousands of free tickets in the public schools. One concert in 1924, titled

"Young Artists' Night," allowed budding musicians to display their skills in a concert of Mozart, Bach, Tchaikovsky, and Rubinstein.[39] This interest in music went further. Los Angeles public schools had long introduced music classes into the curriculum, with an emphasis on singing songs and learning harmony. Artie Mason Carter was keenly aware of the music programs in local elementary and high schools; prior to her involvement in the Bowl, she worked with Hollywood's Children's Chorus. She invited children to orchestral concerts, to perform concerts at school, and even to raise funds for the Bowl.[40]

One annual event in which children could regularly participate was the Easter Sunrise Service. It began in 1921, when the Hollywood Bowl Association asked William Andrews Clark Jr. if he would allow the Los Angeles Philharmonic to perform at the Bowl on Easter Sunday. He agreed, and on March 27, Rothwell led the orchestra in Sibelius's tone poem, *Finlandia*, before an audience of 10,000. Rothwell's wife, Elizabeth Rothwell, sang "Morning Hymn of Henschel" and the Hollywood Community Chorus under the direction of Hugo Kirchhofer sang "Holy, Holy, Holy" and "All Hail the Power of Jesus' Name."[41] The event grew in popularity, and in 1925, an estimated 50,000 people assembled in and around the Bowl on Easter Sunday.[42] A children's choir played a prominent role in these concerts, and dressed in white, the children formed the sign of a cross against the backdrop of the hill, clearly visible from the opposite side of the dale. One woman, Miriam Ziegler, recalled as a ten-year-old chorister in the first Easter Sunrise Service that there "were wooden benches to seat about 800 people. The rest of the people spread blankets on the ground and worshipped picnic-style."[43] The natural acoustics of the site helped ensure that the children's voices would carry over the orchestra, which played below them.

Far more than performances of European art music took place at the Bowl. On May 20, 1925 a concert featured Arapaho Indians, a children's choir, and an orchestra. Two years later, the Bowl hosted a four-day intertribal ceremonial, which featured 52 Indian tribes of the Southwest, and Pueblo Indians set up a make-shift village at the Bowl's site for the occasion.[44] In 1926, a 400-voice African American choir gave a concert, followed later by a Latin American ballet troupe. The Bowl also became a favorite site for dancers, hosting Ruth St. Denis, Norma Gould, and Ernest Belcher, who were strongly influenced by the work of Isadora Duncan in their search for greater freedom in dance.[45] No other venue in Los Angeles offered this degree of cultural diversity.

There are some examples of Asian artists at the Bowl, although not many. One frequent performer was the dancer and choreographer Michio Ito, who emigrated from Japan in 1929 and founded a dance studio in Hollywood. On one occasion, he choreographed a set of dances for an appearance by conductor Viscount Hidemaro Konoye, brother of the Japanese premier, who came with the Japanese Philharmonic Orchestra of Tokyo to perform at the Bowl in August 1937. After a rendition of Dvorak's Symphony No. 5 in E Minor ("From the New World"), a group of Japanese and American dancers under

Figure 3.2 Easter Sunrise Service, 1924

Ito's direction performed two works, *Etenraku* and *The Blue Danube*.[46] On another occasion, soprano Toshiko Sekiya sang during a special La Fiesta program in September 1931, and the Bowl also hosted Madame Chiang Kai-shek in a China War Relief Concert during World War II.[47]

The largest group of Asian Americans in Los Angeles at the time was the Japanese. A limitation on Asian immigration in the 1880s had strong support in California. Yet whereas the number of Chinese in Los Angeles declined, the Japanese population increased, despite a partial government ban on Japanese immigration in 1907, followed by a total ban with the passage of the Immigration Act in 1924. There were an estimated 4,238 Japanese in Los Angeles by 1910, and by 1940 that number had grown to 36,866.[48] Most lived in Little Tokyo, which Carey McWilliams asserts "was the center of Japanese life on the west coast," and which became the site of a second-generation festival, or Nisei Week, in 1934.[49] There were Japanese performers of art music in Los Angeles, such as in July 1922 when mezzo-soprano Suga Umezaki took part in a multiethnic concert at Blanchard Hall with composer Gertrude Ross, among others.[50] While several of the Bowl activists were prominent in social reform causes, they do not appear to have taken up the cause of "Orientals," perhaps, as historian Henry Yu has pointed out, they continued to see Asian immigrants as "foreign and exotic, no matter how long they had resided in the U.S."[51]

The lack of Mexican American performers is more difficult to explain. Here, too, the Progressive spirit that drove many of the Bowl's founders rarely allowed the participation of Latinos. The prominence of Latino musicians during the nineteenth century in art music circles, such as Miguel Arévalo or Ysabel del Valle, was far less in acceptance by the early twentieth century. Only under the more generic title of "Latin American" were performers recognized, such as in the case of the ballet troupe in 1926, and the frequent performances by South American pianist and conductor José Iturbi in the 1930s and '40s, who appeared in several Hollywood films.[52] The policy of relative exclusion of Mexican American performers, however, did not abate until after World War II.

A Permanent Theater

The growth in popularity of the Bowl persuaded its founders to make the venue a permanent site for the arts. Within three years of the Bowl's opening concert, the management received over $16,000 in pledges. In a triumphant moment, Carter burned the mortgage before a cheering audience.[53] The danger of losing the site, however, was by no means over, and the next step was to deed the property to Los Angeles County and to arrange a 99-year lease to protect it from further development.[54] The Hollywood Bowl Association, the name adopted by members of the old Theatre Arts Alliance in 1925, stipulated that it would maintain complete control over artistic decisions and over the finances. At the time, the 60-acre site was conservatively estimated to be worth $1,500,000: a dramatic increase from its original purchase price of $47,500.[55] The main advantage of deeding the property to the county was that real estate developers would never be able to ruin what the Association had worked so hard to achieve. In this way, audiences could be certain of having their local institution remain intact.

From its founding, many Angelenos supported the idea of the Bowl because they saw it very much as *their* institution. They sought "to encourage and develop, through community spirit and civic patriotism, the finest forms of arts and crafts and to promote appreciation of and inculcate love for artistic and beautiful creation and productions of every source, kind, and nature . . . and to present, produce, and exhibit dramatic, operatic, and musical attractions . . . for the edification, entertainment, and benefit of the public."[56] The Bowl represented from the beginning an opportunity to hear fine music outside of the standard settings of "highbrow" culture. People no longer had to sit in a cramped concert hall or theater; they could enjoy the sounds of a professional ensemble in the quiet outdoors of a summer evening.

With the addition of wood benches around a large oak tree in the center of a sloping hill, listeners could look down on the dale below. They may have come to hear music, but the music came to them too, in rolls of sound that, by contemporary accounts, few if any man-made concert halls could match.

Figure 3.3 Founders and patrons signing up, 1927

Little wonder, then, that the choral conductor Hugo Kirchhofer called it the "Hollywood Bowl" because of its natural shape. Virtually the only disturbances in such natural surroundings were those of nature, such as the wind, crickets, or birds. The Bowl offered not only outdoor music concerts, but an important example of community participation in the arts. As manager Raymond Brite once noted, "under the stars we are one!"[57]

The immediate popularity of the venue also brought problems. With the growth in the size of audiences, it became increasingly difficult to provide adequate seating, not to mention adequate parking. Talk of making the Bowl more "permanent" grew louder, while those who had wanted to maintain its natural environment began to lose out. Many questioned whether such natural, idyllic surroundings could last forever. There were some complaints—members of the audience spoke of damp seats or muddy walkways; musicians noted that the sun was always in their eyes when they practiced; and management and audiences alike continued to bemoan the birds squawking during performances. In short, this natural arena was perhaps a little *too* natural. As a result, the Bowl management sought to raise enough money to create a lasting amphitheater.

There were three main goals in building an amphitheater: first, to attempt to emulate the natural acoustics; second, to provide a dramatic backdrop for the performers; and third, to protect the musicians from the elements. Its creators drew on the model of the Greek theater, the first of such structures in southern

California being at San Diego's Point Loma, built in 1901 for use by the Theosophical Society.[58] For the Hollywood Bowl, leading architects vied with each other to design an edifice of visual beauty and elegance. Between 1926 and 1929, several architects designed and built four different shells. Two were the products of Lloyd Wright, son of Frank Lloyd Wright. His first effort, a pyramid shape resembling a kind of pseudo-Mayan temple, remained in place during the 1927 season. His second was a lean, curved shell perfectly in keeping with the ideals of the Bauhaus and Art Deco movements. An engineering firm eventually designed the final structure in 1929, based in part on Wright's ideas.[59]

This planning and constructing proved expensive. The Bowl management marshaled a fund drive in order to raise $100,000, organizing a series of subscription concerts and making continuous appeals to the general public. The management was not always successful. In a cry perhaps familiar to modern orchestra administrators, then-manager Raymond Brite challenged readers at the beginning of one season: "Are you a real lover of Hollywood Bowl? . . . Book sales are behind this time last year, we are sorry to say. Please help!"[60] Nonetheless, the Bowl management was able to pay off its debts, sometimes amounting to over $17,000 per year.

The result was a structure of dramatic beauty, but to the loss of the natural environs that had made the "Bowl experience" so special. Builders graded the hillside in 1926, based on designs by Myron Hunt, the Pasadena architect of the Rose Bowl. They then installed a concrete amphitheatre, with wooden seats to replace the moveable wooden benches originally in place. Perhaps

Figure 3.4 Hollywood Bowl, 1930

nostalgically, manager Raymond Brite wrote that "the toppling wooden benches are gone. The tree has passed into the realm of memory . . ."[61] A permanent outdoor edifice had replaced the more austere, more "natural" Bowl. What remained in place was the ultimate mission of the Bowl's founders: the democratization of art music.

Repertoire

What kinds of music would attract audiences to the Bowl? The first of a concert series romantically titled "Symphonies Under the Stars," which took place on July 11, 1922, provided a taste of things to come: Wagner's "Overture" to the opera *Rienzi*, the "Andante cantabile" movement from Tchaikovsky's Symphony No. 5, and an unspecified number of Brahms's *Hungarian Dances*. The musicians then proceeded with Grieg's Suite No. 1 from *Peer Gynt*, and Fritz Kreisler's *Liebesleid* and *Liebesfreud*. The program closed with Rossini's "Overture" to *William Tell*.[62] The Bowl management chose Alfred Hertz, conductor of the San Francisco Symphony, to lead the concert, since the conductor of the Los Angeles Philharmonic Orchestra, Walter Henry Rothwell, had other engagements on the East Coast during the summer.[63] Hertz proved to be an excellent choice, and led a successful series titled "Hollywood Bowl Summer Popular Concerts" that provided a sound basis for future summer concerts.

As in the East and Midwest, opera was much in demand in southern California. Wagner's music figured prominently in the Bowl's early years, even though American performances of his works declined markedly after World War I amid anti-German sentiment.[64] While few opera companies presented complete operas at the Bowl, probably because of the difficulty in staging opera outdoors, many people came to the performances that did take place. One of the most popular was Bizet's *Carmen*, whose first production at the Bowl in 1922 filled the venue to capacity. For one such production, *Los Angeles Times* drama critic Edwin Schallert noted that the local "Spanish community turned out in force, including many Angelenos of Castillian ancestry as members of the chorus, which was directed by Manuel Sanchez de Lara."[65] During the period 1935 to 1944, with only 21 performances of 15 different operas, about 300,000 people attended, and this interest in opera at the Bowl continued at least until the early 1950s.

While opera productions were scarce, opera *singers* were more common. Soloists such as Ernestine Schumann-Heink from Germany and Amelita Galli-Curci from Italy drew audiences in the tens of thousands. One concert by Galli-Curci in 1924 attracted almost 22,000 people, yielding receipts of almost \$26,000.[66] The record, however, goes to Lily Pons, a coloratura soprano. A total of 26,410 people came to hear her sing in 1936, which was the recorded number *inside* the Bowl. There were thousands more outside who listened to the concert from speakers the Bowl's then-manager, Mrs. Leiland Atherton Irish, had installed for those who could not get in. A long-time radio broadcaster for the classical music station KFAC, Thomas Cassidy, recalled that the audiences went down Highland Avenue, and spilled over onto Cahuenga Boulevard. A clear testament to her popularity, Lily Pons's concert reportedly brought in the largest attendance for *any* genre in the history of the Bowl.[67]

The introduction of "Theme Nights" proved to be an excellent way of attracting audiences. Under the baton of Alfred Hertz and guest-conductor Boris Dunev, a Russian Program took place on July 25, 1922, with works from Tchaikovsky, Rubinstein, Borodin, and Ippolitov-Ivanov.[68] A Wagner Program followed three evenings later, with the "Prelude" from *Lohengrin*, the Overtures of *Rienzi* and *Tannhäuser*, the "Prelude and Love and Death" from *Tristan und Isolde*, and the "Prelude" from *Die Meistersinger*.[69] Virtually every year, Wagner Nights became a staple of the Bowl's offerings; particularly notable was conductor Fritz Reiner's arrival in 1925 to conduct a lengthy Wagner Program.[70] There was even a "Pasadena Program," featuring soloists and composers from that city, as well as a "University of California Night."[71] Particularly notable was a "Request Night," long a popular event at the Boston Pops, for which the management asked the audience for their musical favorites. One such evening in August 1924 indicates popular taste of the time. Bowl audiences selected an overwhelmingly European repertoire: Ambroise Thomas's Overture to the opera *Mignon*, Camille Saint-Saëns's *Danse Macabre*, Tchaikovsky's *Nutcracker Suite* and his "Andante cantabile" from the String Quartet, No. 11, Franz Liszt's *Les Preludes*, and Fritz Kreisler's *Caprice Viennois*, *Liebesleid*, and *Liebesfreud*.[72]

English music also formed part of the repertoire at the Bowl. Audiences heralded a visit in July 1925 by conductor Sir Henry Wood, who first rose to national prominence in England by reviving the Promenade concerts at the Queen's Hall in London in 1895. The *Los Angeles Times* critic noted that about "18,000 persons were present for the debut of the famous English conductor last evening. . . . The public evidenced very enthusiastic approval for the various numbers, both new and familiar, that he included among his selections, and it was apparent that the novel and light character of the program brought an unusual sense of pleasure."[73] Wood strongly supported new music by British composers, and during his week-long engagement, he conducted, among other works, Gustav Holst's *The Planets*; Ralph Vaughan Williams's *A London Symphony*; Ethel M. Smyth's *On the Cliffs of Cornwall*; and the "Luring Scene" from the opera, *The Immortal Hour*, by Rutland Boughton. As if to balance the more modern selections, the conductor presented an orchestral suite of several works by Henry Purcell, which Wood himself arranged.[74] Another English composer, Arthur Bliss, also performed at the Bowl. During his two-year residency in California, which he spent mainly in Pasadena, Bliss conducted his "Finale" from *A Colour Symphony*.[75]

A frequent visitor to the Bowl was the British conductor, Eugene Goossens. He wrote glowingly of his experiences in an issue of the British journal,

The Gramophone:

> Everyone has heard of the Hollywood Bowl, but few people realize the acoustic marvels of this enormous natural amphitheatre in the California hills, where the metaphorical pin dropped on the orchestra stage can be heard on the hill-top a quarter of a mile away. During eight weeks of cloudless summer weather, concerts are held in the Bowl on four evenings out of seven. And the sensation of conducting a fine orchestra under that marvelous blue vault studded with blazing stars, with an audience of twenty or thirty thousand thronging the darkness of the hillsides, remains unforgettable and indescribable.[76]

Figure 3.5 Eugene Goossens

Goossens had the privilege of making possibly the first outdoor recording of a symphony orchestra in America, which took place at the Bowl with the Los Angeles Philharmonic in August 1928 (hear Track no. 11). Six double-sided records comprised the recording, which RCA-Victor made on portable equipment shipped out from New York. Goossens recalled that among the challenges were the breezes, which adversely affected the microphone, as well as having to deal with an airplane that circled lazily overhead, "providing a gratuitous obbligato to Dvorak's *Carnival Overture*."[77]

Modern or "novelty" music was a standard part of the repertoire, and a number of works by American composers had their West Coast premieres at the Bowl. Critic and composer Deems Taylor's orchestral suite *Through the Looking-Glass* premiered during the final week of the 1924 season.[78] The following year, the Director of the Eastman School of Music, Howard Hanson, conducted one of his works for its first performance on the West Coast, the *Nordic Symphony*. In 1928, the West Coast premiere of Aaron Copland's *Concerto for Piano and Orchestra* took place.[79] Musicologist and conductor Nicolas Slonimsky continued this tradition in the 1930s with varying degrees of success, introducing modern music to Bowl audiences. One notorious example was Edgard Varèse's *Ionisation*, which required 41 percussive instruments, including bongos, sleigh bells, two anvils, and two sirens (hear Track no. 12).[80]

Dozens of American and European composers moved to southern California during the first half of the twentieth century, and some saw their works performed at the Bowl. Even before the shell and benches were in place, Gertrude Ross performed her music with singer Anna Ruzena Sprotte. The Indianist composer Charles Wakefield Cadman, who lived in Hollywood, Glendale, and San Diego over a 30-year period, had several of his works performed, including one dedicated to the Hollywood Bowl itself. He fervently supported the Bowl from its earliest days, and "Cadman Nights" were common events during the 1920s. The West Coast premiere took place on June 24 and 28, 1926 of his one-act opera, *Shanewis*, based on the life of Native American Princess Tsianina (also called Redfeather), who sang the title role. Rafaelo Diaz from the Metropolitan Opera and Chief Os-Ke-Non-Ton, a Mohawk Indian baritone and Tsianina's father-in-law, sang the other lead roles.[81] Also significant was a work by the 12-tone composer, Arnold Schoenberg, who moved to Los Angeles in 1933. Like Cadman he composed a decidedly tonal piece dedicated to the Bowl, *Fanfare for a Bowl Concert*.[82] Occasions such as these helped to establish the amphitheater's importance as a venue for both American and European art music.

Changes in the Air

Musical offerings at the Bowl changed significantly during the Great Depression and World War II. Similar to other music institutions around the country, the Bowl saw a decline in revenues during the 1930s. At a time when

Figure 3.6 Princess Tsianina

many Americans turned to radio and movies for their entertainment, it became almost impossible to maintain a continuous series of outdoor summer concerts at the Bowl. As a result, the Bowl management decided to diversify its offerings, and thus to represent more fully the musical needs of Los Angeles. That meant featuring decidedly different performers, as well as playing the works of composers whose music had been insufficiently represented at the Bowl.

One indication of this change was the appearance of several prominent African American artists. When Los Angeles composer William Grant Still came to conduct his music in 1936, it was the first time that an African American conducted a major symphony orchestra in America.[83] Still visited Los Angeles in 1929 while working as an arranger with the Paul Whiteman Orchestra, and he decided to settle permanently in the city the following year. The Los Angeles Philharmonic performed both the "Land of Romance" from Still's symphonic poem *Africa*, and the "Scherzo" from the *Afro-American Symphony*. The concert, which also featured gospel selections from the Hall Johnson Choir, attracted a highly integrated audience. One enthusiastic listener wrote to a friend that the composer "was the hit of the evening."[84] In 1940, Paul Robeson sang to an audience of over 23,000 people—the largest audience at the Bowl that season. Robeson was not merely a music personality, but also a strong supporter for civil rights. In 1944, a "Marian Anderson Night" took place as part of the "Symphonies Under the Stars." One of the country's finest contraltos, Anderson sang mainly an operatic repertoire, including works by Monteverdi and Verdi, under the baton of Dimitri Mitropoulos, then conductor of the Minneapolis Symphony.[85]

Two further events that signified a change were memorial concerts for George Gershwin. Gershwin's musical influences were primarily those of Broadway and Tin Pan Alley. While he regularly composed concert music until the end of his life, his works were almost never played at the Bowl, although he had conducted the Los Angeles Philharmonic in February 1937 at the Philharmonic Auditorium downtown. Yet on July 12, 1937, the day after his death, an orchestra and several soloists turned out at the Bowl to perform selections from his music, which were aired live through the Mutual Broadcast System.[86] The Hollywood music director, Johnny Green, chose a tune from the Gershwin musical, *Girl Crazy*, called "Bidin' My Time" (hear Track no. 15). A male quartet sang the song, which Green accompanied on piano (and guided the group through a false start—an occasional danger with live radio broadcasts). In addition, several figures gave eulogies, including Otto Klemperer, impresario Merle Armitage, and Green himself. Arnold Schoenberg, who was a frequent tennis partner of Gershwin, gave a poignant eulogy in memory of his friend (hear Track no. 16).

A second concert in Gershwin's memory took place in September of that year. For this occasion a group of Euro-American, African American, and Latin American performers assembled, including such notables as conductors Otto Klemperer, Victor Young, and José Iturbi, and soloists Al Jolson, Fred Astaire, Oscar Levant, and Lily Pons. The Hall Johnson Choir, which had performed with Still the previous year, accompanied singers Ruby Elzy, Anne Brown, and Todd Duncan in selections from *Porgy and Bess*. These memorial concerts, which featured both classical and popular music artists, established the tradition of "Gershwin Nights" at the Bowl, several of which Green conducted. Between 1945 and 1962, 12 concerts devoted solely to Gershwin's music attracted more than 200,000 people.[87]

The Gershwin memorial concerts signaled a trend at the Bowl: an increasing emphasis on "popular" music. What had been anathema to Bowl founders 20 years earlier became more common for two reasons: to be more representative of the city's diverse music culture, and to increase revenue. Two years after the Gershwin memorial concert, Benny Goodman's swing band appeared and attracted 7,500 people, a large audience during the 1930s. Frank Sinatra gave the Bowl's first official "pop" concert in 1943, with the Los Angeles Philharmonic providing accompaniment. The Sinatra concert drew the Bowl's limit during wartime of 10,000 people, when the average audience size for that season was 4,596. Other jazz and Broadway artists followed, and included Louis Armstrong, Duke Ellington, Nat King Cole, and Ethel Merman, with well-known conductors such as Paul Whiteman and Nelson Riddle leading the orchestra.[88] The increase in revenue had a further benefit: It enabled performances of classical music to continue. As one writer noted, Sinatra's sole appearance in 1943 "was largely responsible for keeping the Bowl in the black that summer."[89] Although classical music still predominated, jazz and pop music henceforward became a critical part of the Bowl concert schedule, which has continued up to the present day.

The growth of Fascism in Europe and the subsequent outbreak of war brought significant changes to the Bowl concert schedule. Some musicians who left Europe permanently made Los Angeles their home, and were able to appear at the Bowl more frequently. They chose southern California over Boston, New York, or San Francisco for several reasons. One impetus was the movie industry, and the employment opportunities it offered. The climate was also appealing, with its strong similarity to the Mediterranean. A further attraction was the émigré community itself, and as the tide of European refugees to the region increased, their friends and colleagues followed. Within a six-year period, some of Europe's most famous cultural figures arrived, among them directors Otto Preminger and Alfred Hitchcock, composers Ernst Toch, Igor Stravinsky, and Ernst Krenek, actors Peter Lorre and Ingrid Bergman, writers Aldous Huxley, Thomas Mann, and Bertolt Brecht, and the writer/composer Alma Mahler-Werfel with her poet husband, Franz Werfel. This diverse group came to personify "exiles in paradise."[90]

The emphasis on renowned soloists at the Bowl represented an enormous shift from the original intentions of the Bowl's founders. They had first sought to emphasize *music* rather than *performers*, but they soon realized that star soloists attracted audiences. Famed singers set attendance records at the Bowl and helped to "popularize" the classics, among them Ernestine Schumann-Heink, Amelita Galli-Curci, and Lily Pons. Prominent European performers attracted audiences to classical music in a way that native American talent could scarcely achieve, and those who arrived during the 1930s and early 1940s only served to reinforce this trend.

The Los Angeles Philharmonic gained a new conductor almost solely because of the rise of Nazi Germany. Otto Klemperer left in 1933 when the Nazis assumed power, and during a brief engagement in Florence, Italy a representative from the Los Angeles Philharmonic asked if he would be interested in being its new conductor. He agreed, so the Philharmonic management quickly drew up a contract, and Klemperer arrived shortly thereafter. He described the orchestra at that time as "[v]ery good. Not as good as the Boston or the Philadelphia Orchestra, but very good. It had a lot of routine, and sight-reading was no difficulty. I conducted every two weeks and the concerts were all very well attended."[91] For an opening concert at the Bowl on July 16, 1935, he conducted Debussy's *La Mer* and Berlioz's "Queen Mab" scherzo from the *Romeo and Juliet Symphony*, followed by Spanish composer Albéniz's *Triana* and *Navarra*. On the same program, the orchestra also performed Beethoven's

Overture to *Egmont*, Bach's Suite No. 2 in B Minor for Two Lutes and Strings, and Wagner's "Bacchanala" from *Tannhäuser*.[92] During his tenure with the Philharmonic, the towering, 6'7" conductor "elevated performance standards and musical understanding to new heights in Los Angeles."[93]

Another well-known conductor, who like Klemperer came to stay, was Bruno Walter. He had appeared at the Bowl before; for his first visit in 1927, according to Bowl Manager Raymond Brite, he had "come all the way from Berlin mainly for the Bowl concerts," as well as for a music festival in Cleveland.[94] This was but another indication that the fame of the Bowl had spread far beyond California. With the onset of war, Walter settled permanently in Los Angeles and gave a concert in 1940—his first appearance at the Bowl since 1929. It revealed a strong German bent: Weber, Mozart, Wagner, and Brahms. Bowl audiences were thus able once again to hear one of the true master conductors of German music.[95]

Equally notable were the numerous appearances by pianist Artur Rubinstein, who arrived in California with his family in 1940 and bought a house in Brentwood. "The Hollywood Bowl concerts," he wrote, "became more and more popular. All the available conductors showed their diverse interpretations, and as I played there each of the thirteen years I lived in California, I had the opportunity to be soloist with all the following: Stokowski, Ormandy, Szell, Steinberg, Rodzinski, Beecham, Klemperer, Wallenstein, Barbirolli, and Bruno Walter." He added that despite his "dislike for playing in the open air, I enjoyed these summer concerts." One reason was the shell. "In the Hollywood Bowl alone," he exclaimed, "the shell was sufficient to make the piano sound beautifully."[96] At one performance, led by Philadelphia conductor George Szell, Rubinstein played pieces by Weber, Brahms, Smetana, and Chopin. Audiences responded with enthusiasm; as he recalled, he won "in two consecutive years a silver cup for the largest attendance—with Menuhin, Heifetz, Horowitz, and Serkin as runners-up."[97]

Throughout the war, the Bowl remained one of the main venues for classical music in Los Angeles. Although pianist Vladimir Horowitz had been living in America since his departure from Russia following the Revolution, he came to the Bowl for the first time in 1941, which was possibly the first time he had ever given a concert outdoors. Among other pieces, Horowitz played Rachmaninoff's Piano Concerto No. 3, and the composer himself (who lived in Beverly Hills) walked onstage to declare it was how he had always dreamed it would be performed. Horowitz called it "the greatest moment of my life" and agreed to come back the following year.[98] In the summer of 1944, violinist Yehudi Menuhin performed in an all-Brahms concert, and Dimitri Mitropoulos conducted the Los Angeles Philharmonic. Violinist Jascha Heifetz, who like Rachmaninoff moved to Beverly Hills, gave a solo performance.[99] On another occasion, film composer Franz Waxman conducted a concert, which included one of his own compositions for the war effort, *Symphonic Fantasy for Chorus and Orchestra*, based on Martin Luther's hymn, "A Mighty Fortress is our God."[100]

Why did so many concerts take place during a time of war, when the coast was constantly under the threat of attack? Repeated blackouts, rationing, and an imposed limit on audience attendance of 10,000 people all seemed ominous for musical performances. The Bowl management, however, received government permission to continue giving concerts, because the U.S. Army believed the concerts would keep up morale.[101] It was a prime location for the entertainment of troops, and thousands came to see shows before sailing out to fight in the Pacific theater. The Bowl also proved to be a good venue for raising money. One example was the "5th War Bond Show," which took place on July 4, 1944. The American Air Force Symphony Orchestra played a richly diverse repertoire, from Mendelssohn, Chopin, and Wagner to songs by Broadway tunesmiths Jerome Kern and Irving Berlin. Two works by a local composer and conductor, David Rose, opened the show, and Bing Crosby, the Master of Ceremonies, sang three songs. A certain attention-getter was the note at the bottom of the concert brochure: "Land mines will be exploded to open the program."[102] The concert was a smash success.

Conclusion

The Hollywood Bowl was central to Los Angeles's music culture. Men, women, and children were essential to the venue's early popularity by organizing, performing in, and attending concerts.[103] Community activists, not boosters at City Hall, strongly supported the performance of classical music, and dynamic figures such as T. Perceval Gerson and Artie Mason Carter led the way. Because there was no government funding, and admission to orchestral concerts cost only 25 cents, donations from community fund drives helped make the venture possible. Two wealthy philanthropists committed to the arts, Christine Wetherill Stevenson and Marie Rankin Clarke, also made substantial contributions, because they believed strongly in the Bowl's mission of making music accessible to the common people and not merely the elite. This kind of mutual commitment made the democratization of music at the Bowl a reality.

A distinguishing feature of Bowl concerts was diversity, both in terms of repertoire and ethnicity. There were few opportunities to hear entire symphonies or operatic arias outdoors other than at the Bowl, which since the late 1930s also provided a site for swing and other forms of popular music. Similarly, during an era of housing restrictions and school segregation, there were few other locations for diverse ethnic groups to perform before mixed audiences. African Americans, Native Americans, Latin Americans, and Asian Americans all performed at the Bowl during the 1920s and 1930s, thereby helping to fulfill the notion of an arts center that reflected the diversity of the city's population, although with a caveat: Mexican Americans or Asian Americans rarely appeared during this time. Theaters and concerts halls in downtown Los Angeles did not dominate music culture.

Within the decentralized geographic layout of the region, a concert venue on the rim of the mountains became one of the region's leading sites for the performance of music.

The Bowl's renown reached far beyond Los Angeles's borders. While outdoor concerts existed long before the Bowl's founding, visitors from the United States and abroad quickly realized the unique atmosphere of the venue, which became a symbol of a new approach to musical performance. At least five other American cities with less perfect climates built Bowls of their own. Chicago's Grant Park on Lake Michigan became the site for one in 1931; Milwaukee built a Music Shell in 1934; Denver built a Red Rocks amphitheater in 1939; Boston, home of the Boston Pops, built a Hatch Shell in 1940; and a shell was built at Ravinia Park outside of Chicago in 1949.[104] This movement of "Bowl building" affirmed the notion that thousands of people could enjoy music performances in a romantic atmosphere beneath the stars.

Thus while the process of sacralization was certainly at work, with audiences listening reverently to the works of the great masters, a parallel process of desacralization was also taking place. In the great outdoors, the formality of concert halls disappeared, supplanted by hills, dales, and trees, all of which encouraged audiences to listen to music in a unique setting. At the Hollywood Bowl, the enormous variety in repertoire and performers belied any notion of formalizing art music within distinct boundaries. Contributions by men, women, and children made the Bowl's mission a reality, because the purpose from the beginning was to meet the cultural needs of the population. The strong appeal of outdoor theaters in Los Angeles was a result of a conducive environment and community participation, which the popularity of pageantry in the next chapter will further demonstrate.

4

The Art of Pageants, Plays, and Dance

Since the days of the ancient Greeks, dramatic productions have taught us much about what a citizenry held to be important. The Greeks reveled in issues of identity, power, and love, often drawing little distinction between history and myth. So it was with southern California residents and visitors, millions of whom attended outdoor productions during the first half of the twentieth century as a natural product of being in the "Athens of the West."[1] Since many were recent migrants, they sought to resurrect, or create anew, the region's history through a variety of dramatic productions that incorporated elements of pageantry, plays, and dance. How might those inhabitants adopt, or adapt for their needs, the history of the region? And what do these productions tell us about local residents during this era, particularly how they viewed themselves within the context of the region's multiple identities? The use of pageantry and plays as a means of depicting both history and identity forms the subject of this chapter.

Pageantry in the United States arose at the same time as Progressivism, which proved optimal for both movements. In his landmark study of pageantry, historian David Glassberg argues that a reform-minded agenda had a marked presence in the historical presentation of public images. Progressives felt that "history could be made into a dramatic public ritual through which the residents of a town, by acting out the right version of their past, could bring about some kind of future social and political transformation." Many pageants thus had elements of "civic boosterism and moralizing."[2] Acting out local traditions was only one part of its appeal. What made pageantry so powerful was its scale; pageants varied in size from a few hundred in the cast to several thousand, with up to tens of thousands of people attending performances. As a form of mass entertainment that tended to project an uplifting appraisal of a region's history, it proved ideal ground for the Progressive spirit.

Over a period of several decades, three productions in southern California continued to attract audiences: the Mission Play, the Ramona Pageant, and the Mexican Players.[3] Each of these community dramas not only blended several different genres but also drew on the mixing of different cultures common to southern California: Californio, Mexican, Anglo, and American Indian. Religion was an important component of these productions and one reason for their powerful appeal. They all placed a heavy emphasis on music and dance, and a curious feature of these three productions is that while they took place in the same region as the film industry, most of the performers were amateurs, not professionals. Although professional actors did take some of the lead roles in the Mission Play and the Ramona Pageant, most of the casts consisted of people from the adjoining towns or communities.

This is no coincidence, because "community drama" had become very popular in California, as it did in many parts of the country during the early twentieth century. Some of the earliest examples in California took place in outdoor theaters in the north, such as at the Bohemian Grove in Sonoma County, the Forest Theater in Carmel, and the Greek Theater in Berkeley.[4] The type of drama performed at these outdoor theaters had several elements in common. It was above all anti-modern, decrying the emphasis on commercialism and machines that formed the foundation of modern, industrialized society. This nostalgia was in a sense paradoxical to the Progressive movement, yet as Glassberg notes, pageantry did contain a measure of "antimodernism" by appealing to those who rejected the present for an idealized past.[5] It commemorated and romanticized that past by pointing to a time when people supposedly found meaning and happiness in life outside of commercial pursuits. It was anti-elitist, in that it condemned the snobbery around legitimate theater and the patrons who frequented it. Finally, as a by-product of anti-elitism, it was community-oriented, by encouraging people who previously had little to do with the theater to join in and be counted. Thus while providing a platform for community uplift and improvement, this type of theater sought to transform the very notion of theater itself.

Members of the Theosophical Society, an international religious organization that claimed its mystic roots in India, created some of the first pageants in southern California. A colony at Point Loma in San Diego that formed in 1897 built California's first Greek theater, where theosophists staged numerous pageants, concerts, and plays. In Los Angeles, the Society built a 15-acre colony, called Krotona, atop Vista Del Mar Street in the Hollywood Hills in 1910.[6] In an open-air theater they staged the *Light of Asia* pageant in 1918, based on a poem by the English poet Sir Edwin Arnold that celebrated the life of the Buddha. Philanthropist Christine Wetherill Stevenson, a fervent theosophist, was the producer, and she envisioned the pageant as part of a series to dramatize the lives of major religious figures in the world. Playwright Georgina Jones Walton was the dramatist, and choreographer Ruth St. Denis arranged the dance sequences, which featured some of her students from the Denishawn School she had founded with her husband, Ted Shawn.[7] According to one account, the *Light of Asia* pageant profoundly inspired a group of community arts activists to found an open air arts center, the Hollywood Bowl.[8]

Whereas the *Light of Asia* portrayed the life of the Buddha, another Stevenson production, the *Pilgrimage Play*, portrayed the life of Jesus Christ. Stevenson, who wrote the script, even traveled to the Holy Land to gather costumes and do research for the production, and at first insisted that the music should consist solely of flutes and cymbals. The first composer for the pageant, Arthur Farwell, thought otherwise. Since he had already written much of the music and chosen the musicians, his music won out. The following year, however, Stevenson requested modernist composer and a fellow follower of theosophy, Dane Rudhyar, to write a new musical accompaniment, which remained in place until the music of Los Angeles composer Gertrude Ross came to supplement Rudhyar's score in 1936.[9] One of the most important figures of pageantry in California, Garnet Holme, co-directed the pageant with Henry Herbert, both of whom had belonged to the English troupe, the Stratford-on-Avon Players. There was a huge cast of four principal actors, eighty supporting players, twenty singers, and an instrumental ensemble.[10] The Pilgrimage Play opened for an eight-week season in 1920 at a specially-built, open air theater across from the Hollywood Bowl, and it continued to be performed until 1951. During the Depression, the County Supervisor John Anson Ford was instrumental in keeping it going by regular subventions by the city.[11]

Two figures had an enormous influence on twentieth-century community drama in England and the United States: the Englishman Louis Napoleon Parker and the American Percy MacKaye. Parker originated the "new pageantry" movement in England in June 1905, when he organized the *Pageant of Sherborne* in Sherborne, Dorsetshire, in celebration of that city's twelve-hundredth anniversary. He was a retired music teacher who really wanted to be a playwright, and his revolt against modernity found a ready audience. "This modernizing spirit," he wrote, "which destroys all loveliness and has no loveliness of its own to put in its place, is the negation of poetry, the negation of romance. . . . This is just precisely the kind of spirit which a properly organized and properly conducted pageant is designed to kill."[12]

Parker was resurrecting a dramatic form that dates back at least to the thirteenth century, which consisted mainly of ceremonial processions and historical dramas. Ceremonial processions commemorated a range of events, including festival days, the crowing of a king or queen, or a saint's day. Of the latter belonged the mystery plays and passion plays on the life of Jesus Christ, and the oldest continuous pageant in existence remains the Passion Play in the Oberammergau in Bavaria, Germany, which since 1634 has been mounted every ten years. When communities in the modern era resurrected the pageant form, they retained elements of medieval and renaissance pageantry. According to theater historian Thomas H. Dickinson, modern pageants, as their earlier forebears, contained four key elements: historical fact, ceremony, folklore, and what he calls "community life and spirit."[13] Pageantry in its essence was thus a celebration of history and ritual.

Parker merged his pageant with two other forms: the masque and the epic drama. The masque, which also began as a court entertainment in medieval Europe, uses symbolism and allegory by means of poetry, dance, and costumes (hence "masque" or "masquerade"). Music was an integral part of the traditional masque in England, and Parker arranged for an orchestra to perform early music from the period—the only performers in the pageant who received a salary. Where possible they based this music on historical research, which local composers then supplemented with original works. The epic drama proved to be one of the most remarkable and memorable aspects to Parker's pageant, involving huge casts of hundreds of people, much like Hollywood studios would later incorporate in silent films.[14] In the true nature of "community drama," almost all of the players were amateurs, often making their own costumes and scenery. This unique dramatic and historical portrayal attracted the attention of tens of thousands of English people, who flocked to Parker's pageants until after World War I.[15]

Percy MacKaye was the foremost proponent of the "new pageantry" that came to America's shores. Born in 1875 in New York, MacKaye studied at Harvard and taught in New York City for four years before moving to New Hampshire. Much like Parker, MacKaye was a frustrated playwright who wanted to put on plays. He decried the commercialism and vulgarity of modern society, which he felt had corrupted the legitimate theater as well, and which only indulged public taste rather than led it. In his book *The Playhouse and the Play*, published in 1909, he discussed the current problems of theater and offered several solutions. MacKaye plead for a "new drama" that could adapt "to a people of many millions . . . their prairies, their mountains, their vast river valleys"; a "new theatre," with an emphasis on democracy that has "a native appeal and message"; and (naturally) a "new dramatist," one who can understand the past, present, and future, while being "as simply understandable to our American masses as the Greek-stage Zeus and Agamemnon were to the Athenians."[16]

This is a tall order, and we might forgive his contemporaries for getting lost in his message. In the same month and year as Parker, MacKaye and several colleagues mounted the *Saint-Gaudens Pageant* in Cornish, Maine, which helped inspire numerous pageants in other states over the next several years, notably in Boston, Philadelphia, and Chicago.[17] Like Parker, he also wrote several community dramas that he called "pageant-masques," one of which, *The Masque of Saint Louis*, attracted over 150,000 citizens of St. Louis in 1914 and made a profit of $17,000.[18] Unfortunately, as in England, enthusiasm on the East Coast for the "new pageantry" began to decline after World War I, both as a result of the public's exhaustion with historical commemoration and that a key stimulus, the Progressive spirit of renewal, had run its course.[19]

However, MacKaye's achievements and writings in the field of community drama continued to merit the admiration of others, particularly at universities.[20] Among these were Thomas H. Dickinson at the University of Minnesota, Thomas Wood Stevens at Carnegie Institute of Technology, and Paul Green at the University of North Carolina.[21] The latter produced the most successful example of eastern epic-drama, *The Lost Colony* at Manteo,

Roanoke Island, North Carolina, which depicts the tale of the English colonists who vanished without a trace in 1587 for reasons that remain a mystery. Green called it a "symphonic drama," because of its close integration of music and drama, and the pageant first took place in 1937 as a joint production with the Federal Theater Project of the Works Progress Administration and the University of North Carolina at Chapel Hill. Performances of this pageant continue into the twenty-first century.[22]

To sum up, there was an intense, national effort to revive outdoor theater in America during the early twentieth century. This effort resulted in the staging of pageants, masques, and other community dramas throughout the country, which drew heavily on European dramatic traditions for inspiration. While other pageant forms in America exist, such as the Rose Bowl Pageant and even the American Beauty Pageant, these are ceremonial processions and so will not concern us here. In southern California, a series of pageants arose from the 1910s to the 1930s in which music and dance had a prominent role. Inspired by the ideals of community drama, local residents both adopted and revised the pageant form to create historically based plays that sought to express diverse versions of regional identity.

The Mission Play

The Mission Play was a paean to the mission system that flourished in California when the territory was still under the rule of Spain. It was the product of John Steven McGroarty, a journalist, poet, and playwright. He envisioned a colorful, historical depiction of the rise and fall of that system, centered around the life of the Franciscan friar, Junípero Serra, and he chose the pageant form as his vehicle of communication. It worked. Opening on April 29, 1912 at the Mission Theater, a specially built theater near Mission San Gabriel, the pageant took place four months per year during the spring and summer. By 1924, an estimated two million people had seen it, and the pageant continued to have revivals even after McGroarty's death some two decades later.[23] In terms of a community drama getting across its message, the Mission Play has had few equals in American history.

Why would so many people come to see it? Following the true form of the pageant, it offered a continuous stream of entertainment, skillfully blending music, drama, and dance of a bygone era. Yet it was much more than this; the play spoke directly to the fascination the public had with the myth of California's past in a way that many could readily understand and appreciate. As with Parker's pageants, its claim to historical reliability was a hallmark of the Mission Play—a point that caught the attention of theater historian Thomas Dickinson, who lauded the Mission Play as "a true pageant which is at the same time something of a historical chronicle."[24] One program states that the "Mission Play is a dramatization of the early history of California, faithfully and accurately portrayed. Those witnessing tonight's performance may

Figure 4.1 John Steven McGroarty

accept the presentation as a true portrayal of history."[25] Although far from the case, it was nonetheless one version of the colonization of Alta California that had a marked appeal for audiences, due in part to its clear depiction of characters: the fearless friar, the lustful soldier, the devout Indian.

Patriotism was also part of the Mission Play. As one program states: "The Mission Play is given annually at San Gabriel in a theatre specially created for it by patriotic citizens of California."[26] The pageant thus reaffirmed one's sense of place in America. This notion was fully in keeping with the Americanization movement of the early twentieth century, which rigorously defined what was pro-American and what was not. In other words, to see the Mission Play was to affirm one's identity of being an American in California; it provided a sense of belonging. The one twist is that that identity was not "Anglo-Saxon" in the traditional sense, with a corresponding emphasis on Protestantism, but rather reaffirmed the Catholic heritage of California and hence the heritage of millions of immigrants to America.

Given this Progressive bent, it is little surprise that the play attracted some significant figures in southern California who supported it. Henry E. Huntington helped finance the play when it was in its infancy. By the mid-1920s, a Mission Playhouse Corporation was formed with twenty-one directors, among them real estate magnate W. I. Hollingsworth of the Los Angeles Chamber of Commerce, oil baron E. L. Doheny, *Times* publisher Harry Chandler, Mission Inn owner Frank Miller, impresario Lynden Behymer, and businessman Arthur Bent. Also on the board was San Fernando Valley developer William Paul Whitsett, who even suggested that the play would be more financially feasible during the Depression in a specially built theater behind the San Fernando Mission, an idea that the San Gabriel theater supporters sharply rejected.[27]

Significantly, the Mission Play depicted an America that was thoroughly diverse, both racially and culturally, although within a particular racial hierarchy. Latinos, Anglos, and Indians alike took part in the production. Anglos held many of the leading roles, such as the actor R. D. MacLean, who played the part of Father Serra for over a decade.[28] With over one hundred people in the cast, Latinos were involved as actors, dancers, and musicians. One of the actresses in the first performance in 1912 was Lucretia del Valle, the daughter of state senator Reginaldo del Valle and granddaughter of Ysabel del Valle of Rancho Camulos—the model for the rancho in Helen Hunt Jackson's *Ramona*.[29] She was thus a descendant of the Californios and came from the region's upper class. For her debut performance, Lucretia even wore her grandmother's clothes and jewelry.[30] Juan Zorraquinos and Juanita Vigare began in 1912 as dancers, and in the 1920s and early '30s, Leandra Bustamente and Eduardo Corralles played the roles of an Indian mother and father, respectively. Some Indians also had roles, such as Chief Young Turtle, who was the central character in an Indian dance sequence.[31] The use of such performers, who continued with the production often for more than a decade, was to reinforce the notion of authenticity the pageant steadfastly sought to affirm.

This ethnic diversity among the actors was also true among the musicians. One of the first conductors of the "Mission Play Concert Band and Orchestra" was Dr. D. Juan C. Rechy, who came from the Conservatorio Nacional de Musica in Mexico City.[32] His successor was José Ceniceros, and composer Salvador Nuño was the pageant's pianist. One of the directors of music, C. M. Pyke, had served as music director of the Los Angeles Operatic Society and worked in Los Angeles theaters since the late-nineteenth century. He composed at least two of the songs for the play, "El Dia Festivo" and "El Toreador." Native Americans, led by Chief Young Turtle, performed on drums in an Indian Dance sequence. A program claims that Pedro Cahote, Chief Manitou of the Pueblo Indians from New Mexico, was one of the drum beaters.[33]

The Mission Play consisted of three acts and a "Fiesta scene," each reinforcing the play's central theme: that the missions arose through the goodness of Father Junípero Serra and went into decline following Mexico's rebellion against Spain. It begins with a prologue, consisting of a "prelude in pantomime." The prologue symbolizes the three main periods of the play, depicting a clear racial hierarchy:[34]

I. The Savage Sensing the Approach of his White Conquerors.
II. Spectre of the Faded Military Glory of the Spanish Conquest.
III. Spirit of the Ever-Living Faith in the Cross of Christ.

With these images combining race, power, and religion firmly fixed in the audience's mind, the drama begins. The first act depicts the founding of the first mission in 1769 in San Diego, the second act shows the founding of the Mission San Carlos de Borromeo in 1784 near present-day Carmel, and the third act is set in the ruined Mission San Juan Capistrano in 1847—the eve of the American conquest of California. Between the second and third acts there is the vibrant Fiesta scene, filled with music and color, with much

Figure 4.2 Juan Zorraquinos and Juanita Vigare

Figure 4.3 Fiesta scene, The Mission Play

dancing and merrymaking as well as songs of sadness over the decline of the missions. Among the songs the company performed were traditional Mexican folk songs, such as "La Partida," "La Golondrina," and "El Palmar." Thus the pageant was a historical portrayal that depicted the rise and fall of an era, almost like a life itself. It ended on the reaffirming notion of the sanctity and endurance of religious faith, regardless of the historical conditions, thereby seeking to portray the eternal beyond history.

The author of the pageant, John Steven McGroarty, was something of a household name in California during the 1920s and '30s. While his main profession was as a feature writer for the *Los Angeles Times* during the era of Harrison Gray Otis, the paper's editor and publisher, he wrote several collections of poetry and books on history. McGroarty's collection of poems includes *Poets and Poetry of Wyoming Valley* in 1885, *Wander Songs* in 1908, and *The King's Highway* in 1909. He then wrote histories, among them *California—Its History and Romance*, published in 1911; a three-volume *Los Angeles From the Mountains to the Sea*, which the American Historical Society published in 1921; and a three-volume *History of Los Angeles County* in 1923.[35] He also wrote at least three more pageant-plays: *La Golondrina* in 1923 on the early Spanish colonization, *Osceola* in 1927, and *Babylon* in 1927, none of which achieved the renown of the Mission Play. One of his poems, "Just California," was required reading in elementary schools in California during the 1930s. McGroarty's clear love for the state comes across markedly in the poem's four verses. The first verse describes the dramatic coastline:

'Twixt the sea and the deserts,
'Twixt the wastes and the waves,
Between the sands of buried lands

And ocean's coral caves,
It lies not East nor West,
But like a scroll unfurled,
Where the hand of God hath flung it,
Down the middle of the world.

This religious imagery is typical of the text, as we see in the final verse, which is almost bursting in its description of the sheer beauty of the state:

Sun and dew that kiss it,
Balmy winds that blow,
The stars in clustered diadems,
Upon its peaks of snow:
The mighty mountains o'er it,
Below the white seas swirled—
Just California stretching down
The middle of the world.

It was doubtless a comforting thought to thousands of schoolchildren to know they lived in a state that was in the "middle of the world," and the poem renders a clear conviction of McGroarty's vision of the state as the true destination of the holy. Neither the Vatican nor the Holy Land were at the world's epicenter according to McGroarty, a Presbyterian who converted to Roman Catholicism, but California itself. In his books, poems, and plays, McGroarty lauded the very images that many Californians shared in common: a pride in the state's beautiful coastlines, rugged mountains, and fertile valleys—all products of the seeming revelation of God's presence. As the final line in the third verse states, "Morns break again in splendor / O'er the giant newborn West, / But of all the lands God fashioned, / 'Tis this land is the best."[36]

As many before him, McGroarty was a true convert to the state, not having been born in California but in Pennsylvania in 1862.[37] He first worked as a teacher, then a journalist, and was elected county treasurer of Luzerne County in Pennsylvania before being admitted to the bar and practicing as a lawyer. He and his wife, Ida McGroarty, moved to Montana after McGroarty joined the legal staff of Marcus Daly, who bought the Anaconda silver mine in Montana and made millions from copper extraction and other investments in land, banks, and railroads. Following Daly's death in 1900, McGroarty traveled with his wife through the western United States and Mexico before coming to Los Angeles in 1901, where he began writing for the *Los Angeles Times* and later became editor of *West Coast Magazine*. He thus had the unusual background of wide experience in both business and letters, and as one writer put it effusively, "There is no business man and no business enterprise in California that is not indebted in some way or other to the things that John S. McGroarty has said in his writings."[38] While certainly an overstatement, one of his greatest strengths was an ability to communicate with the common man, which became a key virtue of the Mission Play.

The idea of creating a pageant on the missions was not McGroarty's idea at all but that of Frank Miller, the owner of the Mission Inn in Riverside.[39] Miller was born in Wisconsin in 1859 and moved to Riverside in 1870, the year the town was founded on the eastern portion of the old Rancho Jurupa. He herded sheep and worked in farming before building the Mission Inn, a rambling hotel loosely based on the Spanish mission style.[40] Like McGroarty he became fascinated with California's Mexican and Indian past, and a transforming moment came when Miller saw the Passion Play in Oberammergau in Bavaria. Miller wanted to have something similar for California, and chose the story of the missions as the nearest corollary to the theme of the Oberammergau. According to one account, he first asked Professor Henry Van Dyke, chair of the English department at Princeton University and a leading authority on pageantry, if he might write such a play, but Van Dyke declined, stating that he did not have sufficient experience with the state's history. When Van Dyke encouraged him to find someone in California instead, Miller sought out Dr. David Starr Jordan, chancellor of Stanford University, who then recommended McGroarty.

While the idea immediately appealed to McGroarty, he was at first unsure about the task. He explained that he would need four months to write it, and Harrison Gray Otis would have to give his permission for a leave of absence—not at all likely, considering Otis's reputation as a difficult man; his title was "the General" from his service in the military reserve. After a plea by Frank Miller, the General surprisingly consented, and in 1911, Miller set aside a room for McGroarty at the Mission Inn so that he might write in peace.[41] McGroarty wrote the play in two months. Surrounded by desert vistas and orange groves, and living in a hotel fashioned after the mission style that was filled with "old tomes and pictures and relics," he probably drew inspiration as much from his surroundings as from whatever knowledge he gleaned from history books and novels.[42]

The period in which McGroarty wrote the play is significant: Los Angeles was rocked by conflict. The *Times* offices had been bombed by labor activists in 1910, and General Otis was battling against all perceived threats to free markets and the open shop. The following year, Job Harriman ran for mayor on the Socialist ticket, and the Far Western Socialists "cast a larger fraction of the presidential vote in 1912 than did the Socialists of the Northeastern states."[43] McGroarty sympathized with his employer, and his vision of California called on a father figure to see both the state and the country through those arduous times. His position as a booster was clear in the state's history he published in the same year, *California—Its History and Romance*. As he wrote the play, far from the political tumult of Los Angeles, he may have found it at once comforting yet perhaps also daunting that, in his view, the city now had to take the path of righteousness and courage in the face of adversity. The story of Junípero Serra provided that model.

Where should the pageant take place? Miller's original idea was to stage it at the Mission Inn, but when he realized the scale of the project that

McGroarty had in mind, he decided the cost would be too great. The author then tried to find someone else to stage the play, to no avail. Failing in all his efforts, he decided to build his own theater at his own cost. He chose the site of Mission San Gabriel, one of the only missions in Los Angeles County and located about 12 miles from downtown Los Angeles. The church adjacent to the mission readily helped out by donating land for the theater. His wife Ida joined him in the enterprise, designing the costumes, making many of them herself, and even choosing the color schemes for the interior of the theater. On a later trip to Europe, she purchased shawls and dresses in Spain, which women in the play wore from then on.[44] The McGroartys hired a "pageant master" to direct the play, Henry Kabierske from Breslau, Germany, and paid the actors and all other costs. McGroarty claimed his debts rose to over $50,000, although on another occasion he stated that the amount came to $100,000.[45] Whatever the cost, he asserted in 1929 that the play "has paid every dollar of the debts that were incurred to produce it, and it has always since paid its own way as a Play."[46] While not entirely true—Behymer and the Los Angeles Chamber of Commerce launched a campaign to revive sagging ticket sales in 1926—the Mission Play eventually had over 3,000 performances: an extraordinary run by any standard. As the multitudes poured in, it seems that McGroarty's gamble indeed paid off. Long after its premiere in 1912, which religious dignitaries, leading businessmen, and "old Spanish families" witnessed, the pageant was a hit.[47]

One of the pageant's strengths was its consistent focus on Father Serra, who comes across as a veritable savior of the West. He is alternatingly deeply religious, always tender with children, utterly dedicated, and at times capable of rising up in righteous anger. Referring to Serra as an "eighteenth-century Saint Francis," McGroarty depicts him as the guiding force of goodness in a chaotic world.[48] No deed is too small, or too difficult, that Serra might tackle it to achieve his dream: the Christianization of the entire Indian population of California. "His labors in California during the sixteen years of his ministry were herculean and were marked by extreme self-sacrifice and a Christ-like love," McGroarty writes. "Though he never sought for worldly honors, his name is now, nearly a century and a half after his death, the one great, immortal name in California and one of the immortal names in the history of the human race."[49] While his image suffered considerably in later times, Junípero Serra could scarcely have asked for a more laudatory tribute in this pageant, and millions of people imbibed that image at one of the sources, the Mission San Gabriel.

The location of the pageant was a key element in its success, not only in terms of the perception of historical truth, but that the pageant became in part a community enterprise. Two local dancers from the city of San Gabriel, Juanita Vigare and Juan Zorraquinos, led the dance songs "El sombrero blanco" and "La señora," respectively, and Vigare was allegedly "the fourth generation of her family to be baptized in San Gabriel Mission."[50] Both children and adults of San Gabriel filled other roles: "[T]he play as a pageant is a personal pride of San Gabriel. Members of the old Spanish and Mexican families of the Mission town enact the minor roles year after year, sing the songs that their forefathers and mothers sang at the fiestas, and dance the dances of other days. It is this that gives the Mission play its beauty and sincerity."[51] The point here is that the creators of the Mission Play saw their drama as a pageant rather than merely another theatrical work, and indeed referred to it as a "pageant drama." In other words, by incorporating members from the local community, the pageant makers sought to reaffirm the traditional notion of the pageant form in the Los Angeles region. A continuing presence of local actors was also a critical factor in the pageant's continuity for over 20 years; it fostered a tradition of involvement for many residents of San Gabriel, much like the Ramona Pageant did in Hemet in Riverside County.

Although Indians acted in the pageant from the beginning, the play's position on the Indians was strongly paternalistic. They were "a race that was low in the primitive scale and without even traditions. . . . This whole race, so long useless in the world, was made strikingly useful through the efforts of the missionaries."[52] Father Serra, in delivering them from their uselessness, "stands almost without a parallel in human history," and the Indians "were taught to work at fifty-four different European trades." What exactly these trades were is not stated, but the audiences could rest assured that in "the days when the Missions were in their glory California was said to be the happiest land in the world. There was peace and plenty everywhere."[53] The fact that an Indian chief, Chief Young Turtle, took part in the musical celebrations gave this depiction a sense of authenticity, even though there is little evidence that other Indians took part.

As the pageant grew in popularity, so did the plans for the Mission Play. The McGroartys formed the Mission Play Association and began to build a new theater in 1924, complete with a courtyard, gardens, patio, and foyer that featured "a miniature El Camino Real." When they ran into financial difficulties, the Los Angeles Chamber of Commerce took over the project, and the grand opening took place on March 5, 1927. A Spanish Café and tea room served traditional Mexican dishes to happy patrons, who could drink wine from the old vineyard that the Mission Play Association had purchased. The new theater seated 2,500, adjacent to recreation rooms, tennis courts, and that joy of joys for all Angelenos: plentiful parking. The model for the playhouse was of all places one of the five missions of San Antonio, Texas, the Mission San Antonio de Padua, which McGroarty referred to as "the most beautiful of all the missions."[54] Before Christine Sterling's renovation of Olvera Street in downtown Los Angeles during the 1930s, the McGroartys and the Chamber of Commerce had fashioned a kind of miniature theme park built around the mission myth, which continued to regale and fascinate audiences long afterward.

So renowned had the Mission Play become that in 1931 it even had a performance at the Hollywood Bowl—the ultimate bestowal of recognition and approval for the performing arts in Los Angeles during the 1920s and '30s. After two decades of almost continuous performances, something that few productions on Broadway or even in Hollywood could match, it had become one of the most famous pageants in the country. The Hollywood Bowl performance took place on July 1, 1931 in honor of the National Education Association and in celebration of the 3,140th rendition of the Mission Play. We find many of the same actors, still loyally filling their roles, and several of the original dancers and musicians were also there, such as Juanita Vigare and Juan Zorraquinos, although the Indian chief was now Chief Willow Bird, who replaced Chief Young Turtle.[55]

Its glorification of a bygone era remained one of the appeals of the play. The kind, patriarchal image of Serra served to reassure audiences that a charismatic figure who exuded the purity of religious faith could save anyone, and at one point its creators even promoted it as "the historical Oberammergau of California."[56] What made the Mission Play unique among other religious dramatic portrayals in the region, such as the Pilgrimage Play or the *Light of Asia*, was its message that the cultures of Euro-American, Mexican American, and Native American could unite within one religion and indeed within one culture. This message found a ready audience in Los Angeles during the first half of the twentieth century, and the play's combination of drama, music, and religious fervor long proved a powerful attraction for residents and tourists alike.

The Ramona Pageant

No less spectacular was the success of the Ramona Pageant, based on the famous novel by Helen Hunt Jackson. *Ramona* is not merely a story; it is a phenomenon. Few other books have had the same impact on southern California history, tourism, and identity than has Jackson's tale. She wrote it, she said, to reach the heart of Americans over the plight of the Indians in America, rather in the vein of Harriet Beecher Stowe's *Uncle Tom's Cabin* on black slavery in the South. While some reform efforts did eventually result after the publication of Jackson's novel in 1884, *Ramona* is no *Uncle Tom's Cabin*. The public's response, however, was immediate; the book quickly sold out of its initial run and proceeded to go through a stream of reprints and foreign translations. The book remains in print.[57]

Jackson had already tried to emphasize the plight of Native Americans with another publication, *A Century of Dishonor*.[58] Based on exhaustive research and an admirable attention to detail, she listed the hardships that major Indian tribes endured—among them the Cheyenne, the Nez Percé, and the Sioux—and described atrocities that whites committed against them. Even the acerbic writer Carey McWilliams grudgingly admired the work, and it inspired Charles Lummis to found the Sequoya League in 1902 "to make better Indians."[59] American readers, however, found romance and nostalgia for the "old mission days" more to their taste, and *Ramona* became a source of fascination that has scarcely faded with time.

The impact of the novel was far different from what Jackson had planned. As thousands of tourists poured into southern California, tracing the paths that the "true" Ramona allegedly took, a veritable industry arose around the story that came to include books, plays, and at least five motion pictures, beginning in 1910 with one of D. W. Griffith's first full-length features, starring Mary Pickford.[60] The book also became the basis for an outdoor dramatization that integrated music and dance: the Ramona Pageant. Since its debut in 1923, it has been presented on an almost continuous basis into the twenty-first century, making it the longest-running pageant in American history.[61]

The location is highly unlikely for a pageant, consisting mainly of rocks, canyons, and sagebrush. Citizens of the small town of Hemet, located close to Palm Springs, saw that the region had little to interest tourists other than the nearby San Jacinto Hot Mud Sulphur Springs, an array of Indian artifacts, rock drawings, and caves, and the *Ramona* story. Led by the determined Burdette Raynor, secretary of the Hemet Chamber of Commerce, the town's citizens reasoned that a pageant might attract people to the region, both tourists and migrants. Thus a key element in the pageant's creation was tourism.[62]

Like the Mission Play, the founders of the Ramona Pageant claimed historical accuracy. One program states that while Jackson "distorted the actual case with a fiction writer's license . . . it remains true that the foundations of the story are laid in fact, and that the incidents actually took place very nearly as recorded, in the mountains near Hemet and San Jacinto and in the Valley itself."[63] Charles Lummis, who in 1888 published a book of photographs based on the novel, made a similar claim of Jackson's work: "No novel of strong purpose can be pure fiction. . . . No such story was ever true collectively, but there is hardly an individual incident in the book which Mrs. Jackson did not pick from life."[64] As presenters of the pageant wrote: "It is the miracle of pageantry that reincarnates these ghostly figures of a day gone by and breathes into them the breath of life. . . . We the people of the Hemet-San Jacinto Valley, in bringing to you this story, feel that we have contributed something to the world that will live. We feel that we have been instrumental in preserving a bit of California's history in pageant form. . . . We who live amid the scenes described in book and play invite you to enjoy with us the romance, the color, the excitement of a day gone by."[65]

Although *Ramona* is a love story, Jackson's interest in writing the tale began with her hearing of a true-life crime. She integrated several elements of the crime in her novel: that an Indian woman named Ramona existed (even if she had nothing to do with the fictional Ramona), that she was married to an Indian (Juan Diego, but named Alessandro in the novel), and that Diego was shot by a white man (Sam Temple, named Jim Farrar in the novel), whose horse he claimed Diego had stolen. Temple, whom an all-white jury later acquitted, described the event to George Wharton James in a cylinder recording of their talk.[66] It seems Jackson first heard of the crime while staying in April 1883 with a Mrs. J. C. Jordan, who lived in the old district of San Jacinto. While Jackson may have written some of the story while residing in San Jacinto, as the program claims, most of it she actually wrote in a hotel in New York City.[67]

An essential reason for the success of the pageant was the hiring of Garnet Holme, a Shakespearean-trained actor from England who created a series of pageants in northern and southern California during the 1910s and '20s.[68] Born in 1873 and educated at Cambridge University, Holme decided to dedicate his life to the stage. After acting in and directing Shakespearean plays for almost ten years, he became acquainted with Kate Galpin, who founded the Los Angeles Shakespeare Club and visited the Shakespeare Festival at Stratford-on-Avon. Galpin had taught at several different private schools in the Los Angeles area since 1890, and she invited Holme to come to Los Angeles to direct plays at her Shakespeare Club. Holme readily agreed, and in 1904 he made the trek out west. For the next two years, until Galpin's death, he directed a series of student productions, among them *The Merry Wives of Windsor*. After Galpin's death he decided to join a traveling company to perform *A Midsummer Night's Dream* at the Greek Theater at the University of California, Berkeley. He proceeded to direct further productions with the Theater of the Children in San Francisco, and at the Forest Theater at Carmel-by-the-Sea, where writer Mary Austin staged many of her works.[69]

Holme's interest in outdoor theater ultimately persuaded him to join the pageantry movement. He wrote *The Pageant of the Seven Seas*, which was produced in San Francisco in December 1913, and worked in Percy MacKaye's *Caliban by the Yellow Sands* in New York City before returning to California to direct *José* in San Jose, followed by the patriotic *The Pageant of Peace* in San Francisco in December 1918 to celebrate the end of the war. Upon hearing of the strong interest in pageantry in southern California, he returned in 1920 to write or direct a series of pageants and plays over the next two years, gaining much experience as a pageant master. Among these productions were the Pilgrimage Play in Hollywood, a pageant on Spanish explorer Juan Cabrillo at the Cabrillo Festival in San Pedro, and the *Pageant of the Rose* in Redlands. He also created and directed a drama called the Desert Play, which was based on an earlier play by Mary Austin on the old Indian legend of Tahquitz, an evil spirit whose shrieks were said to resound through the desert hills and valleys near Palm Springs.[70]

Holme was thus a seasoned veteran in both drama and pageantry by the time the Hemet Chamber of Commerce approached him to direct the Ramona Pageant. The association had originally asked an English teacher at the town's high school to write the script, yet after seeing the Desert Play, they asked Holme if he might be interested. In November 1922, members of the Chamber of Commerce brought him to a possible location for the pageant that immediately appealed to him, and Holme readily agreed to do the project. It was a natural amphitheater outside Hemet, and in an experience that recalls the founding of the Hollywood Bowl, a writer remarked: "So

Figure 4.4 Garnet Holme

marvelous were the acoustics that the author and later first director of the Pageant became even more enthusiastic than he had been before."[71] Within a few months Holme had completed the script, auditioned and directed the actors, and on April 13, 1923 the first Ramona Pageant took place.

Despite the remote location, the pageant proved to be enormously successful almost immediately. Over 200,000 people came during the first twelve seasons, with each season lasting only three weekends. The peak year was 1929, when 20,451 people attended a total of six performances.[72] To accommodate the pageant-goers, much like at the Hollywood Bowl, in 1926 the owners built concrete and wooden seats to accommodate up to six thousand people. Like the founders of the Mission Play, the members of what became the Ramona Pageant Association (founded in 1927) likened their pageant to the Passion Play of Oberammergau.[73] The Association oversaw a kind of a pilgrimage of pageant-goers, reveling in a mystical past that is part-truth, part-fiction.

One virtue of the pageant is that it follows the novel very closely. The plot intertwines three overlapping cultures: the Indian, the Mexican, and the Anglo. The widow of a prominent Californio family, Señora Moreno, lives on a rancho in the 1850s with her only son, Felipe, and the half-Indian, half-Anglo Ramona, the adopted daughter of Señora Moreno's dead sister. Keeping company with this trio are over a dozen servants and ranch hands. The world they have known for decades is coming to an end, because the Yankees have taken over the country and are moving into southern California. The Morenos' only connection to their glorious past is to maintain both their rancho culture and firm ties to the Catholic Church, represented by the honest, dedicated figure of Father Salvierderra, an aging Franciscan friar. When Ramona falls in love with the full-blooded Luiseño Indian Alessandro, the head of the sheep-shearers on the ranch, the horrified Señora Moreno forbids the match, seeking to keep the honor of the household intact by forbidding any intermarriage between members of her family and the Indians.

What should Ramona do? Claim her inheritance, which she may have only if she stays on the rancho, or leave with the man she truly loves? When Alessandro is left bereft after white men steal his father's land, Ramona agrees to flee the rancho and go south with him, where a priest in San Diego, Father Gaspara, marries them. After two years and the birth of a baby girl, Ramona and Alessandro again face tragedy, losing their land to more white settlers, and are driven from the region. Although taken in by a friendly white woman, Aunt Ri, they soon lose their daughter as well to illness. Driven mad by this stream of misfortunes, Alessandro mistakenly takes the horse of a white man, who hunts him down and kills him in cold blood. Ramona is left destitute, but no! Felipe, who has secretly loved Ramona all his life, traces her path. He arrives a day after Alessandro's murder, and takes Ramona away, deciding to abandon his life as owner of a declining rancho and to leave for Mexico, where they will finally live in peace.

The two-act pageant loyally adheres to this plot:

Act One—The Camulos Rancho

Episode One—Alessandro comes to the rancho. (One month elapse.)
Episode Two—The love story. (Six months elapse.)
Episode Three—The senora discovers the lovers. (Eighteen days elapse.)
Episode Four—The lovers flee from the rancho. (Two years elapse.)

Intermission

Act Two: In Exile

Episode One—The christening of Ramona's child at Pasquale
Episode Two—Soboba Springs
Episode Three—Death of Alessandro on Mt. San Jacinto

Epilogue: The Love of Felipe

What is it about the story that would appeal to so many people around the country, many of whom had probably never been to California or seen real Indians? Like much of nineteenth-century literature, such as Sir Walter Scott's Waverly novels and Charles Dickens's *Great Expectations* and *Oliver*

Twist, highly descriptive stories that moved people's hearts did not require the reader to have actually experienced these scenes before. Several universal themes are present: the conquest of the Anglo-Saxon over brown-skinned natives, the longing for love in a world filled with misfortune and envy, the desire for peace in a time of ceaseless social and technological change. That these themes were all combined so skillfully in a single tome speaks volumes of Jackson's story-telling abilities, even if the work is not on the scale of her model, *Uncle Tom's Cabin*. Jackson's true talent lay in taking events and characters that had truth in them but were not necessarily related, and blending them in a harmonious whole as if the story could *only* have happened this way.[74]

As with the Mission Play, the Ramona Pageant asserts a particular view of the Anglo-Saxon conquest of California. There are few "gray" shades to the characters, who often fall into some common stereotypes; the Indians are predominantly good, the whites invading the land are predominantly bad, and the Californios are on the whole a fun-loving people with a passion for fiesta and siesta. The Indians seek to preserve a sense of self-worth in a world that denies them that self-worth; the Anglos gain their self-worth at least in part through that process of denial; and the Californios appear as a breed apart. That most of the actors over the pageant's history have historically been neither Indian nor Latino may or may not detract from the true historical character of the pageant; that the pageant remains one of the few examples of expressive culture that preserves a link to the history of conquest remains part of its continuing vitality and peculiar fascination. In this sense, the Ramona Pageant represents what McGroarty called California's "romantic history."[75]

One aspect that lends the pageant both its vitality and its historical character is the music. While we do not know which musicians Holme hired during the first year, he asked Los Angeles guitarist and singer José Arias to perform songs for the 1924 season. Arias had worked with Holme on an earlier pageant on the missions, which took place at San Juan Capistrano. He was a perfect choice for the Ramona Pageant, since Arias excelled in the music of Mexico, Spain, and California. At the time he was the founder of the Mexican Troubadours, a string orchestra he formed in the early 1920s that consisted of up to 32 musicians: guitarists, violinists, cellists, and bass and mandolin players. Arias was one of the few musicians who not only seriously sought to retain the culture of old California—a culture that was slowly disappearing, but to communicate its music to the Anglo population. In the words of his son, José Arias Jr., the music of the Californios integrated Spanish and Mexican influences, and thus represented a "longing of being away from the homeland."[76]

Arias began his professional career in the 1910s, performing for several of the old Californio families, including the Sepulvedas, the Verdugos, and the Lugos. Dressed in the old Californio costume of basic black, with a Spanish hat and sash about the waist, strumming tunes on his guitar that evoked a bygone era, he struck a figure of the old world who functioned very well in the new. He became acquainted with several Anglos, such as Frank Miller,

Figure 4.5 José Arías and Troubadours

owner of the Mission Inn in Riverside, where he frequently performed and met his future wife. Arias also began mixing with the Hollywood movie colony by playing guitar on film sets, such as for the 1921 picture *Four Horseman of the Apocalypse* with Rudolph Valentino. He maintained this Hollywood connection for most of his life, performing in the 1928 and 1936 filmed versions of *Ramona*, starring respectively Dolores Del Rio and Loretta Young.[77] One friend was Charles Lummis, who published *Spanish Songs of Old California* in 1923, a collection of 14 traditional songs that Lummis translated and that art music composer Arthur Farwell arranged for piano.[78] Lummis and Farwell worked together on transcribing hundreds of cylinders Lummis had recorded of Mexican American and Native American musicians, and one result was Lummis's songbook, which had several songs that Arias chose to perform for the Ramona Pageant.

Arias selected songs that came from the three cultures of Californio, Mexican, and Spanish. Two examples are "El capotin" (The Rain Song) and "La hamaca" (The Hammock), the former of which Lummis had recorded earlier with local singer Manuela Garcia in 1904 and both of which appear in Lummis's songbook and are traditional Californio songs. "El capotin" is in waltz time, and tells of a man's desperate love for a woman, so that he "takes to wine and . . . Goes to bed without a bite."[79] The strident beat on guitar signifies the "tin-tin-tin" of the rain beating down (hear Track no. 19). By contrast, "La hamaca" is a gentle if plaintive love song, played "[w]ith swaying motion," that describes someone calling for his love to join him in his hammock, where they might rock to sleep to the murmur of nearby waves.[80] "Cielito lindo" (Beautiful Cielito) is an old Mexican song familiar to many, with its vibrant chorus of bittersweet love: "Ay! Ay, ay, ay! / Sing and don't weep / Because singing brings happiness / Beautiful Cielito, / Into our hearts" (hear Track no. 20). A dance song that appeared in both the Mission Play and the Ramona Pageant, "La jota vieja," is based on an old Aragonese dance form that became popular in Mexico and the Southwest, the *jota*. Arias further added a song for which he wrote the lyrics, called "Camila," with music by composer Salvador Nuño, who also performed for the Mission Play.

Aside from the drum players, almost all the musicians came from the Arias clan. Accompanying Arias were at first only his brother-in-law, Antonio Corral, whom he had taught both the guitar and mandolin. The ensemble, called the José Arias Troubadours, soon grew to at least five instrumentalists: a guitarist, two violinists, a mandolin player, and a clarinetist. Except for the clarinetist, whom Arias hired, all of the musicians consisted mainly of brothers-in-law and later his sons. This musical dynasty continued into the twenty-first century, with Arias's sons and grandsons comprising most of the Latino musicians for the pageant.[81]

As with the Mission Play, several Native Americans participated in the acting, dancing, and music. Playing the matriarch of the Indian tribe ("Mara") was Isidore Costo, a member of the Kumeyaay tribe in San Diego who married into the Cahuilla tribe; the Cahuilla reservation is located near the Ramona Bowl. Mrs. Costo played the role on and off over a period of 40 years, from 1923 to 1962.[82] Two of her sons, Rupert and Manuel, danced in the pageant during the 1920s, while her daughter Rose took part in publicity stunts for the pageant, such as riding in an oxcart, portrayed as Ramona. The family may even have known the actual Ramona Lubo, who died in 1922 but was often "put on display" for county fairs and at the Soboba Indian reservation where she lived, also located near the Ramona Bowl. From 1938 to 1941, children from the Sherman Institute in Riverside did the dancing, and also played the drums—the first time that Indians actually did so.[83]

In the true tradition of the pageant form, many people from the neighboring communities of Hemet and San Jacinto took part in the play. They provided most of the actors and dancers, and it was common for family members to begin as children and continue to be involved well into their adult years. Others contributed as greeters, costume makers, or by selling food and drinks. Only the principal characters of Ramona, Alessandro, Felipe (until 1939), and occasionally Margarita were professional actors; all of the others were amateurs—an essential point, since the Ramona Pageant Association was a nonprofit organization and could not afford additional professional actors. Citizens of Hemet were organized in all levels of the production: from actors,

Figure 4.6 Indian Christening scene, Ramona Pageant

singers, and dancers, to greeters and costume makers. This kind of community participation was an essential element in the longevity of the Ramona Pageant.

The Mexican Players

An acting troupe from the Padua Hills Theatre in Claremont, the Mexican Players, is more difficult to categorize. While it integrated elements of pageantry to re-enact historical scenes or events, its management also saw the purpose of the troupe's existence as lying somewhere between sheer entertainment and international relations. This multiplicity of goals is the result of a highly diverse input by both Anglo and Latino performers, organizers, and playwrights during a period lasting over 40 years, from 1931 to 1974. During that time, widely varying interpretations of both Mexican and Californian identity found expression on the Padua Hills stage, making it a continued subject of interest, and controversy, for scholars.[84]

The Padua Hills Theatre owed its existence to the citizens of the nearby city of Claremont, who in 1930 set aside a lot near the foothills as a community center. The land was part of a much larger plot of some 2,000 acres, which a citizens committee purchased five years earlier in an effort to control development and, in the words of one scholar, "to preserve the natural beauty of the small foothill area by carefully planning a residential settlement that would not dominate the delicate landscape."[85] That meant that neighbors of the community center tended to be wealthy whites who had a strong interest in supporting an arts organization, but in doing as little damage as possible to the surrounding environment. They chose the name from the Italian city of Padua because of the Mediterranean atmosphere of the area's hillside. Foremost among their goals was the creation of a theater, with a restaurant and dining area attached to it, rather like the Mission Playhouse, with its Spanish style décor that reflected California's European heritage. After the completion of this complex at a cost of $75,000, "making it among the most expensive community theaters in California," a group that called itself the Claremont Community Players began putting on a series of plays for the 1930–31 season, despite the impact of the Depression.[86]

While it might seem unusual to begin any cultural effort in an economic crisis, the citizens of this community, particularly the industrialist Herman Garner and his wife Bess Garner, were adamant that their theater would go on. They were deeply inspired by the "little theater" movement, which had begun in Europe during the late nineteenth century and came to America shortly before World War I—precisely the movement that Percy MacKaye, Garnet Holme, and many others saw as a way of integrating the local community in theatrical productions and thus to "democratize" the theater across America. Despite efforts by the New Deal program, the Federal Theater Project, to support community theater, the Depression signaled the end of much of this movement in California. This is where the Padua Hills Theatre had a distinct advantage: The wealthy Garners and their neighbors provided the essential economic support to keep the theater going, without government support.

The failure of one troupe led to the creation of another. Although the Claremont Community Players managed to present up to eight plays per year over three years, they soon succumbed to economic hardship, in part from simply trying to find other day jobs to survive. The Garners sought to maintain operations by a two-pronged approach: inviting actors from the Pasadena Playhouse to perform during the week, and arranging for the Mexican American workers at the theater to perform in the restaurant on weekends. This latter group, who otherwise served as waiters, waitresses, gardeners, and cooks, began with an evening of singing and dancing called "Noche Mexicana" (Mexican Night). They soon called themselves the "Mexican Players," and as their input and repertoire increased, the mission of the theater changed in dramatic ways.[87]

The Mexican Players stood on the threshold of a historic event. Most of the troupe came from the local barrios near Claremont and Pomona, where they or their families worked in agriculture, mining, and heavy industry. They were not professional actors, but in performing their own songs and dances, they gave a kind of authenticity to the production that made it unique. If we accept the notion of community as a basis for theater, then the Mexican Players worked within that model but in a somewhat revised form, since the model never implied anything about serving tables. Yet their dual roles added to the unique charm of the theater and certainly to the enjoyment of predominantly Anglo audiences, who were amazed at a demonstration of young Latino men and women singing, dancing, acting, and serving in an environment that resembled "old Mexico." What set these actors apart from the Claremont Community Players, as well as most others acting troupes in the region, was the music.

This model for the productions was not unique to the Padua Hills Theatre. The Garners, on a previous visit to Italy, had come across a similar type of entertainment, in which the boys and girls who served them also sang and danced during the meals. By applying this model to the Padua Hills Theatre, the Garners thus modified the notion of community theater, which provided the basis for the unique character of the Mexican Players. The troupe began to attract not only audiences from the surrounding communities but also some well-known personalities, among them the poet Carl Sandburg, novelist Hugh Wallace, and even Walt Disney, who later used the group in an animated short.[88]

The theater reminds us of a third model, and that is the Italian form, *commedia dell'arte*. As a scholar of Spanish literature, Pauline Deuel, points out, this type of theater presented stock characters in improvised situations, such as the hero, the villain, or the clown involved in a typically comic plot, and always accompanied by music and dancing. Beginning in the sixteenth century, it spread to France, where it became *Theatre-Italienne*, as well as to Spain and even England. Numerous playwrights drew directly on this form, from Molière, to Ben Jonson, to Shakespeare, for some of their characters, and it is possible that through Spain it also came to Mexico. While we have no proof that the troupe drew consciously on this form, the special character of *commedia dell'arte* does characterize the particular style of the Mexican Players, who during the first decade essentially combined music and dancing with improvised dialogue on specific themes.

Let us examine three examples of their work. The first of these was "Serenata Mexicana" (Mexican Serenade), which was their second production and the first one under the name of the Mexican Players. The play took place on Mondays, Tuesdays, Thursdays, and Fridays, at 2:30 P.M. and 8:30 P.M., from July through September, with seats costing 75 cents. It depicts the "simple story of life in a village street somewhere—anywhere in Mexico."[89] In the courtyard of an inn, "Boys sing, girls dance, youth loves." There was little plot to speak of, but that wasn't the point; the goal was to show how young Mexicans might spend the afternoon and early evening in a small village. A graduate student from the Claremont Colleges, Charles Dickinson, directed the play with advice from one of the actors, Juan Matutte y Remus, who 50 years later assembled a scrapbook of the Padua Hills Theatre. Dickinson became heavily involved with the theater, designing costumes and sets, writing plays, and later creating a detailed map of Mexico on the asbestos curtain of the theater, indicating the various states.[90] All of the music from

"Serenata Mexicana" is traditionally Mexican, including the perpetual "Cielito lindo." Matute arranged one of the songs, while four of the songs had appeared earlier in Lummis's song book that the Ramona Pageant players also used, *Spanish Songs of Old California*.[91]

The stereotype of the happy, smiling Mexican that appeared in the original production came to be revised in future productions. Either due to the popularity of "Serenata Mexicana" or the lack of other plays to perform, the troupe decided to repeat it two more times that year, but in a different manner. They give a more complex vision of village life than the mere carousing of boys and girls, depicting "little servant girls going for 'masa' for the morning tortillas, the shivering devout going to early mass, men setting out for market, children going to school, girls and women coming for water for their morning housework, a street musician dawdling the day away, girls dancing in the sun . . ."[92]

The play grew to include a multiplicity of scenes, all occurring simultaneously or consecutively, and with music to accompany each scene. Not all of it is happy or festive; we also see women gossiping, or a "little box coffin of the poor," led by a grieving father. A cockfight takes place in one scene, and a tortilla maker sells her wares in another. This kind of theater is not merely designed to entertain, but also to instruct. Unlike with the *Ramona Pageant* or the *Mission Play*, for which Anglos wrote the scripts, these players were essentially improvising their own words, since they were performing precisely *without* scripts. While the ultimate approval of each scene came from the director, Charles Dickinson, the actors themselves seem to have had much influence in how that scene took place. Therein lay the believability of this syncretic genre and the true power of theater: the notion that the actors were no longer acting.

The music for the production varied greatly in mood and was dominant throughout. At least four musicians performed at various times on the stage: a guitarist, a violinist, a harpist, and a percussionist, who played a total of at least 14 different pieces. We do not know how long the play took to perform, but if we assume that it was 60 minutes long, then there was music every 4 or so minutes; if the play took two hours to perform, then music took place every 9 minutes. This is more on the level of a musical than a play. Adding to the list of music previously arranged, three of the actors, Salvador Sanchez, Miguel Vera, and Catalino Alva, also wrote a piece specifically for the play, titled "Serenata."[93] Thus the play provided a continuous stream of entertainment, with the emphasis on music and dancing rather than on plot.

A second example is "Mi Compadre Juan," which took place twice every Saturday from January to March 1935.[94] In this production, the Garners invited to direct the songs and dancing the dancer Luz Maria Garcés, whose visit the Mexican government and particularly the Secretary of Education arranged.[95] The Mexican Players had grown to 17 actors: nine men and eight women. This production consists of five scenes, and the plot concerns a travel through Mexico by an Anglo-American couple, the Smiths, and their Mexican

American friend Juan as they visit the latter's home in Mexico; "Juan" was Juan Matute, who evidently came from Vera Cruz. On their tour they visit Vera Cruz, Oaxaca, Michoacan, and the Yucatan before ending up in Mexico City. Each location provides an opportunity for singing and dancing.

In this production the music is even more extensive than in "Serenata Mexicana." In all there are at least 21 performances of either a song, dance, or a combination of the two. If we assume that it lasted two hours, then every five to six minutes the audience heard a new piece. The majority of the performances (11 out of 21) were dances, all of which came from the regions the travelers visited, such as the "Sandunga" of Oaxaca or "Los Viejitos" of Lake Patzcuero. Thus the play represented a kind of musical panorama of parts of Mexico, and the music that accompanied the dances also assumedly came from each respective region. The play ended with the national dance of Mexico, the "Jarabe."[96]

As with "Serenata Mexicana," there is an element of education involved here. The goal is to present a musical overview of Mexico, and the plot is minimal, consisting mainly of visiting one place after another. While the play might be a demonstration that "half the fun is getting there," the variety of folk dances seek to attest to the cultural richness of Mexico. Garcés was there to assure the authenticity of each song or dance, since to do otherwise would have been a discredit to the production. The involvement of the Mexican government underlined this intent, as well as the interest in seeking to improve relations between the two countries.

Both politics and research came to be distinguishing features of the Padua Hills Theatre. The Garners formed the Padua Institute in 1935, which had as its goal the dissemination of Mexican culture in the Southland. Its purpose was to study the cultural practices, performances, and history of Mexico, and present the results of these efforts to the public through the Mexican Players. The Institute also published some music that the troupe performed, such as the Christmas songs, *Las Posadas*.[97] There is no evidence that funds from the U.S. government supported the Institute, since it seems to have been entirely privately financed, but the Garners received much recognition from the Mexican government, which eventually gave a medal of honor to Mr. Garner. The Institute established some ties to the Claremont Colleges, particularly with Millard Sheets, who headed the Scripps Art Department since 1932 and became a trustee of the Institute and even a resident in the Padua Hills. Sheets undertook realist murals during the 1930s through commissions with the Works Progress Administration, including one for the Angel's Flight Railway on Bunker Hill.[98] The Padua Institute provided the basis for all future productions by the Mexican Players.

An example of the Padua Institute's efforts was to invite another performer and teacher from Mexico, Graciela Amador, to mount a production with the Mexican Players, called "Aguila y Nopal" (The Eagle and Cactus) in November 1935. This elaborate play consists of five parts, and similar to "Mi Compadre Juan," it is a kind of musical travelogue of Mexico, although with more of a historical approach. The first part contains music and dances from the eighteenth century, such as "Zapatitos de Tatetan" (little shoes of Chinese silk), "Hay un lirio" (the song of the lily) and "Saratoga." The second part represents the nineteenth century, including "El Curripiti" (ballad of the downfall of Maximilian), "Clarin de Campaña" (first song of the Cadets of Chapultepec), and "Aires Nacionales" (the first Mexican Jarabe). The third part takes the listener to the Isthmus region, presenting two *sandungas* and "Daini Tibi," a Zapotec Indian song from Oaxaca. The fourth part has music from the coast of the Gulf of Mexico, including "Uchila" (a song of the Huapango), "Huapango del Pañuelito" (a dance of the handkerchief), and "Huapango del Caracol" (a dance of the snail). Finally, the production closes with three songs and dances from central Mexico: "La Rana" (song of the frog), "El Toro" (the bull), and "El Gallito" (dance of the little rooster). In all, at least 19 songs and dances comprise the show, although there may have been even more, since one of the pieces listed, "El Palomon," consists of "songs and dances of the Port of Alvarado," suggesting a medley of music and dance. Thus for a two-hour show, a song or dance took place almost every six minutes or less, which was on par with earlier productions. This is musical theater in every sense. Although we do not know how many instruments they used, a photograph indicates four guitars and a bass guitar.

Yet as with "Mi Padre Juan," it is not simply entertainment. The Mexican Players were seeking to educate a predominantly white audience about the music and dance of various parts of Mexico, in this case with the guiding hand of a real practitioner in the art, the guitarist, singer, and composer Graciela Amador. The guest artist, who was a distant relative to one of the players, Casilda Amador, taught the Mexican Players how to present the music and how to perform the dances, and she wrote several new songs for the troupe. Although there is no indication that she came through the aide of the Mexican government, there is this element of international relations at work: trying to understand the culture of another country through its music. As one scholar put it, by exposing whites to Mexican culture, such plays "presented the possibility of dispelling antipathies towards Mexican people while attracting large audiences."[99]

Nor are these the only teachers who came from Mexico to work with the Mexican Players. Francisco Sánchez Flores arrived from Guadalajara in 1935 to mount "[¿]Idolos Muertos?" (Are the Idols Dead?), a serious production with little evidence of gaiety. Like Amador, Flores taught the troupe a variety of dances, and a narrator explained the play to the audience. Ema Duarte and Amado López Castillo came in 1936 to teach the troupe folk dances as well.[100] Their visits leant a quality of academic purpose to the Institute, as well as a form of cultural exchange between the two countries.

A final, distinguishing feature of the Padua Hills Theatre was a series of seasonal plays. The first of these was a Christmas play the Mexican Players gave during their second year in operation, called "Christmas at Mi Rancho Bonito." When the production met with delight by audiences, the Garners decided to have a Christmas special each year, titled "Las Posadas" (the shelters), a traditional ceremony of Mexico depicting the journey of Mary and Joseph from house to house until they were finally admitted on the ninth night, Christmas Eve. Bess Garner claims that the stimulus for the production came from one of the actors, Miguel Vera, who told them of his childhood experiences with Christmas at his home in La Cañada de Caracheo, Guanajuoto. Vera sang the lyrics to the melodies while Mrs. Garner and Dickinson wrote them down. Mrs. Garner then visited Vera's home in Mexico in 1933 and saw 18 different variations of Las Posadas. The result of these efforts was the publication by the Padua Institute of six Christmas songs which the Mexican Players sang each year; Mrs. Garner wrote that "whatever one's race or people or creed, in music the age old story of the Holy Babe may still warm and gladden our hearts and widen our sympathies."[101] Similarly, the Mexican Players gave a seasonal play every Easter in a production called "The Fiesta of San Ysidro."

Despite these efforts at historical or cultural accuracy, most of the productions over the 40-year history of the Padua Hills Theatre were comedies or farces. Both Charles Dickinson and Bess Garner commonly served either as directors or sources for themes.[102] Most of the comedies seem to have resulted from their input, with titles such as "Mi Rancho Bonito," or "Rosita," or "Mamacita." "Rosita," mounted in 1933, depicts the simple but happy Rosita falling in and out of love, a common theme of the comic plays. In another comedy of 1938, "The Professor Visits Veracruz," an American entomologist (played by Dickinson) arrives in "the little town of Ixtlan del Rio," which causes quite a stir amongst the inhabitants.[103] Here the stereotype of the ever-smiling Mexicans comes more fully to the fore, and the Mexican Players made it more "authentic" by supplying their own dialogue as well as music. Mrs. Garner seems to have tried to make the costumes and music as realistic as possible, doing research and collecting items during multiple trips to Mexico, much as the McGroartys did on their trips to Spain for the Mission Play. Yet some scholars have criticized the Garners as exploitive or at least paternalistic, by paying the actors relatively little for their work and seeking to keep them away from the "evil influences" of Hollywood.[104]

Despite the Garners' protective attitude, the Mexican Players reached audiences far beyond the Padua Hills Theatre. They made several tours in the state, including one in 1934 to the California missions, where they performed for the local priests and congregations. And despite the efforts of the Garners to keep the Mexican Players away from Hollywood, the troupe made at least two film appearances. Walt Disney was so enamored with the Mexican Players that he decided to integrate them in one of the first animated feature films that combined live action, *The Three Caballeros*, in 1944. The Mexican Players provided the music and dancing in a Latin American setting (in a Burbank studio), interacting with Donald Duck ("Señor Donald") and two other animated figures, a parrot named José Carioca and a rooster, Panchito. One of the scenes, titled "La Piñata," involved one of the Mexican Players' best-known folk plays, Las Posadas, quite appropriate for the film's world premiere in Mexico City on December 21, 1944.[105] The troupe even appeared in a film that the U.S. military produced, titled *Cultural Activities in the United States* in 1950, which the American government showed around the world as an example of cultural awareness and diversity.[106]

The musical theater that the Mexican Players offered thus presents the scholar with a conundrum. On the one hand, there is the serious effort to present Mexican and early Californian music and dance by true practitioners of the art. While most of the productions revolved around Mexico, others depicted scenes in southern California, such as one play on the creation of the Spanish Royal Road ("El Camino Real"). Moreover, the Mexican Players were clearly dedicated to their cause, managing a demanding schedule of at least eight different productions per year, each given on an average of six to eight times per week, and they kept that schedule on a continuous basis over their 40-year history. No amount of "Anglo coercion" could maintain this level of continuity, and as historian Matt Garcia attests, members of the troupe formed close bonds and continued to organize reunions long after the theater had closed.[107]

On the other hand, there is no escaping the framework that the Garners put in place: to present Mexicans and Mexican Americans in the best possible light, often to the point of caricature. Discrimination and exploitation of Latinos in southern California, such as the forced repatriation to Mexico of thousands of Latinos during the Depression, were not the staged themes of this theater. Nonetheless, the Mexican Players offered some of the few opportunities for Anglos to hear and see Mexican music and dance, and thereby to make the connection to Latino culture in Los Angeles. Like the Mission Play and the Ramona Pageant, the music dramas of the Padua Hills Theatre represented a blend of Anglo, Mexican, and Indian identities in Los Angeles's diverse music culture, thus yielding a cornucopia of artistic expression.

Conclusion

These music dramas, with their celebration of the cultural history of the southland, contain some similar elements. Each presents a colorful depiction of the past, seeking to teach as well as to entertain. Music has a central role in all three productions, whether in the Fiesta scene for the Mission Play, or the song and dances in the Ramona Pageant, or the continuous stream of music that the Mexican Players performed. The music thus serves as a unifying principle—as a means of explaining history through the format of song—and with its integration of Anglo, Mexican, and Indian traditions, the music illustrates the ethnic mix that has long defined Californian culture.

An interesting feature of these music dramas is that they continued to attract audiences long after the tourism boom of the 1920s. These plays comforted with their general emphasis on stability and optimism, which were not commonly heard words during the Great Depression. After the almost giddy buoyancy and prosperity of the 1920s, people now saw long lines at soup kitchens in a supposed land of plenty, where the recently unemployed shared the same pavement as families on relief. The notion of a happy, mystical past was not new, but during the 1930s these music dramas served a different purpose: to reassure a deeply troubled world that had seemingly lost its bearings. Audiences could look back at an idealized time and imagine an era when the state's inhabitants seemed truly happy, and the land of plenty was real, when in the words of McGroarty, "desert fields were tilled and made to blossom as the rose."

It is all the more ironic that at a time when thousands of Latinos were being repatriated, or forced into unemployment, many Anglos were celebrating the Latino influence in southern California culture. The powerful role that Mexican cultural traditions had in the region continued to fascinate and regale, almost like a kind of museum display. We see this in the 150th anniversary of the city's founding in its celebration of Latino culture, presented most spectacularly in a seven-day pageant that 110,000 people attended at the Los Angeles Coliseum in 1931, or a "La Fiesta" event at the Hollywood Bowl the same year that celebrated the city's diverse ethnic heritage.[108] Could it be that the declining percentage in the Latino population in southern California, which had begun long before these music dramas were created, led to a kind of worship of a disappearing culture, much as many Anglo composers used Indian melodies for inspiration after the decimation of Indian tribes? Only when Indians were safely tucked away on reservations could the early twentieth-century Indianist movement in musical composition truly take hold; only when the Mexicans had declined as a "threat" to Anglo interests during the same period could they become a source of fascination in music dramas on the region's history.

Ethnicity was not the sole reason for the enduring interest in these plays. Religion, too, played a powerful role. Each music drama emphasized that religious belief could provide a rock of certainty through any time, no matter how desperate. Creators of the Mission Play referred to the play as the "historical Oberammergau of California," and while McGroarty died and audiences moved away or sought other distractions after World War II, the pageant continued to see revivals some 50 years later; the spirit of Father Serra lived on through drama.[109] Religious devotion is central to the Ramona Pageant, too, such as in the model of the Franciscan friar, Father Salvierderra. Many of the serious productions of the Mexican Players similarly drew on religious rituals, especially in the plays at Easter and Christmas, as well as those plays that depicted the cultural life of a Mexican village.

Do these productions simply portray Anglos as they wanted to be portrayed: in glowing terms? Not entirely. In the Mission Play, the Yankee invasion brings an end to the legacy of Father Serra. In the Ramona Pageant, Anglos tend to appear insensitive and caustic, and in the real-life case of Sam

Temple, even murderous. In the Mexican Players productions, when whites do appear, they are generally as students of Mexican or early Californian culture, and are almost always marginal players. This is also expressed in the music; there are essentially no examples of Anglo music, not even by Euro-American composers who sought to integrate Mexican melodies. The emphasis remained on Mexican folk music.

What did audiences learn in attending these productions? The plays demonstrated that southern California represented a mixture of cultures: Californio, Mexican, Anglo, and Indian. They upheld the notion of understanding the region's present through a study of its past, however "romantic" that portrayal may have been. Finally, they presented dramatic portrayals of song and dance, demonstrating a true integration of the arts that the Greeks had first attempted thousands of years ago. In the "Athens of the West," music found a home in drama. In the same way that the creators of these plays reached out to a larger audience through pageantry, others turned to recording and radio: two media that helped define the modern era.

5

Leaving a Legacy: Early Recordings of Indigenous, Classical, and Popular Music

In the summer of 1896, a Texan by the name of Thomas L. Tally opened a phonograph parlor at 311 South Spring Street in the middle of Los Angeles's theater district. As the first such shop in Los Angeles, it immediately brought in paying customers, who dropped a nickel in a slot to listen to two minutes of scratchy music through ear tubes. At first, Tally offered the repertoire that had become standard in such parlors: band music, "coon" songs by minstrel performers, and humorous sketches. Yet over time he recorded several local artists on cylinder, such as the prominent violinist Adolf Lowinsky and his orchestra performing John Philip Sousa's *American Beauty* march, as well as the "Sextet" from the Donizetti opera *Lucia di Lammermoor*. Nor were patrons solely limited to listening to music; six kinetoscopes were also an attraction at Tally's parlor, as was an Edison "Vitascope" that presented a short motion picture through a peephole.[1] Entertainment in Los Angeles was certainly evolving in a new direction.

That "new direction" was a nationwide phenomenon. Phonograph and kinetoscope parlors appeared in cities across the country during the 1890s. San Francisco businessman Louis Glass set up several phonographs in saloons at the beginning of the decade, which he claimed brought in thousands of dollars in revenue.[2] The machines were exhibited in Atlanta, Georgia, Dallas, Texas, and at summer resorts in the Boston area and New York, as well as at state, county, and world's fairs. Costing a nickel for two minutes of music, recordings consisted mainly of popular songs, operatic arias, comic routines, and sound effects. An underground market even developed in vulgar or "profane" subjects. After a slow start, phonographs attracted a particular fascination among the public by the turn of the century. When business owners moved them from saloons to "parlors," they were often enclosed in oak or glass cabinets, and exhibited in fancy settings "with potted palms, ceiling fans, and quasi-Oriental rugs."[3] The upscale marketing transformed the phonograph, like vaudeville before it, into a respectable form of mass entertainment.

Music theorists have a mixed record in their treatment of the role of technology on music performance. Within the European context, sociologist of music Theodor Adorno wrote in 1927 that it "is the bourgeois family that gathers around the gramophone in order to enjoy the music that it itself . . . is unable to perform."[4] Yet recording in America was not necessarily limited by class or race, neither on the part of recording artists nor consumers. One of Adorno's colleagues, Walter Benjamin, was more optimistic; in the words of sociologist Simon Frith, Benjamin "argued that the technology of mass reproduction was a progressive force, the means by which the traditional authority and 'aura' of art was broken." Frith continues, "[m]ass artists were democratic artists; their work was shared with an audience in which everyone was an 'expert.' The technology of the mass media had changed the relationship of the masses to art and opened up new possibilities for cultural work."[5]

In Los Angeles that meant that the recording of music not only made different forms of music accessible to a wider public, but left a permanent record, as it were, of men and women who were active musicians in the region during the first half of the twentieth century. In a world where aesthetics, business, and ethnicity all influenced Los Angeles's music culture, early recordings give us a window on some of the musicians who made up that culture. Given the scope of this field, in the interest of clarity we will focus on individual examples from the 1910s to the '30s: the recordings of Charles Lummis and Andrae Nordskog, as well as the recording of jazz artists during the thirties. The purpose of the chapter is to demonstrate that a diversity of artists had access to recordings in Los Angeles during the first half of the twentieth century.

The Lummis Recordings

One of the first Angelenos to put recording technology to constructive use was Charles Fletcher Lummis. The tireless booster of southern California, as well as a prolific writer and general bon vivant, Lummis sought to record for posterity Hispanic and Indian music of the Southwest, which he first encountered during a trip through New Mexico and Arizona in 1885. As he came to know both Indian and Hispanic inhabitants of the Los Angeles region, he set out to get as much of their music as he could on cylinder before it was too late. Here Lummis was following an illustrious tradition of recording indigenous music, which the anthropologist Franz Boas had begun as early as the 1890s.[6] But few in southern California were equal to the task. Lummis was, and his collection of cylinders has continued to fascinate scholars, one of whom, John Koegel, has done pioneering work in this field.[7]

Lummis's contacts with people on both the East and West Coasts served him well in this endeavor. To purchase recording equipment and wax cylinders, he received $1,500 in grants from the Archaeological Institute of

America (AIA), an organization based in New Haven, Connecticut, which founded the Classical Schools in Rome and Athens. At the time of Lummis's request, the president of the AIA was a professor of classics at Yale, Dr. Thomas Day Seymour. Lummis was a well-known personality, in part because he cofounded the Southwest Society in 1903, a research and preservation organization that was a member society of AIA. One of the goals of that Society was to collect artifacts of "old California" for a museum, representing both the Native American and Spanish heritage of the Southwest; another goal was to record the music that Lummis feared was dying out. As he stated in a letter to Seymour, "the matter of the songs is not only of wider popular appeal, it is far more urgent, because far more perishable."[8]

In a publication titled *The Southwest Society of the Archaeological Institute of America: The Southwest Museum, Three Years of Success*, Lummis described his undertaking as "catching our archaeology alive."[9] He saw this project as very much a scientific endeavor, despite having to deal with naysayers: "When the Southwest Society of the Archaeological Institute of America began, as the very forefront of its scientific activities, to record on a large scale the old folk songs of the Southwest, there were not lacking formal persons in the East to protest: 'But that isn't archaeology, you know.' " Lummis was out to prove them wrong. "These songs are the very earliest American Classics," he claimed, "and Live Classics are quite as essential to science, and quite as interesting to mere human beings, as are Dead Classics."[10] He thus enthusiastically set out to preserve this music.

Lummis drew on the talents of many people for his project. He already knew at least 35 of the musicians who would record for him, some of whom had spent many an evening at his home, "El Alisal," singing and strumming under the stars. Part of what we could call the "Lummis community," these men and women happily complied by singing or strumming into his transportable Edison wax cylinder phonograph, and furthermore, they did it almost entirely for free.[11] At once mythologizing and preserving their music, Lummis amassed a unique collection that is a blend of both popular and serious traditions, particularly in Mexican music: the *canción* (lyric song), the *romance* (historical ballad), and the *corrido* (contemporary ballad).

The songs came from diverse locations dispersed throughout southern California. He made almost all of the recordings in 1904 and 1905 at four places: Rancho Camulos; the house of Adalaida Kamp in the city of Ventura; the Sherman Institute (now the Sherman Indian School) in Riverside; and El Alisal, Lummis's home, about 5 miles from downtown Los Angeles.[12] Many of the Spanish-language songs Angelenos would have commonly heard during the nineteenth and early twentieth century. Lummis's recordings comprise at least 460 cylinders; of these, 300 are Spanish-language songs, while the remaining 160 cylinders consist of 62 American Indian songs in 24 languages—some of the first known recordings of southwestern Indian music. Almost all of the songs are between two to three minutes long, which was the standard recording time of the cylinders. The total number of cylinders he recorded is not known, since some were probably lost or damaged, but he may have made between 550 to 600 cylinders.[13]

Like many other boosters, Lummis arrived from the East Coast and came to love Los Angeles and the rugged environs of southern California. Dropping out of Harvard shortly before graduating in 1880, he did odd jobs at his first wife's home in Ohio before trekking across the country to Los Angeles, arriving at the Mission San Gabriel on February 1, 1885. Similar to the preparations Mark Twain made prior to his trip out west, Lummis had astutely written of his intent to the publisher and editor of the three-year-old *Los Angeles Times*, General Harrison Gray Otis, who immediately contracted him to write dispatches along the way as he traveled from Ohio through the Midwest and Southwest: Indiana, Illinois, Missouri, Kansas, Colorado, New Mexico, Arizona, and finally California.[14] When he arrived in Los Angeles, Lummis was already a known entity to *Times* readers, and "the General" immediately hired him to be city editor of the paper, which Lummis did for the next three years.

One experience from his travels that fascinated Lummis was coming across the enormous repertoire of southwest Hispanic and Indian songs he heard along the way. After his first three years in Los Angeles, he returned to New Mexico for health reasons, where from 1888 to 1892 he began compiling many Mexican folk songs, writing down the words and memorizing the melodies, 12 of which he published in an October 1892 issue of *Cosmopolitan*.[15] While he had little formal musical training and did not collect the songs in any systematic fashion, he did have some musical gifts, such as being able to play guitar. Driven by the infectious enthusiasm of the amateur, he sought to learn as much as he could about the music of the region. As he related it, "[a] great factor in my upbuilding [*sic*] was the deep interest I took in New Mexican folk songs. In California I had learned many beautiful Spanish songs. Out here [in New Mexico] I learned hundreds of others. For months I hung by night around the sheep camps of Don Amado [Chaves], squatting with the quiet Mexican herders in the little semi-circular brush shelter by a crackling fire of juniper . . . we sang and talked and smoked cigarettes under the infinite stars of a New Mexican sky or the even more numerous flakes of a mountain snowstorm."[16]

Over a decade after his return to Los Angeles Lummis began his recording project. Most of the singers he recorded were women, and foremost among these was Manuela García, the daughter of commercial agent Ygnacio García. She was born in 1869 and grew up in a close web of social relations, since her father played an important role in Los Angeles business and social life during the second half of the nineteenth century. He was an agent for ranch owner Ygnacio del Valle, who not only owned the ranch that Helen Hunt Jackson made famous with the novel *Ramona*, but was also manager of the store of the merchant John Temple, who built Temple's Theater. Also part of this network was Harris Newmark, a local businessman who wrote of his "sixty years in southern California," and Professor Miguel Arévalo, who even lived with the

García family for several years in the 1890s at their home on 1115 South Olive in Los Angeles.[17]

Manuela García received training in art music. As a mezzo soprano who may have taken lessons from Arévalo, she studied vocal music for two terms at the State Normal School (now UCLA), where one of her teachers was Emily Valentine, cofounder of the Los Angeles Conservatory of Music and Arts. While she never took a degree, García was listed for many years as a music teacher in the city's directories.[18] Lummis recorded a total of 107 cylinders of her songs, singing alone or accompanied on guitar by either her brother Ygnacio or a blind musician, Rosendo Uruchurtu. Most are love songs, although some are satirical, such as "Las puglas de Morelia," a comment on the fleas of the Mexican city Morelia. Together these *romances* and *canciónes* reveal a rich folkloric tradition that flourished in the Southwest during the second half of the nineteenth century.[19]

One love song that Arthur Farwell transcribed, translated, and then arranged is the Serenade, "La Noche Está Serena."[20] It describes feelings of

Figure 5.1 Manuela García

true passion that contrast with the calm of night:

> La noche está serena, tranquilo et aquilon;
> Tu dulce centinela te guarda el corazon.
> Y en alas de los céfiros, que vagan por doquier,
> Volando van mis suplicas, á ti, bella mujer,
> Volando van mis suplicas, á ti, bella mujer.
>
> De un corazon que te ama, recibe el tierno amor;
> No aumentes mas la llama, piedad á un trobador.
> Y si te mueve á lastima mi eterno padecer,
> Como te amo, amame, bellisima mujer!
> Como te amo, amame, bellisima mujer!

(So still and calm the night is, / The very winds asleep; / Thy heart's so tender sentinel / His watch and ward doth keep. / And on the wings of zephyrs soft / That wander how they will / To thee, oh woman fair, to thee / My prayers go fluttering still, / To thee, oh woman fair, to thee / My prayers go fluttering still.

Oh take the heart's love to thy heart / Of one that doth adore! / Have pity—add not to the flame / That burns thy troubadour! / And if compassion stir thy breast / For my eternal woe, / Oh, as I love thee, loveliest / Of women, love me so! / Oh, as I love thee, loveliest / Of women, love me so!)

Both Lummis and Farwell were fascinated with such songs. In their eyes, this music represented a culture, and a people, that were in the process of simply disappearing, yet the music contained passion and devotion that might well enervate or inspire their own culture. As "archaeologists of music," they saw their mission as both uncovering and preserving not just music for its own sake, but songs of astonishing beauty and grace.

Adalaida Kamp provided more songs. Like García, she was related to several old Californian families, such as that of General Mariano Guadalupe Vallejo, commander of the San Francisco Presidio. Lummis recorded 65 songs by Kamp between June and July 1904, many of which, like García's songs, date from the Mexican period in California (1821–46). Others are more recent, such as "El gachupin" which celebrates Mexico's independence from Spain, or "Napoleón y Miramón," a *corrido* that criticizes the French invaders and Mexican collaborators of the 1860s: monarch Napoleon III, military officer Manuel Losada, and President Miguel Miramón.[21] García also recorded *canciones* that show a strong influence from Italian opera, such as "El destino de la joven encarcelada," based on the aria "Tu che a Dio spiegasti l'ali" from Donizetti's *Lucia di Lammermoor*. According to Koegel, Mexican love songs that reflect this Italian opera influence tend to have "[c]hromatic and melismatic inflections at cadence points (ends of phrases), the use of *portamento* (a sliding between pitches) in performance, and an expanded melodic range."[22]

Most of the songs have similarities with traditional American folk music. They are either strophic (using the same music in successive stanzas) or in verse-refrain form, and are from 16 to 32 bars in length. A few of the songs are waltzes, consisting of melodic pairs of eight measures each. The remaining Spanish-language recordings illustrate the talents of such figures as guitarists José de la Rosa and Rosendo Uruchurtu, as well as musicians from the Villa family, who immigrated from Baja California to Los Angeles after the Gold Rush and became friends with Arévalo, García, and Uruchurtu.[23] Rosa Villa taught the guitar and mandolin, and her vocal duets with her sister Luisa, such as the waltz "La Serenata," are among the highlights of the Lummis wax cylinder collection. Unfortunately, because of the collection's age and fragility, very few cylinders have escaped unscathed; many are filled with scratches and "pops" from repeated use, rendering them almost unplayable. The cylinder for "La Serenata," which Lummis recorded in Los Angeles on January 31, 1904, is an exception (hear Track no. 1).

Lummis drew on two main sources for the Native American songs. One was the Sherman Institute, a school that real estate developer Frank Miller, founder of the Mission Inn, built in Riverside in 1901. Miller moved the school from its original location about 15 miles from Riverside, where it was called the Perris Indian School during the 1890s. This federal government-run institution sought to Americanize Indians by removing them from their parents at an early age and training them to acquire skills to live in white society. One of these skills appears to have been courses in music, since among its virtues the school boasted one of the few Indian bands in the country, which gained a national reputation from touring.[24] The cylinders consist mainly of

Figure 5.2 Rosendo Uruchurtu

solo artists, such as of Martin Villegas, who was possibly a Cahuilla Indian assistant at the school. His unaccompanied solo from April 25, 1904 of a repeated melody with variations, "Song of Las Cruces," is an indication of the musical tradition that existed in the Southwest long before the Mexican or American settlers arrived. Lummis also recorded Procopio Montoya and Ramón Zuñi, two men from the Isleta Pueblo, a nearby reservation. Conveniently, Lummis met them when they helped build his home, El Alisal. Their songs are a vital part of the collection, representing nineteenth-century music not only from Isleta but other reservations of southern California.[25]

These recordings of Indian music were not merely curiosity pieces for interested scientists; they also had an impact on contemporary American music and hence the modernist movement. During the early twentieth century, many American composers sought to integrate Indian melodies and rhythms in their own works, thereby seeking to create a uniquely American music that stood apart from either European art music traditions or African American music. Such efforts were not new. American composer Thomas Hastings harmonized Indian melodies by Thomas Commuck, a Narragansett Indian, in 1845; Hastings claimed that at least one of the tunes dated back to before the arrival of white settlers in America.[26] While one could argue that much of this output was "Indian" in name only, compositions that evoked Indian themes rather than preserved original melodies, it nonetheless remained a defining movement in American music.[27]

Several of the Indianist composers either visited or lived in southern California. Charles Wakefield Cadman was a prominent example: his music was popular enough to garner "Cadman Nights" at the Hollywood Bowl during the 1920s. Three other composers were Arthur Farwell, Harvey Worthington Loomis, and Harry Partch—all of whom at different times aided in transcribing the cylinders. Both the Spanish-language and Indian recordings seem to have had an enormous impact on how they viewed indigenous music as well as how they went about composing their own works.

Farwell was one of the high priests of the Indianist movement, and had the most to do with the transcriptions. He first met Lummis in January 1904 during a lecture-recital trip to Los Angeles, which he described as "an Eastern city with the possibilities of a Western."[28] As a guest at Lummis's house he heard first hand some of the singers whom Lummis recorded, and became immediately intrigued by their music. Farwell had already begun his own press for publishing American music, Wa-Wan Press in Massachusetts, which lasted from 1901 to 1911, and he was eager to tackle the Lummis recordings. After he personally received a guarantee for compensation of $200 by the president of the AIA, Dr. Thomas Seymour, Farwell decided to return to begin transcribing the songs later that summer.[29] This time he was able to hear more songs from the Lummis community, such as by Adelaida Kamp and Rosendo Uruchurtu. These experiences gave him a unique insight into working with the songs, prompting him to note that a "good number are of high quality, and some are remarkable finds, nuggets of folksong of the greatest rarity and beauty."[30]

Farwell was not the first musician to begin transcribing this music. He took over from Albert Stanley, a composer, organist, and professor of music at the University of Michigan, whom Lummis had appointed in 1904 to work on the songs during Stanley's visiting professorship at UC Berkeley. Previous commitments made it impossible for Stanley to proceed, however, so Farwell arrived at the perfect time. Working closely with Harvey Worthington Loomis, Farwell managed to notate the melodies, adding piano accompaniment, of 283 of the Spanish-language songs. While he printed only two of these songs in 1905 in a collection titled *Folk Songs of the West and South*, he contributed 14 more songs almost 20 years later in the Spanish-language songbook, *Spanish Songs of Old California*.[31] Some of the songs he used while conducting Community Choruses in Santa Barbara and Pasadena in 1920, part of a larger American movement to advance singing through amateur choral groups.[32]

The Indian songs took on a special meaning for Farwell. After becoming editor of *Musical America* from 1909 to 1914, he noted frankly that "[t]he Indian songs were much more exciting to work with—the field being far less familiar, and the songs being of so surprising and extraordinary a nature. These records had been made by Mr. Lummis during his various sojourns among the desert Indians. Some of them were of such complicated rhythmic structure, and such unusual melodic nature as to require hundreds of repetitions before I could transcribe them to my own satisfaction."[33] Farwell may have been exaggerating on the number of repetitions, since such frequent playbacks of the cylinders would probably have damaged them irreparably, but he certainly showed a fascination with the music the Indians produced. Strongly inspired by the ideas of composers George W. Chadwick, Edward MacDowell, and Antonín Dvorák, all of whom were fascinated by indigenous music, Farwell wrote that the "mass of characteristic and poetic folksong peculiar to the soil of America—Indian, negro, cowboy, Spanish-Californian and other varieties—appeared to me to be a vast mine of valuable musical ore, to be wrought into music of new types and colors."[34]

While he published few transcriptions of Indian songs in his *Folk Songs of the West and South*, such as "Cahuilla Bird Dance Song," others eventually took up where Farwell left off. Composer Harry Partch transcribed 24 of the Indian songs in 1933, while ethnomusicologist Helen Heffron Roberts duplicated the Indian cylinders onto aluminum discs during the 1930s at Yale University—one of several attempts to rerecord the Lummis cylinders using modern technology. The Spanish-language songs were recorded onto ten-inch acetate discs in the 1940s, then on reel-to-reel tapes in 1960 by Capitol Records engineers through an Irvine Foundation grant, and then again in 1984 by the owner of Mark 56 Records in Los Angeles, George

Garabedian. Some cylinders were duplicated again onto reel-to-reel tape in the 1990s.[35]

Lummis's recording project is significant for several reasons. First, he sought to capture the music of descendants of some of the state's first inhabitants. Few others at this time were working on similar projects that sought to preserve the rich cultural life of Hispanic and Indian California. Second, the cylinders tie in directly to the Indianist movement, one of the leading efforts during the first half of the twentieth century to establish a truly American school of composition. Four composers, Farwell, Loomis, Partch, and Stanley, all helped transcribe the cylinders to make this music more available to scholars and the public.

Finally, many people in California and across the country were able to hear this music. He often played the songs to Angelenos to promote the Southwest Society and gain members. In 1904 he wrote to Dr. Seymour that "the overwhelming majority of these [members] have come in because of the interest in the folk-song work," and he added that "nothing appeals to so many people so quickly as this campaign to preserve and record the old songs of the soil."[36] After numerous local presentations, Lummis used the collection as the basis for a tour of Midwestern and eastern cities, in which he "spread the gospel" of the American Southwest. From December 1904 to January 1905, again with financial support from the AIA, he spoke in New York; Boston; Washington, D.C.; Pittsburgh; Detroit; Cleveland; and Chicago, among other cities large and small, inciting both curiosity and enthusiasm about the music. In a letter to Farwell, he wrote happily that "the lecture tour was a great success. Every audience cottoned to the songs; and there is no doubt that the propaganda has taken hold of several thousands of our good Americans."[37] While Lummis was a master at such self-promotion, and often claimed more than he actually achieved, he was nonetheless able to publicize types of music that audiences outside the Southwest rarely, if ever, had the opportunity to hear.

It is important to place Lummis's remarkable efforts in context. Despite the enormous cultural value of his recordings, they do not represent all forms of Hispanic music of the era. As Koegel reminds us, sacred songs, such as *cánticos, himnos*, and *alabados*, are nonexistent in the collection, probably because Lummis felt them inappropriate for his designs. Nor was Lummis the only one interested in preserving Mexican and Indian music of early California; the composers William J. McCoy and Antoni van der Voort, ethnomusicologists Frances Densmore and Laura Boulton, folklore researcher Eleanor Hague, and the song collector Aurelio Macdeonio Espinosa similarly sought to preserve this music by transcribing and publishing several song collections. However, few actually recorded the music for the purposes of preservation until the 1930s, when efforts to record Indian, African American, and rural white musicians became much more common in America, such as the field recordings of Alan Lomax. Lummis therefore ranks as a true pioneer in recording the music of indigenous people in southern California.

Nordskog Records

Andrae ("Arne") Nordskog was a multitalented individual. At various stages in his career he was a singer, inventor, concert manager, writer, and political activist, and like Lummis he recorded many musicians in southern California. Yet unlike Lummis, his interest was primarily commercial, and he sought out men and women who performed "marketable" music. In 1921 Nordskog founded a record company, Nordskog Records, which he claimed was the first of its kind on the West Coast. While he could not compete with the likes of Victor, U.S. Decca, or Columbia, who had far greater resources and so could contract with major artists, he could, like Lummis, draw on a broad network of friends and associates who might otherwise have little opportunity of being recorded.[38] Nordskog's mission was thus to record predominantly Los Angeles musicians, and he sought to include a wide variety of both popular and concert music.

Nordskog had a richly varied musical career. Born to Norwegian immigrants in 1885, he made a name for himself in his hometown of Story City, Iowa as the "Norwegian Tenor," singing mainly in local churches or at music festivals. In 1914 he moved to the West Coast to sing lead tenor for two years with the Standard Grand Opera Company of Seattle, where he also took voice lessons from a Professor Edmund Myer. Nordskog had many interests; at the same time he worked on several electrical devices, eventually taking out a patent for an improved block signal system for railroads, which he invented while working and singing in Seattle. Technology fascinated him; rather like Edison, he had tinkered with electronics as a young man, and established two of the first wireless telegraph stations in Iowa in 1909, which prompted a life-long fascination with both recorded and broadcast sound.[39] But unlike Edison, technology remained only a hobby, and he continued to seek a career in music, singing lead tenor in 1917 with a touring company, the Knickerbocker Light Opera Company. His career was briefly interrupted by World War I, when he applied his technical knowledge by serving as a telephone engineer.

It is not clear why he settled in Los Angeles. He visited while on tour after the war, and may have decided to stay because of the city's allure as a growing entertainment center.[40] What is certain is that he chose Santa Monica as his home, and after opening a studio on 1685 Ocean Avenue to teach voice, he wasted no time getting involved in several community musical activities. He created the Santa Monica Bay Cities Philharmonic Courses, a concert series of art music he managed from 1919 to 1924. Some of the artists who came to perform were singer Ernestine Schumann-Heink and the Minneapolis Symphony Orchestra with conductor Emil Oberhoffer. He also gave a joint concert with the African American tenor Roland Hayes at the Woman's Club Auditorium in Santa Monica in July 1919, which helped launch that artist's career and began a life-long friendship between the two singers.[41] These activities attracted the attention of Los Angeles's main impresario, Lynden Behymer. Although he may have seen Nordskog as a threat to his business, he did try to book some musicians with Nordskog's help, and their correspondence was cordial enough.[42]

Nordskog's involvement with the Hollywood music community gave him even more recognition. Because of the publicity he received from his Philharmonic Courses, he became General Manager of the Hollywood May Festival, an enormous outdoor festival of music and drama in 1920 that celebrated the rich musical diversity of the region. The success of this venture persuaded the organizers of the newly founded Hollywood Bowl Association to invite him to organize the first series of musical concerts at the Hollywood Bowl in 1920 and 1921. At least two concerts featured the music of local composers Carrie Jacobs Bond and Charles Wakefield Cadman, and among the artists who performed at other concerts were choral leader Hugo Kirchhofer and the Hollywood Community Sing, violinist Sol Cohen, contralto Anna Ruzena Sprotte, and Professor Antonio Sarli and the Greater Los Angeles Municipal Symphonic Band.[43] Several of these artists provided Nordskog with his first recordings.

The first step in setting up his record company at his studio in Santa Monica was to acquire the necessary equipment. In a letter to his vocal instructor in Seattle, Professor Myer, he describes buying a recording machine for $750 from a Mr. Hartwell Webb in New York.[44] "I have a friend who manufactures phonographs," he writes, "and he has a very good instrument, nearest thing to the human voice I have heard."[45] All we know concerning the technology lies in another letter he wrote to the Chamber of Commerce of Los Angeles: the lateral cut system of recording was "the same as that used by the Victor Co."[46]

The actual production process involved several steps. He first had to cut a record on a wax disc, which he then sent across the country by rail to New York, where the vast majority of pressing plants were located. After an electroplater treated the discs in Brooklyn, another plant in West Orange, New Jersey, called the Arto Company, made the pressings (called mothers and stampers) as well as the record labels. Under a reciprocity agreement, some of the recordings appeared under the Nordskog label for sales on the West Coast, while sales on the East Coast had the Arto label. The company then shipped the finished product out to Los Angeles, where Nordskog contracted an international distribution company, the Yale Corporation, to sell the records worldwide. Nordskog had met the president of Yale Corporation, Kelly Monroe Turner, when Turner served as president of the Hollywood May Festival Association in 1920.[47]

Here was a truly East Coast–West Coast arrangement: while the recordings took place in Santa Monica, the actual production of the records took place in New York and New Jersey. Yet one problem with this arrangement is that during the shipment of records back to the West Coast, the wax discs often cracked or otherwise were damaged. As a result, Nordskog decided to perform the entire process at his studio in Santa Monica, and he traveled to New York in June 1922 to have Webb personally show him how to produce records. Here his technical background proved very useful, and he also learned some recording techniques from a German recording engineer who had worked for the Brunswick Company. Taking out several loans, Nordskog proceeded to purchase a 500-gallon electroplating tank, 1,200 pounds of recording wax, and six used hydraulic presses, all of which he shipped out to Los Angeles.[48] This equipment was potentially capable of producing one million discs per year. The modern era of recording technology in Los Angeles had begun.

This was no run-of-the-mill operation. To persuade potential inventors, Nordskog formed a board of four directors, all of whom had impressive credentials. One director was vice-president of the Marine Bank of Santa Monica, another the owner and publisher of the *Western Music Trades Journal*, another a lawyer with a Los Angeles law firm, and the fourth director was president of the Music Trades Association of Los Angeles County and manager of Barker Brothers music department.[49] The company also had an "Industrial Development Syndicate," consisting of four more businessmen, one of whom was president of the California Fruit Juice Company and president and general manager of the National Motion Picture Finance Corporation.[50] The arrangement had impressed the Chamber of Commerce of Santa Monica enough to write: "It is the opinion of the Industrial Committee of the Santa Monica-Ocean Park Chamber of Commerce that the Nordskog Phonograph Record Company is an institution well worth developing; that it has infinite possibilities for furnishing publicity to the City of Santa Monica, and that it will serve to bring here nationally and internationally known artists."[51]

Within two years, Nordskog Records had a list of 22 artists, including 10 dance bands. Most of the musicians worked in the field of popular music, but he also recorded several performers of art music. By far the best known artist at the time was the comedienne and singer "Cyclonic" Eva Tanguay, whom Nordskog recorded in the spring of 1922. Known as the "I Don't Care Girl," Tanguay was in Los Angeles performing at the Pantages Theater and preparing to act in a movie for Fox Films. Nordskog paid the San Francisco singer the enormous sum of $1,000, and it represents possibly the only recording she ever made of the hit that made her famous, "I Don't Care."[52] She was one of the few artists not from southern California that Nordskog had on his list.

Another musician Nordskog recorded was the African American trombonist, Ed "Kid" Ory, who moved to Los Angeles from New Orleans in 1919. He had started a band in New Orleans in 1904 called the "Brownskin Babies," which included horn players King Oliver, Louis Armstrong, and Johnny Dodds, and Ory joined a growing coterie of jazz musicians who migrated out to the West Coast during the 1910s and early '20s, including Jelly Roll Morton, Paul Howard, Sonny Clay, and Lionel Hampton.[53] With a new group called "Spikes' Seven Pods of Pepper," which included the brothers John and

Reb Spikes, he recorded two songs in June 1922, "Ory's Creole Trombone" and "Society Blues," representing the first jazz recording ever made on the West Coast, or indeed of a black New Orleans jazz band—a point of fact that later earned Nordskog a write-up in the jazz publication *Dig Magazine* in 1957 (hear Track no. 3).[54]

However, the records did not go out under the Nordskog label. Ory and his colleagues paid Nordskog for the pressings, then created their own label, Sunshine Records, and pasted it over the Nordskog label with the new name of "Kid Ory's Sunshine Orchestra."[55] They sold the records mainly through the Spikes Brothers Music Store on Central Avenue and 12th Street, which the two brothers had opened in December 1919. The band recorded two more songs under its new name, backing the singers Roberta Dudley and Ruth Lee. Unfortunately, four of the six masters that Ory recorded "melted in the sun while being transported through the California desert."[56] What survived is of inestimable value to the early history of West Coast jazz.

Among Nordskog's recordings of musicians of art music, only the pianist and composer Charles Wakefield Cadman had a national reputation. One of the few American composers not trained in the European tradition, Cadman felt drawn early on to Native American melodies, a fascination he described in an article in *Musical Quarterly* in 1915, "The 'Idealization' of Indian Music."[57] Like Lummis, his first experiences with such melodies came from visits to reservations in New Mexico, and on the recommendation of ethnologist Alice Fletcher, he visited the Omaha Indians in Nebraska. With the half-Indian Francis La Flesche, he made cylinder recordings of the tribe's music and learned to play their instruments. By placing Indian-like melodies in a late-Romantic harmonic idiom, with melodies by close friend and associate Nelle Richmond Eberhart, he achieved a niche in the burgeoning American Indianist movement.

Two of Cadman's songs, "From the Land of the Sky Blue Water" and "At Dawning," assured his reputation and early success. Soprano Lillian Nordica sang the first of these in 1909, while tenor John McCormack subsequently popularized the second. Nordskog recorded six Cadman songs, including "Spring Song of the Robin Woman" from his opera, *Shanewis*, which later premiered at the Hollywood Bowl in 1926. Soprano Margaret Messer Morris sang all of the selections, with Cadman himself accompanying her on piano; the composer later recorded several piano solos of his songs as well (hear Tracks no. 4 and 5).[58]

As with other recording companies, the category of music determined the price of the recording. Nordskog's art music records sold for either \$1 or \$1.25, while most of the popular music records sold for 75 cents. These and other recordings in dance music assured Nordskog a highly diverse catalog in an effort to attract sales, with the 1923 catalog listing a total of 56 titles. The project seemed destined to work. Nordskog claims that within the first several weeks, the Yale Corporation received orders for over 300,000 records from around the world, including Australia, England, Spain, South Africa,

Figure 5.3 (l. to r.) Charles Wakefield Cadman, Margaret Messer Morris, Arthur Alexander

and British, French, and Dutch Guineas in South America, although this may have been more hype than fact.[59] It is not known how many records were actually sold.

Unfortunately, Nordskog had less luck with his banker than with most of his recording artists. Merchants signed contracts for shipments requiring notes for payment in periods of 30, 60, or 90 days, with a bank agreeing to make loans on these notes. However, his banker at the Ocean Park Bank in Santa Monica, T. H. Dudley, received brokerage fees of two percent in exchange for extending credit to pay for short term loans on the paper notes: apparently a criminal offense at the time. This ultimately proved destructive for Nordskog Records when a banking war began in southern California, with large banks taking over smaller ones. The State Bank Examiners were looking into the financial dealings of smaller banks, and when the Ocean Park Bank merged with the Pacific Southwest Bank, Dudley decided no longer to honor the short term loans. The impact on Nordskog's business was disastrous.

Nor was this unfortunate scenario the end of Nordskog's problems. While one might fault him for choosing a minor bank for his business, he clearly hadn't counted on a criminal banker. Unbeknownst to the firm, Dudley removed money from the firm's bank account to apply interest to the short term loans. When checks came back stamped "NSF" ("not sufficient funds"), the reputation of the company plummeted, and in Nordskog's words, it "caused untold damage from which our corporation never recovered."[60] This meant that attempting to begin the business anew would probably have proved impossible because of bad credit. Although Nordskog sued for damages, he was unable to recoup his losses. Contributing to this malaise, independent of Nordskog's troubles, was the bankruptcy of the Arto Company in 1923, which held 80 masters, stampers, and mothers belonging to Nordskog. Since Nordskog did not have the finances to recoup these items crucial to his business, most of these masters were lost, despite his filing a claim in the bankruptcy court in New Jersey. Were it not for these twin tragedies, Nordskog Records may well have become one of the leading companies to promote Los Angeles musicians during the first half of the twentieth century.

Despite the failure of Nordskog's company, it was not the only recording enterprise on the West Coast by 1924. Small companies in Los Angeles formed to meet local market demands; among these were the Blue-Bird Talking Machine Company in 1921, the Golden Record Company in 1922, and the Hollywood Record Company in 1924, which recorded under the Sunset label. The last of these established a direct link with a Hollywood studio by recording *Echoes from the Iron Horse*, which theater organist and composer Erno Rapée arranged for the John Ford silent western on the transcontinental railroad, and is discussed in more detail in chapter 7 (hear Track no. 8).[61] Yet these companies could scarcely compete with the "Big Three"—Victor, Columbia, and U.S. Decca—who came to dominate the record industry in the Los Angeles region during the 1930s and whose history has been well documented elsewhere.[62]

As for Nordskog, the music business proved too much for him, and he left it for other projects. He soon became deeply involved in political reform, and in 1927 entered the Los Angeles-Owens Valley water controversy. In appearing before the California Legislature, he criticized city boosters William Mulholland, J. B. Lippencott, and Harry Chandler of making millions of dollars from unethical property deals in the Owens Valley, from which Los Angeles received much of its water. In applying the same energy that he had placed in his recording company, Nordskog dedicated his life toward promoting reform legislation and clean government. But he had already made his mark in Los Angeles cultural history, as both a musician and entrepreneur in the fields of both art and popular music.

Jazz Recording in Black and White

One field of recording in which the Los Angeles recording industry played a major part was in the burgeoning jazz and swing movement during the 1920s and '30s. It is precisely in this field that Los Angeles became a recording center of national stature, although the city was at first not a main recording destination for jazz musicians. The overwhelming majority of jazz recording took place in New York, followed by Chicago and Camden, New Jersey (until 1929), while Los Angeles placed a distant fourth.[63] Swing changed that.

A case in point is the recording career of Paul Whiteman, called the "King of Jazz," who had been leading a highly successful dance orchestra at the Alexandria Hotel in Los Angeles after World War I. Although the city was an excellent starting point for Whiteman, who hobnobbed with the small but growing Hollywood movie colony, it was still on the periphery of the entertainment industry. New York was the center, and Whiteman decided to relocate there. This relocation led to precisely what the Whiteman orchestra needed: a recording contract. The Victor Talking Machine Company approached Whiteman after executives heard his orchestra perform not in Los Angeles but in Atlantic City. Victor had already signed two major, classical music conductors, Leopold Stokowski in 1917 and Arturo Toscanini in 1920, and was seeking to build its roster of dance bands. Whiteman provided that balance, and having developed his particular form of "symphonic jazz" in Los Angeles, he recorded that sound in New York.[64]

By 1920, the American recording industry was proving highly profitable. Annual sales totaled $100 million, and Victor, as the leading record company in the world, earned almost half of those sales. The other two major competitors, the Edison and Columbia companies (both of which made acoustic recordings on cylinders and discs), were struggling competitors. One of the major problems of acoustic recording was the poor quality of sound. Even Stokowski's early recordings seemed "more like a brass band than the Philadelphia Orchestra."[65] Yet until the introduction of electric recording in 1925, the old acoustic method was the only option musicians had. None of this seemed to matter to a public hungry for recorded music, and the production of recordings continued apace, from about 27 million units in 1914 to 106 million six years later.[66]

Despite the strong allure of New York and Chicago, a few major jazz musicians did come to the West Coast both to reside and to record, and during the 1920s Los Angeles became the leading recording center on the West Coast. African American musicians were among the first to do so, contributing to a ready market for "race records." Kid Ory joined other black jazz musicians who began performing regularly in clubs along Central Avenue. Numerous scholars have written on the growth of Central Avenue jazz, which operated quite separately from the circle of black musicians who focused on serious music, such as William Wilkins and Paul Gray.[67]

The first nucleus of the black jazz community was a store on Central Avenue, the Spikes Brothers Music Store. It became not only a meeting place for black musicians but was a source of pride. Although whites owned most of the businesses along Central Avenue, about 40 percent of the population of the district had become African American by 1920, a percentage that continued to increase during the decade.[68] The Spikes brothers, who came to Los Angeles from Dallas in 1897 and toured Arizona and San Francisco for several years in the 1910s before returning to the Southland permanently, performed in local clubs in addition to maintaining their music store. Reb Spikes made a few recordings—with at least one record notable because of the presence of Lionel Hampton on drums and Les Hite on clarinet and alto saxophone.[69] Yet the brothers' chief importance remained in the field of booking black bands, thereby providing an indispensable service for local musicians as well as touring ensembles.

One of those musicians was Sonny Clay, a top bandleader of the 1920s and '30s in Los Angeles who achieved a national reputation. In the words of jazz scholar Michael Bakan, however, Clay became "one of the great but forgotten masters of early jazz."[70] The reason for this relative anonymity is difficult to explain. Like the Spikes brothers he hailed from Texas; he was born in Chapel Hill in 1899 and moved to Los Angeles in 1921. Before that time he lived in both Phoenix, Arizona and Tijuana, Mexico, learning much from Mexican bands and playing afterwards with a "Spanish tinge" to his music, as another Los Angeles-based jazz musician, Jelly Roll Morton, referred to Clay's unique style.[71] He played several instruments but preferred piano and drums, performing regularly at the whites-only club, Plantation Café at 108th Street and Central Avenue, and later Clay headlined at the Vernon Country Club, which was also restricted. On the Sunset label, Clay first recorded two songs with a blues vocalist, Camille Allen, before recording two of his own compositions in 1923 with a group called the California Poppies.[72]

Clay continued to make records throughout the decade, primarily with an ensemble named The Stompin' Six, which recorded five sides with the Sunset label in 1924 before switching to a more prestigious label, Vocalion, the following year. One of the best known of these was "Bogaloosa Blues," which sold about 8,000 copies in Chicago alone.[73] If one measure of respect is emulation, then Clay had much respect; several white bands performed his arrangements, including Herb Wiedoeft's band, one of the most popular and widely toured dance groups in southern California.[74] It is possible, however, that Clay never maintained his national celebrity because of his geographic location: Those who left for Chicago or New York had a better chance of entering the annals of jazz history, which largely ignored the achievements of those on the West Coast.[75]

Another bandleader who joined the local network of jazz musicians was Paul Howard. He arrived in Los Angeles even earlier than Clay, in 1913, and could soon be found practicing and playing piano at the swank Clark Hotel. Like Clay, he led his own ensemble, the Quality Serenaders, and performed at the Cadillac Café and Blue Bird Inn, "an exclusive club at 12th and Central for the ultra rich."[76] His nine-member band, which in itself represented a distinct step towards the "big band" movement, recorded 16 sides for the Victor label in 1929 and 1930.[77] The 1929 recordings took place in Culver City, where Victor rented a studio from the movie director and producer, Hal Roach, although conditions were less than optimal. One of the musicians, Lionel Hampton, complained that "it was like a steambath in that studio—to keep out the noise, they kept out the air." Since Victor merged with RCA-NBC later that year, it was able to use the company's recording studio in Hollywood in 1930, where conditions were far more pleasant and the technology was state-of-the-art.[78]

The Quality Serenaders had an excellent local reputation. Marshall Royal, who was a saxophonist with Les Hite's band in the 1930s, claimed that the Quality Serenaders was "the best band around at that time when the bands were just getting into jazz."[79] Lionel Hampton, who left Clay's group to join Howard's band, readily agreed: The Quality Serenaders "was the most popular band among the quality black folks. . . . [It] played every dance and ball and cotillion there was."[80] Howard further made his mark in the jazz community by serving for many years as treasurer of the Musicians Protective Association, otherwise known as Local 767.

Howard's involvement in Local 767 was important, because what made these musicians more of a "community" was the founding of a union. Nine charter members from diverse backgrounds, working in either serious or popular music, formed Local 767 in 1920, and received their charter from the American Federation of Musicians (AFM). The presence of a formal association sought to enforce that members not only worked within a pay scale (although not as high as that of the white union, Local 47), but that they had access to bookings in the best clubs, hotels, and recording gigs. Equally important, the union sought to ensure that the large number of black musicians living in Los Angeles had a sense of belonging; we can truly speak of a community of artists, many of whom met together and socialized on a regular basis.

The union was a symbol of pride not only for black musicians but for the Central Avenue community as well. The original site for the union was on 41st Street, across from Jefferson High School, before members were able to purchase a rambling old house in the middle of an orange grove on 1710 South Central.[81] According to Florence "Tiny" Brantley, who was the union's secretary for 16 years and perhaps its first female officer, the auditorium provided a convenient rehearsal hall not only for members but for many of the black musicians who passed through the area, including Jimmie Lunceford, Duke Ellington, and Nat King Cole. Bentley further claims that after the Chicago Local 208 it was the largest black musicians union in America, with over one thousand members.[82] Of the 673 AFM locals in the United States by the 1940s, only 32 locals represented African Americans; most musicians unions in major cities were segregated, with the sole exceptions in 1943 of New York's Local 802 and Detroit's Local 5.[83] Local 767 continued to represent the interests of black musicians of Los Angeles until, after a long and divisive battle among members of both unions, it agreed to amalgamate with Local 47 in 1953.[84]

Even before the creation of Local 47, white musicians, too, found ways to organize. A cigar store on 110 Spring Street provided the musicians' first headquarters in 1882 until the founding of the Los Angeles Musical Protective Association six years later, when the union's headquarters moved to a brick building on the southwest corner of Second and Main Streets.[85] It first chose affiliation with the National League of Musicians of the United States, which was founded in 1886. When Local 19 published its first musicians directory in 1895, it listed 114 members, 108 of whom were men. When the AFM formed in 1896 under a charter by the American Federation of Labor, the Los Angeles union opted to change its affiliation to the AFM. Once it was accepted, it changed its name to Local 47 in 1897, and less than a decade later moved to 230 ½ S. Spring Street downtown. By 1925, Local 47 had 3,000 members, making it the fourth-largest musicians union in the entire AFM.[86]

It is an accepted fact among historians of southern California that Los Angeles had the reputation of being "open shop" or anti-union. Workers in Los Angeles, this school of thought claims, had little power or influence over their employers, at least until the late 1930s. However, this situation was far less true in the field of music, due to the increasing power of the musicians union. Not all musicians belonged to the union, nor did all businesses respect its laws when they hired musicians, but major institutions depended regularly on maintaining the union's good will, such as the film studios, reputable hotels, theaters, night clubs, and popular dance halls. In return, the union regularly published lists of businesses to patronize as well as those to avoid.[87] The union became significant on a national scale, because thousands of musicians flocked to the region in search of the high-paying jobs that the film and recording studios seemed to promise.

Several white jazz musicians followed their black colleagues by recording in Los Angeles, at first with relatively small labels. Herb Wiedoeft recorded a total of ten songs for Brunswick with two different groups, while the West Coast commercial dance band Vic Meyers and His Orchestra recorded eight songs for Brunswick in 1923 and 1924. Bing Crosby, who hailed from Spokane, Washington and came to Los Angeles in 1925 with his childhood friend Al Rinker, got a job singing at the Biltmore Hotel at Pershing Square downtown. Crosby's first recording was "I've Got the Girl," a duet with Rinker that they recorded with Don Clark's Biltmore Hotel Orchestra in 1926 (hear Track no. 10).[88] In the following decade, Variety recorded four songs with the band of clarinetist and tenor saxophone player Jack Pettis, as well as four songs with Ben Pollack and His Orchestra (who later signed with Decca).[89] These and other recordings indicate that Los Angeles was gradually becoming a favored destination for recording artists.

Although initially hesitant, Decca and RCA Victor (affiliated with NBC), nonetheless went on to record the lion's share of artists in southern California during the 1930s. These companies seemed to sign one musician after another in the hopes of "striking it rich" with the next Paul Whiteman. Decca recorded Matty Malneck and His Orchestra, and Ben Pollack and His Orchestra, who moved to southern California and persuaded a young Benny

Goodman to make the move out to the West Coast.[90] Decca even recorded three jazz songs in 1936 with actress Ginger Rogers. One song was a duet with songwriter Johnny Mercer and accompanied by Victor Young and His Orchestra, and the other two were with Jimmy Dorsey and His Orchestra, which suggest "crossover" efforts by Rogers to reach greater audiences. In a similar crossover vein, Victor recorded the legendary guitarist and songwriter Jimmie Rodgers, a country music singer who decided to include some jazz arrangements while in Los Angeles. Rodgers even recorded two sides with Louis Armstrong and his wife Lil Armstrong, on trumpet and piano respectively, in what must have been a unique experience for the "Yodeling Brakeman."[91] Such records suggest a rich and diverse recording culture of syncopated music.

With the swing movement of the thirties, jazz recording in Los Angeles took on a whole new meaning. Between 1936 and 1942, a veritable explosion in making records took place, for several reasons. After an extraordinarily successful summer concert by Benny Goodman and His Orchestra at the Palomar Ballroom in Los Angeles in 1935, big band "hot" jazz became a goldmine for record companies during what musicologists and historians have dubbed the "swing era."[92] The sudden demand for this type of music resuscitated the music industry out of its Depression-era doldrums, and as a consequence it drove bands either to adopt the new style or risk entering musical obsolescence. Moreover, during the Depression and the onset of war, young people needed an upbeat, highly danceable music that could allow them to forget the times, however briefly. Swing provided that opportunity, and it confronted earlier taboos of listening to "hot" jazz bands, black or white.

Another reason for the increase in recording in Los Angeles concerned the musicians union. The president of the AFM, James Petrillo, called for a recording ban on July 31, 1942 to force record companies to pay royalties on all records sold, which prompted countless bands to rush to the studios to get their music on record. Since the film industry was a further attraction, bands recorded in Los Angeles because they often stayed for extended periods of time while on tour. As a result, several groups recorded a large number of songs prior to 1942. The top three groups, in order of number of jazz songs recorded, were Bob Crosby and His Orchestra, Benny Goodman and His Orchestra, and Duke Ellington and His Famous Orchestra. Los Angeles and Hollywood had finally begun to vie seriously with New York as prime locations for recording music.

Bob Crosby may come as a surprise, since his name scarcely appears in jazz histories or biographies. Yet at the time he led one of the most popular bands in California. Born in Spokane, Washington in 1913 and the brother of the far more famous entertainer Bing Crosby, Bob was a singer and crooner like his brother in addition to being a bandleader. He sang with several groups, including the Dorsey Brothers' Orchestra from 1934 to 1935, before deciding to form his own group. He drew on Ben Pollack's band for several of his musicians, and the ensemble of ten instrumentalists produced an unusual combination of "big-band dixieland jazz," or a combination of New Orleans-style jazz with a more contemporary sound.[93] Between November 1937 and July 1942, Bob Crosby and His Orchestra made the astounding total of 93 recordings of this music, all in Los Angeles on the Decca label, such as the song "Panama" (hear Track no. 17). Crosby also recorded six songs with his elite group, the Bob Cats, in addition to several songs in Los Angeles for Decca with his brother Bing in 1940 and 1942.[94] While New York still remained the recording location of choice for Bob Crosby and His Orchestra, Los Angeles was the second favorite site for the band.

Benny Goodman, too, took advantage of the recording facilities that Los Angeles offered. On a variety of different labels, Benny Goodman and His Orchestra, a 15-member big band, recorded 73 songs between August 1936 and July 1940, and like Crosby Goodman also recorded a further 18 songs with his Trio, Quartet, and Sextet. RCA Victor, Columbia, MGM, and even Philipps all vied for the chance to sell a record by Goodman, who became a cornerstone of the new sound, in part by drawing on the arrangements of African American bandleaders Fletcher Henderson and Count Basie in addition to those by Jimmy Mundy, Budd Johnson, Eddie Sauter, and Mary Lou Williams.[95]

To emphasize the roots of the music, Goodman was renowned for playing and recording in mixed ensembles. He invited Lionel Hampton to play the vibraphone in his Quartet in 1936 after hearing him at the Paradise Café on Main Street in Los Angeles, then later asked Charlie Christian to play electric guitar with his Sextet.[96] He further played and recorded with pianists Teddy Wilson and Fletcher Henderson. The sessions were a breakthrough in the field, since Goodman recorded with black musicians at least one year before he began appearing with them on stage.[97] Part of Goodman's appeal was precisely this assimilationist aspect of bridging ethnic divisions, and historians ignore swing at their peril, because Goodman's efforts took place a decade before Jackie Robinson "broke the color line" in baseball. Goodman maintained a bond with the network of southland musicians throughout his peak years as a touring and recording star, particularly in his association with Lionel Hampton, who moved to Los Angeles in 1923 and appeared frequently at local jazz clubs during the 1920s and '30s.[98]

Finally, Duke Ellington and His Famous Orchestra also maintained ties to Los Angeles. This connection was primarily through the film industry, and the orchestra frequently performed and recorded in Hollywood as a result. Between December 1936 and June 1942, Ellington and his 15-member band recorded 67 songs, almost all for the RCA Victor label.[99] Just as Ellington achieved fame in the 1920s performing at the Cotton Club in Harlem, during his stays in Los Angeles he often played at the New Cotton Club in Culver City at 8781 Washington Street, which was a whites-only locale featuring black musicians.[100]

These bands held several aspects in common. First, they established strong networks with musicians in Los Angeles. Bob Crosby chose the city as his home base; Benny Goodman saw a renewal in his career in Los Angeles; and

Duke Ellington enjoyed a close association with Local 767 and with jazz players at Central Avenue clubs. Second, they chose to record extensively in Los Angeles in addition to recording in New York and Chicago, because of the attraction of Los Angeles for touring and performing, and the benefit of being near the film industry. Third, the bands were models in musicianship, continuously employing some of the best musicians in the popular music industry. As symbols of the swing era, their frequent presence in Los Angeles during this time added to the glamour of the city's music culture and its importance in the swing movement. Ultimately, this period provided the basis for the role Los Angeles would have in the postwar era as the epicenter for entertainment in America, no longer playing "second fiddle" to New York.

Conclusion

The cultural history of southern California, and of Los Angeles in particular, is closely aligned with the development of the recording industry. Yet a history of recording in Los Angeles does not simply comprise a roster of top artists by the major recording companies, but of less significant artists on smaller labels as well, and in the case of Charles Lummis, no label at all. Lummis's intent was to preserve the cultural heritage of southwestern musicians as best as he knew how: through recordings. By "catching archaeology alive," he sought to bring to a wider public the beautiful songs and melodies he had heard almost twenty years before. Nordskog, by contrast, was not on a scientific mission, but he also wanted to capture on record the startling diversity of performers in the Los Angeles region. Founding possibly the first record company on the West Coast, he did not seek to enforce a cultural hierarchy. Rather, as both a performer and impresario, he was well acquainted with the fields of popular and art music, and happily recorded musicians in both fields, much as Thomas Tally had done almost 20 years before him.

A history of recording in Los Angeles reveal a strongly diverse music culture that was a product of a series of different, if occasionally overlapping, musical communities. Black and white musicians tended to remain separate, and were represented by separate unions until those unions amalgamated in 1953, one year before the *Brown v. Board of Education* decision by the Supreme Court to integrate schools and other facilities. However, there were some opportunities for mixing during the 1930s, such as in the cases of Benny Goodman's Orchestra and his smaller ensembles. The recording of swing music thus represented a watershed for the Los Angeles recording industry. We can clearly point to the *creation* of an industry, often with close ties to the film industry, from which musicians such as Ellington, Goodman, and Crosby benefited.[101] As the technology of recording improved and as the allure of Hollywood increased, musicians found themselves drawn to film studios and the riches that they could offer, as well as the fact that Hollywood had some of the best recording studios in the region.

As the fifth-largest city in the United States, with an estimated population of 1,325,000 in 1935, Los Angeles had certainly achieved national status as a metropolis.[102] Whether or not it had also achieved respect among New Yorkers, Chicagoans, or even San Franciscans is another matter. Yet by the late 1930s few could deny the growing importance of Los Angeles as a diverse entertainment center: diverse both in terms of ethnicity and what we could call "media diversity"—the recording of music on records or film. By the end of the decade, more and more top artists in swing music chose studios in the cities of Los Angeles and Hollywood for recording and producing their records, leaving a rich legacy indeed.

Recording also had a clear connection to the radio industry. In the fields of swing and popular music, it was commonplace for bands to seek to augment record sales by appearing on radio, which was also true in the field of art music. When RCA Victor produced a series of inexpensive "Music Appreciation" albums, consisting of famous classical works performed by unknown musicians, the albums by the winter of 1938–39 sold over 300,000 copies nationally: a phenomenal number for classical albums even by today's standards.[103] They sold well because the public had heard much of this music on radio and wanted to purchase the albums, either for home use or for schools. As historian Roland Gelatt asserts: "Radio, which once had laid the phonograph low, was now bringing it millions of new customers."[104] As with recordings, radio transformed the very notion of listening to music.

6

"An Invisible Empire in the Air": Broadcasting the Classics during the Golden Age

The emergence of radio as a mass medium by the mid-1920s had an immediate impact on the recording industry. Record sales across all categories, whether of art music or popular songs (with the exception of race records), declined drastically and only rebounded during the swing era of the late 1930s. Whether programs involved live broadcasting, which was the norm, or recordings, the impact of radio on listening patterns and of the formation of "virtual communities" of listeners was undeniable—a development that the American Federation of Musicians (AFM) found increasingly disturbing. While there is a growing interest among scholars in radio studies, relatively little discussion centers on classical or art music, even though at one point the programming of that music during the Golden Age of the 1920s and '30s made up over a quarter of the daily programming on American radio.[1] One of the longest-running sponsored programs in the history of radio in Los Angeles was with the Los Angeles Philharmonic. The purpose of this chapter is to determine how and why a symphony orchestra, an institution of high culture, was able to reach out to audiences far beyond the concert hall.

Americans enthusiastically took to radio. The number of radio sets they purchased skyrocketed from 60,000 in January 1922 to 1.5 million only one year later. Percentage of ownership further demonstrates this trend. In 1924, with an average price of $76 per set, 11.1 percent of the population owned a radio receiver; in 1931, at an average or $62 per set, over 50 percent owned one; and by 1940, at $40 per set, over 80 percent of all Americans had a radio.[2] Saturation levels varied by region, with 51.1 percent in the North by 1930, compared to 43.9 percent in the Rocky Mountain and Pacific States, to 16.2 percent in the South.[3]

As with the first recording companies in Los Angeles, radio stations before the 1930s were a regional endeavor. Most western stations were not linked to those in the Midwest and East Coast. When the National Broadcasting

Corporation (NBC) created its national network in 1926, its broadcasts reached nineteen states, but only as far west as Kansas City. When it formed the "Red" and "Blue" networks in January the following year, it expanded its reach eventually to San Francisco, sending music scores and scripts by rail each week after it broadcast the same material on the East Coast.[4] Yet Los Angeles came to usurp that role by the end of the decade, becoming the broadcasting center on the West Coast, as broadcasting joined with the film and recording industries to make Los Angeles the premier location for entertainment in the western United States.

One inventor who moved to southern California had an enormous impact on the development of radio technology: Lee De Forest. Although a largely unheralded figure, his discoveries helped pave the way for further research and development in several related fields that defined the modern era: recording, radio, and film. Born in 1873 to missionary parents, De Forest grew up in the South, where his father, a dedicated white Northerner, headed a black college during the era of Reconstruction.[5] A lonely and intense young man, the son went to Yale University for his undergraduate degree, staying on to earn a Ph.D. in electrical engineering in 1899. After getting a job with the Western Electric Company in Chicago and then founding his own company, De Forest Wireless Telegraph Company in 1902, he eventually ended up doing research at the Pacific Wireless Telephone Company on Santa Catalina Island, about 22 miles from mainland California.[6]

Surrounded by seagulls and sailing ships, De Forest developed in 1904 what he called the "Audion," which provided a means of amplifying sound. The obstacle of achieving amplified sound had confounded earlier inventors working on sound transmission, such as the Italian/British pioneer of radio, Guglielmo Marconi. De Forest's invention was a clear improvement on patents that the English scientist working in Marconi's company, John Ambrose Fleming, had already taken out on a glass-bulb detector, based on Edison's work with the incandescent lamp. De Forest added a "grid" in the vacuum tube that enabled the amplification of weak signals. Radio was only one technology that benefited; the vacuum tube was also instrumental in the development of the microphone and the corresponding transition from acoustical to electrical recording in the mid-1920s. With his invention, as De Forest wrote in his diary, he had discovered "an Invisible Empire in the Air."[7] In the realm of this empire, one of his key goals was to transmit music, or as he poetically described it, "to distribute sweet melody broadcast over the city and sea so that even the mariner far out across the silent waves may hear the music of his homeland."[8] Out on Catalina Island, De Forest had stumbled across precisely the link that made those broadcasts possible.

Few could capitalize at first on De Forest's invention, but immediately following World War I, several radio stations appeared in Los Angeles using this technology. As on the East Coast and in the Midwest, enthusiastic ham operators, many operating without a license, created their own "virtual communities" that at first may have had fewer audiences than participants.

The first station to be actually granted a radiotelephone license in Los Angeles was KQL on October 13, 1921, a year after the creation of the first radio station in America, KDKA in Pittsburgh.[9] Others soon joined the air waves; by May of 1922, there were at least 13 stations in southern California, and within six years the *Los Angeles Times* listed 22 local stations, representing a true Golden Age of radio.[10] Most programs involved live broadcasting, although recordings occasionally supplanted live programs.

One ham operator was Kelly Monroe Turner, who founded KMTR in a two-story building at the corner of Sunset Boulevard and Wilton Place in Hollywood.[11] Turner had long shown an interest in broadcasting classical music. With the help of De Forest, he installed the recording equipment at the Metropolitan Opera House in New York to make possibly the first radio broadcast of an opera in America: the double bill of Enrico Caruso and Riccardo Martin in *I pagliacci* and *Cavalleria rusticana*, respectively, on January 13, 1910. While only a handful of people with ham radios in Newark and New York City heard the broadcast, along with 11 wireless telegraph operators on board United States Navy ships in New York Harbor, the event signaled the enormous potential of the new medium.[12] When Turner moved to Los Angeles, he immediately became involved in the Hollywood musical community, where he met Andrae Nordskog, among others, and served as president of the Hollywood May Festival Association in 1920.[13]

As businessmen sensed a golden commercial opportunity, they founded a series of stations that shared the local airwaves with ham operators. Immediately recognizing another outlet for boosterism, Harry Chandler, publisher of the *Los Angeles Times*, began KHJ with a 50-watt station on April 14, 1922. This formed part of a national trend; by 1940, newspaper publishers owned over one-third of all radio stations in America.[14] It was a natural choice for Chandler's driving mission to make Los Angeles a prominent metropolis, but he also described the station as a form of public service, with an emphasis on "musical entertainment and the dissemination of educational matter."[15] As the technology improved, so did the reach of the radio stations, taking them far beyond their original coastal audiences. A year after the founding of KHJ, Chandler greatly expanded its broadcasting capability, and boasted that the station now operated "on a 500-watt set that covers every corner of the United States and the greater part of Mexico and Canada. Its voice has been heard in Cuba, in Hawaii and in the Samoan Islands of the South Seas."[16]

Who precisely was listening? Market research of radio audiences demonstrated that the majority of listeners in the morning and early afternoon hours were women, followed by children in the late afternoon after school, and both men and women in the evenings during the prime time period of 7 to 9 P.M.[17] The programs of the radio stations, duly listed in the *Los Angeles Times*, solidly reflect these demographics. Morning programs have titles such as "Georgia O. George Hour," "Martha Lee's Hour," and "New Idea Shopping Hour," while in the afternoon children could hear such programs as

"Educational Hour" on KFJ or "Children's Hour" on KFI.[18] On Sundays, the devout could enjoy church music on shows by the pentecostal preacher Aimee Semple McPherson during the 1920s, who sang songs like "I Ain't Gonna Grieve" (hear Track no. 9). Both McPherson and the fundamentalist Charles Fuller in the 1930s reached huge audiences; Fuller's "Old Fashioned Revival Hour," broadcast from Long Beach, had an estimated audience of ten million people by 1939.[19]

Programs featuring classical and popular music were common throughout the week, either in the form of recordings or live broadcasts. In daytime programming, the notation "Records" in some time slots occurs frequently enough in the radio listings of the *Los Angeles Times*, although radio station owners tended to look down on them as a misuse of the airwaves.[20] It was far more likely that during the evening one could hear live music, either remote broadcasts from a hotel or from the station's studio; the largest stations also had their own studio orchestras. Listeners could expect a rich diversity of choice, from "string music," to "organ," to violin and piano duets, to ensembles ranging from dance bands to symphony orchestras.

The Standard Hour

When the Los Angeles Philharmonic began broadcasting its concerts in 1925, it was in good company. Two of the first orchestras to do so were the New York Philharmonic and the Cleveland Orchestra, both of which began airing concerts in 1922. Conductor Walter Rothwell and the Los Angeles Philharmonic made their first appearance on radio on January 24, 1925. The *Los Angeles Times* station KHJ broadcast the concert from the First Methodist Church, located at Eighth and Hope Streets downtown.[21] In the same year, the Boston Symphony Orchestra and the Chicago Symphony Orchestra began airing their concerts, followed in 1926 by the San Francisco Symphony and the New York Symphony Orchestra.[22] In stark contrast, the Philadelphia Orchestra under Leopold Stokowski, who was fascinated with modern technology, curiously refused to air its concerts. Its Board of Directors felt it to be "unfair to patrons of the orchestra, who pay for tickets and take the trouble to attend the concerts in person, to broadcast the music throughout the country."[23]

The Los Angeles Philharmonic radio concerts represented a turning point for the orchestra. Unlike the San Francisco Symphony, which began recording with RCA in 1925, the Los Angeles Philharmonic had few outlets beyond live performance to get its music across to a wider public.[24] Now it did, thanks to a regular series of sponsors willing to finance the program, beginning with the Standard Oil Company. In a program called the "Standard Hour" on Sunday afternoons, with Rothwell at the helm, the audience was the entire Pacific Coast, linked by five radio stations—what would eventually become part of the NBC Pacific Network. During the 1926–27 season alone, there were five such Sunday afternoon concerts, each potentially reaching hundreds of thousands of listeners.

Standard Oil could well afford to finance such programs, since it had become one of the richest oil companies in the southland. At its peak in 1923, its production reached 113,000 barrels of oil per day, all tapped at its plant at Huntington Beach, and it was still producing over 100 million barrels per year by 1926. Even deep into the Depression, the company had 16,000 employees—one of the largest employers in southern California.[25] Its dominant presence gave it enormous clout, which potentially meant a large audience for the Standard Hour. In the community of El Segundo, the site of Standard Oil's second major California refinery, residents "shopped at the Standard Market, attended Standard Elementary School, played baseball at the Standard Park, and were treated at the Standard Hospital." (Independence from the company seems only to have come with death, since "Standard did not have its own cemetery."[26]) Now residents could listen to Standard's radio program as well, and as a major employer in the region, the name had widespread recognition across class and ethnic lines.[27]

Standard Oil was thus the perfect sponsor for a program that sought to "popularize" art music, complete with regular broadcasts and educational programs provided by the leading orchestras in California. The benefit for Standard Oil itself was the "prestige factor," as music commentator José Rodriguez pointed out: The Standard Hour belonged to the category of "institutional or prestige programs . . . meant to testify to the integrity and standing of the sponsor."[28] Unlike, say, General Foods sponsoring the Jack Benny Show, with the expectation that the program would boost sales, Standard Oil's primary goal was to present itself as a "good citizen" company. It helped set the standard for high quality cultural programs, similar to the Ford Sunday Evening Hour, or the General Motors Hour, both of which broadcast classical music.

Standard Oil needed this kind of public relations, because oil companies had suffered in the public's eye, particularly since the Teapot Dome scandal. The scandal got its name from the Teapot Dome reserves in Wyoming, which Secretary of the Interior of President Warren Harding's administration, Harry Sinclair, had secretly leased to the Mammoth Oil Company in 1922 in return for gifts in cash and no-interest loans. Also involved in this affair was Edward Doheny, owner of Pan American Petroleum and a Los Angeles resident, to whom Sinclair leased the Elk Hills Reserves and Buena Vista Reserves in California in 1921 and 1922. Although Doheny was eventually acquitted of charges of bribery and Standard Oil was not directly involved in the scandal, its image suffered along with the others. Programs such as the Standard Hour gave the company the perception of serving in the public interest, and as a result, both Standard Oil Company and the Los Angeles Philharmonic benefited.

Projecting its message to a wider public had long been a key goal of the orchestra. Walter Rothwell, since the founding of the Los Angeles Philharmonic in 1919, had sought to make it a truly regional orchestra, giving concerts around the southland: in auditoriums, churches, and schools. He continued this tradition with the advent of radio by broadcasting from different locations, both inside and outside Los Angeles, much like jazz bands and other entertainers were doing with their remote broadcasts. The Standard Hour was certainly a hit with the public; when the 1927 season ended and the Los Angeles Philharmonic broadcasts went off the air, listeners clamored for more radio concerts. Standard Oil, sensing a public relations boon, agreed to continue financing concerts on radio, thereby supporting one of the most effective means of popularization of symphonic music possible at the time.[29]

The radio concerts had a further purpose: to unite the supposedly dueling cultural centers on the West Coast: San Francisco and Los Angeles. It occurred during the tenure of Artur Rodzinski, conductor of the Los Angeles Philharmonic from 1929 to 1933. Rothwell died suddenly in 1927, and his successor, Finnish conductor Georg Schnéevoigt, only served for two years and showed little interest in broadcasting. Rodzinski, however, was eager to take advantage of radio, and he conducted the first program on station KFI on Thursday evening, October 17, 1929 from 7:30 to 8:30 P.M. The orchestra alternated every other week with the San Francisco Symphony Orchestra, under conductor Alfred Hertz, who was already a known figure in Los Angeles with the "Symphonies Under the Stars" concerts at the Hollywood Bowl. A *Los Angeles Times* article on the Standard Symphony Hour noted that "this splendid radio concert series will introduce Artur Rodzinski, new conductor of the local orchestra, to the air audience."[30] Since KFI was part of the NBC network, that audience consisted of anyone with access to a radio on the West Coast. An accompanying advertisement proclaiming "The Pacific Coast's Greatest Radio Feature" stated: "In presenting these two famous musical organizations—amongst the greatest in the world—the Standard Symphony Hour becomes one of the outstanding features of American radio. Each Thursday evening between ninety and one hundred talented artists, under the distinguished leadership of Alfred Hertz or Artur Rodzinski, will play the finest and most beautiful of the world's music."[31] In essence, living rooms on the West Coast became their mutual theater, creating "virtual communities" united by an interest in classical music.

These programs were part of a nationwide phenomenon, what musicologist Joseph Horowitz calls "a new phase in sacralized classical music: its popularization."[32] Like Rothwell, conductor Walter Damrosch was a leader in this field. Not only did Damrosch arrange the New York Philharmonic-Symphony Sunday afternoon concerts, but in the same year he began the NBC *Music Appreciation Hour* aimed at schoolchildren, which reached 1,500,000 children in its first season, growing to an estimated seven million children in 70,000 schools across the country by 1940.[33] Similarly, the president of the Radio Corporation of America (RCA), David Sarnoff, created an entire orchestra for classical music programs in 1937: the NBC Orchestra under Arturo Toscanini. NBC was truly dominant in the broadcasting of art music; in 1938 alone, it broadcast over 40 symphony orchestras, 23 smaller or secondary orchestras, the Radio City Music Hall Orchestra, and performances by the Metropolitan Opera.[34] Beginning in 1935, it also broadcast the Los Angeles Philharmonic over its West Coast network. We know that the potential audience for such programs was significant; *Fortune* magazine at the time noted that 62.5 percent of Americans enjoyed listening to classical music on radio, while *Life* magazine stated that Toscanini was as famous as Joe DiMaggio.[35]

As with Damrosch's series, children were part of the target audience for the Standard Hour broadcasts. The oil company sponsored the "Standard School Broadcast," a music education program begun in 1928 that took place on Thursday mornings from 11 to 11:45 A.M. on NBC's West Coast network. An advertisement exclaimed that in "hundreds of schools of the Pacific Coast students are listening each Thursday morning to these musical lectures, while thousands of mothers in the homes receive the same program."[36] The idea behind these broadcasts was to prepare students (and interested adults) for the radio concert they would hear that evening. To be effective, such a program demanded the cooperation of school teachers and administrators alike, and the widespread music education programs in California during the twenties and thirties dovetailed perfectly with the mission behind the broadcasts: to make art music available to children as well as adults. The educational role such programs promoted could scarcely find a more appropriate medium, and the Standard School Broadcasts continued for over thirty years—a testament to the value these programs had in the eyes of broadcasters, sponsors, musicians, and parents.[37]

If we look at the content of the Standard Hour radio concerts from 1929 to 1935, a period for which we have complete records, we find a rigorous emphasis on European art music. More precisely, "the finest and most beautiful of the world's music" consisted primarily of works from the late-Romantic era.[38] It underlines a point that Joseph Horowitz has made several times, that America "borrowed its classical music tradition from Europe."[39] Yet there is a rich diversity in that field; in the 60 broadcasts during this period, the orchestra performed a total of 319 works by 70 different composers. Of these, all but 6 were European. Music by Wagner predominated, with 11.3 percent of all pieces performed, followed by Tchaikovsky, with 6.6 percent, and Beethoven ties with Johann Strauss Jr. with only 4.4 percent of all works performed. This emphasis on Wagner was a common feature of American orchestral repertoires since the late-nineteenth century, when music scholars and the concert-going public often thought of Wagner's music as the "Music of the Future" (*Zukunftsmusik*).[40] The following table of the top 12 composers in the radio broadcasts shows a general partiality towards nineteenth-century composers, with only a few from the eighteenth and twentieth centuries.

Table 6.1 Top 12 Composers on Standard Hour Broadcasts, 1929–35

Composer	*Number of Works Performed*	*Percentage of Total*
Richard Wagner	36	11.3
Piotr Tchaikovsky	21	6.6
Johann Strauss Jr.	14	4.4
Ludwig van Beethoven	14	4.4
Nikolay Rimsky-Korsakov	12	3.8
Felix Mendelssohn	11	3.4
Wolfgang Amadeus Mozart	11	3.4
Hector Berlioz	11	3.4
Jean Sibelius	11	3.4
Carl Maria von Weber	11	3.4
Georges Bizet	10	3.1
Claude Debussy	8	2.5

Source: Radio Broadcast Programs, Los Angeles Philharmonic Archives, 1929–35

Table 6.2 Origin of Composers on Standard Hour Broadcasts, 1929–35

Country/Region of Origin	*Number of Composers Whose Works Were Performed*	*Percentage of Total*
German/Austrian	20	28.6
French	20	28.6
Russian	10	14.3
Scandinavian	7	10.0
American	6	8.5
Slavic	3	4.2
English	2	2.9
Italian	2	2.9
Total	70	100

Source: Radio Broadcast Programs, Los Angeles Philharmonic Archives, 1929–35

While this repertoire suggests a dominance of German or Austrian composers, a different picture emerges when we take all 70 composers into account, some of whom had only one or two works performed. Table 6.2 shows that the number of pieces by French composers in fact equaled that by German and Austrian composers, and that the music by Russian composers was also well represented.

Why did American composers fare so poorly? In part this may have been due to the music interests of the two conductors who followed Rothwell: Artur Rodzinski and Otto Klemperer (who served from 1933 to 1939), since their repertoire was almost entirely European and they assumedly helped program these concerts. In her master's thesis, Natalie Bowen Ritter tabulated the frequency of composers performed per conductor throughout their tenures in regular, nonbroadcast concerts. Rodzinski and Klemperer had a clear interest in the music of nineteenth-century European composers, although they also frequently conducted works from the Baroque and Classical periods, especially Bach, Beethoven, and Mozart. Given in order of frequency, Rodzinski conducted Bach the most, or 8.6 percent of total works performed during his tenure, followed by Wagner with 6.3 percent, Tchaikovsky with almost 6 percent, and with both Brahms and Richard Strauss tied at 5.2 percent. Klemperer conducted the music of Beethoven and Brahms most frequently, with both composers at 8.6 percent of all works he performed, followed by Bach with 7.9 percent, Wagner at 6.2 percent, and Mozart with 5.9 percent. Twentieth-century composers are naturally on the list as well, such as Maurice Ravel, Igor Stravinsky, Jean Sibelius, and Claude Debussy, but they are all under 4 percent of all the music these two conductors programmed.[41]

A further reason for the paucity of modern American music was cost. The Depression years were not good times for the orchestra. It had run heavily into debt, in part because its prime benefactor, William Andrews Clark Jr., had died in 1934 without leaving it an endowment. The businessman and philanthropist Harvey S. Mudd, who became president of the Southern California Symphony Association in 1935, made these financial problems clear when he began a fund drive to raise $80,000. He stated that the orchestra desperately needed this money to remain in operation, and while such calls for help were by no means unusual among arts institutions at the time, the situation for the Los Angeles Philharmonic was particularly dire. The orchestra was in the red to the tune of $150,000, and Mudd claimed that if the Association could not raise its current goal of $80,000, "there is grave question whether the orchestra can be preserved."[42] One factor that kept the Los Angeles Philharmonic in the minds, and ears, of Angelenos was the medium of radio, but it could scarcely afford to pay royalty fees on modern music—American or European. As a result, listeners heard primarily music in the public domain, consisting of works mainly from the eighteenth and nineteenth centuries.

In terms of American composers, no one composer predominates in the radio broadcasts. On three occasions the orchestra performed works by an immigrant from Australia who took American citizenship in 1918, Percy Grainger, whereas the orchestra broadcast only one work each of composers George Chadwick, Edward MacDowell, Charles Skilton, and Charles Wakefield Cadman.[43] Of these, only Cadman spent a significant period of time in southern California, although Grainger visited on several occasions and even got married at the Hollywood Bowl. What unites them is that they all composed in the Romantic or post-Romantic vein. Together, American works comprised 8.5 percent of the program total during this period, so while the Standard Hour did not ignore American composers, neither did it actively promote them.

The disinterest of the Los Angeles Philharmonic in performing American music, while striking, should not surprise us. If we look at the data concerning American works that Rodzinski and Klemperer performed during their tenures during the regular concert season, the results are not too encouraging, at a total of 5.6 percent and 2.8 percent, respectively. Nor are these figures much different for all of the permanent conductors of the

Los Angeles Philharmonic during the period 1919 to 1970; only with guest conductors in the period 1939 to 1942, when the Philharmonic had no permanent conductor, does that percentage rise to almost 14 percent. The best period that American composers fared among the orchestra's permanent conductors was during the tenure of its only conductor born in America (and indeed who grew up in Los Angeles), Alfred Wallenstein, who served from 1943 to 1955. Almost 10 percent of all works he conducted were by American composers, and during two seasons the percentage was over 15 percent—by far the largest amount by any permanent conductor of the orchestra.[44] By contrast, at least two other major American orchestras could afford to be more supportive of American music: the Boston Symphony Orchestra under conductor Serge Koussevitsky and the Philadelphia Orchestra under Leopold Stokowski.[45]

What an orchestra programmed is one issue; how radio stations presented that music is another. Beginning in 1936, it appears that station KFI sought to broaden the audience base for the Standard Hour, in part by programming popular shows before it. "Classical music stations" were unknown at the time, and stations tended to broadcast a diverse, even eclectic, variety of programs, often including popular music, classical music, comedy, and drama on the same day. On January 2, 1936, the day of the first evening concert for that year, KFI listeners at 5 P.M. could hear the *Rudy Vallee Show*; at 6 P.M. it was *Capt. Henry's Showboat*; at 7 P.M. was the *Paul Whiteman Hour*; and at 8:15 P.M., programmed after *Amos 'n' Andy*, the Los Angeles Philharmonic had its turn. Guest conductor Henry Svedrofsky led the orchestra in this concert, which featured one work each by composers Édouard Lalo, Franz Schubert, Georges Bizet, Johann Strauss Jr., and Victor Herbert.[46] As with the previous series, almost all of the concerts featured solely music by European composers, with the exception being the final radio concert of the season, with pieces by Deems Taylor, Ferde Grofé, and Stephen Foster.[47] That year Standard Oil sponsored a total of six broadcasts on KFI, which formed part of the NBC coast network. All of them continued to follow the same evening line-up of programming, although the *Bing Crosby's Show* soon replaced the *Paul Whiteman Hour*.[48]

At first it seems that the Los Angeles Philharmonic Orchestra's permanent conductor, Otto Klemperer, wanted no part in this "popularizing" effort. He began personally conducting radio broadcast programs only in 1938, five years after he had begun with the Philharmonic. The Standard Oil Company continued to sponsor these programs, starting the year off right with a concert on New Year's Day. As if to emphasize the seriousness of the venture, he returned to the earlier format of Rodzinski, with plentiful Bach, Wagner, Debussy, and Beethoven, conducting a cross-section of European art music: German, Austrian, French, English, Russian, and Spanish, with but one composer from North America, Edward MacDowell. A work by the Spaniard Enrique Granados, *Romanza*, marks the first time the orchestra broadcast a work by a Spanish-speaking composer. Yet despite this difference in content, the radio station continued to program popular shows preceding the Los Angeles Philharmonic. Thus Klemperer followed *Amos 'n' Andy*, and the difference with the earlier series on KFI is that this series aired over the Columbia Broadcasting System, from the sound stage of Paramount Studio.[49] "High art" on radio finally met Hollywood.

These broadcasts were by no means the only classical programs available to Los Angeles listeners. At least four other stations broadcast art music on a regular basis: KECA, KMTR, KHJ, and a new station owned by the *Los Angeles Times*, KFAC, which after 1945 broadcast solely classical music.[50] KECA was especially active in the field. Car salesman Earle C. Anthony founded the station in 1929, and with the slogan of "Aristocrat of the Air" sought to establish it as the "prestige" channel. This meant devoting about 40 percent of the station's programming to classical music, the remaining time taken up with drama, children's programs, and community service programs such as "Spanish Lesson," "Care of the Eyes," and "KECA News Period." Much like public broadcasting stations today, it allowed only limited advertising. To emphasize its role as the station for what it called "lovers of fine music," in October 1935 KECA began publishing a *Program Magazine*, which subscribers could receive for one dollar per year.[51] Music commentator José Rodriguez was the editor, and each month he highlighted the works of a particular composer, such as Beethoven, Brahms, Sibelius, or Stravinsky.[52]

Rodriguez was a remarkable figure in the Los Angeles music world. He was born in Guatemala in 1898 and immigrated as a youth to Los Angeles, where he attended Manual Arts High School, which had a renowned music program.[53] He then served in World War I, for which he received a Distinguished Conduct Medal, and went on to study piano and earn degrees in music at Balliol College in Oxford. Rodriguez settled definitively in Los Angeles during the 1920s, and worked as a reporter and editor for the Hearst newspapers and United Press before becoming a radio commentator for KFI in 1928 and later KECA. In 1929 he joined a group of intellectuals that included poet and bookseller Jacob Israel Zeitlin, writer Carey McWilliams, and impresario Merle Armitage to found the journal *Opinion* that had "no particular axe to grind . . . [but] rather to grind all axes."[54] The journal, which only lasted one year due to evident disagreement among its editors, featured poetry, painting, and literary journalism.

Rodriguez thus already had editorial experience before taking the position as editor of the *Program Magazine*, which he did with great enthusiasm. For each issue he gave a synopsis of a composer's life and work, and a local artist, Paul Landacre, designed a wood engraving for the magazine covers. Although like *Opinion* the magazine lasted only one year, it underlined the seriousness that the station went about its mission. As it stated in one program, "KECA assumes that its audience is whole-heartedly in favor of dignified, intelligent broadcasting of fine things; that a station that attempts this work will attract the most solid and responsible elements of the community; that such an example will bear fruit in the general improvement of radio standards; that

Figure 6.1 KECA Program: Beethoven, 1935

although the development will be slow and gradual, it will gather momentum and force to achieve permanence."[55]

This mission demonstrates a surprising optimism and determination to provide Angelenos with an alternative to what had become a common broadcasting format by the mid-1930s: popular dance music and extensive advertising. Few program directors had the will to attempt such a venture. But could it work? Evidently the KECA staff thought so: "We believe firmly, even obstinately, that it is possible and quite feasible to awaken a popular movement for fine music. . . . Popular music, which we recognize and respect, enjoys such a determined following; so does sport, fashion, motion pictures. BEETHOVEN, BACH AND STRAVINSKY deserve a proportional representation. If one out of every hundred persons who attend a football game or a feature movie can be won to the cause of good music, the battle is won."[56]

Not surprisingly, however, KECA's policy of allowing only limited advertising was not lucrative. The station appears to have lost hundreds of thousands of dollars since its founding in 1929. Earle C. Anthony absorbed the loss, much as Clark paid for the annual deficit of the Los Angeles Philharmonic.[57] But this could not go on forever, and like many before it, KECA decided to join the NBC-Blue Network in February 1936 to remain financially viable. What KECA lost in independence it made up for in expanding its programming to include much live classical music from the East Coast. Since most of its previous programs appear to have consisted of recordings, this represented a major shift indeed. The station could now broadcast concerts by the Boston Symphony Orchestra and Metropolitan Opera, the Library of Congress Chamber Music, and Rochester Civic Concerts. These and other concerts regularly appeared in the newspaper radio column, which along with a "Colleges of Southern California Music Series" listed live broadcasts such as of Arturo Toscanini and the NBC Symphony Orchestra and concerts from Artur Rodzinski and the Cleveland Orchestra.[58]

For a while, this programming was a success. Following the distribution of a listener's survey, program director Glenn R. Dolberg decided to switch the station's format by May 1936 to almost 100 percent classical music for its 16 hours each day on the air.[59] Since KECA's signal was comparatively weak, most of its audience came from the city of Los Angeles; only when the station built a more powerful transmitter in August 1936 could it reach neighboring communities in Pasadena, Glendale, Long Beach, Santa Monica, and Beverly Hills.[60] The following year, however, KECA greatly scaled back its classical music selections. Although it remained the premier classical music station in Los Angeles, at least half of its programming soon consisted of talk shows, drama, dance music, and public information programs. With the increased presence of NBC, Los Angeles radio was even further on the national map. The loss, of course, was that KECA was now one of many stations that NBC owned, and so was less of a local product and had much less control over its programming.

One group that benefited from the growth in radio broadcasting were local composers. Elinor Remick Warren, who grew up in Los Angeles, made good use of the airwaves. Her music was readily accessible, mainly because it blended a neo-Romanticism with distinctly American themes, such as in Los Angeles baritone Lawrence Tibbett's rendition in 1935 of her song, "Sweetgrass Range" (hear Track no. 14). Warren specialized in vocal music but also wrote many orchestral pieces. Similarly, William Grant Still had much experience with radio. In 1935 he wrote music for a ballet on the theme of Central Avenue, describing the various scenes he saw there: "Dancing Boys," "Intervention of the Law," "The Philosopher," and so on. When he received a commission from CBS in New York for an orchestral suite, he completed the score and retitled it *Lenox Avenue* after a street in Harlem.[61] The New Deal program, the Works Progress Administration (WPA), paid for an orchestra and African American chorus so that Still could make transcriptions of the music in Los Angeles, which were then aired across the country (hear Track no. 18).

Although on a less extensive basis than KECA, KMTR broadcast art music as well. Echoing an idea that KECA began, it created a "Musical Vignettes" series in 1936, which presented a half hour of short biographies of famous composers, accompanied by selections of their music. The first such program consisted of a "dramatization of the life and loves of Franz Schubert, together with the presentation of his best-known compositions."[62] Subsequent broadcasts, which also went under the title of "Musical Immortals," continued this trend. Along with the offerings of KHJ and KFAC, both of which programmed recordings and live concerts, art music was readily available to the radio-listening public in Los Angeles.

Audience Surveys

Who was actually listening to classical music on radio? Two surveys that took place during the 1930s attempted to answer this question: one by KECA, the other by an independent research team. KECA's audience survey in 1936 sought to determine the listening habits, interests, and background of its listeners. Questions varied from "How many hours a day do you listen to KECA?," to more personal questions, such as "Do you own your own home?," or "How many automobiles?" It received over one thousand replies, representing about 25 percent of its subscribers to the *Program Magazine*.[63]

This survey gives us one of the first composite pictures of an audience that listened predominantly to classical music. The average age of listeners was 44 years, although unfortunately the breakdown in terms of sex or ethnicity was not given. The average income of respondents was substantial, at $3,259; over 200 listeners were professionals, such as doctors, lawyers, engineers, and teachers, while housewives made up 116 of the viewers and 52 were students. The rest were in the miscellaneous category, which ranged from policemen and soldiers to salesmen and clerks. Almost half, or 41 percent, owned their own home, 71 percent owned automobiles, and 100 percent owned radio receivers. Interestingly, 47 percent claimed to be "definitely influenced by radio advertising." In terms of musical interests, a majority wanted to hear instrumental music, and 65 percent approved of organ music; on average, listeners tuned in to about four hours per day.[64]

KECA WANTS TO KNOW

PLEASE fill out this questionnaire, but do not sign your name. KECA wants to know all about its audience, for many reasons. Only by reliable facts about the sort of person who listens to KECA and subscribes to this magazine, can the station determine the character of its audience and thus adapt its program schedule the better to satisfy it. We are most interested in knowing the kind of person you are, and you can tell us this in confidence without telling us your name or address. Mail to Program Department, KECA, 1000 South Hope Street, Los Angeles.

1. How many hours a day do you listen to KECA?
   a. Morning (3 weekends) b. Afternoon (3)
   c. Evening 3
2. What type of music do you prefer?
   a. Symphony 1 b. Opera 2 c. Chamber ....
   d. Solos .... e. Light concerts & ballads 3
3. Do you listen to KECA's news broadcast?
   a. Noon .... b. Six P.M. if at home c. Nine P.M. if not in bed
4. KECA now signs off at 11:00 P.M. Would you prefer it to remain on the air until midnight? don't stay up so late With what type of music? ....
5. How old are you? 19 What business are you in? sophomore U.C.L.A. Married or single? Single
   How many children? none Their ages? ....
6. What is your average income? —— Are you an employee? no employer? no
   Are you in business for yourself? no
7. Do you own your own home? parent does Estimated value $1,000 How many automobiles? 1
   Make and year? 1934 Studebaker
8. How old is your radio set? 2 yrs Make? Sparton
9. When merchandize is advertised by radio, does that influence you to buy it? no
10. Do you like organ music? no Do you listen to Twilight Reveries? rarely
11. What magazines do you read? American, Sat. Eve. Post, Lit. Digest, Ladies Home Journal, Sunset, Calif. Alumni News, etc.
12. Are you a high-school yes college graduate? not yet
13. How many times a week do you attend:
    a. Motion pictures? 1 b. Theaters? once a year
    c. Concerts? twice a year d. Dances? once every two or three months
    Opera 5 or 6 times a year
14. Comments Don't care much for talks.

Figure 6.2 KECA Survey, 1936

The survey demonstrates several things. First, listeners to KECA were comparatively well-off, which would have been of certain interest to advertisers on the NBC-Blue Network. That almost half the respondents indicated being influenced in their purchasing decisions by advertisers would reinforce this interest. Second, the average listener was approaching middle age, which agrees with more modern surveys of classical music audiences. Finally, if we can extrapolate from the survey, the program of KECA continued to appeal to its almost 4,000 subscribers and over 50,000 listeners. Overwhelmingly the respondents preferred instrumental music. In other words, these Angelenos wanted an alternative in their radio listening habits, and KECA offered them that alternative. However, KECA was an experiment in broadcasting, and had not yet proven itself to be financially viable prior to the takeover by NBC. This survey indicates a definite target group that other stations overlooked.

Los Angeles audiences attracted the attention of two other researchers during this period: Margaret Grant and Herman Hettinger. The purpose of their study was to discover why people attended symphony concerts. To set up a comparative basis, they drew some of their conclusions from questionnaires they distributed to audiences at concerts in both Los Angeles and Grand Rapids, Michigan; no reason was given for the choice of Grand Rapids. In Los Angeles they received 869 responses, compared to 1,009 in Grand Rapids. The majority of respondents were subscribers to symphony concerts: 59 percent in Los Angeles and 64 percent in Grand Rapids, and the median age was comparatively young by current standards: 33 years old in Los Angeles and 27 years old in Grand Rapids. Almost three-fourths of the respondents were women (74 percent in Los Angeles, 70 percent in Grand Rapids), and most were either housewives, clerical workers, or students, with 72 percent of the respondents in Los Angeles having attended college, compared to 49 percent in Grand Rapids. The overwhelming majority were native-born Americans, with 90 percent in Los Angeles and 96 percent in Grand Rapids, although fewer were of American parentage, at 60 percent for both cities. The ethnicity of respondents was not given, but was probably predominantly white.[65]

The authors concluded that aside from the experience of attending symphony concerts, "broadcasting has been the most importance force in building interest in symphonic music among the audiences surveyed."[66] Almost a third of nonsubscribers in Los Angeles listed radio as an influential factor in encouraging them to attend, while 22 percent of subscribers noted this as a major reason. Curiously, 84 percent of nonsubscribers listed symphony music as their preference, compared to only 68 percent of subscribers. Instrumental solos were their second preference. In ranking their favorite composers, about a fifth of the Los Angeles respondents mentioned Ludwig van Beethoven in first place, followed by Johannes Brahms (13 percent), Piotr Tchaikovsky (11 percent), and Jean Sibelius (6 percent). These choices roughly correlated with respondents in Grand Rapids, who listed in order Beethoven, Tchaikovsky, Wagner, and Brahms.

When asked which symphony broadcasts they listened to the most, respondents mentioned several programs. The leading program was with the New York Philharmonic Orchestra, which conductor Dr. Walter Damrosch led on the Columbia network. Of the Los Angeles respondents, 84 percent ranked it first among their favorite art music broadcasts, compared to only 63 percent in Grand Rapids. Tied in second place were both the Standard

Symphony Hour and Arturo Toscanini's NBC Symphony concerts. The Los Angeles respondents put the Ford Sunday Evening Hour in third place, at 41 percent, of their favorite radio programs of art music.

These results suggest several things. First, radio broadcasting of classical music had become a regular part of many listeners' lives. It ranked even above listening to records; 82 percent of the Los Angeles respondents reported that they preferred radio to records, compared to 66 percent in Grand Rapids.[67] Second, programs broadcast in other parts of the country had a devoted following in Los Angeles. This would seem to reinforce one of the goals of such programs, such as broadcasts by the New York Philharmonic: to make listeners aware of the country's leading orchestras, since listeners could hear them on a regular basis. Third, the programs must have served their original purpose: to inform the public about the value of art music in a manner that they found appealing. As a result, radio had become the most powerful medium in the popularization of classical music.

The Musicians Union

A final question to pose here is: How did the musicians union respond to the challenges posed by both the recording and radio industries? In the employment of musicians, the two industries were closely linked. At first, the AFM saw little threat to musicians' jobs with the advent of recordings. Quite the contrary, there was the perception that recordings actually improved the situation for musicians by enabling "musical education of large numbers of people and the ensuing demand for musical performances."[68]

That view changed markedly, however, following the improvement of sound quality with electrical recording after 1925. The "recording industry" by the 1920s encompassed two main fields: records, which were primarily for home use, and electrical transcriptions, which were primarily for use by radio broadcasters. Transcriptions came on ten-, twelve-, and sixteen-inch records, and served both noncommercial and commercial purposes.[69] Libraries that rented transcriptions were among the main customers for noncommercial use, and they could play these transcriptions as often as they wished. Commercial transcriptions, however, were different: these were for broadcasts which advertisers sponsored. NBC, in particular, produced most commercial transcriptions, and it also owned one of the largest record companies, RCA-Victor. Since royalties were not part of musicians' contracts at this time, they received nothing for these broadcasts.

Musicians also suffered from the introduction of sound films. In 1929, there were over 19,000 musicians employed in theaters throughout the country. The effects of the transition from silent to sound films were at first scarcely felt, due to the time it took to outfit theaters with the appropriate sound equipment. Many symphony orchestras still had difficulties getting well-qualified players on a permanent basis, since theater jobs tended to pay much better. In that year, musicians were receiving a total of almost $1 million a week in wages, or about $53 per week per player—far more than symphony orchestras could offer. Within a year the number of theater musicians had fallen to 14,000, and the following year to 5,000 musicians, where it remained fairly constant for the next two decades.[70] The impact of the Depression was in part responsible for this ruinous situation, but recorded sound had also clearly played a role. Why pay for live musicians when the recorded version sufficed?

During the Depression, when radio became a much more popular form of entertainment, relations between the musicians union and the recording and radio industries became truly antagonistic. By contrast, despite the loss of theater musicians from sound films, the AFM had relatively few actual complaints with Hollywood film studios over working conditions, since contracts tended to be met with satisfaction on both sides. But the AFM also sought control over all other forms of recorded sound, namely records bought by the public, transcriptions, and recordings in juke boxes. The repeated use of recordings in any form clearly meant that musicians were not performing live and so were not getting work. A 1942 report by the Federal Communications Commission (FCC) found that of the total time that an average radio station broadcast music, over half, or 55.9 percent, consisted of recorded music.[71] This was bad enough, yet what particularly riled the AFM is that it had become a common practice among some stations to play recordings in order to mislead the public into thinking that what they were hearing *was* live. Regulation of the industry, in the eyes of the musicians union, had become essential.

Under a president who minced few words, James Petrillo, the AFM thus launched an all-out war against the record companies, in part as a way of getting at the radio stations. Petrillo called for a recording ban to take effect on August 1, 1942. It lasted over 27 months. Although wartime inhibited overt gestures that may have been taken as unpatriotic, Petrillo continued to use inflammatory rhetoric, such as claiming that the ban on recordings was permanent, in order to force a better deal with the record companies. The AFM was not alone on this issue; it had the full support not only of many labor unions in the United States, but also musicians unions abroad: in Great Britain, Mexico, Cuba, Chile, and South Africa.[72]

Battle lines were drawn. Two of the largest record producers, RCA-Victor and CBS, both major broadcasters, saw the ban as particularly ominous. Not surprisingly, most newspapers were against the ban as well, in part because many papers, such as the *Los Angeles Times*, owned radio stations themselves.[73] Nor was the ban popular among the American public. A Gallup poll taken in 1942 concluded that 73 percent of respondents wanted the federal government to stop Petrillo by legal means if necessary, while only 12 percent were against such action.[74] Ironically, Petrillo was no friend of Los Angeles musicians, whom he later referred to as those "$800-a-week Communist fiddle-players in Hollywood."[75] Yet Petrillo and the AFM claimed they had little choice but to draw battle lines, since they feared being run over entirely.

Even the federal government joined the fight. Although it had little influence over the recording industry, Congress sought to control the airwaves first through the Federal Radio Commission from 1927 to 1934, and then through the FCC. However, it did not yet have legislative means to combat the musicians union, and strongly resented some of Petrillo's other actions, such as blocking the broadcasting of youth orchestras, or requiring radio stations to hire more musicians. In retaliation, Congress investigated the musicians union in 1943, and the AFM became "the first union to have legislation passed specifically to control its actions."[76] Congress passed the Lea Act during the war, known as the "Anti-Petrillo Law." The Act, which formed the basis for the Taft-Hartley Act of 1947 to reduce the power of unions, made it a criminal offense to attempt to force radio stations to comply with union regulations. Although the union challenged the Lea Act in court, the Supreme Court ultimately ruled it constitutional in 1947.[77]

While radio stations were safe, record companies were not. Despite their avowed determination to resist the ban, the record companies gradually relented. The third-largest record producer, Decca, was the first to yield to the AFM's demands in September 1943, agreeing to pay a set fee for every recording and transcription it made with union members. About one hundred smaller record companies followed Decca's lead in early 1944, although RCA-Victor and Columbia submitted a formal complaint before the War Labor Board, which called for an end to the ban. Even President Roosevelt wired Petrillo in October 1944, requesting him to end the ban, which Petrillo refused to do until all of the record companies had finally acquiesced.[78] That occurred the following month, when both RCA-Victor and Columbia signed a contract with the AFM, fearing that their competitors were gaining market share.

The agreements brought substantial changes for the AFM, which grew from 135,000 members in 1940 to 231,000 in 1948.[79] Record companies had to pay the union between 1/4 cent to five cents for each record costing up to two dollars. For more expensive records, companies paid 2.5 percent of the sale price. In addition, there were fees for library transcriptions, although curiously none for commercial transcriptions of single broadcasts. These fees went into a separate Recording and Transcription Fund, which paid for free live music in parks, schools, hospitals, and similar institutions. The fund, which disbursed $10.43 to each local for each member in good standing, resulted in a total of $4,500,000 through 1947, paying for almost 19,000 performances and 45,000 paychecks at union scale.[80]

The AFM's demands for regulation did not stop there. After the war, not only radio but television had to be made part of the contracts. The AFM achieved a settlement in 1954 with radio and television stations, who agreed to a 15 percent wage rate increase, among other demands. While these agreements affected musicians all over the country, locals particularly benefited in Los Angeles, New York, and Chicago, where most recording and broadcasting took place. This battle had some unintended consequences, such as radio stations broadcasting race records and rock 'n' roll as a way of avoiding the new regulations and royalties. Nonetheless, the union had achieved what it had set out to do over a decade earlier: to receive some reimbursement for the music that listeners heard from both recordings and radio.

Conclusion

Broadcasting on radio transformed Los Angeles's music culture, mainly because it provided opportunities that simply did not exist with any other medium. Advances in radio technology combined with a civic interest on the part of radio station managers had some wide-ranging results for orchestras across the country, such as breaking down the barriers to what had literally been concert music, that is, music intended primarily for the concert hall. Now the strength of a radio transmitter determined the size of these new "empires of the air," and conductors such as Rothwell were quick to see radio's virtues in reaching new audiences. Curiously, it seems that Rothwell was uninterested in recording the Los Angeles Philharmonic, which is possibly a reason why his name is so little known in music circles today, despite his innovations in music education and radio. Nor were his successors, Rodzinski and Klemperer, much interested in recording, preferring like Rothwell to rely on broadcasting to make the orchestra known beyond the boundaries of Los Angeles. One of the few early examples we have of the Los Angeles Philharmonic on record is its outdoor recording in 1928, as noted in chapter 3 (hear Track no. 11).[81] Thus while the Los Angeles Philharmonic at this time had no recording contract like other major orchestras enjoyed, it did have a long-running radio program with the Standard Hour. Only under Alfred Wallenstein was the orchestra able to secure recording contracts: first with Decca shortly after the recording ban ended, then with RCA-Victor and later London Records.

As these and other conductors recognized, one of the great virtues of radio was its role in the field of music education. It is significant that many radio performances before World War II were live, because the management of radio stations tended to frown on recorded programs. Almost anyone with access to a wireless could hear concerts by the New York Philharmonic, the Cleveland Orchestra, or the Los Angeles Philharmonic, almost as if they were in a concert hall. In 1940, music commentator José Rodriguez enthusiastically noted the importance of radio as part of a wider trend in music education in America: "The enormous output of radio, which in variety alone does in a week what no single orchestra or company could do in a year, the growing literature on the history, meaning and importance of music, the increased activity of our schools in practical musical education, the widening consumption of phonographs and records, all point to a popular stimulation and interest which will find spontaneously the best means of organizing and exploiting successfully all forms of musical activity."[82]

The large number of radio stations that sprang up during the 1920s and '30s thus demonstrated that a veritable "radio culture" had developed, bringing together virtual communities of listeners who enjoyed a variety of music programs, something that the musicians union saw with an increasingly wary eye. Only after intensive resistance on the part of Petrillo and his followers could union members, white or black, receive royalties for the recordings they made and that radio stations broadcast. This was not a major issue yet for the Los Angeles Philharmonic, with few recordings to its name, but it would become so during and after the tenure of Wallenstein, when the orchestra began to make more recordings that stations could then broadcast.

It becomes difficult to uphold the notions of cultural hierarchy and "sacralization" when we begin looking at the development of radio. While symphony orchestras had certainly become a fixture in most major American cities, those that sought to broadcast their music were not closing doors; they were opening them. Audience surveys suggest that many Americans were receptive to those efforts and tuned in to classical music on a regular basis. Under the leadership of Walter Rothwell, the Los Angeles Philharmonic was a pioneer in radio broadcasts in California, as it was in the field of music education. Although the music it performed was primarily European in origin, the variety of composers from different countries offered a broad range of the orchestral repertoire to a diverse "air audience" of men, women, and children. Similarly, radio enabled local composers to reach far more people than mere concerts would allow, thereby greatly diversifying the kinds of art music available to the radio listening public.

The recording and radio industries helped define modern entertainment in Los Angeles as much as in other major cities. Los Angeles, and not San Francisco, became the prime location for broadcasting as well as recording on the West Coast—a factor that would have enormous significance for Los Angeles's entertainment industry in the years that followed. The final capstone in that development lay in the fact that no other American city, either on the West or the East Coast, became more identified with the medium that truly defined the modern age: film.

7

Music on Film: Hollywood and the Conversion to Sound

Few industries have had as much impact on Los Angeles's music culture than the film industry. With the exorbitant salaries and the allure of Hollywood, thousands of talented musicians from across America and abroad came to southern California in a kind of second Gold Rush, particularly once the industry converted to sound during the late 1920s. The rush turned into a stampede during the Depression, when Hollywood offered some of the few lucrative positions for musicians in the country. Like the skills of actors, directors, and writers, studios urgently required composers and orchestral musicians, even though film music was typically in the background, perhaps scarcely noticed by the audience. The purpose of this chapter is to demonstrate how music was vital in creating an atmosphere or mood in both non-animated and animated films following the conversion to sound.

When motion pictures surpassed vaudeville in popularity during the 1920s, theater owners gradually converted their variety houses to movie theaters, which people flocked to in growing numbers. Film, like vaudeville before it, provided a common thread of experience for Americans, often across ethnic and economic boundaries. Movies represented a dream world in which patrons could laugh, cry, or in some way react to that entertainment *together*. One reason film has survived over time is that it has been, from the beginning, an essentially communal medium.

Orchestral musicians and organists were in great demand in silent movie houses, in part to drown out the not-so-silent film projectors.[1] These musicians frequently used excerpts from classical music, with the result that some of the first applications of music for films involved the use of scores never originally intended for that purpose. In using music by European composers, theater musicians brought a whole new meaning to the term "light classics." As early as 1909, the Edison company began using sections of pieces by famous composers under the category of "specific suggestions for music" for the films that it produced, otherwise known as "cue sheets." Musicians also used catalogues for this purpose, such as *The Sam Fox Moving Picture Music*

Volumes, published in 1913 by J. S. Zamecnik, a pupil of the Czech composer Antonin Dvorák, and *Kinobibliothek* by Giuseppe Becce, published in 1919. The composer and conductor Erno Rapée published *Motion Picture Moods for Pianists and Organists* in 1924, which featured 52 different categories or "moods," drawn primarily from pieces by art music composers.[2] Catalogues such as these greatly helped musicians in their choice of musical accompaniment, and music became virtually inseparable from the very experience of sitting in the theater and watching a film.

The idea of composing music for American films came only gradually. Joseph Carl Breil composed and arranged music for D. W. Griffith's epic 1915 film, *The Birth of a Nation*, which premiered at Temple Auditorium at Fifth and Olive Streets in downtown Los Angeles—the same location as the earlier Hazard's Pavilion.[3] An orchestra accompanied the event and then toured with the film, causing a sensation. Several composers began to write scores for silent films; Louis Gottschalk, for example, composed music in 1921 for *The Three Musketeers*, and Douglas Fairbanks hired Mortimer Wilson to compose scores for Fairbanks's pictures while they were actually being filmed.[4] Yet a problem with these scores is that they were for live performances, and not every theater in the country had the benefit of an orchestra.

A sign of things to come was when John Ford made his epic silent film in 1924 on the transcontinental railroad, *The Iron Horse*, and he asked Erno Rapée to arrange and write live music to accompany it. Rapée included several folk tunes, such as "Turkey in the Straw" and "Pop Goes the Weasel," as well as a male ensemble singing an old railroad song, "Drill, Ye Tarriers, Drill." The following year, Rapée published a piano arrangement of the title song, "March of the Iron Horse," and the Hollywood Record Company released the first known recording of prologue music to a motion picture in Los Angeles. Since the film had played at Sid Grauman's Egyptian Theatre in Hollywood, the Grauman's Egyptian Orchestra under conductor Ulderico Marcelli made the recording, *Echoes From the Iron Horse* (hear Track no. 8).[5]

The advent of sound in motion pictures transformed the kinds of music that audiences heard. Lee De Forest, who invented the vacuum-tube amplifier, was a pioneer in the field. He took out a patent for a process called the Phonofilm system in 1920, which recorded sound directly onto the film itself. He filmed President Calvin Coolidge and Wisconsin Senator Robert La Follette giving speeches, as well as vaudeville performers Eddie Cantor, Noble Sissle and Eubie Blake singing or playing the piano.[6] De Forest's system ultimately failed commercially, mainly because the Hollywood studios, fearful of losing profits, managed to block his efforts to distribute his invention. But the attempt to record sound with films continued.

An alternative technology was Vitaphone, which consisted of accompanying a film with a record. With the 1926 release of *Don Juan*, a swashbuckling picture in the true Hollywood tradition, Warner Brothers sought to blend orchestral music (though no dialogue) with action. An orchestra was roughly synchronized with the image through the Vitaphone recording process, "which made [the film] a sensation and led directly to the talkie revolution."[7] Although it provided musical accompaniment, it was far from satisfactory. If the record broke or was in any way damaged, it became almost impossible to coordinate the music to the action on the screen. Because the records were made of thick wax, film companies had to ship out several copies of the record in the case of breakage, which ultimately proved wasteful.

Nonetheless, the release by the same studio of the even more influential *The Jazz Singer* the following year confirmed what many already suspected: that "talkies" would be primarily responsible for future profits in the industry. The few sections with sound included almost solely music, with very little dialogue, and there was a rich variety in that music. The narrative revolves around a singer who is torn between two worlds: the highly traditional, religious world of his father, a cantor in a synagogue, and the wild, secular world of the stage, where sin and revelry prevail. The latter entices the youth away, which leaves his father broken-hearted. The singer, whom vaudeville performer Al Jolson portrayed, finds fame and fortune and falls in love with a *shiksa*, or a non-Jewish woman. When his father is on his deathbed, however, the dutiful son responds to his last wish, that he take his place as cantor in the synagogue.

The film provided several opportunities for musical innovation. Jolson performed five songs in the vaudeville tradition, and one song, "Mother of Mine," depicted Jolson in blackface. But there is more to the music than that; the music director, Louis Silvers, included themes from Tchaikovsky's *Romeo and Juliet* in the opening credits, and the closing scene finds Jolson singing "Kol Nidre" in the synagogue. Along with providing a model for future films in its depiction of both class and cultural conflict, *The Jazz Singer* demonstrated with finality that audiences wanted to hear music on film.[8]

The invention of sound in motion pictures did not mean that theater orchestras *immediately* disappeared. Some orchestras continued to perform in large movie theaters, if only as entertainment between viewings, much as orchestras had done in vaudeville theaters between acts or shows. At the Carthay Circle Theater in Los Angeles, for example, Carli Elinor's Concert Orchestra performed pieces before and after the showing of films.[9] Similarly, composer and conductor Erno Rapée led an orchestra at one of the largest theaters in the country, the Roxy in New York City. At least within the first few years of sound, orchestras could still lend a more festive atmosphere to the proceedings. In 1929, theaters were by far the largest employers of musicians in the country, but the combined result of sound in films and theater owners' difficulty in paying musicians during the Depression immediately changed that situation. The impact was all the more devastating since theater musicians often earned more than did those performing in symphony orchestras.[10] Thus, studio work became even more enticing, and thousands made the move out to Hollywood for the limited number of jobs available.

While the nation's first films at the turn of the century were produced on the East Coast, by the time *The Jazz Singer* appeared, Hollywood studios accounted for at least 80 percent of all films made in the country.[11] By the 1930s, eight studios dominated film production: Warner Brothers, Metro-Goldwyn-Mayer (MGM), Radio-Keith-Orpheum (RKO), Universal, Twentieth Century-Fox, Paramount, United Artists, and Columbia.[12] The studio system was highly decentralized; belying the generic name "Hollywood," they were also located in Culver City, Beverly Hills, and the San Fernando Valley. The studios worked on a production method, and during the Golden Age of the 1930s and '40s, they produced and distributed over 500 feature films annually. Eighty million Americans, or 65 percent of the population, were going to the movies on a weekly basis by 1938, and films exerted a powerful influence on American mores, fashion, and taste.[13] In the words of one film historian, "the entertainment industry was no longer simply a source of relaxation. . . . It was also a major ideological force."[14]

Because music had become an essential part of filmmaking, each of the studios formed a music department following the conversion to sound. In great demand were experienced music directors to run these departments, who not only knew how to compose quickly and conduct orchestras but could also manage the business end: to work within a budget, to hire and fire musicians, and to get along with the upper management. At first, conditions were relatively primitive. When MGM's chief producer, Irving Thalberg, invited bandleader and arranger Arthur Lange to run the studio's music department in 1929, Lange found less than what he expected: "It was one little room with a piano in it. . . . All they gave us was a little two-by-four building. . . . It was like the old piano rooms that they had in publishing houses."[15] Despite the slow start, MGM developed a reputation for investing heavily in its music department, mainly because one of its most popular genres during the 1930s was the musical.

These music departments provided employment for hundreds of musicians. Three of the largest studios, MGM, Twentieth Century-Fox, and Warner Brothers, each hired orchestras of 50 musicians, whereas smaller studios, such as RKO and Columbia, had orchestras of 45 musicians. Additional staff also proved necessary. In 1930, the music director at Paramount, Nathaniel Finston, had on his staff four conductors, five arrangers, twelve composers and songwriters, and five librarians in addition to the studio orchestra of twenty-five musicians, plus seventy-five "outside players employed on a weekly basis."[16] Some of the best musicians in the country came out to Hollywood, because the musicians union established a minimum wage of $30 for a full day's work, more than most musicians could typically make in a symphony orchestra or theater orchestra.[17]

Although the high pay was attractive, the studios required a particular kind of musician. Studio musicians had to work under the tight schedules of film recording, and they had to be able to sight-read quickly and efficiently—a trait that characterizes studio musicians to this day. They worked under contract, but one that the studio could make or break at will. They could not afford to be dismissive of simple music, and they needed endless patience in dealing with those who demanded changes, from the studio head down to the film director, most of whom rarely demonstrated much musical talent. Finally, they had to habituate themselves to the highly commercial aspect of their work, because in Hollywood, music was big business.

As with studio musicians, experienced composers and arrangers were essential to the making of films. The production method left little time for reflection or even rewriting the musical accompaniment. Because the studio usually arranged for the music to be added in the last three to four weeks of production, the ability to compose quickly and collaborate with other composers and arrangers was standard practice. Studios rushed to hire some of the best composers they could find, most of whom had backgrounds in either the theater or concert hall. The kind of film music they typically wrote, the symphonic score, predominated in Hollywood from the 1930s to the 1950s. Three composers, in particular, excelled in the symphonic score: Max Steiner, Erich Wolfgang Korngold, and Alfred Newman.

Max Steiner

Few film composers were as prolific as Max Steiner. During the 37 years that he spent in Hollywood, he wrote the music for over 300 films, and was principal composer for more than 100 of those films.[18] A third of his total output he accomplished as music director at RKO from 1929 to 1935, before moving on to Warner Brothers, where he remained for the rest of his career.[19] Like many of his colleagues he was an immigrant; Maximilian Raoul Walter Steiner was born into a theatrical family in Vienna, Austria in 1888. His namesake, his grandfather Maximilian Steiner, was an impresario who worked closely with Franz von Suppé and Johann Strauss Jr. in mounting several of their operettas at one of the city's leading theaters, the Theatre an der Wien. Max Steiner had a thorough classical training, which included studying under composer and conductor Gustav Mahler, and he earned a degree at the four-year program at the Imperial Academy of Music in one year, for which he received a gold medal.[20]

Steiner wasted no time in making a name as a composer. At the age of 17 he composed an opera, *Beautiful Greek Girl*, which the Viennese impresario Karl Tuschl produced. Its commercial success brought Steiner offers to conduct theater orchestras in Austria and Germany, and while still a teenager he traveled to London to work for impresario George Edwardes, who tried to emulate the Viennese musical theater of Suppé and Strauss. After working in London for seven years and a brief stint in Paris, Steiner immigrated to the United States after the outbreak of war in Europe in 1914. His work with Edwardes guaranteed him a position with Flo Ziegfield in New York, who hired Steiner as a conductor and orchestrator of musical comedies, including one in 1927 titled *Rio Rita* by songwriter Harry Tierney. The film studio RKO contracted Tierney to make a film of the show, and Tierney recommended that RKO hire Steiner.[21]

Figure 7.1 Max Steiner

Steiner arrived in Hollywood at the perfect time. Warner Brothers' *The Jazz Singer* had only been released two years before, and film studios desperately needed composers and arrangers who had theater experience.[22] When the 30-year old David Selznick became executive producer at RKO, he immediately set out looking for strong talent in all creative fields to improve the studio's output. Steiner's remarkable abilities brought him to Selznick's attention, who arranged for him to become the studio's music director. Steiner brought several innovations to the film music genre that continued to influence film composers long afterward. He used original compositions in his scores, typically using a leitmotif, or musical theme, for each major character: a practice long common in opera but new to film. He wrote mimetic music, or musical phrases that reflected what was on the screen for dramatic emphasis, what film scholar Kathryn Kalinak calls "synchronization between music and narrative action."[23] He also introduced underscoring, or playing music in the background even if no instrument was in sight. The standard format for an earlier film score was to write music for the opening credits, then highlight some dramatic scenes during the film (or fill in where the dialogue or plot was lacking in sparkle), and to write music for the film's end. By contrast, Steiner's music demanded attention by the sheer length of the score.

Steiner achieved major recognition in Hollywood in 1932, when he was the principal composer for 18 films. One of these was *Bird of Paradise*, which dealt with an interracial romance in the South Seas: an Anglo man, Jonny (Joel McCrea), and a Polynesian woman, Luana (Dolores Del Rio). Steiner used drums and ukuleles to evince the exotic atmosphere, which provided source music in the score. But there is also plentiful underscoring, a prominent feature of the film. Composers were initially reluctant to try this technique, fearing that audiences would wonder what connection the music had with the film, but Steiner proved these fears groundless; the music consistently sets a mood, mimics or reflects the action, and emphasizes the love story between Jonny and Luana. When they are swimming and cavorting in the water, the music is playful; when they kiss, a theme in three-quarter time rises up. Each main character has a leitmotif, and a descending four-note theme is symbolic of their sad fate: the islanders do not accept the couple's relationship, and they must part.[24]

Steiner quickly followed on this success with *King Kong*, which RKO released in 1933. Similar to *Bird of Paradise*, the narrative depicts a confrontation between the "modern" and the "primitive." An American film team goes on a safari, led by a maniacal director, Carl Denham (Robert Armstrong). An African tribe captures the lead actress, Ann (Fay Wray), to feed a giant ape, King Kong, who demands constant sacrifice. After subduing the animal, the film team brings it back to New York to exhibit, and the ape then proceeds to run amok. With Ann clenched in his huge fist, King Kong climbs the newly opened Empire State Building—a symbol of pride, modernism, and American manhood, swatting airplanes as he scales the heights. King Kong sends the city of New York into an uproar before he eventually falls to his death, prompting the closing words of an onlooker, "It was beauty [that] killed the beast."

The film's music was a triumphant example of what a symphonic score could accomplish. As with *Bird of Paradise*, music ran for most of the film's length, as if to demonstrate the central value of musical themes in the early stages of the sound era. In the scenes in Africa, the heavy emphasis on strings and brass contrasts starkly with the powerful, almost hypnotic effect of the pounding of African drums and wild chants of the tribesmen. The music reflects the actors' movements, including that of the beast, such as when he takes Ann to his lair, and deep notes in the bass echo his heavy tread, or in a more playful moment, he tickles her to a vibrato in the strings.[25] The foreboding "King Kong" theme appears throughout the film, and when the film crew returns to New York, the theme provides the link between the abrupt change in scene between the streets of Manhattan and the African jungle. The result is a striking unity in its dichotomy of sound, symbolizing the two contrasting worlds of urban America and deepest Africa. Only a highly skilled composer could achieve this aim.

The public's reaction to *King Kong* was phenomenal. At the height of the Depression, Americans from coast to coast lined up to see the film, which within four days had grossed $89,931 at the box office—a staggering figure at the time. For good measure, in the same year Steiner also conducted Vincent

Youmans's score for a musical starring Dolores Del Rio, Fred Astaire, and Ginger Rogers, *Flying Down to Rio*, whose main song, "Carioca," earned an Academy Award nomination (hear Track no. 13). The success of these two films was welcome news for RKO, which was in equity receivership with $4,384,064 in losses at the time, and profits from the films helped keep RKO out of bankruptcy.[26] Ironically, David Selznick at first showed little faith in *King Kong* and did not want to spend much on musical accompaniment, but the director, Merian C. Cooper, insisted that Steiner write an effective score. The events proved Cooper right. David Raksin noted later that the sheer power of Steiner's music was a prominent factor in the film's success.[27]

The growing importance of film music was revealing in itself: a composer from Hollywood was able to move a mass audience, something few art music composers at the time could claim. The notion of the film composer as someone less than worthy, as an artist of lesser value, is a burden film composers have not worn lightly. The position demanded the utmost in flexibility, and given the time constraints such composers suffered under, it seems remarkable that they were able to create anything of lasting value at all. In *King Kong*, Steiner employed an 80-piece orchestra at a cost of $50,000.[28] Not only did such films mean substantial employment for local musicians, but even audiences in the smallest theater in the country could enjoy the benefit of a large orchestra. Hollywood films in essence popularized orchestral music.

Possibly Steiner's most famous score was for *Gone With the Wind*, released in 1939. Producer David Selznick personally chose Steiner to write the score, who composed almost 300 musical sections with the aid of at least five orchestrators, among whom were two film composers who would later achieve renown, Hugo Friedhofer and Adolph Deutsch. Steiner worked 12 weeks on the score, far longer than the usual time most composers received. He wrote over three hours of music, which provided an almost continuous stream of musical accompaniment for the film, much as he had done with *Bird of Paradise* and *King Kong*.[29] The opening sequence alone has 23 minutes of music.[30]

Steiner came up with 11 different musical themes for the main characters. At Selznick's insistence, Steiner and his orchestrators also integrated a further 16 ideas based on folk tunes and songs from Stephen Foster, among them "Old Folks at Home," "Louisiana Belle," and "Ring de Banjo." The film has often been criticized for lapsing into stereotypes of African Americans, and the music reflects this portrayal in the leitmotif for the slave Mammy (Hattie McDaniel), which is in ragtime.[31] The theme is also anachronistic, since ragtime did not develop until the end of the nineteenth century. Other leitmotifs are less blatantly racist and serve to reinforce the personality of each character: the noble Ashley (Leslie Howard), his sweet fiancée Melanie (Olivia de Havilland), and the virile Rhett Butler (Clark Gable).

The film's most famous theme, however, is not for a character at all but for the land itself: the Georgia plantation, Tara. The emphasis is apt, for it is what the main character, Scarlett O'Hara (Vivien Leigh), prizes more than anything. When she declares, "Land is the only thing that matters," or "It's the only thing worth dying for," the soaring, four-note initial motif emphasizes her strength of purpose and defiance. When Scarlett tries to escape Atlanta, the theme reminds us of her home, as it does when she returns to find Tara largely intact, although damaged, after the war.[32] In the final scenes, when she agonizes over her relationship with Rhett, a full orchestra plays the "Tara" theme that gives her a sense of renewal. It is impossible to avoid the music, and while the film can be criticized for relying too much on the score for emotional impact, the music was a stunning achievement at the time. While Steiner did not get an Academy Award, which went to composer Herbert Stothart at MGM for *The Wizard of Oz*, the score remains a hallmark of the genre.[33]

Steiner helped set the standard for the film composers who followed him. His extensive use of creative themes for characters, mimetic composition, and underscoring became commonplace in Hollywood's symphonic style, which depended on composers and arrangers well-versed in concert music and theater music. Steiner had weaknesses; for example, he was less strong on rhythmic and harmonic innovation than melodic invention, and he freely borrowed from classical and folk music, and even from his own scores—a form of musical theft that was a common practice in film scoring. Whether or not one had heard a Steiner score, it soon became impossible to avoid his music. His opening theme for the 1936 film, *The Charge of the Light Brigade* was such a favorite for studio head Jack Warner that it became the opening fanfare for major film releases over the next 20 years and even for video and DVD releases into the twenty-first century.[34] The conversion to sound enabled talented composers like Steiner to experiment with an array of techniques to reinforce the action on the screen.

Erich Wolfgang Korngold

Another Viennese composer who achieved prominence in Hollywood was Erich Wolfgang Korngold. Although he worked on only 20 films, almost entirely in adventure films and romantic melodramas at Warner Brothers, his influence on his colleagues and the symphonic score went beyond mere numbers. Korngold was a far more accomplished composer than Steiner when he came to Hollywood. He was born in 1897 in Brünn (currently in the Czech Republic but then part of Austria-Hungary), and grew up in the vibrant musical world that the Viennese enjoyed. He wrote a sonata, a trio, and a ballet-pantomime called *Der Schneemann* (The Snowman) before he was 13 years old, and for his astonishing musical gifts he received the praise of numerous musical luminaries of the era: conductors Bruno Walter, Arthur Nikisch, and Felix Weingartner, composers Richard Strauss, Gustav Mahler, Engelbert Humperdinck, and Giacomo Puccini, and pianist Artur Schnabel.[35] Korngold studied two years with composer Alexander von Zemlinsky, who

Figure 7.2 Erich Wolfgang Korngold

taught him piano and composition, but there was little else that his instructors could teach him. He had perfect pitch, excellent piano technique, and could compose in seemingly any musical style. He could thank his father, the Viennese music critic Dr. Julius Korngold, for his musical upbringing, although Dr. Korngold never approved of his son's decision to work in films.[36]

In some ways it is curious that Korngold came to Hollywood at all. Unlike in Europe, independent composers of concert music have not traditionally done well in Hollywood, nor have they had the steadfast support of film producers and directors that might result in a more refined product. Korngold was by no means the only prominent composer to write a film score; during the 1930s, George Antheil, Virgil Thomson, and Aaron Copland all did so. But his enthusiasm, wit, and affability, as well as his international reputation, set him apart. Korngold had at first expressed great reluctance to join the industry, yet when he saw film music as something akin to writing for opera, he saw an artistic purpose as well as a financial one. In 1934, Warner Brothers arranged with Viennese impresario Max Reinhardt to direct the Shakespearean drama, *A Midsummer Night's Dream*, and Reinhardt insisted on hiring Korngold, who had conducted several operettas to great acclaim, including Johann Strauss Jr.'s *Die Fledermaus* and Jacques Offenbach's

La Belle Hélène. Once Korngold finally agreed to do the music for the picture, he became fascinated with the industry, to Hollywood's great fortune.

Whereas Steiner came from the world of musical comedy and operetta, Korngold came from the world of opera. He had already written four operas before his arrival in America: *Der Ring von Polykrates* (The Ring of Polycrates), *Violanta*, *Die tote Stadt* (The Dead City), and *Das Wunder der Heliane* (The Wonder of Heliane), all of which were well-received in Europe. As Korngold stated, "Never have I differentiated between my music for the films and that for the operas and concert pieces. Just as I do for the operatic stage, I try to invent for the motion picture dramatically melodious music with symphonic development and variation of the themes."[37] His astounding talent beguiled Hollywood, and Warner Brothers allowed him a flexibility that virtually no other composer, including Steiner, enjoyed: to choose the films he wanted to work on, to have complete control over the final product, and even to have ownership over his own music. It is testament to the studio's respect for Korngold that it gave him this almost dangerous degree of freedom, but it gave the studio something it desperately wanted: international respectability.

This point is significant. Up until this time, Hollywood studios had employed hundreds of songwriters and composers, but no one of the stature of Korngold. Both the artistic challenge that Korngold saw in films, along with his desire to escape the growing political turmoil in Europe, meant that at last Hollywood could claim a composer whom Europeans greatly admired. The allure of the Old World, and the fascination with European sophistication, were common among the movie colony elite, who lived a lifestyle patterned after the European nobility, with landed estates and servants.[38] Studios rushed to hire the best actors from Europe they could find, such as Laurence Olivier, David Niven, and Marlene Dietrich, as well as noted directors as diverse in style as Fritz Lang, Ernst Lubitsch, and Michael Curtiz. Outsiders might condemn the crass materialism that Hollywood represented, but they were less likely to scoff at the artistic achievements of highly talented Europeans. Korngold was as important to Warner Brothers for what he represented as for what he achieved, and the longer he stayed in Hollywood, the more Hollywood could claim him as one of its own.

During the 1930s, Warner Brothers created a series of lavishly produced costume dramas, and Korngold's music was perfectly suited to them. Among the pictures he wrote music for were *Captain Blood* and *The Adventures of Robin Hood*, both of which starred one of the decade's most popular actors, Errol Flynn. Significantly, these pictures were for a general audience, which enabled children as well as adults to hear a symphonic score. Korngold's lush, orchestral writing recalled the era of Strauss, Puccini, and Mahler, and he lent a classical aura to film scores that perfectly complemented their historical character.

Captain Blood, released in 1936, was one of the first films for which Korngold wrote the music. Based on a famous novel by Rafael Sabatini, the narrative revolves around a British surgeon who is falsely condemned for aiding rebels, and he escapes to become a pirate, Captain Blood (Errol Flynn), in the Caribbean. The composer treated the film like an opera. He used leitmotifs for each of the characters to provide melodic contrast, an operatic technique that Wagner had particularly emphasized. One innovation was to have music play continuously during spoken dialogue, which provided a sense of continuity throughout the film. Although Steiner introduced underscoring, Korngold took it a step further in never allowing the music to dominate the dialogue. Since he was allowed only three weeks to write the score, Korngold worked closely with an orchestrator who had learned the craft with Steiner, Hugo Friedhofer. Friedhofer was ideally suited for the task, and had a thorough knowledge of Wagner, Strauss, and Mahler—some of the very role models for Korngold. The two continued to work together on almost all of Korngold's films.[39]

The score for *The Adventures of Robin Hood*, released in 1938, used similar techniques. The narrative takes place in 1191, when King Richard the Lion-Heart (Ian Hunter) leaves to join the Crusades. The king's wicked brother, Prince John (Claude Rains), seizes his chance and takes over the throne with the help of Sir Guy of Gisbourne (Basil Rathbone). As they proceed to oppress the common folk, Sir Robin of Locksley, or Robin Hood (Errol Flynn), assembles a band of "merry thieves" to rob from the rich in order to help out the poor. He treats all women with courtesy, including the Lady Marian (Olivia de Havilland), with whom he falls in love. The story provided Korngold a rich tapestry to apply his operatic skills.

Operatic techniques are common throughout the film. The music is constantly present and takes up 73 minutes out of 102 minutes, or about three-fourths of the film's length. Each major character has a leitmotif: "Robin Hood's theme," "Little John's theme," and so on, as well as leitmotifs for particular situations or locations, such as a love theme or an "England theme." Korngold excelled in combining these themes together to create a broader textual score, and he paid special attention to dramatic phrasing, never dominating the action but always accenting it. Rather than constantly seeking to mimic the action, as Steiner would have done, he frequently employed silence for dramatic impact.[40]

A key aspect of Korngold's technique was to integrate diegetic music, or source music, in his scores. When a drummer beats out a rhythm, it becomes part of the symphonic score rather than letting it stand on its own; when trumpets blare, or one of the "merry thieves" plays a lute, the instruments become an integral part of the music in the background, thereby maintaining the pace of the action rather than serving to interrupt it. Korngold deftly employed these techniques in an almost continuous flow of sound, and the music earned him an Academy Award as "the quintessential romantic epic score."[41]

One question, particularly following a renewed interest in Korngold's concert music after his death, concerns the impact that the film industry had on Korngold's career. There is a story, perhaps apocryphal, of Korngold meeting Steiner at the Warner Brothers studio. Steiner declared, "Erich, we've both been working at Warners for ten years now, and during that time, it seems to me, your music has gotten worse whereas mine has gotten better—now why do you suppose that is?" Korngold replied, "That's easy, Steiner: it's because you have been stealing from me and I have been stealing from you!"[42] While his film work naturally paid very well at a time when he would have had few opportunities in Europe with the onset of fascism in Austria and Germany, he occasionally expressed regret that he had ever become a film composer.[43] At first glance this might seem surprising, considering that he was principal composer for only thirteen films, and provided arrangements or contributed melodies to seven others. Yet he seemed at times to want to leave Hollywood behind, as his father had constantly encouraged him to do. The long debate of "art" versus "commerce" almost inevitably came down against Hollywood film music for being primarily commercial in nature, and hence the distrust that people like Korngold's father had for the medium. Nonetheless, like Steiner, Korngold's impact on film music was profound, because he brought the symphonic score to a new level of sophistication.

Alfred Newman

Alfred Newman saw himself more as a conductor than a composer. "Composing is a lonely business," he said. "Conducting is gregarious, you work with anywhere from five to a hundred men, the lights are always on, and there's an excitement to being with talented musicians and making music."[44] This talent served him well ever since he came to Hollywood in 1930 and especially when he became head of the music department for Twentieth Century-Fox in 1940, where he remained for the next two decades. Despite this reluctance to compose, Newman helped shape the symphonic style that Steiner and Korngold had pioneered.

Newman had few of the opportunities that either Steiner or Korngold enjoyed. Born in a working-class family in 1900 in New Haven, Connecticut, only when he showed an inclination to playing the piano did his parents arrange for him to play on a neighbor's instrument. His musical training was unremarkable until the age of nine, when he was able to study composition and piano with Zygmunt (or Sigismond) Stojowski, a Polish composer, pianist, and teacher who immigrated in 1906 to New York and headed the Institute of Musical Art. Stojowski's music showed a strong French influence, since he had studied at the Paris Conservatory with composers Léo Delibes, Camille Saint-Saëns, and Jules Massenet. He was impressed enough with Newman's abilities, despite the young boy's limited education, to arrange for him to have a piano scholarship. Unfortunately, at the age of 12 Newman had to end his musical training because of financial hardship, and he began working in vaudeville theaters.[45]

Figure 7.3 Alfred Newman

Newman's training in the theater, as with Steiner, provided the perfect foundation for his later film work. He became one of the youngest conductors on Broadway, where he worked for 12 years. At the age of 17 he led a theater orchestra for *The George White Scandals*, and he befriended songwriter Irving Berlin, who urged him to come to Hollywood. Berlin was working on a film called *Reaching for the Moon* in 1930, and he mentioned Newman's talents to United Artists studio head Joe Schenck, who also urged the young conductor to come out to the West Coast.[46] Newman proceeded to do in Hollywood what he had done on Broadway for years: to arrange and conduct musical comedies. He soon became a mentor to many musicians, providing work for them or suggesting their names to other studios.

As with Steiner and Korngold, Newman wrote musical themes for specific situations, but unlike them he was less concerned about associating a theme with a particular character. Above all, he tried to create a mood, and unlike Steiner or Korngold his music remained very much in the background. Newman was thus a master at subtle but evocative music. One indicative work is the 1939 film based on Emily Brontë's novel, *Wuthering Heights*. Cathy (Merle Oberon) is from a middle-class family in Yorkshire who falls in love with a gypsy, Heathcliff (Laurence Olivier) with whom she grew up. Newman wrote a theme for a memory that Cathy has of playing with

Heathcliff as children in the countryside. The musical theme returns in several scenes, such as during her agonizing longing for Heathcliff in spite of a different life she has chosen, wondering what kind of life they may have had together. When Heathcliff and Cathy hear dance music at someone's home, the sprightly yet uneasy leitmotif suggests the mixed emotions they feel when seeing other couples dancing together.[47] In each case, Newman was less descriptive of people than of situations, which required an abstract, and hence subtle, form of composition.

Newman used a similar approach with *The Song of Bernadette* in 1943, which earned him an Academy Award. While the award is traditionally no guarantee of quality, it is an indication of the esteem a composer is held by colleagues. This is only surprising when considering the subject matter, which involved the true story of a young woman in the southern French town of Lourdes in the 1850s and her experience of seeing the Virgin in a grotto—not exactly a "typical" Hollywood narrative. It is based on a book by poet Franz Werfel, an Austrian émigré to Los Angeles in the 1930s, and wartime perhaps persuaded studio executives at Twentieth Century-Fox to be more accepting of films with religious themes. Unaccustomed to the genre, Newman at first encountered problems in coming up with appropriate musical material. He then experienced a breakthrough: "I read back over Werfel's book and found that Bernadette had never claimed to have seen anything other than a 'beautiful lady.' I now wrote music I thought would describe this extraordinary experience of a young girl who was neither sophisticated enough nor knowledgeable enough to evaluate it as anything more than a lovely vision."[48] In imagining the "gusts of wind and the rustling bushes" that Bernadette experienced in seeing her vision, Newman was trying to evoke a mood: not to describe Bernadette as such but the emotional response to her experience.

Newman used other techniques in the film. The leitmotif he wrote for Bernadette's encounter with the Virgin is illustrative. When she speaks to Mary, the theme echoes slightly in the background, and becomes in essence the "Bernadette theme," although it is scarcely employed in the way Steiner or Korngold would have done with constant repetitions in almost Wagnerian fashion. The rising first half of the theme suggests Mary's presence, while the descending second half of the theme evokes the earthly Bernadette's response. Elsewhere in the film there is source music, such as church bells and organ, which Newman integrates into the symphonic score. But he does not allow the cliché of a standard hymn or liturgical work to take precedence; only at the end of the film, when skeptical townspeople are finally swayed by her vision, does one hear "Ave Maria" sung by a church choir.

Newman's contributions as a conductor and composer were many and varied. Though a reluctant composer, he took his craft seriously. He does not appear to have agonized over his position as a film composer as Korngold later did, although to improve his technique Newman took lessons with Arnold Schoenberg when the composer moved to Los Angeles, and studied privately with other composers as well. There was scarcely a film genre in which Newman did not compose, and he earned the admiration of other film composers and studio musicians, many of whose careers he helped further. The subtlety that characterized his scores belied the extraordinary degree of influence he had over his colleagues and successors, and his ability to write music in almost any style remained one of his most enviable qualities.

Disney Animation

The worlds of "highbrow" and "lowbrow" came together in creative ways in animation. Whereas in nonanimated features, music was almost always determined at the end of the production, music in animation often determined the action itself. Walt Disney was fascinated in juxtaposing the two fields of high and low art. Like many of his colleagues in the film industry, he often turned to classical music to symbolize the highbrow. Cartoons have enabled millions of people to hear classical music, primarily works by eighteenth- and nineteenth-century European composers, on a scale inconceivable in variety theaters or concert halls. Much of this music appeared in the form of single movements or short, orchestral passages, but in some cases entire works were featured. Both Walt Disney Studios and Warner Brothers experimented extensively with different types of music in animation. Cartoons, which quickly became much loved among American audiences and indeed around the world, offered the perfect format for popularizing the classics.

Disney's first venture in using sound with animated shorts was *Steamboat Willie*. It came out in 1928, two years after the advent of sound in motion pictures. The highlight of the feature is the creation of an orchestra of animals on a steamboat, with Mickey Mouse and his friends performing on improvised instruments: the animals themselves. The film score consisted primarily of two songs, "Turkey in the Straw" and "Steamboat Bill."[49] The orchestration was no afterthought; Disney was very specific about what he wanted the orchestra to play on the accompanying soundtrack. On the main title sheet describing the layout of the cartoon, he wrote: "Orchestra starts playing opening verses of 'Steamboat Bill,' as soon as title flashes on. The orchestration can be so arrainged [*sic*] that many variations may be included before the title fades out. It would be best if the music was arrainged so that the end of a verse would end at the end of the title . . . and a new verse start at [the] beginning of the first scene."[50]

Disney even went to great lengths to secure top musicians. As he explained in a letter to his brother and business partner Roy Disney, begging him to wire more money: "They get ten dollars an hour for this work. It will take three hours to do it, plus the time the effect men put in today." He eventually paid between $5,000 and $10,000 solely to record the music.[51] Fortunately for

Disney, the film, which premiered on November 18, 1928 in New York's Colony Theater, was "an instant success."[52] Thousands not only laughed at the antics of a small mouse and his comrades, but heard the recording of an orchestra that performed popular songs on film.

With this early success providing both psychological and financial stimulus, Disney and his colleagues began pioneering the use of classical music in animation. Beginning with the series titled the "Silly Symphonies," his animators allowed their imaginations free reign in using the classics, jazz, and folk music to apply to humorous scenes or situations. Disney was fortunate in being able to persuade Carl Stalling, a composer and conductor with whom he had worked in Kansas City, to move out to Hollywood. Stalling, born in 1891, had already arranged music and played the organ for silent movies, as well as conducted theater orchestras.[53] After writing music for several short features, he discussed with Disney the different ways in which music might be the *determining* factor in a cartoon series. Out of these discussions arose the Silly Symphonies.[54]

A short feature produced in 1929, called *The Skeleton Dance*, was the first of the series, and it represented a genuinely innovative use of the medium. Four skeletons emerge from their graves at midnight, and dance to a variety of music, some of it borrowed from Grieg's "March of the Dwarfs."[55] The skeletons even fashion their own instruments, such as the use of a fellow skeleton for a xylophone, or a cat's tail for a violin (to the clear annoyance of the cat). At dawn, the skeletons race back to their graves. The unusual choice of a graveyard for the film's setting was apparently Stalling's, who recalled that "since I was a kid I wanted to see real skeletons dancing and had always enjoyed seeing skeleton-dancing acts in vaudeville."[56] Using the music of Grieg, Stalling could make that dream a reality, although one might hesitate to think what Grieg would have thought of the idea.

Ironically, *The Skeleton Dance* was so far removed from Disney's previous work that some theater owners were reluctant to show it. Disney managed to persuade the owner of Los Angeles's Carthay Circle Theater to screen the short. The reviews were excellent, and after this remarkable West Coast debut, the feature had a successful run in New York, which firmly established the series nationwide.[57] With titles such as *Babes in the Woods*, *Lullaby Land*, *Old King Cole*, and *Spring*, youngsters and oldsters alike delighted in the antics of characters which themselves often reveled to the sounds of an orchestra. Either implicitly or explicitly, audiences made the association of classical music with humor, something distinctly unusual in the concert hall. The cartoons, which Disney no longer drew but rather produced and provided creative input, soon earned him and his animators critical acclaim. Beginning in 1932 with *Flowers and Trees*, which featured music by Mendelssohn and Schubert, Disney Studios eventually won a series of Academy Awards in the newly created category, "Short Subjects: Cartoons."[58]

The combination of classical music with other forms, such as jazz or folk music, produced some particularly entertaining results. In some ways there was a natural juxtaposition for comedic effect; as one writer has noted, classical music "connotes what some might refer to as 'highbrow' music, music that stands in opposition to the more popular forms of the art, whether songs, dance tunes, [or] jazz."[59] An attempt to literally bridge the gap between classical music and jazz occurs in the 1935 Silly Symphony, *Music Land*. In this cartoon, anthropomorphized musical instruments "speak" by the tones from their instruments. A narrative unfolds concerning the prince of the Isle of Jazz, who falls in love with the daughter of the Queen of the Land of Symphony, a country primarily of string instruments surrounded by a Sea of Discord. In one scene, the enamored saxophone writes a note to his violin ladylove, literally in musical notes, and when the two are barred from seeing each other, a musical war between the two countries breaks out. The Isle of Jazz blows jazz tunes at the Land of Symphony, which retaliates with Wagner's *Ride of the Valkyries*.[60] All ends happily, however, when the King of the Isle of Jazz falls in love with the Queen of the Land of Symphony, and the two couples are finally wed. Both forms of music are thereby united in syncretism, and a Bridge of Harmony literally brings the two kingdoms together. Such contrasts of the presumably "high" culture of classical music and the "low" culture of jazz provided Disney's cartoonists with almost endless possibilities for humor.

The Silly Symphonies were far from the studio's only applications of classical music. This same juxtaposition of musical styles was used in several of the Mickey Mouse cartoons. In the 1929 cartoon *The Opry House*, Mickey is the leader of a small-town vaudeville show, but the music he performs is far from the usual variety fare. At the piano he plays various renditions of classical works, such as Rachmaninoff's Prelude in C-sharp Minor.[61] Meanwhile, an ill-rehearsed orchestra of farm animals attempts to get through selections from *Carmen*. As the scene becomes increasingly chaotic, Mickey finds his stool and piano swaying in time to the music, and as the stool sinks lower, musical tones descend the scale.[62] In presenting classical works in a humorous way and in a fundamentally American setting, a theater akin to the Grand Old Opry in Nashville, Tennessee, the effect is frankly astonishing; pieces of "high" culture, drawn from the categories of classical music and opera, no longer seem so formidable in a cartoon feature.

Disney put this interplay of "high" and "low" culture to further use in 1935 in the first Mickey Mouse cartoon to appear in Technicolor, *The Band Concert*. As with *The Opry House*, Mickey is the director of an orchestra in a small, Midwestern town, conducting a series of popular classics for an appreciative audience. When the band launches into Rossini's *William Tell* Overture, however, chaos ensues, a common enough theme in Disney cartoons. Donald Duck attempts to get the orchestra to join him in a spirited version of "Turkey in the Straw," while a persistent bee distracts both conductor and orchestra. Finally, a tornado touches down and spins up Mickey and his ensemble, but the determined conductor continues, and finishes, the performance.[63] Much as in *Music Land* and *The Opry House*, Disney presents two kinds of music, in this case folk and classical, and through juxtaposing them makes the point of "sending up" high art with the democratizing impact of folk songs.

Each of these features provided a basis for perhaps Disney's foremost experiment in classical music, the feature-length film produced in 1940, *Fantasia*. Since classical music inspired the animation, the film was in some ways a continuation of the Silly Symphonies. As one historian stated, the "first thing to be decided upon was the program of music that would form the basis of this film."[64] But it was on a far grander scale, as Disney himself duly noted: "We are picturing music. This music is not serving as background to a picture."[65] And what music! Bach's Toccata and Fugue in D Minor, Tchaikovsky's *Nutcracker Suite*, Stravinsky's *Rite of Spring*, Beethoven's Sixth Symphony ("Pastoral"), the "Dance of the Hours" from Ponchielli's opera, *La Giocanda*, Mussorgsky's *Night on Bald Mountain*, and Schubert's *Ave Maria*. With "the exception of the Stravinsky piece, all of the final selections for *Fantasia* fell into the category of popular classics—tunes with which many people would be familiar."[66]

The conductor of the music was already legendary. Leopold Stokowski became deeply involved in the *Fantasia* project once Disney asked him to participate, and the choice of music selections grew under his leadership. Stokowski had shown far more interest in Hollywood than did most of his fellow conductors, and he had already appeared in several Hollywood films prior to his involvement with *Fantasia*. One picture was *100 Men and a Girl*, which Universal released in 1937. It starred the 15-year old singer Deanna Durbin, and Stokowski conducted a range of works we could also call popular classics, among them the "Rakoczky March" by Berlioz, the Scherzo from Beethoven's Second Symphony, and the Prelude to Act II of Wagner's *Lohengrin*. Stokowski also included two of his own arrangements: Bach's Toccata and Fugue in D Minor (which later reappeared in Disney's *Fantasia*) and Liszt's second *Hungarian Rhapsody*. Unlike *Fantasia*, not every piece appears in its entirety—anywhere from fifteen seconds to almost six minutes of each classical piece is performed—but the film does present both classical and popular music, and the famed conductor plays (appropriately) a conductor of a symphony orchestra.[67] Stokowski, who appeared the same year with the Philadelphia Orchestra in *The Big Broadcast of 1937*, was making a statement: that while the film musical might be a popular art, it does offer distinct possibilities for art music.[68]

Fantasia proved to be an extraordinary opportunity for Stokowski's "instrument," the Philadelphia Orchestra. It reached far more people through the film than it possibly could have from concert performances. While Stokowski used studio musicians for one of the film's main scenes, the "Sorcerer's Apprentice," he used his own orchestra for the rest of the score. Nor was the orchestra merely a backdrop for the film, but at times became the primary subject in several scenes, such as in explaining the various instruments that made up the ensemble.

While not all segments of *Fantasia* are of equal quality, several stand out: "The Sorcerer's Apprentice," the "Nutcracker Suite," and "Dance of the Hours." The central scene of the film is "The Sorcerer's Apprentice," which Disney had finished first and eventually joined with other scenes for a full-length feature. The story presents Mickey Mouse as an assistant to a wizard. When the sorcerer is away, the assistant puts on his master's hat to try out his prowess as a magician. He sets a broom to the task of filling a large vat with water, and promptly falls asleep, leaving the broom to do the work. After disaster strikes and the room is flooded with water, the master returns to set everything straight. The sleep sequence is an ironic play on the image of conductor; Mickey dreams that he is capable of controlling the planets and stars with dramatic flourishes of his hands, and the music crashes forth with every one of his movements. In this sense, the scene is reminiscent of *The Band Concert*, with its swirling passages of sound and image, as well as for its rather chaotic representation of the conductor.

By contrast, "Nutcracker Suite," a work for ballet, presents magical effects in an entirely different way. Dragonfly sprites dance about groups of flowers, and as they touch the flowers with their wands, small droplets of dew shine forth. Buds of flowers open up, other fairies awaken, and the scene is one of beautiful splendor to Tchaikovsky's music. The effect is light and dazzling. Disney seems to have been fascinated with the scene, for he continued to use a sprite with a magic wand in the opening credits of his Sunday evening television program, "Walt Disney's Wonderful World of Color," long afterwards.[69]

Whereas the effect in "Nutcracker Suite" borders on the magical, "Dance of the Hours" is pure comic relief. A group of hippos, elephants, alligators, and ostriches, some dressed in scant tutus, pirouette about the stage, in a delightful take on ballerinas. The supposedly awkward rhinos swing themselves around with the greatest of ease, their every movement grace itself. Disney achieves two main, musical objectives: first, to present operatic music as a background to an animated feature; and second, to introduce viewers, particularly children, to the ballet by presenting a parody of it.

Fantasia was an orchestral concert on film, complete with an intermission—something rare in movies up to that time. It seems ironic, then, that it was not a success when it was first released. In part this was due to timing, since the picture came out during World War, but it may also have been that the film was simply too advanced for its era. Certainly, the soundtrack was; it consisted of a multichannel, 35 mm film called "Fantasound," at least 15 years before stereo had become standard in the recording industry. Unfortunately, most theaters were not equipped for this kind of soundtrack, so the technical achievements in sound were lost to many audiences at the time. Despite its disappointing debut, the film eventually became a cult classic, earning the studio an estimated $2 million per year from "reissue revenue" alone.[70] While some scenes in the film are arguably more effective than others, Disney still saw *Fantasia* as "what the future of this medium may well turn out to be."[71]

Disney's films presented classical music to children and adults alike, not only in North America but also in Europe and Asia. Italians called the mouse "Topolino" and the Japanese called him "Miki Kuchi."[72] The conductor Arturo Toscanini was apparently so taken with *The Band Concert* that he saw it at least six times and invited Disney to visit him in Italy. The Broadway lyricist Jerome Kern exclaimed: Disney "has made use of music as language. In the synchronization of humorous episodes with humorous music, he has unquestionably given us the outstanding contribution of our time."[73] The comment, which was made before Disney commenced with his series of full-length features, is an amazing accolade for someone whose cartoons rarely lasted longer than eight minutes. By blending different forms of music, Disney made innovative contributions to the medium of animation, a form perfectly adapted to "picturing music."

Not everyone has lauded Disney's efforts. The critic Richard Schickel, of *Time* magazine, was particularly harsh, depicting Disney as a member of the "lumpen bourgeoisie," who aspired to high culture of which he was largely ignorant. Disney, he wrote, "had no real musical knowledge or, indeed, standards, as his cheerful chopping and bowdlerizing of music testifies."[74] A veritable "anti-Disney" industry has since arisen, criticizing him for his stereotyped portrayals of women and minorities, and his looseness with original texts and material on which many Disney cartoons were based, such as *Snow White and the Seven Dwarfs* and *Pinocchio*.

Others, however, have steadfastly defended Disney and his use of classical music. One writer stated that "Disney did not have pretensions toward high culture. Nor did he claim any extensive knowledge of classical music, though, according to his daughter Diane, he enjoyed it tremendously."[75] This was the attitude of many Americans, who did not necessarily have a great knowledge of classical music, but went to classical music concerts. Through his animated series that gave this music a central role, Disney encouraged his public to enjoy, or at least listen to, the very works that he did. Whether Disney was showcasing or merely mocking classical music is still a matter of debate. One thing is certain: He *did* use these different forms of music when other cartoonists were more focused on the visual, and this frequent interaction between different musical styles made the films truly revolutionary.

Warner Brothers' Animation

Disney Studios' main competitor, Warner Brothers, also sought to use classical music in its own features. Warner Brothers was a pioneer in sound pictures and had large cash reserves since the enormous commercial success of *The Jazz Singer*. The head of Warner Brothers' animation, Leon Schlesinger, could thus lure several key animators away, some of whom had been with Disney virtually since his start in Hollywood. Among these were Charlie Thorson, Hugh Harman, and Rudolf Ising, as well as Disney's original music collaborator, Carl Stalling.[76] With the creation of the series titled "Looney Tunes" in 1930 by Harman and Ising, Warner Brothers followed Disney by integrating both popular and classical music in its features.

Unlike the Silly Symphonies, however, the first subjects for the Looney Tunes series arose not out of the classics but rather vaudeville. Vaudevillian skits and gimmicks, such as topical references, ethnic jokes, and physical gags, were all reformulated for a new generation. "Vaudeville and its performance traditions," writes one film scholar, "were a temporary solution to the problem of how to use sound and how sound might change the structure of cartoons."[77] The Looney Tunes series began with a black ink figure as its first main character, Bosko. Bosko spoke a southern dialect, was vaguely suggestive of a small, black boy, and appeared in a variety of features in which music was a prominent part. In the very first Looney Tune, *Sinkin' in the Bathtub*, produced in 1930, the animators "followed the pattern established by Walt Disney in *Steamboat Willie* (1928), showcasing music and letting songs dictate the development of the cartoon."[78] Bosko plays around to music in a bathtub, and the music is derived from a popular song of the period. In the 1930 short *Congo Jazz*, Bosko learns about the foundations of jazz by going to an African jungle. He begins making music with the animals, and they use a variety of objects in the jungle for their instruments.[79] The cartoon is really a throwback to blackface minstrelsy, one of the most common forms of vaudeville.

This vaudevillian basis gradually gave way to more classically oriented fare. Following its rival's experiment with classical music in *Fantasia*, Warner Brothers came out in 1941 with a cartoon in a similar vein: *Rhapsody in Rivets*. To the music of Liszt's second *Hungarian Rhapsody*, a lion as a conductor and foreman urges on his crew of a symphonic orchestra, building the "Umpire State" skyscraper. An octopus lays down bricks in time to the 32nd notes, and brushes cement over the bricks during the *glissandro*. A kind of musical extravaganza, it has been referred to as "a working class *Fantasia*."[80] The studio followed this feature two years later with *Pigs in a Polka*, which parodied Disney's Three Little Pigs, and is set entirely to Brahms's *Hungarian Dances*. At the same time, the feature presents "new forms of eccentrically timed, stop-and-start action that were noticeably nonnaturalistic and pointedly anti-Disney."[81] Each of these cartoons received Oscar nominations—something that only the Disney studio had achieved in the world of animation. Warner Brothers, like Disney, had found the perfect theme for its particular brand of humor: cartoon characters sending up the world of "high" culture. The series provided strong competition; one critic even stated that the Looney Tunes "surpassed Disney's Silly Symphonies to become the number-one short subject during the war years."[82]

Another rival to Disney consisted of Warner Brothers' Merrie Melodies series, which began in 1931. In these cartoons, classical music was not the focus but provided comic background for popular songs. The animated shorts in fact were vehicles to market the studio's catalogue of popular songs, since in its original contract, the studio asserted that each cartoon would include "a performance of at least one complete chorus of a Warner-owned tune."[83] The series did not exist entirely of songs, however; occasionally there was a juxtaposition with classical, jazz, and folk songs as well. For example, in a 1941 Porky Pig feature, titled *Notes to You*, for which Carl Stalling both arranged and conducted the music, a musical cat sets up his notes on a music stand and tries to sing Rossini's "Figaro" theme at night, to the annoyance of Porky. But he also conducts an orchestra on the radio, singing a series of hits, such as "When Irish Eyes are Smiling," "Jeepers Creepers," and "Farewell to Thee." He even does a fair rendition of Donizetti's Sextette from *Lucia di Lammermoor*. In this blending of musical styles, audiences heard opera alongside popular songs, like a true variety show.[84]

With the creation of Bugs Bunny, Warner Brothers had found the perfect personality with which to blend classical music and humor. The indomitable Bugs appeared in numerous features, often engaged in upsetting the serious work of high art. One early example was the 1943 animated short, *A Corny Concerto*, which consists of two cartoons set to the music of Johann Strauss Jr. It begins in "Corny-gie Hall," with Elmer Fudd introducing the music audiences will hear, with Tchaikovsky's Piano Concerto No. 1 playing in the background. The first features Elmer Fudd, gun in hand and dog in tow, hunting for rabbit to the tune of Strauss's *Tales from the Vienna Woods*. Bugs evades all of Elmer's efforts to shoot him, and even enlists the help of the dog. When Bugs appears shot, the hunting dog cries in tune to the melody. In the next short, three white ducklings are swimming gracefully with their mother to the *Blue Danube* waltz. A black duckling tries to join them, but the mother swan quickly pushes him out. When a vulture appears and grabs all three of the ducklings, the black duckling turns into a B-52 bomber (this is wartime) and downs the vulture. When the black duckling returns the other ducklings to the mother, the group of four swims away to the closing refrain of the waltz. Warner Brothers followed up this feature in 1946 with the *Rhapsody Rabbit*. In this feature, Bugs Bunny attempts to get through a performance of Liszt's second *Hungarian Rhapsody* at a grand piano, grabbing up keys during one passage and laying them all down in another. The Liszt work was a favorite of Warner Brothers' head of animation, Friz Freleng, and the film critic James Agee wrote in *The Nation* that "[t]he funniest thing I have seen since the decline of sociological dancing is 'Rhapsody Rabbit.' "[85]

It was only a notion of things to come. In the 1949 feature called *Long-Haired Hare*, a tenor, "Giovanni Jones," is practicing for a concert at the Hollywood Bowl. While the singer is going through an aria ("Largo al factotum") from Rossini's *Barber of Seville*, Bugs Bunny happily plucks out folk tunes on a banjo. After several altercations, including the tenor's destruction of the banjo, Bugs aims to get even. He upsets the evening performance at the Bowl, in a variety of ways. In one scene, he bangs on the hard shell; hearing it resonate, Bugs comments: "Acoustically perfect!" When the orchestra is performing Wagner's *Ride of the Valkyries* and the tenor is about to go on again, Bugs offers him a lighted dynamite stick in place of a pen to sign his autograph. The climax comes when Bugs appears on stage dressed as Leopold Stokowski, while musicians excitedly whisper, "Leopold! Leopold!" Bugs calls on the tenor to display some of his impressive range, and in forcing him to hit a high tone, the Hollywood Bowl comes crashing down on him. Bugs ends by plucking away on a new banjo, symbolizing the triumph of popular music over high art.[86] Warner Brothers' animators went beyond Disney by not only juxtaposing different musical styles but also clearly declaring popular music (or at the very least, songs from Warner Brothers' catalogue), the winner. With the destruction of both the tenor and the Hollywood Bowl, Bugs is free to engage in his own music, no longer repressed by the supposedly elitist, and indeed foreign, world that the tenor represents. Classical music appears more as whipping boy in cartoons that were arguably more violent and hard-edged than Disney's efforts. If you wanted animation with punch, you went to Warner Brothers. Nonetheless, whether the animators of these studios were praising or condemning classical music, they at least used it frequently as a backdrop for the action in cartoons, and at times that music could be at the forefront of the action itself.

One reason why these studios used classical music so freely is that they did not have to pay copyright costs. Works by eighteenth- and nineteenth-century European composers were in the public domain, and the studio had only to hire musicians to perform the music, with perhaps a staff composer to arrange or add orchestration. It was quite a different matter with controlling the copyright for popular songs and other contemporary music, for which the studios either hired songwriters or purchased rights to the material. Warner Brothers continually drew upon its catalog of popular songs, and the American Society of Composers and Artists (ASCAP) went along with the songs' use in films. When Disney used the music of twentieth-century composer Igor Stravinsky, he paid him a generous sum, but this kind of arrangement with modern composers was the exception.[87] The works of long-dead composers were happily brought to life on the silver screen, and Disney and Warner Brothers became animation's foremost "popularizers" of classical music.

Conclusion

Music has been a critical aspect of films since the early days of the silent era. Orchestras or keyboard players from the beginning served an important function by enhancing the action on the screen. The development of talkies transformed the role of music in films, greatly increasing the variety of works that composers and arrangers used, and enabling composers to develop innovative and experimental techniques to make film music a true art. Through animated and nonanimated features alike, audiences could hear orchestral arrangements without the benefit of actually having an orchestra in the theater. Although he was exaggerating the point, Harry Warner, one of the founders of Warner Brothers, stated a clear advantage of sound in films: "From now on we can give every small town in America, and every moviehouse, its own 110-piece orchestra."[88]

Yet despite their important contributions to motion pictures, film composers have long had to fight for respectability in their profession as composers. A debate has long raged concerning the role of film music as an art form and hence its role in American music. Composers of art music, or "concert music," have traditionally looked down on film music and film composers.[89] One reason may be that composers in America who considered themselves primarily as creators of art music have not tended to fare well in the movie industry, the example of Korngold notwithstanding. Virgil Thomson, Aaron Copland, and Ernst Krenek all sought to experiment with the new medium by providing a different "sound" than the usual orchestral effects that were then common. But these composers were attempting to achieve something that was simply incompatible with most commercial films, for they sought to bring "art music," or music less adaptable to popular taste, to a medium that was primarily intended for a large audience.[90] Not surprisingly, they composed but a handful of film scores. An executive for Paramount Studios, Boris Morros, tried to get both Arnold Schoenberg and Igor Stravinsky, both of whom lived in Los Angeles, to write film scores during the late 1930s. They laid down terms so onerous that the studio refused to hire them.[91] One lesson which Hollywood studios quickly learned was that the medium of film, in part because of its strongly commercial nature, was not a proper format for art music composers not willing to compromise their art.

The composer George Antheil, who wrote both film and art music, pondered why European composers of art music were loved at the same time that Hollywood film composers were denigrated. "Listening, as I often do, to new and highly touted European composers . . . we here in Hollywood could do such a piece in an afternoon and call it a motion-picture cue and think nothing more about it."[92] However, music for the movies has still received widespread condescension by "serious" composers, despite the fact that a growing number of composers who have worked primarily in films have also written a considerable body of work for the concert hall: not only Erich Korngold and David Raksin, but also Miklós Rózsa, André Previn, Bernard Herrmann, and Franz Waxman, to name only a few.[93]

This rivalry between film and art composers is not merely due to snobbishness. The pianist and composer Oscar Levant referred to film scores from the early period of Hollywood, roughly 1926 to 1940, as either "generic" or "derivative." If generic, it was intended to sound much like other film music; if derivative, it was meant simply to offer a backdrop to the action on the screen. What united much of this music is that it tended to be imbued with a strong, nineteenth-century Romanticism, in part because many early film composers admired what Wagner had done for opera: to present lush scores as a background to the drama. Unlike Wagner, however, that music had to remain in the background.

Despite such concerns, film composers contributed to the music culture of Los Angeles both inside and outside the studio. In the studio system, composers and arrangers learned their craft by working closely with other composers, and so music directors were often mentors to younger musicians. David Raksin, who wrote the music for the 1944 *film noir* classic, *Laura*, learned film scoring from both Steiner and Newman, the latter of whom had also assigned Raksin to write the music for *Laura*.[94] Korngold, whose concert works were performed in Los Angeles, put his talent to local use. When one of the leading rabbis in Los Angeles, Jacob Sonderling, asked Korngold to write liturgical music, Korngold, though not a practicing Jew, agreed. He composed two works, *A Passover Psalm*, Op. 30 and *Prayer*, Op. 32, and he conducted the world premiere of *A Passover Psalm* at the Hollywood Bowl in June 1945.[95] Other film composers, such as Franz Waxman, took part in local concerts or organized music festivals, as Waxman did in the 1950s and 1960s.

Music for animation became an art form following the conversion to sound. Both animated shorts and features often contained classical music, either in the relatively serious manner of Disney's *Fantasia* or in the uproarious comedy of Warner Brothers' *Long-Haired Hare*. These studios juxtaposed the classics with popular or folk tunes to comic effect, thereby demonstrating the differences between "highbrow" and "lowbrow" forms but also uniting them in a single feature, as if to demonstrate that they did not have to exist separately. MGM continued the path that Disney and Warner Brothers had laid out with its "Tom and Jerry" series, several of which contained excerpts of classical music or which were even based on classical themes.[96] That these cartoons reached millions of children as well as adults suggests the powerful message that animated features could deliver. Cartoons, after all, were not just fun and games.

The film studios provided highly lucrative employment to those willing to play by their rules. Each year, the music departments of these studios required hundreds of musicians for performing, arranging, editing, and even appearing in films. Composers wrote the melodies and often worked with arrangers to write the orchestration, which provided a means for younger composers to learn the trade. Those who began their careers as orchestrators, such as Hugo Friedhofer and Adolf Deutsch, could thus hone and perfect their skills in the community of musicians that each studio maintained—a community that all but disappeared with the demise of the studio system in the 1960s. During Hollywood's Golden Age, unprecedented opportunities arose for musicians in the region to ply their talents. With the widespread distribution of films, the work of these composers, arrangers, and performers reached millions of men, women, and children in theaters around the country. As a result, music for motion pictures, long an important part of Los Angeles's music culture, became vital to American culture.

Epilogue

Two features characterized Los Angeles's music culture: diversity and decentralization. I have examined diversity on several levels: gender, age, class, and ethnicity, both in terms of performers and audiences. Whether at indoor or outdoor theaters, in schools, or from the media of recording, radio, and film, Angelenos had access to a rich variety of music. Similarly, just as Los Angeles County was highly decentralized, so was its music culture. Despite the importance of the central city, cultural institutions far from downtown played a vital role in the production, performance, and teaching of music. I thus suggest that an understanding of the region's music helps us understand the identity of that region; through the arts we have a window into what it meant to men, women, and children to live in Los Angeles.

Women long had a presence in Los Angeles's music culture. They took part as performers, organizers, teachers, and philanthropists. That the majority of musicians in Los Angeles by 1890 were women reflects the extraordinary appeal the region offered, and the founding of the Woman's Symphony Orchestra in 1893, possibly the first of its kind in the country, attests to the presence of women musicians of talent and interest in forming orchestral institutions. They also took part in the growing tradition of community choruses, such as the Hollywood Community Chorus that Artie Mason Carter led. They appeared as leading singers and dancers in two of the major pageants of Los Angeles, the Mission Play and the Ramona Pageant, and they comprised almost half of the performers of one of the most popular troupes of the San Gabriel Valley, the Mexican Players.

Other avenues in music were open to women of Los Angeles. They founded or cofounded music schools, among them the Los Angeles Conservatory of Music and Arts, the Von Stein Academy of Music, and the Olga Steeb Piano School. A circle of women composers, notably Elinor Remick Warren, Gertrude Ross, and Mary Carr Moore, had their work performed in Los Angeles during a time when women composers received little support elsewhere. The founding of the Hollywood Bowl owed much to the dedication of at least two women, Christine Wetherill Stevenson and Carter. Their roles as philanthropist and fundraiser, respectively, helped assure the financial solvency of what was an experimental venture in the community arts, and other women, notably the manager Mrs. Leiland Atherton Irish, oversaw the development of the Bowl over the next several decades.

Women provided many opportunities for young people to study and perform music: a hallmark of the cultural life of Los Angeles. Caroline Severance and the Friday Morning Club founded kindergartens as early as the 1870s, which encouraged children to learn simple harmonies and songs. One of the city's first Supervisors of Music, Kathryn Emilie Stone, was a pioneer in using recordings in class instruction, and Jennie L. Jones founded an Orchestration Department in the Los Angeles Public Schools to enable children of modest means to play on quality instruments. The founding of the Neighborhood Music Settlement by Pearle Odell strengthened this prospect, targeting poor, immigrant children by means of the settlement model and integrating them in a process of Americanization through music. The school, whose teachers included members of the Los Angeles Philharmonic among its ranks, remains the only music school from this period in Los Angeles to survive intact into the modern era. Odell's school was a symbol of the Progressive movement, when the teaching and performance of music became a means of transforming and improving society, and what better place to start than with the children?

There were other ways to instruct young people in music. Youth concerts by the Los Angeles Philharmonic, at the Hollywood Bowl, and in Behymer's Philharmonic Courses enabled children and adolescents to attend art music concerts as well as participate in them. When a statewide committee of elementary, high school, and college music teachers met over a three-year period, they produced the textbook, *Music Education in the Elementary School*, which sought to inspire children in the study of music and thoroughly integrate them in musical and dramatic performances. Its authors did not emphasize solely European art music but also songs from Mexico, China, and other countries, and by studying and performing a country's music, the manual maintained, one could also learn about that country's history. Because of the combined efforts of the hundreds of instructors who taught at elementary school through high school, countless schoolchildren across Los Angeles County before World War II could learn about and perform music.

In terms of ethnicity, while Los Angeles was overwhelmingly Anglo during this period, within that category were many different traditions. Germans, Italians, Jews, and English were among the most prominent, but by the 1920s immigrants came from at least 25 different European countries. We see this diversity in the city's music. The German immigrants who created Turnverein Hall in the 1870s helped establish ensembles for the performance of art music in the 1880s and '90s. Two such immigrants, Adolph Willhartitz and A. J. Stamm, founded the Philharmonic Society in 1888 and the Philharmonic Orchestra in 1892, respectively, and musicians with German surnames made up almost a third of the Philharmonic Orchestra. Both Heinrich von Stein and Olga Steeb were the children of German immigrants.

Other Euro-American groups made their mark. Italians constantly turned out to support visiting opera troupes, such as the Del Conte Opera Company from Milan that gave the first performance of *La Bohème* in North America in

1897, which the comanager of the Los Angeles Theatre and descendant of Italian immigrants, Charles Modini-Wood, arranged. Other Italian performers made their mark, such as coloratura soprano Amelita Galli-Curci and theater conductor Ulderico Marcelli. Jews long saw Los Angeles as a haven, and until the 1950s the largest Jewish community in the region was in Boyle Heights, where the Neighborhood Music Settlement served a predominantly German and Russian Jewish immigrant population. Jews also numbered heavily in the film industry, and became some of the leading film composers of the era, notably Max Steiner and Erich Wolfgang Korngold. The talents of a Shakespearean-trained actor and director, the Englishman Garnet Holme, helped assure the success of the longest-running pageant in American history, the Ramona Pageant.

African Americans contributed in several ways to the city's music. The establishment of a series of churches in the Central Avenue region provided a foundation for black religious music and subsequently gospel. Adding to this musical heritage during the age of the Los Angeles Renaissance was the founding of two music conservatories, which taught primarily European art music to black children, and possibly to Japanese and white children as well. The presence of a large black middle class, a greater proportion of whom were homeowners compared to blacks elsewhere in the country before the Depression, enabled these music schools to prosper. The founders, William Wilkins and John Gray, were leaders of their communities and also active in church music. They created schools that went beyond the mere giving of lessons and student concerts; they sought to create permanent institutions that were examples of cultural and racial pride.

On a quite different level, black musicians from the South helped make Los Angeles an important city for jazz shortly after World War I. Trombonist Kid Ory and the brothers John and Reb Spikes, who owned a music store on Central Avenue, made the first recording of a black New Orleans band with Nordskog Records in 1922. Other musicians made their way out to the West Coast, including Jelly Roll Morton, Paul Howard, Sonny Clay, and Lionel Hampton, who all took part in Central Avenue's vibrant club scene. With the growth of the recording industry, Los Angeles increasingly attracted jazz musicians through the swing era, and Benny Goodman made the major step of recording and performing with black musicians.

Latinos played an important role in Los Angeles music culture. When the guitarist and composer Miguel Arévalo arrived in Los Angeles in 1871, he found a welcoming home for his talents, and gave concerts with Latinos and Anglos alike during his 30-year career in the city. His many performances of Mexican, Spanish, and Italian works were major community events, and he further enjoyed a reputation as a fine teacher. When friends arranged a benefit concert in his honor in 1889, courtesy of the mayor and other leading citizens, Arévalo's colleagues and students performed a diverse repertoire of European and Latino composers. Two students, María Pruneda and Ysabel del Valle, continued this tradition in pedagogy and art music, and Pruneda became one of two music instructors at the newly founded University of Southern California in 1880.

The Lummis cylinder recordings are an indication of the rich Mexican and Indian folk music tradition. Musicians Manuela García, Adalaida Kamp, Rosendo Uruchurtu, and Rosa and Luisa Villa recorded many songs that demonstrated the wide diversity of vocal and instrumental music. The music of southwestern Indian tribes formed an important part of the collection, comprising songs from numerous different sources: the Maricopa, Papago, Pima, Cahuilla, Hupa, Luiseño, Mono, and Pomo.[1] The songs inspired the "Indianist" composer and choral leader Arthur Farwell, among others, to try to write a specifically American music that had few ties to European traditions. Farwell further transcribed the songs by the Latino musicians, which resulted in the publication by Lummis of 14 Californio, Mexican, and Spanish melodies in *Spanish Songs of Old California* in 1923. It was well received, selling over 7,000 copies nationwide.[2] Several of these songs were integral to the music of the Ramona Pageant, and the songbook provided material for the Mexican Players as well. If one wanted to break down the barriers of race and expressive culture that remained in place during the first half of the twentieth century, one means of doing so was in the field of music.

Similarly, when José Arias visited the homes of the Californio families in the 1910s, such as the Sepulvedas and the Lugos, he performed the music of early California and kept that music alive in a process of cultural preservation. He mixed easily with Anglos, as had Arévalo, and he befriended the growing movie colony in Hollywood, where he appeared in films and made several recordings during the 1920s and '30s. Arias's appearances at the Mission Inn in Riverside and with the Ramona Pageant were merely extensions of what he had been doing for years: to play Californian, Mexican, and Spanish music to diverse audiences. The efforts of such troubadours assured that the music would not die.

The media diversity of recording, radio, and film was a distinguishing feature of the city's music culture. While the existence of these media in one city was by no means unique to Los Angeles, their combined role helped make Los Angeles the epicenter of entertainment in the country. The recordings by Andrae Nordskog in the early 1920s demonstrate a legacy of both popular and art music in Los Angeles, because like Lummis he focused on musicians who lived in the region. The dramatic growth of the recording industry during the swing era made Los Angeles a recording center, which had close ties to the film industry. For those ensembles or artists with few recordings, such as the Los Angeles Philharmonic, radio provided the perfect means to reach a wider audience. One indication of the importance of these media was the growth of musicians unions, both white and black, in a city that was distinctly anti-union. The enormous prosperity of the recording, radio, and film industries assured that many local musicians would benefit from lucrative recording and film contracts, and one reason for the amalgamation of the two unions in 1953 was that black musicians could have greater access to these contracts.

The decentralized layout of Los Angeles contributed definitively to making its music culture decentralized as well. Downtown Los Angeles was the location for the city's first theaters, and later the Philharmonic Auditorium, but other major cultural institutions thrived away from downtown. Founders of the Hollywood Bowl saw the site as a distinct alternative to traditional theaters or concert halls, but probably did not foresee its eventual use for jazz and popular music. They envisioned an arts center to serve Angelenos across ethnic and class lines, despite the scant appearance of Mexican Americans and Asian Americans. When Michio Ito came to Los Angeles in 1929, he chose not to live downtown or in Little Tokyo but in Hollywood, where he worked in the film industry and choreographed dances at the Bowl. Some of the region's most successful pageants and community dramas were far from the city of Los Angeles, such as the Mission Play in San Gabriel and the Ramona Pageant in Hemet. The Padua Hills Theatre, the venue for the Mexican Players in Claremont, was located at the far eastern border of Los Angeles County yet still attracted Angelenos elsewhere, among them Walt Disney, with the production's unique combination of music and dance.

Similarly, music schools were not established solely downtown but spread out across Los Angeles County. While both the Los Angeles Conservatory of Music and Arts and the Von Stein Academy were both close to the theater district, other schools soon formed that were away from it. The Olga Steeb Piano School was on Wilshire Boulevard near Hancock Park, and the Neighborhood Music Settlement was in Boyle Heights in East Los Angeles. Both the Wilkins School of Music and the Gray Conservatory were on or near Central Avenue. Music conservatories formed in Pasadena and Long Beach as well, and the relative ease of transport with the electric rail line enabled youth to attend schools that were miles from their places of residence, without the need to be shuttled about by automobile.

Finally, the film studios were also decentralized. The eight major studios were in at least three different locations: Hollywood, Culver City, and the San Fernando Valley. This decentralization was essential in order to have access to large tracts of land for film sets, but it also meant that the studios' music departments would not be in the same, localized area, as the generic term "Hollywood" might imply. Each studio created its own "corporate culture" quite independent of the other studios. The decentralization that defined the film industry thus allowed a degree of individualism and competition that characterized the industry long afterwards.

The model of sacralization that Lawrence Levine and other scholars have used to describe a key transformation in the country's expressive culture has considerable merit in its application to Los Angeles. The founding of orchestras and opera troupes with predominantly European repertoires as symbols of Culture, and the disciplining of audiences in concert halls, all point toward an increasing view of high art as something to be admired from afar, as something to worship. Levine is doubtless correct in defining the "sacred spirit" artists claimed for inspiration, although there is an almost

Hegelian connotation in defining music composition "as a valuable indicator of the spirit of the age."[3] Yet a study of music does help us reveal what people held to be important at the time, and the deification of performing artists or a reverence for art music was as true in Los Angeles by the first half of the twentieth century as it was in New York, Boston, or Chicago.

I suggest, however, that there was a parallel process at work, a desacralization of culture that made examples of high art immediately accessible across race, class, and gender. Music education programs served not merely to foster music appreciation but a true practice of music itself: the ability to play it as well as understand it. Their goal of competent amateurs was an important feature of music education in Los Angeles as well as in California as a whole before World War II, because teachers and administrators saw these programs as fruitful for students' general education as well as a means of Americanization. To attend the Hollywood Bowl in audiences of tens of thousands of people integrated both elements of sacralized and desacralized culture: They came to worship at the shrine of a natural, outdoor theater but with few of the restrictions they would have found in standard concert halls, with the insistence on stylized forms of dress, strict behavioral codes, and hierarchal seating arrangements. On a similar note, pageant masters, trained in high art, sought to resolve the problems of legitimate theater by fostering community drama, which in the form of pageantry integrated music with drama and dance. Community participation was at the heart of removing the barriers between artists and audiences, thereby democratizing, or desacralizing, expressive culture.

In the media of broadcasting and film, we find further evidence of both sacralization and desacralization at work. The Los Angeles Philharmonic performed almost entirely a European repertoire in its radio broadcasts during the late 1920s and '30s, which was true of its concert performances as well. The inherent message was that this repertoire represented the ideal of what orchestral music should sound like. At the same time, however, the stations that broadcast this music did not play solely classical works but an eclectic programming of popular and classical music, in addition to comedy, variety, and informational shows. The inherent message here is that the music of the Los Angeles Philharmonic belonged with all of these cultural forms, and did not stand alone on a pedestal to be worshipped. Quite the contrary: KFI saw no difficulty in programming the orchestra after the *Paul Whiteman Hour* or *Amos 'n' Andy*. This kind of programming demanded that classical music was an integral part of America's cultural heritage, and should not be "ghettoized" to a station that broadcast solely one type of music. Although KECA specialized in classical music, and almost solely so in 1936, the notion of serving the public interest by broadcasting a variety of genres was a common national feature of radio during the Golden Age.

Radio commentator and pianist José Rodriguez strongly upheld this point. Value judgments on the inherent worth of classical music versus popular music provided a disservice to musical expression as well as to the musicians themselves: "The accusation that popular musicians are technically incompetent, that they write popular music *faute de mieux*," he argued, "is clearly an absurdity. From the standpoint of sheer technique, of pure musicality, the popular [musicians] are extremely competent and gifted. If it were possible to measure their comparative abilities, they might not excel their academic colleagues in these elements, but they certainly would not fall below them."[4] Since one of the stations where Rodriguez had worked, KFI, broadcast both classical and popular music, he was speaking from first-hand knowledge; the programming of both kinds of music well served the interests of the station's listeners. "Southern California stations," he wrote in a different context, "have high rank among the nation's broadcasters as purveyors of music in any form. . . . They need for this a clear mandate of their listeners; the listeners who love Beethoven and Franck as well as those who prefer [Irving] Berlin and [bandleader] Abe Lyman."[5] During much of radio's Golden Age, a true democratization of music was possible.

Desacralization formed the very essence of Hollywood film music, which was essential to Los Angeles's music culture. The three major film composers of the 1930s and '40s, Max Steiner, Erich Wolfgang Korngold, and Alfred Newman, were all highly-trained musicians who experienced both worlds of the concert hall and the popular theater early on in their careers. Their positions called for the utmost in musical flexibility: the ability to write scores that integrated classical, popular, or folk music, and the musicians who staffed the studios' music departments had to be capable of performing these works. Composers applied the techniques of opera in creating the symphonic score that accompanied most pictures of the period. The message was clear: Orchestral music was not separate from but rather integral to a medium intended for a mass audience.

Musical eclecticism defined much animation of the era. In the features of Disney and Warner Brothers, the juxtaposition of high and low art was commonplace. Disney and his colleagues created the Silly Symphonies, several of which won Academy Awards, and the studio pioneered the use of classical music in animation with *Fantasia*. Warner Brothers responded in kind, combining humor and classical and folk music in its Bugs Bunny cartoons that mocked the highbrow yet also brought classical music to millions of children. The integration of these musical styles was a common feature of Los Angeles's music culture.

Numerous other fields remain to be explored. The rise of community orchestras, choral groups, and marching bands would all doubtless further enrich our understanding of music production and performance in Los Angeles. The legacy of religious music that found enormous audiences would greatly benefit from an analysis of the historical context in which that music arose. If I have not tried to tell "the whole story," it is because to do so in a single volume would be an impossible task. Research into these other fields would demonstrate communal or amateur music making, and could well support the thesis of diversity and decentralization: that participants consisted of men, women, and children across ethnic or class lines, and that they engaged in these musical activities throughout the region.

The purpose of this book has been to demonstrate why diversity and decentralization were characteristic of the music culture of Los Angeles. In the production, performance, and teaching of music, some of the city's most vital cultural institutions represented a diverse blend of traditions and practices. There are several successes in this story, and if there is more ethnic cooperation than discrimination in these pages, it is because the diverse fields of expressive culture made that cooperation possible. This is not to say that discrimination or marginalization of ethnic groups did not exist, for they certainly did, but there is also a story of cultural integration that formed an important part of Los Angeles history before World War II.

One sign of the strength of the city's music culture is that most of the institutions that appear in this book survived long after their creation. The establishment of an orchestra that performed regularly in public schools and adjoining cities, the founding of the Hollywood Bowl as a forum for music and dance, the rise of pageantry that combined music with drama, the expansion of the recording industry, and the widespread use of classical and popular music in the film industry are some of the more notable examples of that culture. The dual processes of sacralization and desacralization characterized all of these institutions, whose renown reached far beyond the borders of Los Angeles. In becoming a major metropolis, Los Angeles had become a musical metropolis.

Notes

Introduction

1. *Los Angeles County Culture and the Community* (Los Angeles: Civic Bureau of Music and Art, 1929).
2. Carey McWilliams, "Culture and the Community," *Opinion* 1 (October 1929): 9–10.
3. I use the term "expressive culture" to denote the decorative and performing arts, as Lawrence Levine has employed it in *Highbrow/Lowbrow: The Emergence of Cultural Hierarchy in America* (Cambridge, MA: Harvard University Press, 1988), 8.
4. John Russell Taylor, *Strangers in Paradise: The Hollywood Émigrés, 1933–1950* (New York: Holt, Rinehart and Winston, 1983), 33. Although many of the towns and cities of Los Angeles County were separated by fields for agriculture, especially in the San Gabriel Valley and San Fernando Valley, inhabitants from these urban areas participated in forms of music that were accessible to the entire County. In this sense we may speak of a regional music culture rather than merely a localized culture in the central city.
5. Gloria Ricci Lothrop, "The Boom of the '80s Revisited," *Southern California Quarterly* 75 (Fall/Winter 1993): 269.
6. Philip J. Ethington, "Segregated Diversity: Race-Ethnicity, Space, and Political Fragmentation in Los Angeles County, 1940–1994," available at <http://www.rcf.usc.edu/~philipje/CENSUS_MAPS/Haynes_Reports/FINAL_REPORT_20000719g.pdf>. Accessed on January 21, 2004.
7. Among the Committee's estimates, Jews were the largest ethnic group at 45,000, followed by Italians at 14,000, English and Germans at 11,000 each, and Jugoslavs at 10,000. *Map Showing Foreign Born Population in Los Angeles County, California.* Estimated by the Americanization Committee of the Los Angeles District of the California Federation of Women's Clubs, June 1921, HL.
8. Phil Ethington estimates that of the 2.6 million people in Los Angeles County by 1940, 93.3 percent were European/white, 2.7 percent (75,206) were African American, 2.2 percent (61,248) were Latino, and 1.9 percent (52,911) were Asian. "Segregated Diversity: Race-Ethnicity, Space, and Political Fragmentation in Los Angeles County, 1940–1994."
9. *Proceedings of the First Regional Planning Conference of Los Angeles County* (Los Angeles: Regional Planning Commission, 1922); also cited in Greg Hise, Michael J. Dear, and H. Eric Schockman, "Rethinking Los Angeles," in *Rethinking Los Angeles*, ed. Greg Hise, Michael J. Dear, and H. Eric Schockman (Thousand Oaks, CA: Sage Publications, 1996), 7.
10. In order to provide some planning sense to this development, the consultants Harland Bartholomew and Frederick Olmsted Jr. proposed a system of large

boulevards at one-mile intervals, something akin to Paris and Washington, D.C., although their wider vision of a city with plentiful parks and open spaces was ultimately unsuccessful. See Greg Hise and William Deverell, *Eden by Design: The 1930 Olmsted-Bartholomew Plan for the Los Angeles Region* (Berkeley and Los Angeles: University of California Press, 2000).

11. Hise, Dear, and Schockman, "Rethinking Los Angeles," 8.
12. H. Eric Schockman, "Is Los Angeles Governable?" in *Rethinking Los Angeles*, ed. Greg Hise, Michael J. Dear, and H. Eric Schockman (Thousand Oaks, CA: Sage Publications, 1996), 58–59.
13. Philip J. Ethington, "Waiting for the 'L.A. School': A Book Review Essay," *Southern California Quarterly* 80 (Fall 1998): 349–62. Michael Engh, in a similar review, notes "the near absence of serious discussion of the vast number of informal social networks that knit the civic community together and create the means for the city to cohere," in "At Home in the Heteropolis: Understanding the Postmodern L.A.," *American Historical Review* 105 (December 2000): 1680.
14. William Deverell, "Writing the History of Los Angeles," paper presented at the Haynes Foundation Conference on the History of Los Angeles, The Huntington Library, San Marino, CA, Fall 2001.
15. Carey McWilliams, *Southern California Country: An Island on the Land* (New York: Duell, Sloan & Pearce, 1946), 101.
16. Glen Gendzel, "Pioneers and Padres: Competing Mythologies in Northern and Southern California, 1850–1930," *The Western Historical Quarterly* 32 (Spring 2001): 1, 4.
17. Carey McWilliams devoted a whole chapter to the "Island of Hollywood," in *Southern California Country*, chap. 16.
18. To name but a few: Robert Stevenson, "Music in Southern California: A Tale of Two Cities," *Inter-American Music Review* 10 (Fall–Winter 1988): 39–111; Stevenson, "Local Music History Research in Los Angeles Area Libraries, Part I," *Inter-American Review* 10 (Fall–Winter 1988): 19–38; Stevenson, "Carreño's 1875 California Appearances," *Inter-American Music Review* 10 (Spring–Summer 1983): 9–15.
19. Robert Stevenson, "William Andrews Clark, Jr., Founder of the Los Angeles Philharmonic Orchestra," *William Andrews Clark, Jr.: His Cultural Legacy. Papers read at a Clark Library Seminar, 7 November 1981, by William E. Conway, Robert Stevenson* (UCLA: William Andrews Clark Memorial Library, 1985), 31–52.
20. Catherine Parsons Smith and Cynthia S. Richardson, *Mary Carr Moore, American Composer* (Ann Arbor: The University of Michigan Press, 1987); Catherine Parsons Smith, with contributed essays by Gayle Murchison and Willard B. Gatewood, chronology by Carolyn L. Quin, *William Grant Still: A Study in Contradictions* (Berkeley and Los Angeles: University of California Press, 2000).
21. Catherine Parsons Smith, "Founding the Hollywood Bowl," *American Music* 11 (Summer 1993): 206–42; Smith, " 'Something of Good for the Future': The People's Orchestra of Los Angeles," *Nineteenth-Century Music* 16 (Fall 1992): 146–60; Smith, " 'Popular Prices Will Prevail': Setting the Social Role of European-based Concert Music," in *Musical Aesthetics and Multiculturalism in Los Angeles*, ed. Steven Loza, Selected Reports in Ethnomusicology, vol. 10 (Los Angeles: Regents of the University of California, 1994), 207–21; Smith, "Of Pageantry and Politics," *American Quarterly* 44 (March 1992): 115–22.
22. John Koegel, "Mexican-American Music in Nineteenth-Century Southern California: The Lummis Wax Cylinder Collection at the Southwest Museum, Los

Angeles" (Ph.D. diss., The Claremont Graduate School, 1994); Koegel, "Mexican-American Music in Nineteenth-Century California: The Lummis Wax Cylinder Collection at the Southwest Museum, Los Angeles." *Revista de Musicología* 16, no. 4 (1993): 26–41; Koegel, "Preserving the Sounds of the 'Old' Southwest: Charles Lummis and his Cylinder Collection of Mexican-American and Indian Music." ARSC *Journal* 29 (Spring 1998): 1–29.

23. John Koegel, "*Canciones del país:* Mexican Musical Life in California after the Gold Rush," *California History* 78 (Fall 1999): 161–87; Koegel, "Calendar of Southern California Amusements 1852–1897 Designed for the Spanish-Speaking Public," *Inter-American Music Review* 13 (Spring–Summer 1993): 115–43.
24. Levine, *Highbrow/Lowbrow*, 9, 241.
25. Levine, *Highbrow/Lowbrow*, 241; Paul DiMaggio, "Cultural Entrepreneurship in Nineteenth-Century Boston, Part II," *Media, Culture and Society* 4 (1982): 320.
26. Levine, *Highbrow/Lowbrow*, 186, who cites Frederick Law Olmsted, *Public Parks and the Enlargement of Towns* (Brookline, MA, 1902), 69.
27. Joseph Horowitz, *Wagner Nights: An American History* (Berkeley and Los Angeles: University of California Press, 1994), 3.
28. Horowitz, *Wagner Nights*, 324; Horowitz, *Understanding Toscanini: A Social History of American Concert Life* (Berkeley and Los Angeles: University of California Press, 1994); Horowitz, " 'Sermons in Tones': Sacralization as a Theme in American Classical Music," *American Music* 16 (Fall 1998): 311–39. See also Levine, *Highbrow/Lowbrow*, 101–4.
29. Horowitz, " 'Sermons in Tones,' " 328, 332.

Chapter 1

1. *The Mirror*, September 25, 1893, p. 3, Album No. 23, Behymer Collection. George D. Betts was the editor of the Los Angeles Theatre program, which took the name of *The Mirror* in October 1892, and then became *The Players* in April 1894. Lynden Behymer took over as editor of the program in February 1894.
2. *The Mirror*, September 25, 1893, p. 3, Album No. 23, Behymer Collection. The theater was for plays, and was called the Burbank Opera House, located on Main Street.
3. Bernard Marchand, *The Emergence of Los Angeles: Population and Housing in the City of Dreams, 1940–1970* (London: Pion, 1986), 63.
4. "By 1885, the Santa Fe Railroad also reached Los Angeles. This event gave the city a second rail connection to the East Coast—one free of the subsidies of cash and land the S[outhern] P[acific] had forced the city to pay." Andrew Rolle, *Los Angeles: From Pueblo to City of the Future*, 2nd ed. (San Francisco: MTL, 1995), 36. See also William Deverell, *Railroad Crossing: Californians and the Railroad, 1850–1910* (Berkeley and Los Angeles: University of California Press, 1994), 62; Lothrop, "The Boom of the '80s Revisited," 263–301.
5. The theater was the Grand Opera House. *The Footlights*, May 28, 1893, frontispiece, Album No. 23, Behymer Collection.
6. Robert M. Fogelson, *The Fragmented Metropolis: Los Angeles, 1850–1930* (1967; reprint, with a foreword by Robert Fishman, Berkeley and Los Angeles: University of California Press, 1993), chap. 3.
7. David Lavender, *Los Angeles Two Hundred: A Pictorial and Entertaining Commentary on the Growth and Development of Los Angeles, California* (Tulsa,

OK: Continental Heritage Press, 1980), 169–70; Rolle, *Los Angeles*, 37–38. On lighting, see Eddy S. Feldman, *The Art of Street Lighting in Los Angeles* (Los Angeles: Dawson's Book Shop, 1972), 26–30.

8. Glenn S. Dumke, *The Boom of the Eighties in Southern California* (San Marino, CA: The Huntington Library, 1944), 47.
9. Kevin Starr, *Material Dreams: Southern California Through the 1920s* (New York: Oxford University Press, 1990), chap. 1. Starr discusses the realization of this dream in chap. 2.
10. Lothrop, "The Boom of the '80s Revisted," 290; Fogelson, *The Fragmented Metropolis*, 95–107.
11. Marchand, *The Emergence of Los Angeles*, 63; Rolle, *Los Angeles*, 36.
12. Rolle, *Los Angeles*, 37.
13. A pioneer in Los Angeles wrote this comment in his diary in 1842, cited by the historian James Miller Guinn; see Koegel, "*Canciones del país*," 177.
14. Stearns's Hall remained open at least until 1875. On groups who performed there, see Koegel, "*Canciones del país*," 178–79; Koegel, "Calendar of Southern California Amusements," 123–24; Stevenson, "Music in Southern California," 57–58.
15. On Temple Theater: Koegel, "*Canciones del país*," 179; Koegel, "Calendar of Southern California Amusements," 124. On the Merced Theater, see Moshe Yaari, "The Merced Theater," *Historical Society of Southern California Quarterly* 37 (September 1955), 195–210; Howard Swan, *Music in the Southwest, 1825–1950* (1952; reprint, Da Capo Press, 1977), 120.
16. Swan, *Music in the Southwest*, 122. Until 1893, it was located at 231 South Spring Street, and then at other sites between 1893 and about 1944. Koegel, "*Canciones del país*," 180; Stevenson, "Music in Southern California," 59–60. Stevenson describes the original theater as "a shingle[d] two-story building with three windows and a middle entrance." See his "Carreño's 1875 California Appearances," 13.
17. *Los Angeles Times*, Tuesday, December 13, 1881, p. 3; *Los Angeles Times*, Thursday morning, January 5, 1882, p. 3.
18. The letter by Clara Brown was published in the *San Diego Union*, March 25, 1883. Cited by Sue Wolfer Earnest, "An Historical Study of the Growth of the Theatre in Southern California, 1848–1894" (Ph.D. diss., University of Southern California, 1947), vol. 1: 388.
19. Horticulturist and real estate tycoon Ozro W. Childs opened the Grand Opera House, which was first known as Childs' Opera House and renamed the Orpheum in 1895. It was located on 110 South Main Street between First and Second Streets, and the office for its weekly program (called first *Footlights* and later *The Stage*), which Lynden Behymer edited, was at 202 North Main Street, at the corner of Requena Street. See *Los Angeles Times*, Wednesday, January 2, 1895, p. 1; *Footlights*, May 8, 1893, p. 3, Album No. 23, Behymer Collection.
20. The dimensions of the building were reported as being 72 × 20 feet. *Los Angeles Daily Herald*, May 25, 1884; *Los Angeles Times Illustrated Weekly*, March 28, 1914; both articles are cited by Earnest, "An Historical Study," vol. 1: 396.
21. Two early residents, Harris Newmark and J. A. Graves, both claim that the Grand Opera House had a seating capacity of 1,800 people: Harris Newmark, *Sixty Years in Southern California, 1853–1913* (Boston: Houghton Mifflin, 1930), 543; J. A. Graves, *My Seventy Years in California, 1857–1927* (Los Angeles: Times-Mirror Press, 1927), 128.

22. Earnest, "An Historical Study," vol. I: 401; John Northcutt, "Music Halls of Yesterday" (pamphlet, publisher unknown, 1931), California Historical Society Collection, Doheny.
23. Although the Philharmonic Auditorium was declared a monument in 1969, it was demolished 15 years later.
24. The Los Angeles Theatre, located on 227 South Spring Street between Second and Third Streets, became the New Los Angeles Theatre on October 13, 1890, but by 1899 had resumed its earlier name. It will be referred to here by its original title throughout. The office for the weekly program for the Los Angeles Theatre, *The Mirror*, was located at the northeast corner of Second and Broadway. Its seating capacity was 1,454. Program, Los Angeles Theatre, February 7–10, 1898, Box 8, Collection no. 1146, Seaver.
25. Program [no title], Los Angeles Theatre, Grand Opening Week, December 17–24, 1888, Box 7, Collection no. 1146, Seaver; Theater Programs, Dobinson Collection.
26. Program [no title], Los Angeles Theatre, Grand Opening Week, December 17–24, 1888, Box 7, Collection no. 1146, Seaver; Theater Programs, Dobinson Collection.
27. The theaters included Horton Hall (est. 1870); Leach's Opera House (est. 1885); Louis Opera House (est. 1887) and Fisher Opera House (est. 1892). Stevenson, "Music in Southern California," 41–42.
28. Music hall variety shows became the common form of vaudeville by the nineteenth century; see Clifford Barnes, "Vaudeville," *The New Grove Dictionary of Music and Musicians*, ed. Stanley Sadie, 20 vols. (London: Macmillan, 1980), vol. 19: 564–67. See also Douglas Gilbert, *American Vaudeville: Its Life and Times* (New York: Whittlesey House, 1940), 3–4.
29. The term "vaudeville" comes from the "Vau-de-Vire," or valley of the Vire River in Normandy, France, where townspeople sang satirical and bawdy songs during the fifteenth century. See Henry Gidel, *Le vaudeville* (Paris: Presses universitaires de France, 1986), 7. A contemporary description of the genre's origins is in *The Footlights*, May 8, 1893, p. 3, Album No. 23, Behymer Collection.
30. The French troupe also played at the Adelphi Theater, later called the French Theater, during the 1850s. Claudine Chalmers, "Françoise, Lucienne, Rosalie: French Women-Adventurers in the Early Days of the California Gold Rush," *California History* 78 (Fall 1999): 147. With the opening of actual vaudeville theaters, such performances quickly became common throughout the country, in which both male and female performers thrived. Susan A. Glenn, " 'Give an Imitation of Me': Vaudeville Mimics and the Play of the Self," *American Quarterly* 50 (March 1998): 47–76, esp. 47–53; Barnes, "Vaudeville," 566–67.
31. Gilbert, *American Vaudeville*, 61–62,
32. Robert C. Toll, *On With the Show! The First Century of Show Business in America* (New York: Oxford University Press, 1976), 267–72; Robert C. Allen, *Horrible Prettiness: Burlesque and American Culture* (Chapel Hill: University of North Carolina Press, 1991), 179–80.
33. Allen states that "Vaudeville and burlesque were negative reflections of each other. Each defined itself in terms of what the other was not," in *Horrible Prettiness*, 179. See also Levine, *Highbrow/Lowbrow*, 195–97.
34. The evening's entertainment took place at the Turnverein Hall and was titled "Entertainment and Ball of the Confidence Engine Co. No. 2," a firemen's association. The comic burlesque opera was *Il Jacobi. The Evening Express*, Tuesday, February 10, 1880, p. 2.

35. Program [no title], Grand Opera House [n.d.], 1888, Dobinson Collection.
36. For Lydia Thompson's New York appearances and the sensation they caused, see Toll, *On With the Show!*, 216–21; Allen, *Horrible Prettiness*, 18–19.
37. Review [anonymous, n.d.], 1888, Album No. 42, Behymer Collection. According to historian Ralph Schaffer, all critics of the *Los Angeles Times* were anonymous during this period, although Dr. Dorothea Lummis, the first wife of Charles Lummis, wrote critical reviews, as did Eliza Otis, who "performed nearly all the editorial functions at the paper."
38. Review [anonymous, n.d.], 1888, Album No. 42, Behymer Collection. A year later, another work by the same composer and lyricist team of Stephens and Solomon appeared at the Los Angeles Theatre: *Virginia*, performed by the Wyatt English Opera Company. A critic stated that the music was "strongly reminiscent of Gilbert and Sullivan, especially of [H.M.S.] *Pinafore* and *The Sorcerer*." Review [anonymous, n.d.], 1889, Album No. 42, Behymer Collection.
39. Review [anonymous], May 27, 1890, Album No. 56, Behymer Collection.
40. *Los Angeles Times*, Thursday, January 3, 1895, p. 6.
41. Ibid., p. 6.
42. *Los Angeles Times*, Tuesday, January 1, 1895, p. 28; Wednesday, January 2, 1895, p. 1. Brenda Dixon Gottschild discusses the opportunities for blacks in minstrelsy in *Waltzing in the Dark: African American Vaudeville and Race Politics in the Swing Era* (New York: St. Martin's Press, 2000), 8–9.
43. Program [no title], Los Angeles Theatre, January 23, 1900, Album No. 52, f. 18, Behymer Collection. The accompanying vaudeville acts were Teal and Baker, Dan Allman, Morton and Elliott, and "The European Marvels, The Couture Brothers."
44. Program [no title], Los Angeles Theatre, July 24, 1892, Album No. 26, Behymer Collection.
45. *Los Angeles Times*, Monday, July 25, 1892, p. 4.
46. A description of their life and career together is in Menetta S. Behymer, *Starlit Trails: A Biography of L. E. Behymer, Impresario of the West, 1862–1947* (Oklahoma City, OK: Glen Behymer, 1998). I would like to thank Glenarvon Behymer Jr. for providing me with a copy of this work. Behymer was a controversial figure and could exaggerate his influence; Catherine Parsons Smith discussed his role in Los Angeles's cultural life in a paper, " 'Our Awe Struck Vision': The Emergence of L. E. Behymer as an Impresario," paper presented at the fiftieth anniversary of the Music Library Association, Pasadena Public Library, Pasadena, CA, October 18, 1991.
47. *The Footlights*, May 8, 1893, p. 3, Album No. 23, Behymer Collection.
48. The review cited here is in *Los Angeles Times*, Sunday, November 17, 1895, p. 35. The critic noted specifically the Ovide Musin Concert Company, which featured the violinist Ovide Musin and his wife, the soprano Annie Louise Tanner-Musin, and others, and had come "directly here from a triumphal tour of the Mexican republic." Their contract was for $1,200 for a week's engagement at the Orpheum: "Double Dates for Musin," *Los Angeles Times*, Saturday, November 16, 1895, p. 6. The husband and wife duo had already appeared at the Los Angeles Theatre on April 11 and 12, 1892. Program, Los Angeles Theatre, Album No. 26, Behymer Collection.
49. See Richard Traubner, *Operetta: A Theatrical History* (Garden City, NY: Doubleday, 1983).
50. Program [no title], Los Angeles Theatre, April 9, 1891, Album No. 26, Behymer Collection. The critic also noted that the "tuneful composition has been heard

here before, rendered by the same company and almost by the same cast." *Los Angeles Times*, Friday, April 10, 1891, p. 4.

51. *Los Angeles Times*, Thursday, March 9, 1893, p. 4. The same company also gave a performance of Franz von Suppé's operetta, *Boccaccio. The Mirror*, March 7, 1893, p. 7, Album No. 23, Behymer Collection. In an unusual instance, a comic opera by a German troupe of 20 people was performed in German: *Robert und Bertram* (also billed as *The Jolly Robbers*). Presumably the German community in Los Angeles was large enough to justify the production. *The Mirror*, January 1, 1893, p. 5, Album No. 23, Behymer Collection.
52. Program [no title], Los Angeles Theatre, April 11, 1891, Album No. 26; *The Mirror*, April 12, 1893, p. 5, Album No. 23, Behymer Collection.
53. *Los Angeles Times*, Tuesday, April 7, 1891, p. 4.
54. Ibid., p. 4. The reviewer wrote more on this operetta than most other productions reviewed in the *Los Angeles Times*.
55. "In compliance with the suggestion made in these columns, the management has determined to present *Robin Hood* again tonight, instead of *Mignon*, as advertised. The change will gratify a large number of people who have hitherto been unable to get seats to witness this popular opera. It will also be given for the last time at the matinée tomorrow." *Los Angeles Times*, Friday, April 10, 1891, p. 4.
56. *Los Angeles Times*, Thursday, April 13, 1893, p. 4. They repeated their success in 1895, the local critic referring to them as "the cleverest company on the American highway of melody." *Los Angeles Times*, Saturday, November 16, 1895, p. 6.
57. *Los Angeles Times*, Thursday, April 13, 1893, p. 4.
58. *The Mirror*, April 13, 1893, p. 7, Album No. 23, Behymer Collection.
59. *Los Angeles Times*, Friday, April 14, 1893, p. 4.
60. Program [*The Play Bill*], Grand Opera House, February 28, 1893, Album No. 23, Behymer Collection. Almost all the members of the cast have German names, so it seems possible that the group originated in Germany.
61. *Los Angeles Times*, Wednesday, March 1, 1893, p. 4. The advertisement for the show states that they had enjoyed a long run at the Baldwin Theater in San Francisco.
62. *The Mirror*, April 9, 1894, p. 5; *The Players*, June 22–23, 1894, p. 5, Album No. 27, Behymer Collection.
63. *Los Angeles Times*, Saturday, June 23, 1894, p. 1.
64. Ibid., p. 4.
65. *The Mirror*, April 19, 1893, p. 9, Album No. 23, Behymer Collection. Professor Willhartitz contributed much to the city's musical life. In 1894 he oversaw a musical evening of the Unity Club (which met each month at the Unity Church) devoted to the music of Carl Maria von Weber; he gave a paper titled "Weber and His Works," and took part in the evening's musical performances. *Los Angeles Times*, Thursday, February 8, 1894, p. 6.
66. Program [no title], Los Angeles Theatre, July 8, 1892, pp. 1–2, Album No. 26, Behymer Collection. The conductor of the orchestra was Ludomir Tomaszewicz. Mr. Tomaszewicz directed a series of concerts by the "Orchestral Society Lute" (e.g., Program, Los Angeles Theatre, August 18, 1892, Album No. 26, Behymer Collection) as well as a production of *The Chimes of Normandy* the previous year at the Los Angeles Theatre with an orchestra of twenty musicians. C. L. Bagley, "History of the Band and Orchestra Business in Los Angeles," *The Overture* 5 (March 15, 1926): 8.

67. *Los Angeles Times*, Saturday, July 9, 1892, p. 4.
68. *The Mirror*, August 21, 1893, p. 3, Album No. 23, Behymer Collection. The then editor of the program, George Betts, solicited "Communications of a theatrical nature" from the public, so the comment may have come from a local patron.
69. The musicians in the orchestra at the time of the opening of the Los Angeles Theatre consisted of Harley Hamilton, director and first violin; Elmer Wachtel, second violin; Robert Nelson, viola; Tom Connor, bass; Max Lenzberg, flute; V. Hurka, clarinet; W. H. Brown, cornet; E. Binder, trombone; and George R. Held, drums. C. L. Bagley, "History of the Band and Orchestra Business in Los Angeles," *The Overture* 5 (June 15, 1925): 4. On Harley Hamilton, see Smith, " 'Something of Good for the Future,' " 152–53; Earnest, "An Historical Study," vol. 1: 623–24.
70. The McFadden Company, the Boston troupe who performed the play, was booked for the entire week, December 31, 1888–January 6, 1889. The company also had its own ensemble, "McFadden's Famous Eclipse Quartette," which played between Acts I and II. Program [no title], Los Angeles Theatre, January 1, 1889, Album No. 25, Behymer Collection.
71. Program [no title], Los Angeles Theatre, October 21, 1898 [?], Album No. 51, f. 88, Behymer Collection.
72. *The Mirror*, October 16, 1893, p. 6, Album No. 23, Behymer Collection. C. L. Bagley described Romandy as "a great leader and handles the violin like an old master," in "History of the Band and Orchestra Business in Los Angeles," *The Overture* 5 (January 1, 1926): 11–12.
73. *The Mirror*, January 22–24, 1894, p. 5, Album No. 27, Behymer Collection.
74. *The Mirror*, March 26, 1894, p. 6, Album No. 27, Behymer Collection. Curiously, the *Los Angeles Times* states that the play *Hamlet* was performed on this night in the same theater. For the play *The Butterflies*, see Program [no title], Los Angeles Theatre, August 8–11, 1894, Dobinson Collection.
75. *The Mirror*, December 25, 1893, p. 3, Album No. 23, Behymer Collection.
76. Koegel, "*Canciones del país*," 178.
77. The Gerardo López del Castillo Company from Mexico City performed this work at the Temple Theater in November 1865. Koegel, "*Canciones del país*," 179.
78. The wine merchant was O. G. Weyse. See Henry Winfred Splitter, "Music in Los Angeles," *Historical Society of Southern California Quarterly* 38 (December 1956): 324. See also Catherine Parsons Smith, "Inventing Tradition: Symphony and Opera in Progressive-Era Los Angeles," in *Music and Culture in America, 1861–1918*, ed. Michael Saffle (New York: Garland, 1998), 305–6.
79. Program [no title], Los Angeles Theatre, January 24, 1895, p. 6, Album No. 27, Behymer Collection.
80. *Los Angeles Times*, Friday, January 25, 1895, p. 6.
81. *Los Angeles Times*, Saturday, January 26, 1895, p. 6; *The Players*, January 25, 1895, pp. 5–6, Album No. 27, Behymer Collection.
82. Libby Slate, "Robert Stack and the 'La Bohème' Connection," *Los Angeles Times*, September 11, 1987. See also Program [no title], Los Angeles Theatre, October 14 and 16, 1897; Dobinson Collection. I would like to thank Lance Bowling for providing me with information on this event.
83. Behymer, *Starlit Trails*, 43; Smith, " 'Our Awe Struck Vision,' " 6.
84. Susan Naulty, Notes, p. 1, Behymer Collection Reference Papers, HL. During one five-day visit, the Emma Juch Grand English Opera Company presented Wagner's *Tannhäuser*, Gounod's *Faust*, Bizet's *Carmen*, Donizetti's *Lucia di Lammermoor*,

Mascagni's *Cavalleria rusticana*, Gounod's *Romeo and Juliet*, Verdi's *Il trovatore*, and Wagner's *Lohengrin*. Program [no title], Grand Opera House, March 21, 1892, Box 5, Collection no. 1146, Seaver.

85. Program [no title], Los Angeles Theatre, May 15–August 18, 1899, Album No. 52, ff. 4–17, Behymer Collection. Also performed were Thomas's *Mignon;* Verdi's *Il trovatore* and *La traviata;* and Mascagni's *Cavalleria rusticana.*
86. Program [no title], Los Angeles Theatre, March 18, 1899, Album No. 52, f. 14, Behymer Collection. Luigi Ricci wrote over 30 operas, several of them comic operas, a well as 20 masses and numerous orchestral pieces. He wrote three to four works with his brother Federico. *Die Musik in Geschichte und Gegenwart* (Basel: Bärenreiter, 1949–86), vol. 11: cols. 423–26.
87. The opera consists of three acts, with Act I in a "Forest Roadside in the Far West," Act II in an "Indian Encampment," and Act III in a "Mexican Camp." *The Mirror*, April 14, 1893, p. 9, Album No. 23, Behymer Collection. Joseph Horowitz notes that Waller was pleased by comments on his opera by the conductor Anton Seidl, in *Wagner Nights*, 167. While I have been unable to locate the libretto for the opera, there was a Lakota tribe called the Oglala, forced to migrate to a reservation in Nebraska following the Wounded Knee Massacre in South Dakota; see Catherine Price, *The Oglala People, 1841–1879: A Political History* (Lincoln: University of Nebraska Press, 1996).
88. *Los Angeles Times*, Saturday, April 15, 1893, p. 4.
89. Instrumentation was as follows: six first violins, seven second violins, three violas, two violincellos, three contrabass, one piccolo, two flutes, one oboe, three clarinets ("clarionettes"), two bassoons ("fagotti"), four horns, two cornets, three trombones, and timpani. *Bartlett's Musical and Home Journal* 5 (September 1888): 9, Cambria.
90. Caroline Estes Smith, *The Philharmonic Orchestra of Los Angeles, "The First Decade" 1919-1929* (Los Angeles: Caroline Estes Smith, 1930).
91. Rossini, Overture, *La Gazza Ladra;* Wagner, selections from *Lohengrin;* De Koven, "The Legend of the Chimes"; Kretschmer, Coronation March from *Folkunger;* Mendelssohn, Piano Concerto in G Minor, Op. 25; Thomas, Overture, *Raymond;* Strauss, *Tales From the Vienna Woods;* Nevin, "One Spring Morning, Op. 3, No. 2," and "The Night Has a Thousand Eyes"; Rubinstein, *Toréador et Andalouse;* Meyerbeer, *Fackeltanz in B-flat Major*. The concert took place on January 9, 1893. Smith, *The Philharmonic Orchestra of Los Angeles*, 17–21.
92. *The Mirror*, February 20, 1893, p. 9; May 1, 1893, p. 3; May 8, 1893, p. 3, and backpage, Album No. 23, Behymer Collection. The Fourth Grand Concert took place on May 29, 1893. On Stamm, see Earnest, "An Historical Study," vol. 1: 623; Smith, *The Philharmonic Orchestra of Los Angeles*, 17–21.
93. Program [no title], Los Angeles Theatre, June 3, 1897, Album No. 51, f. 31, Behymer Collection. The program listed the coming attractions the following week, but did not list the repertoire the orchestra would perform.
94. William Andrews Clark Jr. founded the Los Angeles Philharmonic Orchestra in 1919, which was under the management of Lynden Behymer until 1922, when Caroline E. Smith (who was also Clark's personal secretary) assumed control. Lynn Moody Hoffman, "Starlit Trails," Research Summary Report (unpublished manuscript, 1977), p. 5, Behymer Collection Reference Papers, HL. On Clark, see Stevenson, "William Andrews Clark, Jr.," 31–52.
95. The orchestra grew to 77 members by 1912. Stevenson, "Music in Southern California," 73–76.

96. Alfred Metzger, "Symphony Orchestra is Leading Organization," *Musical Review* 9 (June 1906): 13–17.
97. Smith, *The Philharmonic Orchestra of Los Angeles*, 21–24; Swan, *Music in the Southwest*, 177–78.
98. On Behymer and the Woman's Orchestra, see *Pacific Coast Musical Review* 28 (September 25, 1915): 64. More generally, see Rae Linda Brown, "The Woman's Symphony Orchestra of Chicago and Florence B. Price's Piano Concerto in One Movement," *American Music* 11 (Summer 1993): 185–87.
99. Levine, *Highbrow/Lowbrow*, 146.
100. For an example of a church concert, see *Los Angeles Times*, Thursday, February 8, 1894, p. 6.
101. Three organizations dedicated solely to classical music, the Apollo Club, Treble Clef Club, and Ellis Club, also booked the Los Angeles Theatre for their concerts, usually featuring quartets or soloists. For example, the Apollo Club booked the theater on June 30, 1891; October 19, 1891; February 2, 1892; April 29, 1892, and June 30, 1892; the Treble Clef on April 1, 1891 and October 13, 1891; and the Ellis Club on June 4, 1891. Programs, Los Angeles Theatre, Album No. 26, Behymer Collection.
102. Lynden Behymer himself seems to have owned a business, a printing office called Kitts and Behymer, located at 202 N. Main Street, which he duly advertised in the programs: for example, *The Footlights*, June 19, 1893, p. 6, Album No. 23, Behymer Collection. His brother, Aaron Sargent Behymer, a local merchant, may also have been involved in the business; see Behymer, *Starlit Trails*, 719.
103. *Los Angeles Advertiser* 1 (March 1887).
104. *The Footlights*, June 19, 1893, p. 6, Album No. 23, Behymer Collection.
105. *The Mirror*, November 13, 1893, p. 6, Album No. 23, Behymer Collection.
106. *The Footlights*, December 25, 1893, p. 4, Album No. 23, Behymer Collection. Emphasis in original.
107. Ibid., p. 5, Album No. 23, Behymer Collection.
108. Hair cutting was 25 cents, curling hair 25 cents, curling bangs 15 cents, and cutting bangs 15 cents. *The Mirror*, November 21, 1893, p. 5, Album No. 23, Behymer Collection.
109. The following prices were given: Children in the 1st, 2nd, and 3rd grades could have 20 lessons for $40, while children in the 4th, 5th and 6th grades had to pay $60 for 20 lessons. *The Mirror*, October 2, 1893, p. 2, Album No. 23, Behymer Collection.
110. *The Players*, November 13–16, 1895, Album No. 28; *The Stage*, October 1, 1894, p. 3, Album No. 23, Behymer Collection.
111. *The Mirror*, May 1, 1893, back cover, Album No. 23, Behymer Collection.
112. *The Players*, November 13–16, 1895, p. 5, Album No. 28, Behymer Collection. Similarly, an ad for the American Steam Dye Works states: "Ladies and Gent's Garments cleaned, dyed and renovated in superior styles at short notice. Blankets, Curtains and Merchants' Goods, Ostrich Plumes cleaned and curled." *The Mirror*, February 20, 1893, p. 7, Album No. 23, Behymer Collection.
113. *The Footlights*, June 26, 1894, back cover, Album No. 23, Behymer Collection.
114. *The Footlights*, December 25, 1893, p. 3, Album No. 23, Behymer Collection.
115. *The Mirror*, December 26, 1892, back cover, Album No. 23; *The Footlights*, June 19, 1893, p. 6, Album No. 23, Behymer Collection.
116. Levine, *Highbrow/Lowbrow*, 195–97; Toll, *On With the Show!*, 265–71.

117. L. E. Behymer, "The Manager's Lot in the Southland. The Eternal Triangle of Artist, Public and Impresario," in *Who's Who in Music and Dance in Southern California*, ed. Bruno David Ussher (Hollywood: Bureau of Musical Research, 1933), 79–80.
118. Levine, *Highbrow/Lowbrow*, 184–98.
119. *Los Angeles Times*, Tuesday, August 29, 1893, p. 4.
120. Levine, *Highbrow/Lowbrow*, 234.

Chapter 2

1. Anthony Macías, "From Progressivism to Policing: Youth Culture and Public Space in Postwar Los Angeles," paper presented to the Los Angeles History Research Group, The Huntington Library, September 21, 2002. See also *Los Angeles County Culture and the Community* (Los Angeles: Civic Bureau of Music and Art, 1929), 42.
2. On Americanization in Los Angeles, see Judith Raftery, *Land of Fair Promise: Politics and Reform in Los Angeles Schools, 1885–1941* (Stanford, CA: Stanford University Press, 1992), esp. chap. 4; William Deverell, "My America or Yours? Americanization and the Battle for the Youth of Los Angeles," in *Metropolis in the Making: Los Angeles in the 1920s*, ed. Tom Sitton and William Deverell (Berkeley and Los Angeles: University of California Press, 2001), 282–83.
3. The listing for private teachers rose to 12 by 1884, and 30 in 1887. By 1888, 71 private teachers were listed, 165 in 1896, and 808 in 1916. Stevenson, "Music in Southern California," 65; Henry Winfred Splitter, "Music in Los Angeles," *The Historical Society of Southern California Quarterly* 38 (December 1956): 327.
4. United States Bureau of the Census, *Occupations of the Twelfth Census* (Washington, D.C., 1904), 590–93; cited in Smith, " 'Something of Good for the Future,' " 159, n. 46.
5. The latter two were also business partners, having co-founded in 1871 the highly successful Farmers and Merchants Bank, and so had the financial means to launch the new college. Members of the Vincentian order founded St. Vincent's College in 1865, with the aid of Jews and Protestants during a period of interfaith cooperation in Los Angeles. However, it did not give Bachelor of Arts degrees until 1885, and classes numbered no more than 12 students until it closed its doors in 1911. A Jesuit institution, Loyola University, later purchased the site. Michael E. Engh, S. J., *Frontier Faiths: Church, Temple, and Synagogue in Los Angeles, 1846–1888* (Albuquerque: University of New Mexico Press, 1992), 84–90.
6. Engh, *Frontier Faiths*, 192–93. The music department at La Verne College opened in 1893; see Gladdys Esther Muir, "The Founding of La Verne College," *Pomona Valley Historian* 6 (January 1970): 93–109. Another institution, Throop University, was also founded in 1891 (renamed California Institute of Technology in 1921), although there is no indication it offered courses or degrees in music. In 1907, Baptists opened the University of Redlands.
7. On the hiring of musicians at USC and the State Normal School, see Stevenson, "Music in Southern California," 65–67.
8. Raftery, *Land of Fair Promise*, 67.

9. Gloria Ricci Lothrop, "Nurturing Society's Children," *California History* 65 (December 1986), 274–83. On Froebel's educational philosophy, see Friedrich Froebel, *The Education of Man*, trans. W. N. Hailmann (New York: D. Appleton, 1901); on the value of music and singing, see pp. 265–72.
10. Cited in William Warren Ferrier, *Ninety Years of Education in California, 1846–1936: A Presentation of Educational Movements and Their Outcome in Education Today* (Berkeley, CA: Sather Gate Book Shop, 1937), 163.
11. Ferrier, *Ninety Years of Education in California*, 163.
12. Lothrop, "Nurturing Society's Children," 277–80; Virginia Elwood-Akers, "George Henry Hewes and the Neighborhood Settlement in Los Angeles," *Southern California Quarterly* 83 (Winter 2001): 384–86.
13. Judith Raftery, "Los Angeles Clubwomen and Progressive Reform," in *California Progressivism Revisited*, ed. William Deverell and Tom Sitton (Berkeley and Los Angeles: University of California Press, 1994), 147–52; Elwood-Akers, "George Henry Hewes," 385.
14. Vermont, Indiana, and Connecticut all made kindergartens part of the public school system during the period 1880 to 1890. Ferrier, *Ninety Years of Education in California*, 174.
15. Lothrop, "Nurturing Society's Children," 279–80; Ferrier, *Ninety Years of Education in California*, 175.
16. Lowell Mason, *Mason's Normal Singer* (New York: Mason Brothers, 1856). Mason founded the Boston Academy of Music in 1833 and the Normal Musical Institute for music teachers in New York; see Gilbert Chase, *America's Music: From the Pilgrims to the Present*, 3rd ed. (Urbana: University of Illinois Press, 1987), 131–38.
17. Stevenson, "Music in Southern California," 67. In 1893, the school board required teachers to learn singing so that they could teach it to their students. *Los Angeles Times*, Monday, March 20, 1893, p. 2.
18. The Superintendent of Los Angeles Schools also hired a part-time music instructor for Los Angeles High School in 1885, which had 143 students. Kathryn Emilie Stone succeeded the first Supervisor of Music in Los Angeles Public Schools, Gertrude E. Parsons, who served from 1897 to 1900.
19. "Music in Business and Education," *The Overture* 1 (September 15, 1921): 2. See also Mark Katz, "Making America More Musical Through the Phonograph, 1900–1930," *American Music* 16 (Winter 1988): 449–50.
20. Founded in 1880, the Southern California Music Company was one of the city's largest music stores. Its main office was first located in a six-story building on Hill Street downtown before moving to an eight-story building on South Broadway, and there were branch offices throughout southern California. *Who's Who in Music and Dance in Southern California*, ed. Bruno David Ussher, 250–51.
21. At least 600 students, Jones estimates, were thus able to study an instrument who otherwise could not. Jennie L. Jones, "Grade School Orchestras: What Los Angeles City Teachers are Doing," in *Who's Who in Music and Dance in Southern California*, ed. Bruno David Ussher, 85–87.
22. Wallenstein moved to Los Angeles in 1906. He also studied with Elsa von Grofé, mother of composer Ferde Grofé, who was educated at St. Vincent's College in Los Angeles. Natalie Bowen Ritter, "The Los Angeles Philharmonic Orchestra: An Artistic History, 1919–1961" (master's thesis, The Claremont Graduate School, 1974), 57. See also John Orlando Northcutt, *Symphony: The Story of the Los Angeles Philharmonic Orchestra* (Los Angeles: Southern California Symphony Association, 1963), 57.

23. "Instrumental Music in Public Schools," *The Overture* 1 (October 1, 1921): 1.
24. "Instrumental Music in Public Schools," *The Overture* 1 (October 1, 1921): 1, 6.
25. "Index of Public School Music Teachers in Southern California," in *Who's Who in Music and Dance in Southern California*, ed. Bruno David Ussher, 93–98.
26. *Music Education in the Elementary School* (Sacramento: California State Department of Education, 1939), v–vi. No author or editor is given.
27. *Music Education in the Elementary School*, 1. The passage is quoted from Lilla Belle Pitts, "The Place of Music in a System of Education," in *Music Education*, Thirty-fifth Yearbook of the National Society for the Study of Education, Part II (Bloomington, IL: Public School Publishing Company, 1936), 18.
28. *Music Education in the Elementary School*, ix, 6–36. See Appendix.
29. *Music Education in the Elementary School*, 13–14.
30. *Music Education in the Elementary School*, ix, 36–68. See Appendix.
31. *Music Education in the Elementary School*, 41–46, 59–67.
32. *Music Education in the Elementary School*, 59–66.
33. *Music Education in the Elementary School* (Sacramento: California State Department of Education, 1944).
34. Changing priorities in education, such as an emphasis on math and science during the Cold War, as well as the passage of Proposition 13 in 1978, which froze property taxes in California, had a direct impact on the cutting of music education budgets, which contributed towards a demise of music education programs in the public schools.
35. *Southern California Musicians' Directory, 1916–1917*, ed. Herman A. Horowitz (Los Angeles: The National Musicians Directory Company, 1916), iv.
36. Agnes Woodward, the founder and director of the California School for Artistic Whistling, wrote a textbook on the subject and prepared students for Chautauqua performances, vaudeville, and the concert stage. She noted that bird calls by concert performers "bring much delight and wonderment to an audience." *Southern California Musicians' Directory, 1916–1917*, 60, 62.
37. On Arévalo's life and career, see John Koegel, "*Canciones del país*," 160, 163, 184–87; Koegel, "Calendar of Southern California Amusements 1852–1897," 125, n. 18. Two composers from Guadalajara whom Arévalo met were Miguel Meneses and Clemente Aguirre.
38. Little is known about the school or how long it was open. An advertisement of 1891 states that Arévalo's studio was located in Wilson Block no. 24, First Street, Room 16. Koegel, "Calendar of Southern California Amusements 1852–1897," 126, 141. On Knell, see Swan, *Music in the Southwest*, 145.
39. Luis Toribio Romero, born around 1854, died in 1893. Koegel, "*Canciones del país*," 186.
40. The concert, which also featured another Arévalo student, Kate Slauson, "was a success financially and otherwise." *Los Angeles Times*, Friday, January 13, 1882, p. 3; see also Stevenson, "Music in Southern California," 61, 65.
41. Koegel, "*Canciones del país*," 186–87. On recordings at Rancho Camulos, see Koegel, "Preserving the Sounds of the 'Old' Southwest," 4; and Joan M. Jensen and Gloria Ricci Lothrop, *California Women: A History* (San Francisco: Boyd and Fraser, 1987), 15–16.
42. He appeared at the Merced Theater on August 31, 1871; April 15, 1872; March 5, 1873; April 26 and 28, 1873; February 7, 1874; March 7, 1874; May 2 and 4, 1874; November 5, 1876; and April 19, 1877. He appeared at Turnverein Hall on July 19,

1873, December 15, 1873; June 13 and 17, 1874; June 28, 1875; September 4, 1875; April 19, 1876; July 28, 1877; April 10, 1878; February 21, 1880; January 12, 1882; and May 13, 1889. Koegel, "Calendar of Southern California Amusements 1852–1897," 126–40.

43. Examples of pieces Arévalo performed are *Himno Nacional Mexicano;* Donizetti's *Duo*, Verdi's "Infelice" from *Ernani;* and by Arévalo himself: *The Mocking Bird*, the waltz *El ave errante, Carnival de Venetia*, and *La Súplica, Danza Habanera*. Koegel, "Calendar of Southern California Amusements 1852–1897," 126–27, 141.
44. Arévalo served as vice-president of the organization in 1877. Koegel, "Calendar of Southern California Amusements 1852–1897," 133. The Musicians' Mutual Protective Association (MMPA) was formed on October 30, 1894, which the *Overture* writer and MMPA member C. L. Bagley praised highly and noted that "the history of the [Los Angeles music] business and the Association are practically identical varying only in detail." C. L. Bagley, "History of the Band and Orchestra Business in Los Angeles," *The Overture* 4 (November 15, 1924): 9.
45. The concert began with a piece titled "Phalanx March" by the local teacher and conductor, Professor A. J. Stamm, followed by "Quintette" from Donizetti's *Lucia di Lammermoor;* "Infelice" from *Ernani* by Verdi; and *Grand Valse* and *Carnival de Venetia* by Arévalo. Works by composers Harper, Millard, Ascher, and White were also performed. Arévalo's students were Ellen Roth, Bertha Roth, Mabel McFarland, Lizzie Hobbs, and M. Carrizosa. Koegel, "Calendar of Southern California Amusements 1852–1897," 140–41.
46. Stevenson, "Music in Southern California," 65. On Mrs. Valentine, see also Koegel, "*Canciones del país*," 163; and C. L. Bagley, "History of the Band and Orchestra Business in Los Angeles," *The Overture* 5 (January 1, 1926): 10–11.
47. Joseph A. Mussulman, *Music in the Cultured Generation: A Social History of Music in America, 1870–1900* (Evanston, IL: Northwestern University Press, 1971), 100.
48. C. L. Bagley, "History of the Band and Orchestra Business in Los Angeles," *The Overture* 5 (January 1, 1926): 10–11.
49. By 1906, the conservatory moved to the Blanchard Building at 232 South Hill Street, where faculty gave lessons not only in piano, organ, violin, voice, and harmony, but also in drama and fencing. *Musical Review* 9 (June 1906): 37.
50. *Who's Who in Music and Dance in Southern California*, ed. Bruno David Ussher, 217. Leonard Pitt and Dale Pitt, *Los Angeles A to Z* (Berkeley and Los Angeles: University of California Press, 1997), 72–73.
51. *Notables of the Southwest, Being the Portraits and Biographies of Progressive Men of the Southwest* (Los Angeles: The Los Angeles Examiner, 1912), 385.
52. The Von Stein Academy was originally located at 1502 South Grand Avenue in 1905 before moving to 958 South Hill Street in 1910. *Notables of the Southwest*, 385; Prospectus, *Von Stein Academy of Music, 1911–12*, pp. 9–10, Cambria. I would like to thank Lance Bowling for bringing these materials to my attention.
53. Instruction was given for piano, violin, cello, voice, clarinet, oboe, flute, saxophone, cornet, baritone, tuba, trombone, and percussion. Prospectus, *Von Stein Academy of Music, 1911–12*, pp. 27–28, Cambria.
54. Prospectus, *Von Stein Academy of Music, 1911–12*, pp. 12–19, Cambria.
55. Rasbach moved to Los Angeles with his family in 1894; the other three instructors were cellist Earl Bright, trombone player Bertram Hitt, and cornet player George Brigden. Prospectus, *Von Stein Academy of Music, 1911–12*, pp. 17–20, Cambria.

56. Prospectus, *Von Stein Academy of Music, 1911–12*, pp. 23, 27, Cambria.
57. A translated version by C. E. R. Müller of the manual's eleventh German edition was published under the title *Grand Theoretical and Practical Piano-school for Systematic Instruction in All Branches of Piano-playing: From the First Elements to the Highest proficiency/by Sigismund Lebert and Louis Stark* (San Francisco: Sherman, Clay & Co., n.d.). G. Schirmer also published an English edition in 1899.
58. Richard K. Lieberman, *Steinway & Sons* (New Haven, CT: Yale University Press, 1995), 338, n. 59. Lebert and Stark published *Grosse theoretische-praktische Klavierschule* in 1858.
59. Prospectus, *Von Stein Academy of Music, 1911–12*, pp. 24, 27–28, Cambria.
60. Prospectus, *Von Stein Academy of Music, 1911–12*, p. 25, Cambria.
61. Judith Raftery notes that "out of a total school enrollment of 33,422, 2,431 students were German-born or children of Germans," in *Land of Fair Promise*, 64.
62. Delilah Beasley, *Negro Trail Blazers of California* (1919; reprint, New York: Negro Universities Press [1969]), 209.
63. Prospectus, *Von Stein Academy of Music, 1911–12*, p. 21, Cambria.
64. *Pacific Coast Musical Review* 28 (September 25, 1915): 16.
65. See Catherine Parsons Smith and Cynthia S. Richardson, *Mary Carr Moore, American Composer* (Ann Arbor: The University of Michigan Press, 1987), 113–16; *Music and Dance in California*, ed. José Rodriguez (Hollywood: Bureau of Musical Research, 1940), 446.
66. Jose Cardenas, "Music School Humming Along at 87," *Los Angeles Times*, Wednesday, May 9, 2001, B3.
67. Boyle Heights by the 1920s had become "the major immigrant district of Los Angeles." James P. Allen and Eugene Turner, *The Ethnic Quilt: Population Diversity in Southern California* (Northridge: California State University, Northridge, 1997), 73. But Wendy Elliott-Scheinberg claims that in 1910, "all sections contained more American-born residents than immigrants," in "Boyle Heights: Jewish Ambiance in a Multicultural Neighborhood" (Ph.D. diss., Claremont Graduate University, 2001), 219. Between 1900 and 1929, the number of Jews in Los Angeles grew from 2,500 to almost 70,000, representing over 17 percent of the city's population. While some settled in the wealthier areas of Wilshire Boulevard, West Adams, and Hollywood, Boyle Heights was the location of choice for middle- and working-class Jews, and so "became the most important Jewish enclave in the 1920s." Allen and Turner, *The Ethnic Quilt*, 50, 95.
68. The house in Boyle Heights was owned by wealthy landowners in the neighborhood, the Hollenbeck family. Robert Kursinski, President, Neighborhood Music School, interview with author, January 24, 2003. The school is currently located in Boyle Heights near the corner of Fourth and Boyle Streets. Anthony Macías brought this school to my attention in his paper, "From Progressivism to Policing: Youth Culture and Public Space in Postwar Los Angeles," who cites a description of the school in "Los Angeles Neighborhood Music School Fills Need in Community," *The Southwestern Musician* 15 (June 1949).
69. *Los Angeles County Culture and the Community*, 42. On the board of directors of the Civic Bureau were David Faries, Arthur Bent, John Mott, Colonel J. B. Chaffey, Antoinette Sabel, Colonel William Eric Fowler, William Lacy, William Garland, Mrs. J. F. Sartori, and Judge Gavin Craig.

70. Robert Kursinski, interview with author, January 24, 2003. Sam Goldwyn Studios produced the film, *They Shall Have Music*.
71. Two major sponsors were Burkell Richardson during the 1930s, who owned a music store, and Dr. Norman Wright during the 1940s, who was an organist at First Methodist in Hollywood.
72. "Los Angeles Neighborhood Music School Fills Need in Community," *The Southwestern Musician* 15 (June 1949). Although the board officially changed the name to the Neighborhood Music School Association, it was still called the Neighborhood Music Settlement until the mid-1990s, when it changed to the Neighborhood Music School. Odell left the Settlement in 1963 to found the Los Angeles Music and Art School (LAMAS) on Third Street near Indiana Street. Robert Kursinski, interview with author, January 24, 2003; Cardenas, "Music School Humming Along at 87," B3.
73. Robert Kursinski, interview with author, January 24, 2003.
74. Raphael Sonenshein, *Politics in Black and White: Race and Power in Los Angeles* (Princeton: Princeton University Press, 1993), 22. John Laslett gives the figure at 15,579 blacks in 1910, or 3 percent of the city's population, in "Historical Perspectives: Immigration and the Rise of a Distinctive Urban Region, 1900–1970," in *Ethnic Los Angeles*, ed. Robert Waldinger and Mehdi Bozorgmehr (New York: Russell Sage Foundation, 1996), 43.
75. The five areas were Central Avenue, Boyle Heights, West Side on Jefferson Avenue (between Normandie and Western Avenue), Temple Street, and the Furlong Tract. Don Lee White, "Black Churches and Black Church Music in Los Angeles" (unpublished manuscript, 1998), pp. 7–8, SCL. On black musicians, see Bette Yarbrough Cox, *Central Avenue—Its Rise and Fall (1890–c. 1955), Including the Musical Renaissance of Black Los Angeles* (Los Angeles: BEEM, 1996), 10.
76. Sonenshein, *Politics in Black and White*, 28.
77. Cox, *Central Avenue*, 14.
78. At Polytechnic High School he studied music with Mr. M. H. Grist. Beasley, *Negro Trail Blazers of California*, 209.
79. *Negro Who's Who in California* (Los Angeles [?]: Negro Who's Who, 1948), 89. Wilkins may also have studied briefly at the Sherwood Music School, located on 715 Park View Avenue in Los Angeles, possibly a branch of the same school in Chicago, which advertised its services in *The Overture* 4 (November 15, 1924): 13.
80. Samuel Browne taught at Jefferson High School in 1936 before moving to Pacific Palisades School in the 1960s. He describes Wilkins in Cox, *Central Avenue*, 15.
81. Cox, *Central Avenue*, 17, 97.
82. Labeled the "4th Commencement," over 60 certificates of merit and promotion and over 12 diplomas were given out. "Wilkink' [sic] Piano Academy in Recital," *The California Eagle*, Friday, June 29, 1928, p. 6. The article also noted that Lena Dorsey, from "branch one of Wilkins' Piano Academy" planned to bring six pupils to participate in the event.
83. Cox, *Central Avenue*, 18, 100–1. The Independent Church (founded in 1915) was located at the corner of 18th and Paloma Streets. White, "Black Churches and Black Church Music in Los Angeles," SCL.
84. Cox, *Central Avenue*, 100–1.

85. Pianist Genevieve Barnes Lewis, who taught at the Academy, recalls that teachers at the branches in Los Angeles were Lucille Blanton, Shelone Brewster, Gilbert Allen, and Mildred Emmett, and in Bakersfield, Lena Dorsey Reid. Among prominent students of the Academy were organist Fannie Benjamin and Florence Cadrez Brantley, the Secretary to the Local 767 Musicians' Union. Cox, *Central Avenue*, 17–18.
86. Cox, *Central Avenue*, 18–19; and *Who's Who in Colored Los Angeles, 1930–31* (Los Angeles: California Eagle Publishing, 1931). Cortot founded the Ecole Normale de Musique de Paris in 1919; see <http://www.ecolenormalecortot.com/>. Accessed on November 27, 2003. Gray's diploma was confirmed by Nadia Dufruit, Admissions Office, Ecole Normale de Musique de Paris, communication with author, December 1, 2003.
87. Cox, *Central Avenue*, 51. An advertisement claims, "Systematic instruction based on scientific principles that guide the student from the earliest to the most advanced stage of proficiency. European system." Ibid., 100.
88. Cox, *Central Avenue*, 18–19. Charlotta Bass, editor of the *California Eagle*, notes that the Second Baptist Church, originally located on Regina Street, was founded about the same time as the First African Methodist Episcopal Church in 1872, in *Forty Years: Memoirs From the Pages of a Newspaper* (Los Angeles: Charlotta Bass, 1960), 16. Church organist and writer Don Lee White, however, claims it was founded in 1885 and was eventually located near the corner of 24th Street and Central Avenue. White, "Black Churches and Black Church Music in Los Angeles," SCL; see also Engh, *Frontier Faiths*, 59–60. St. Philips Episcopal was founded in 1907.
89. Cox, *Central Avenue*, 19, 46. It is not known when the Musicians' Association in Los Angeles was founded. The music editor of the *Chicago Defender*, Nora Holt, founded the National Association of Negro Musicians (NANM) in 1919. Eileen Southern, *The Music of Black Americans: A History*, 2nd ed. (New York: W. W. Norton, 1983), 305–6.
90. The student was Jack Kelson. Clora Bryant, ed., *Central Avenue Sounds: Jazz in Los Angeles* (Berkeley and Los Angeles: University of California Press, 1998), 209.
91. Alfred Metzger, "Symphony Orchestra is Leading Organization," *Musical Review* 9 (June 1906): 15. The *Musical Review* was founded in 1901.
92. *Pacific Coast Musical Review* 28 (September 25, 1915): 32.
93. By 1920, Joseph Zoellner Sr. had become head of the violin department of the University of Redlands, while Amandus Zoellner was head of the violin department of Pomona College. *Who's Who in Music in California* (Los Angeles: Colby and Pryibil, 1920), 148.
94. Beatrice de Troost managed the concerts from 1927 to 1945, which later took place on Thursday afternoons. Behymer, *Starlit Trails*, 657–58. Anne Bollinger sang at the Met from 1949 to 1953, and Brian Sullivan from 1948 to 1961. Metropolitan Opera Annals (CD-ROM, 2000). I would like to thank John Koegel for bringing this latter reference to my attention.
95. Stevenson, "William Andrews Clark, Jr.," 31–52. On the founding of the Los Angeles Philharmonic, see also Smith, *The Philharmonic Orchestra of Los Angeles*.
96. C. L. Bagley, "History of the Band and Orchestra Business in Los Angeles," *The Overture* 1 (October 1, 1921): 5.
97. Swan, *Music in the Southwest*, 244–45.

98. Programs, Philharmonic Orchestra of Los Angeles, 1923–1924, LAPA. See also Smith, *The Philharmonic Orchestra of Los Angeles*, 61–64.
99. William C. Hartshorn and Helen S. Leavitt, *The Mentor: Making Friends With Music* (Boston: Ginn, 1940), 3. I would like to thank Gloria Ricci Lothrop for bringing this work to my attention.
100. Trinity Auditorium, on South Grand Avenue between Eighth and Ninth Streets, opened in September 1914. For the elementary schools: Elgar, Military March No. 1, "Pomp and Circumstance"; Massenet, Ballet Music from *El Cid;* Tchaikovsky, "Andante cantabile" from String Quartet, Op. 11; Godard, *Adagio Pathetique;* and Chabrier, *España*, Rhapsody for Orchestra. For the intermediate schools two weeks later, Bizet's *Carmen* Suite No. 2 was substituted for the Massenet piece, and the Tchaikovsky work was dropped. Programs, Philharmonic Orchestra of Los Angeles, 1919–20, LAPA.
101. Examples of black students who attended these schools were the piano teachers William Wilkins and John Gray at Polytechnic High School, and composer Bruce Forsythe at Manual Arts High School. Los Angeles Polytechnic High School was founded in 1897 at the corner of Washington Boulevard and Flower Streets downtown. See <http://poly.lausd.k12.ca.us/>. Manual Arts High School was founded in 1910 and soon moved to 4131 South Vermont Avenue. See <http://www.lausd.k12.ca.us/Manual_Arts_HS/>. Lincoln High School is located at 3501 North Broadway, and Los Angeles High School, the city's oldest, was founded in 1873 and moved to its current site at 4650 West Olympic Boulevard in 1917. See <http://www.lausd.k12.ca.us/Los_Angeles_HS/>. Accessed on December 1, 2003. See also Marshall Stimson, "History of Los Angeles High School," *Historical Society of Southern California Quarterly* 24 (September 1942): 98–109.
102. For the first program: Elgar, Military March No. 1, "Pomp and Circumstance"; Tchaikovsky, "Andante cantabile" from String Quartet, Op. 11; Massenet, Ballet Music from *Le Cid;* Saint-Saëns, Prelude to *Le Deluge;* Wagner, Prelude to Act III of *Lohengrin*. For the second program: Wagner, March from *Tannhäuser;* Tchaikovsky, "Andante cantabile" from String Quartet, Op. 11; Grieg, Suite No. 1 from *Peer Gynt;* Massenet, excerpt from *Scenes Alsaciennes;* Chabrier, *España*, Rhapsody for Orchestra. Programs, Philharmonic Orchestra of Los Angeles, 1919–20, LAPA.
103. Smith, *The Philharmonic Orchestra of Los Angeles*, 63.
104. These took place on November 8, November 16, December 6, December 14, February 23, March 15, April 4, and April 19. Programs, Philharmonic Orchestra of Los Angeles, 1921–22, LAPA.
105. These concerts took place on November 10, January 12, and April 30. Programs, Philharmonic Orchestra of Los Angeles, 1921–22, LAPA.
106. The Hibler School of Music was located on 95 S. Madison Avenue in Pasadena. *Southern California Musicians' Directory, 1916–1917*, iv.
107. These concerts took place on December 8, January 13, February 24, and April 3. Programs, Philharmonic Orchestra of Los Angeles, 1921–22, LAPA.
108. Programs, Philharmonic Orchestra of Los Angeles, 1922–40, LAPA.
109. Hartshorn and Leavitt, *The Mentor*, 4.
110. Hartshorn and Leavitt, *The Mentor*, 74.
111. Among the pieces performed on December 4, 1937 were the Overture to Beethoven's *Leonore*, the First Movement of Mozart's Violin Concerto, and the

Prelude to Wagner's *Die Meistersinger;* on January 19, 1938, Stravinsky's *Little Suite;* on February 17, 1938, Sibelius's *Swan of Tuonela;* and on February 26, 1938, an arrangement for trumpet and orchestra of Scriabin's Etude No. 2. Programs, Philharmonic Orchestra of Los Angeles, 1937–38, LAPA.

112. Leni Boorstin, Director of Public Affairs and Community Relations, Los Angeles Philharmonic Orchestra, interview with author, tape recording, June 21, 2000. I would also like to thank Gloria Lothrop for her recollections as a schoolgirl in Los Angeles attending orchestral concerts at Dorothy Chandler Pavilion.
113. Deverell, "My America or Yours?," 277–301.
114. Margaret Hindle Hazen and Robert M. Hazen, *The Music Men: An Illustrated History of Brass Bands in America, 1800–1920* (Washington, D.C.: Smithsonian Institution Press, 1987).
115. *Fortune* (August 1939): 49, also quoted in Lieberman, *Steinway & Sons*, 188.
116. Levine discusses the distance that sacralization created between amateur and professional musicians in *Highbrow/Lowbrow*, 139.

Chapter 3

1. There is a comparatively large historiography on the Bowl's development. See especially Smith, "Founding the Hollywood Bowl," 206–42; and the collection of articles in *The Hollywood Bowl: Tales of Summer Nights*, ed. Michael Buckland and John Henken (Los Angeles: Balcony Press, 1996). See also Isabel Morse Jones, *Hollywood Bowl* (New York and Los Angeles: G. Schirmer, 1936); Thomas Perry Stricker, *The Hollywood Bowl* (Los Angeles: Pepper Tree Press, 1939); John Orlando Northcutt, *The Hollywood Bowl Story* (Hollywood: Hollywood Bowl Association, 1962); John Orlando Northcutt, *Magic Valley: The Story of Hollywood Bowl* (Los Angeles: Fashion Press, 1967); and Grace Koopal, *Miracle of Music: The History of the Hollywood Bowl* (Los Angeles: Charles E. Toberman, 1972). There are also two fascinating, if very different, unpublished versions of the Bowl's founding: T. Perceval Gerson, "Hollywood Bowl: A Personal Narrative" [unpublished manuscript, n.d.], Box 89, Folder 6, Gerson Papers/YRL; and Andrae Nordskog, "The Earliest Musical History in the Hollywood Bowl 1920 and 1921" [unpublished manuscript, 1957], Fol. 20–12, Nordskog Collection.
2. On the history of brass bands, see Hazen and Hazen, *The Music Men*. Damrosch's recollection is in *My Musical Life* (New York: Charles Scribner's Sons, 1926), 203. The concert at Lewisohn Stadium took place in 1918; see Northcutt, *Magic Valley*, 47.
3. Jones, *Hollywood Bowl*, 9–10; Smith, "Founding the Hollywood Bowl," 209.
4. Northcutt, *The Hollywood Bowl Story*, 5–6. The Theatre Arts Alliance went through several changes in name over the next two decades. It became the Community Park and Art Association in 1920, then the Hollywood Bowl Association (1925–1932), and it went through further reincarnations. Between 1935 and 1944, it was called the Southern California Symphony Association. Carol Merrill-Mirsky, *Hollywood Bowl Souvenir Book* (Los Angeles: Los Angeles Philharmonic Association, 2000), 29.
5. Joshua Alper, "The Cahuenga Pass Treasure," *Southern California Quarterly* 81 (Spring 1999): 89–116. The Battle of Cahuenga took place on February 20, 1845,

near present-day Ventura Boulevard and Coldwater Canyon: James J. Rawls and Walton Bean, *California: An Interpretive History*, 12th ed. (Boston: McGraw Hill, 1998), 60.

6. Lynn Moody Hoffman, "Starlit Trails," Research Summary Report (unpublished manuscript, 1977), p. 5, Behymer Collection Reference Papers, HL. See also Jones, *Hollywood Bowl*, 28.
7. Northcutt, *Magic Valley*, 39.
8. Glenarvon Behymer Jr., interview with author, tape recording, Pasadena, CA, May 25, 1999.
9. David Fine, *Imagining Los Angeles: A City in Fiction* (Albuquerque: University of New Mexico Press, 2000), 7.
10. "California 1900 . . . on the Threshold of a New Century," *California History* 79 (Fall 2000): 113–14.
11. Rolle, *Los Angeles*, 5.
12. The Los Angeles Aqueduct was built in 1913. Oil discoveries in 1920–22 were at Huntington Beach, Signal Hill, Santa Fe Springs, and Torrance. At least since the production of *The Squaw Man* by Jesse L. Lasky, Samuel Goldwyn and Cecil B. DeMille in 1914, motion pictures had become one of the region's most important industries: Earl Pomeroy, "From War Profits to Peace Profits," in *Los Angeles: Biography of a City*, ed. John and LaRee Caughey (Berkeley and Los Angeles: University of California Press, 1977), 394–95.
13. Starr, *Material Dreams*, chap. 4–5.
14. Hollywood was bounded by the Santa Monica Mountains to the north, Beverly Boulevard to the south, Vermont Avenue to the east, and La Brea Avenue to the west. Richard Longstreth, *City Center to Regional Mall: Architecture, the Automobile, and Retailing in Los Angeles, 1920–1950* (Cambridge, MA: MIT Press, 1997), 81–82.
15. Marc Wanamaker, "Southern California Culture and Film, 1908–1930," paper presented at conference on Community and Culture in Los Angeles, University of La Verne, CA, October 5, 2002.
16. Tom Sitton, *John Randolph Haynes: California Progressive* (Stanford, CA: Stanford University Press, 1992), 236.
17. Correspondence from these figures are in Box 2, Gerson Papers/HL. I would like to thank Bill Deverell for bringing these archival materials to my attention.
18. Smith, "Founding the Hollywood Bowl," 209, 214–15.
19. Smith, "Founding the Hollywood Bowl," 5; and written communication from Catherine Parsons Smith to Lance Bowling, November 13, 1991. I thank Lance Bowling for providing me with a copy of this letter.
20. Smith, "Founding the Hollywood Bowl," 207, 216, 233 n. 8; and Smith, " 'Popular Prices Will Prevail,' " 208–11.
21. Among Toberman's many projects were Grauman's Egyptian Theater (est. 1922), Grauman's Chinese Theater (est. 1927), and the Hollywood Roosevelt Hotel (est. 1927). Jones, *Hollywood Bowl*, 18.
22. Carol McMichael Reese, "Architecture for Performance," *The Hollywood Bowl*, ed. Michael Buckland and John Henken, 42.
23. Koopal, *Miracle of Music*, chap. 7.
24. Henken, "A Bowl Resounding," 10. On Carter, see also Smith, "Founding the Hollywood Bowl," 207, 216–25.
25. Jones, *Hollywood Bowl*, 32; Program, Hollywood Bowl Summer Concerts, July 5–9, 1927, p. 64, HBA.

26. Gerson, "Hollywood Bowl: A Personal Narrative," p. 4, Gerson Papers/YRL.
27. On the decorative arts, see Kathleen D. McCarthy, *Women's Culture: American Philanthropy and Art, 1830–1930* (Chicago: The University of Chicago Press, 1991).
28. Jones, *Hollywood Bowl*, 11–14. See also Northcutt, *Magic Valley*, 37–41.
29. Gerson, "Hollywood Bowl: A Personal Narrative," Gerson Papers/YRL.
30. The Alliance eventually repaid Mrs. Stevenson and Mrs. Clarke in full, including interest and expenses. Jones, *Hollywood Bowl*, 17; Northcutt, *Magic Valley*, 40. Mrs. Stevenson wanted to create a cycle of seven plays based on major religious figures, which the Theatre Arts Alliance resisted. She sold her interest in the Bowl property in 1920 and died two years later traveling in what was then Palestine. Smith, "Founding the Hollywood Bowl," 212–14.
31. Swan, *Music in the Southwest*, 239.
32. Jane Addams, *The Spirit of Youth and the City Streets* (New York: Macmillan, 1910), 98.
33. Schockman, "Is Los Angeles Governable?," 57–66.
34. Henken, "A Bowl Resounding," 13; and Gerald Woods, "A Penchant for Probity: California Progressives and the Disreputable Pleasures," in *California Progressivism Revisited*, ed. William Deverell and Tom Sitton (Berkeley and Los Angeles: University of California Press, 1994), 99–113. On women in California during the Progressive era, see Jensen and Lothrop, *California Women*, chap. 3.
35. Program, Hollywood Bowl Summer Concerts, July 7–11, 1925, p. 1, HBA.
36. Olin Downes, "The Hollywood 'Bowl' Association and Its Artistic Destinies," *The New York Times*, Sunday, July 19, 1924, sec. 7, p. 5.
37. Downes, "The Hollywood 'Bowl' Association," 5.
38. Among the pieces were the Minuet from Mozart's *Symphony in G Minor*, Mendelssohn's *Spring Song* and *Spinning Song;* Beethoven's *Minuet in G;* and Dvorak's *Humoresque*. Debussy's *Golliwog's Cake-walk* from *Children's Corner* was also included, and the concert closed with Kreisler's *Liebesleid* and *Liebesfreud*. Program, Hollywood Bowl Summer Popular Concerts, August 6, 1922, pp. 19–21, HBA.
39. Program, Hollywood Bowl Summer Concerts, August 28, 1924, pp. 285–91, HBA.
40. Students at Hollywood High School carried "penny banks" for donations for the Bowl, and also frequently served as ushers at concerts. While they were unpaid, they did get car fare. As a result of Hollywood High School's involvement, its graduation ceremonies continue to take place at the Bowl each year. Carol Merrill-Mirsky, discussion with author, Hollywood Bowl Museum, October 25, 2002.
41. Jones, *Hollywood Bowl*, 33; Smith, *The Philharmonic Orchestra of Los Angeles*, 81; Smith, "Founding the Hollywood Bowl," 219, 230.
42. "Multitudes Assemble in Easter Sunrise Worship," *Los Angeles Times*, Monday, April 13, 1925, Part I, p. 1.
43. Quoted in Henken, "A Bowl Resounding," 10.
44. Program, Hollywood Bowl Summer Concerts, July 5, 1927, p. 20, HBA. The Native American ceremonial took place on September 12, 14, 16, and 17, 1927.
45. Henken, "A Bowl Resounding," 10–11; Naima Prevots, "How the Bowl Danced: An Era of Exploration," in *The Hollywood Bowl*, ed. Michael Buckland and John Henken, 47–51. On Duncan, see also Jensen and Lothrop, *California Women*, 50, 55.
46. Program, Hollywood Bowl, Symphony Under the Stars, Sixth Week, August 17–20, 1937, HBA. I would like to thank Carol Merill-Mirsky for bringing this concert to my attention.

47. Program, La Fiesta, Hollywood Bowl, September 8, 1931, MCA; China War Relief Concert Program, April 4, 1943, HBA.
48. Laslett, "Historical Perspectives," 43; McWilliams, *Southern California Country*, 321.
49. McWilliams, *Southern California Country*, 321. On the founding of Nisei Week, see Lon Kurashige, *Japanese American Celebration and Conflict: A History of Ethnic Identity and Festival, 1934–1990* (Berkeley and Los Angeles: University of California Press, 2002), chap. 2.
50. The concert was for the benefit of the Japanese Children's Home, and included vocalists E. R. Ellis and Myrtle Ouellet Cockburn, and violist Taye Kojima, who performed selections of primarily nineteenth-century European art music. "Will Sing for Jap Children," *Los Angeles Times*, Sunday, July 9, 1922, Part II, p. 9.
51. Henry Yu, *Thinking Orientals: Migration, Contact, and Exoticism in Modern America* (New York: Oxford University Press, 2001), 63.
52. One film, *Anchors Aweigh* (1945), with Frank Sinatra and Gene Kelly, featured Iturbi playing the piano at the Bowl. Lisa Mitchell, "Hollywood and the Bowl," in *The Hollywood Bowl*, ed. Michael Buckland and John Henken, 78–79.
53. Swan, *Music in the Southwest*, 239.
54. The 99-year lease was renegotiated several times since then, but the site is still leased from the County. Carol Merill-Mirsky, discussion with author, October 25, 2002.
55. "County Gets $1,500,000 Art, Music Center," *Los Angeles Herald*, October 16, 1924, Box 5, Folder 5/3, Gerson Papers/YRL.
56. Cited in Glenn M. Tindall, "A Page About Next Season," Program, Hollywood Bowl, Symphony Under the Stars, August 29–31, September 1–3, 1933, p. 5, Box 89, Folder 5, Gerson Papers/YRL.
57. Souvenir Program, Grand Dedicatory Benefit Opening of the New Hollywood Bowl, June 22, 1926, HBA.
58. "Made in California: Art, Image, and Identity, 1900–2000," Exhibit at Los Angeles County Museum of Art, October 22, 2000–February 25, 2001.
59. The engineering firm was Elliot, Bowen and Walz, whose designs the firm Allied Architects used to construct the final shell. Reese, "Architecture for Performance," 34–42; Merrill-Mirsky, *Hollywood Bowl*, 7–9. On the Bowl's construction, see also Northcutt, *Magic Valley*, chap. 20.
60. Program, Hollywood Bowl Summer Concerts, July 12, 1927, p. 64, HBA.
61. Souvenir Program, Grand Dedicatory Benefit Opening of the New Hollywood Bowl, June 22, 1926, p. 3, HBA.
62. Henken, "A Bowl Resounding," 12.
63. Program, Philharmonic Orchestra of Los Angeles, 1923–24, LAPA; Smith, *The Philharmonic Orchestra of Los Angeles*, 61–64. Rothwell was no stranger to outdoor concerts; he gave about 70 concerts at the Lewisohn Stadium in New York during the summer of 1920 alone, and gave popular concerts at the Los Angeles Coliseum each March.
64. Horowitz, *Wagner Nights*, 295–301.
65. Edwin Schallert, *Los Angeles Times* [n.d.], quoted in Herbert Glass, "A Home for Opera," in *The Hollywood Bowl*, ed. Michael Buckland and John Henken, 62. The first production of *Carmen* at the Bowl took place on July 8, 1922. See also Northcutt, *Hollywood Bowl Story*, 10.
66. Permanent Exhibit, Hollywood Bowl Museum.
67. Thomas Cassidy, interview with author, tape recording, Van Nuys, CA, June 25, 1999. See also Northcutt, *Hollywood Bowl Story*, 15; and Northcutt, *Magic*

Valley, 121. The Bowl's audience capacity decreased over the years, in part due to fire regulations, so that it currently can hold less then 18,000 people.

68. Tchaikovsky, "Allegro molto vivace" from Symphony No. 6; Anton Rubinstein, *Serenade Russe, No. 2*; Alexander Borodin, March from *Prince Igor*; Mikhail Ippolitov-Ivanov, *Caucasian Sketches*; Tchaikovsky, *1812 Overture*. Program, Hollywood Bowl Summer Popular Concerts, Tuesday, July 25, 1922, pp. 5–7, HBA.
69. Program, Hollywood Bowl Summer Popular Concerts, July 28, 1922, pp. 9–13, HBA.
70. Program, Hollywood Bowl Summer Concerts, July 28, 1925, pp. 13–15, HBA.
71. Two composers then living in Pasadena were featured: Morton Mason, *Introduction and Polonaise*, and Arthur Farwell, *The Domain of Hurakan*, with soloists Mr. and Mrs. Norman Hassler, also from Pasadena. Will Rounds, conductor of the Pasadena Community Orchestra, led the Sunday afternoon concert. Program, Hollywood Bowl Summer Popular Concerts, July 30, 1922, p. 19, HBA.
72. Program, Hollywood Bowl Summer Concerts, August 22, 1924, p. 251, HBA.
73. Edwin Schallert, "Wood Triumphs," *Los Angeles Times*, July 15, 1925, part II, p. 9.
74. Program, Hollywood Bowl Summer Concerts, July 14–17, 1925, pp. 13–29. HBA.
75. Program, Hollywood Bowl Summer Concerts, August 23, 1924, pp. 259–61, HBA.
76. Quoted from a 1930 issue of *The Gramophone*, cited in Henken, "A Bowl Resounding," 14.
77. Lance Bowling, "The Evolution of the Recording Industry in Los Angeles, 1896–1950," paper presented at the Los Angeles Musical Heritage Conference, Biltmore Hotel, Los Angeles, CA, October 31, 1987.
78. Program, Hollywood Bowl Summer Concerts, August 30, 1924, p. 299, HBA. The piece was first written for chamber orchestra in 1919, then adapted for full orchestra in 1922.
79. Henken, "A Bowl Resounding," 17.
80. Dorothy Lamb Crawford, *Evenings On and Off the Roof: Pioneering Concerts in Los Angeles, 1939–1971* (Berkeley and Los Angeles: University of California Press, 1995), 18.
81. Glass, "A Home for Opera," 64–65. Cadman lived in southern California from 1916 to 1946. Chief Os-Ke-Non-Ton recorded seven Mohawk songs in New York from 1915 to 1923; see Richard K. Spottswood, *Ethnic Music on Records: A Discography of Ethnic Recordings Produced in the United States, 1893 to 1942*, 7 vols. (Urbana: University of Illinois Press, 1990), 5, 2931.
82. Schoenberg wrote it for Leopold Stokowski and the Hollywood Bowl Orchestra in 1945, based on three themes from a cantata he composed in 1911, called *Gurrelieder*. Liner notes, *Hollywood Dreams*, Hollywood Bowl Orchestra, Philips 432, 109–2.
83. Judith Anne Still, Michael J. Dabrishus, and Carolyn L. Quin, *William Grant Still: A Bio-Bibliography* (Westport, CT: Greenwood Press, 1996), 32.
84. "Chappie" to Harold Bruce Forsythe, July 29, 1936, Box 13, Harold Bruce Forsythe Papers, HL.
85. Anderson sang Monteverdi's "Lamento d'Ariana," and Verdi's "O Don Fatale" from *Don Carlos*, on July 18, 1944. *Hollywood Bowl Magazine*, July 11–16, 1944, MHL.
86. Program, George Gershwin Memorial Concert, July 12, 1937, HBA. I would like to thank Lance Bowling for providing me with a recording of the concert.
87. Northcutt, *Hollywood Bowl Story*, 25. The first Gershwin Night in America was probably at Lewisohn Stadium in 1931 in New York, where Gershwin performed *Rhapsody in Blue* and his *March for Two Pianos and Orchestra*. A close friend of

Gershwin, the pianist, film composer, and laconic wit Oscar Levant, also performed. Oscar Levant, *A Smattering of Ignorance* (Garden City, NY: Garden City Publishing, 1942), 164.

88. "Having a Ball at the Bowl," *Festivals '89*, Supplement to *Musical America*, p. 17.
89. Northcutt, *Hollywood Bowl Story*, 113.
90. Carol Merrill-Mirsky, ed., *Exiles in Paradise* (Los Angeles: Hollywood Bowl Museum, 1991). See also Taylor, *Strangers in Paradise*, chap. 4.
91. Peter Heyworth, ed., *Conversations with Klemperer* (London: Victor Gollancz, 1973), 72; see also Merrill-Mirsky, *Exiles in Paradise*, 19.
92. Composer Enrique Fernandez Arbos orchestrated the Albéniz pieces. Program, Hollywood Bowl Summer Concerts, July 16, 1935, facsimile in Merrill-Mirsky, *Exiles in Paradise*, 18.
93. Crawford, *Evenings On and Off the Roof*, 18.
94. Program, Hollywood Bowl Summer Concerts, July 12, 1927, p. 64, HBA.
95. Weber, *Oberon* Overture; Mozart, Symphony in E-flat Major, K. 543; Wagner, Funeral March from *Götterdämmerung*, Prelude to Act I of *Lohengrin*; and Brahms, Symphony No. 1 in C Minor, Op. 68. Program, Hollywood Bowl Summer Concerts, Friday, July 26, 1940, facsimile in Merrill-Mirsky, *Exiles in Paradise*, 24. Walter died in Beverly Hills in 1962.
96. Artur Rubinstein, *My Many Years* (New York: Alfred A. Knopf, 1980), 500–1, 491; see also Merrill-Mirsky, *Exiles in Paradise*, 37.
97. Weber, *Oberon* Overture; Brahms, Concerto No. 2 for Piano and Orchestra in B-flat Major, Op. 83; Smetana, *The Moldau*; and three piano solos by Chopin: Nocturne in F-sharp Major, Waltz in C-sharp Minor, and Polonaise in A-flat Major. Program, Hollywood Bowl Summer Concerts, Thursday, July 17, 1941, facsimile in Merrill-Mirsky, *Exiles in Paradise*, 36. See also Rubinstein, *My Many Years*, 538.
98. Shortly afterward, Rachmaninoff died at his home in Beverly Hills. Henken, "A Bowl Resounding," 21.
99. *Hollywood Bowl Magazine*, July 11–16, 1944, Hollywood Bowl (1944–1946), MHL.
100. Announcer's Notes [anonymous], Film Music Concert [n.d.], Hollywood Bowl (1945), MHL.
101. The government had first imposed a limit of 5,000 people, but Mrs. Leiland Atherton Irish argued for 10,000, due in part to the large number of servicemen in Los Angeles, and the government concurred. Carol Merrill-Mirsky, discussion with author, October 25, 2002.
102. Program, "5th War Loan Bond Show," July 4, 1944, Actors and Actresses: Fund and Bond Drives, MHL.
103. The successor to Mrs. Carter, Mrs. Leiland Atherton Irish, continued to support this tradition. She organized the Bowl's first association of volunteers, and "would accept any challenge, contribute to any organization, or participate with that organization in any activity" to further the arts in southern California. Thomas Cassidy, interview with author, tape recording, Van Nuys, CA, June 25, 1999.
104. The A. C. Frost Company, a subsidiary of the Chicago and Milwaukee Electric Railroad, built an open-air pavilion at Ravinia Park in 1905 as part of a larger amusement park to attract customers for the railroad. A 3,000-seat theater and shell was built following a fire in 1949.

Chapter 4

1. Several Western cities have laid claim to this title, among them San Francisco and Berkeley. I borrow its usage relating to Los Angeles from art historian Nancy Moure, who writes: "Even late into the 1920's, art lovers were confident Los Angeles' climate gave it the potential of becoming the Athens of the West." *Plein Air Painters of California: The Southland*, ed. Ruth Lilly Westphal (Irvine, CA: Westphal, 1982), 14.
2. David Glassberg, *American Historical Pageantry: The Uses of Tradition in the Early Twentieth Century* (Chapel Hill: University of North Carolina Press, 1990), 4, 155. See also Smith, "Of Pageantry and Politics," 116.
3. Although the Ramona Pageant took place in Riverside County and the geographic focus of this book is metropolitan Los Angeles, I am including it here because most of the pageant was written in Los Angeles, most of the leading actors and musicians were from Los Angeles, and most of the audiences probably came from Los Angeles as well.
4. Kevin Starr, *Inventing the Dream: California Through the Progressive Era* (New York: Oxford University Press, 1985), 88; Naima Prevots, *American Pageantry: A Movement for Art and Democracy* (Ann Arbor: University of Michigan Press, 1990), 146–47.
5. Glassberg, *American Historical Pageantry*, 4.
6. For an institutional history of Krotona, see Joseph E. Ross, *Krotona of Old Hollywood, 1866–1913* (Montecito, CA: El Montecito Oaks Press, 1989).
7. Prevots, *American Pageantry*, 147–48.
8. [Ellis Reed], "Summary of Hollywood Bowl History" (manuscript, dated August 8, 1938), Box 40, Music and the Arts, BIII 9e bb3 (1), Ford Collection.
9. Programs, *The Pilgrimage Play*, 1922–1936; Theater Collection, Box 10/59, 10/92, HL. On Rudhyar and theosophy, see Carol Oja, "Dane Rudhyar's Vision of American Dissonance," *American Music* 17 (Summer 1998), 129–37. Rudhyar's original name was Daniel Chennevière, but his interest in East Indian philosophy led him to adopt the pseudonym Rudhyar. I thank Bill Thomson for this insight.
10. Evelyn Davis Culbertson, *He Heard America Singing: Arthur Farwell, Composer and Crusading Music Educator* (Metuchen, NJ: The Scarecrow Press, 1992), 208–10.
11. Program, *The Pilgrimage Play* [1936]; untitled article in *Daily News*, July 16, 1951, Box 40, Music and the Arts, BIII 9e bb4, Ford Collection.
12. Robert Withington, *English Pageantry: An Historical Outline*, 2 vols. (Cambridge, MA: Harvard University Press, 1918), 2: 195; also quoted in William Augustus Pullen, "The Ramona Pageant: An Historical and Analytical Study" (master's thesis, University of Southern California, 1973), 20.
13. Thomas H. Dickinson, *The Case of American Drama* (Boston: Houghton Mifflin, 1915), 149–50, 153. Three types of pageantry are biographical drama, which focuses on the life of a single person; pageant drama, which integrates music and dance to tell a historical tale, such as of a town or a specific event; and epic drama, which can involve casts in the hundreds or even thousands in a large-scale historical presentation. See also George McCalmon and Christian Moe, *Creating Historical Drama* (Carbondale: Southern Illinois University Press, 1965), 190–341; and Pullen, "The Ramona Pageant," 6 n. 4.

14. Glassberg points out that D. W. Griffith's *The Birth of a Nation* "resembled a pageant, with its abstract symbolism, allegorical finale, and tableaux vivants of famous historical scenes." Glassberg, *American Historical Pageantry*, 155.
15. Withington, *English Pageantry*, 2: 198–201; Pullen, "The Ramona Pageant," 21–26. On the masque, see also Dickinson, *The Case of American Drama*, 151–52.
16. Percy MacKaye, *The Playhouse and the Play* (New York: Macmillan, 1909), 114–15, 118; Pullen, "The Ramona Pageant," 31–32.
17. These were the Educational Pageant in Boston and the Philadelphia Pageant in 1908, and the Pageant of the Italian Renaissance in Chicago in 1909. Dickinson, *The Case of American Drama*, 160–61.
18. Percy MacKaye, *Caliban, by the Yellow Sands* (Garden City, NY: Doubleday, Page & Company, 1916), 156; Pullen, "The Ramona Pageant," 34 n. 57.
19. However, Michael Kammen points out that the "new pageantry" did not die out entirely during the interwar years, particularly in the South and the Pacific Northwest, in *Mystic Chords of Memory: The Transformation of Tradition in American Culture* (New York: Alfred A. Knopf, 1991), 422–26.
20. Percy MacKaye, *Community Drama: Its Motive and Method of Neighborliness* (Boston: Houghton Mifflin, 1917), esp. 5–7.
21. Pullen, "The Ramona Pageant," 35–36.
22. A description of this and other outdoor plays is on the Institute of Outdoor Drama website, in collaboration with the University of North Carolina at Chapel Hill: <http://www.unc.edu/depts/outdoor/>. The pageant website is http://www.thelostcolony.org/. Accessed on October 31, 2003.
23. Program, *The Mission Play by John Steven McGroarty, presented in the Mission play house at old San Gabriel Mission, California* [1924], Doheny; Program, *The Mission Play*, Hollywood Bowl, July 1, 1931, HBA; David Colker, " 'Mother' Revives Pioneer Spirit of 'Mission Play,' " *Los Angeles Times*, Friday, August 2, 1991, A23.
24. Dickinson, *The Case of American Drama*, 171.
25. Program, *The Mission Play*, Hollywood Bowl, July 1, 1931, HBA.
26. Program, *The Mission Play*, Hollywood Bowl, July 1, 1931, HBA.
27. Program, *The Mission Play* [1929], Honnold. On Whitsett, see Francis J. Weber, *Memories of an Old Mission: San Fernando, Rey de España* (Mission Hills, CA: Saint Francis Historical Society, 1997), 67–68. I would like to thank Gloria Lothrop for bringing this book to my attention.
28. MacLean began acting in the role in 1924. Among other actors prior to him were Benjamin Horning, Monroe Salisbury, and Frederick Warde. Programs, *The Mission Play*, Theater Collection, Box 10/2, 10/6 a, b, 10/7, 10/8, HL.
29. Reginaldo del Valle was state senator for two years, from 1882 to 1884. He then served as a delegate to Democratic Party conventions and as an elector, and was appointed by President Woodrow Wilson as his representative to Mexico. Online at <http://www.ranchocamulos.org/History/>. Accessed on November 1, 2003.
30. Program, *The Mission Play* [1913], Theater Collection, Box 10/24, HL. See also Cecilia Rasmussen, "L.A. Then and Now: Del Valle Family Played a Starring Role in Early California," *Los Angeles Times*, November 11, 2001, B4.
31. Programs, *The Mission Play*, Theater Collection, Box 10/1, 10/3 (2), HL; Program, *The Mission Play*, [1924], Doheny.
32. Program, *The Mission Play* [1913], Theater Collection, Box 10/24, HL.
33. Programs, *California: Seventeen Sixty Nine–Nineteen Nineteen, Speech to the Lions Club, Los Angeles, California [1919]*; *The Mission Play* [1924], Doheny. There is no record of the tribal affiliation of Chief Young Turtle.

34. Program, *The Mission Play* [1924], Doheny.
35. John Steven McGroarty, *California—Its History and Romance* (Los Angeles: Grafton Publishing Co., 1911); McGroarty, *Los Angeles From the Mountains to the Sea*, 3 vols. (Chicago and New York: American Historical Society, 1921); McGroarty, *History of Los Angeles County*, 3 vols. (Chicago: American Historical Society, 1923).
36. *Just California* (1903), reprinted in Program, *California: Seventeen Sixty Nine–Nineteen Nineteen*, Doheny.
37. E. K. Hoak, "John Steven McGroarty and the Mission Play," *California: Seventeen Sixty Nine—Nineteen Nineteen*; Program, *The Mission Play* [1924], Doheny. See also Starr, *Inventing the Dream*, 87–89.
38. Hoak, "John Steven McGroarty and the Mission Play," Doheny.
39. Hoak, "John Steven McGroarty and the Mission Play," Doheny. See also Earl Pomeroy, *The Pacific Slope: A History of California, Oregon, Washington, Idaho, Utah, and Nevada* (New York: Alfred A. Knopf, 1965), 348.
40. Miller was an early producer of navel oranges; see *Who's Who in the Pacific Southwest: A Compilation of Authentic Biographical Sketches of Citizens of Southern California and Arizona* (Los Angeles: The Times-Mirror Printing and Binding House, 1913), 257. On Riverside and the Rancho Jurupa, see Mildred Brooke Hoover, Hero Eugene Rensch, and Ethel Grace Rensch, *Historic Spots in California*, revised by Ruth Teiser with an introduction by Robert Glass Cleland (Stanford, CA: Stanford University Press, 1948), 35–36.
41. John Steven McGroarty, *The Golden Scroll* [n.p., n.d. [1927?]], HL. See also Program, *The Mission Play* [1924], pp. 6–9, Doheny.
42. Program, *The Mission Play* [1924], p. 8, Doheny.
43. Pomeroy, *The Pacific Slope*, 182, 184.
44. Program, *The Mission Play* [1924], p. 5, Doheny.
45. Program, *The Mission Play* [1924], p. 9, Doheny. On pageant master Henry Kabierske, see McGroarty, *Los Angeles From the Mountains to the Sea*, 382.
46. Program, *The Mission Play*, Hollywood Bowl, July 1, 1931, HBA.
47. Program, *The Mission Play* [1924], p. 9, Doheny. On the 1926 sales campaign, see William Deverell, *Whitewashed Adobe: The Rise of Los Angeles and the Remaking of its Mexican Past* (Berkeley and Los Angeles: University of California Press, 2004), 231–48.
48. Program, *The Mission Play* [1924], pp. 12–13, Doheny.
49. Program, *The Mission Play* [1924], pp. 12–13, Doheny.
50. Program, *The Mission Play* [1924], Doheny.
51. Program, *The Mission Play* [1924], p. 3, Doheny.
52. Program, *The Mission Play*, Hollywood Bowl, July 1, 1931, HBA.
53. Program, *The Mission Play*, Hollywood Bowl, July 1, 1931, HBA.
54. Program, *The Mission Play* [1924], pp. 4–5, Doheny. See also Deverell, *Whitewashed Adobe*, 244–45.
55. R. D. MacLean was Father Serra, Jane Rupple was Anita (who was half-Indian), portraying the same role since the play's inception in 1912, and William Maginetti played one of the Catalonian soldiers. Program, *The Mission Play*, Hollywood Bowl, July 1, 1931, HBA.
56. Program, *The Mission Play* [1926], Theater Collection, Box 10/10, HL.
57. Helen Hunt Jackson, *Ramona: A Story* (Boston: Roberts Bros., 1884).
58. Helen Hunt Jackson, *A Century of Dishonor* (Boston: Roberts Bros., 1881).
59. McWilliams, *Southern California Country*, 76.

60. The picture was entitled *Ramona: A Story of the White Man's Injustice to the Indian*, which the Biograph Company released in May 1910.
61. The only two years in which no pageant took place were in 1924, when an outbreak of Foot and Mouth Disease prevented people from crossing county lines, and in 1934, when the effects of the Great Depression briefly made it impossible to obtain funding for the pageant. Phil Brigandi, discussion with author, May 10, 2003. The second—longest-running pageant is probably *The Lost Colony*, which began in 1937.
62. "Ramona Pageant Almost Certain," *The Hemet News*, November 17, 1922, p. 1, RPA.
63. Program, *Ramona: California's Greatest Outdoor Play* [1936]), p. 3 (pages not numbered), HL.
64. Charles Lummis, *The Home of Ramona: Photographs of Camulos, the fine old Spanish Estate described by Mrs. Helen Hunt Jackson, as the Home of "Ramona"* (Los Angeles: Charles F. Lummis, 1888), p. 1.
65. Program, *Ramona: California's Greatest Outdoor Play* [1936]), p. 1, HL.
66. The original cylinder recording currently resides in the Southwest Museum, and a copy is in the Ramona Pageant Association Archives.
67. Mrs. J. C. Jordan may have been the basis for the character of Aunti Ri in the novel. Jackson wrote *Ramona* during a five-month period at the Berkeley Hotel in New York. Phil Brigandi and John W. Robinson, "The Killing of Juan Diego: From Murder to Mythology," *Journal of San Diego History* 5 (Winter/Spring 1994): 11.
68. The only full-length study on Holme is Phil Brigandi, *Garnet Holme: California's Pageant Master* (Hemet, CA: Ramona Pageant Association, 1991).
69. Brigandi, *Garnet Holme*, 1–21.
70. Brigandi, *Garnet Holme*, 21–31. The Desert Play, based on a Mary Austin play called *Fire* about an Indian tribe's search for fire, took play at Tahquitz Canyon in November 1921.
71. Program, *Ramona: California's Greatest Outdoor Play* [1936]), p. 31, HL.
72. Program, *Ramona: California's Greatest Outdoor Play* [1936]), p. 31, HL.
73. Program, *Ramona Pageant* [1932]), RPA.
74. The actual Rancho Camulos (an Indian word meaning "Juniper") is located near Píru in the lower half of Ventura County. It is this ranch, consisting of about 1,400 acres, that Lummis visited, and his book depicts the inner court, the "Ramona tree," and other artifacts. Lummis managed to meet the family, and in a strange re-creation of the novel, he promptly fell in love with the widow's daughter, although the widow quashed the match. Lummis relates that when Jackson arrived in Los Angeles, she asked Señor Don Antonio F. Coronel where she might find a "typical old Spanish home." He pointed her to Rancho Camulos, where she stayed a few hours, which she duly noted in a letter to Don Coronel. The region, Lummis asserts in his typical florid style, "comprises of as fair a valley as the sun ever shone on." Lummis, *The Home of Ramona*, p. 2. An excellent analysis of Rancho Camulos and the "Ramona myth" is Phil Brigandi, "The Rancho and the Romance Rancho Camulos: The Home of Ramona," *Ventura County Historical Society Quarterly* 42, nos. 3 and 4 (1998): 5–45.
75. McGroarty, *California—Its History and Romance.*
76. José Arias Jr., telephone interview with author, Pasadena, CA, June 3, 2003.
77. José Arias Jr., interview with author, Pasadena, CA, March 14, 2004.

78. *Spanish Songs of Old California*, collected and translated by Charles F. Lummis, with pianoforte accompaniments by Arthur Farwell (Los Angeles: Charles F. Lummis, 1923).
79. *Spanish Songs of Old California*, 14–15.
80. *Spanish Songs of Old California*, 6–7.
81. In addition to his brother-in-law Antonio Corral, accompanying José Arias Sr. were his sons José Jr., Alfonzo, and Antonio; in 2003 José Arias III played in the group. José Arias Jr., interview with author, March 14, 2004.
82. She originated the role in 1923, returned in 1925 and again in 1931, when she played it until 1962, for a total of 29 years. Pullen, "The Ramona Pageant," 226.
83. Phil Brigandi, discussion with author, May 10, 2003. See also *The Ramona Pageant: A Pictorial History, 1923–1998* (Marceline, MO: Heritage House, 1997), 33.
84. The first scholarly analyses, which were highly laudatory, were by Pauline B. Deuel, *Mexican Serenade: The Story of the Mexican Players and the Padua Hills Theatre* (Padua Hills, Claremont, CA: Padua Institute, 1961); and Norma Hopland Blakeslee, "History of Padua Hills Theatre," *Pomona Valley Historian* 9 (Spring 1973): 47–68. More critical analyses are by Alicia Arrízon, "Contemporizing Performance: Mexican California and the Padua Hills Theater," *Mester* 22 and 23 (Special Double Issue, Chicana/o Discourse, Fall 1993/Spring 1994): 5–30; and Matt Garcia, " 'Just Put On That Padua Hills Smile': The Mexican Players and the Padua Hills Theatre, 1931–1974," *California History* 74 (Fall 1995): 244–61. See also Matt Garcia, *A World of Its Own: Race, Labor, and Citrus in the Making of Greater Los Angeles, 1900–1970* (Chapel Hill: University of North Carolina Press, 2001), chap. 4.
85. Garcia, " 'Just Put On That Padua Hills Smile,' " 249.
86. Norma Hopland Blakeslee, "History of Padua Hills Theatre," *Pomona Valley Historian* 9 (Spring 1973): 47–48.
87. Program, Claremont Community Players, April 20, 21, 1931, PHC/PPL.
88. Deuel, *Mexican Serenade*, 39–40.
89. Program, Little Theatre Padua Hills, July–September [1931], PHC/PPL.
90. On Dickinson, see Blakeslee, "History of Padua Hills Theatre," 54.
91. These are "La hamaca," "El quelele," "El zapatero," and "Adios, adios amores." Lummis, *Spanish Songs of Old California*, 6–7, 10–11, 20–21, 34–35.
92. Program, Padua Hills Theatre, July 28–September 16 [?], 1931, PHC/PPL.
93. Program, Padua Hills Theatre, July 28–September 16 [?], 1931, PHC/PPL.
94. Performance times were at 2:30 P.M. and 8:30 P.M. Program, Padua Hills Theatre, July 28–September 16 [?], 1931, PHC/PPL.
95. Program, Padua Hills Theatre, January 19–March 9, 1935, PHC/PPL.
96. Program, Padua Hills Theatre, January 19–March 9, 1935, PHC/PPL.
97. *Las Posadas: The Songs of Christmas in Mexico As Sung Each Christmas at the Padua Hills Theatre* (Padua Hills, CA: Bess Garner, 1935), HL.
98. Garcia, " 'Put On That Padua Hills Smile,' " 249, 358 n. 20.
99. Garcia, " 'Put On That Padua Hills Smile,' " 252.
100. Blakeslee, "History of Padua Hills Theatre," 53.
101. Introduction, *Las Posadas*.
102. Deuel, *Mexican Serenade*, 45–47.
103. Program, Padua Hills Theatre, January 5–February 19, 1938, PHC/PPL.

104. Garcia, " 'Put On That Padua Hills Smile,' " 259–60; Arrízon, "Contemporizing Performance."
105. The film was released in the United States on February 3, 1945. Dave Smith, *Disney A to Z: The Updated Official Encyclopedia* (New York: Hyperion, 1998), 552; see also Deuel, *Mexican Serenade*, 31, 40.
106. Deuel, *Mexican Serenade*, 42.
107. Garcia, " 'Put On That Padua Hills Smile,' " 260.
108. Hollywood Bowl Collection, MCA.
109. David Colker, " 'Mother' Revives Pioneer Spirit of 'Mission Play,' "*Los Angeles Times*, Friday, August 2, 1991, A23.

Chapter 5

1. Lance Bowling, "The Evolution of the Recording Industry in Los Angeles, 1896–1950," paper presented at the Los Angeles Musical Heritage Conference, Biltmore Hotel, Los Angeles, CA, October 31, 1987. I would like to thank Lance Bowling for providing me with a copy of the paper.
2. Glass claimed to have made $4,019 from fifteen phonographs in 1890. David Nasaw, *Going Out: The Rise and Fall of Public Amusements* (Cambridge, MA: Harvard University Press, 1993), 121–22.
3. Nasaw, *Going Out*, 126.
4. Theodor W. Adorno, "The Curves of the Needle," in *Essays on Music*, ed. Richard Leppert (Berkeley and Los Angeles: University of California Press, 2002), 272.
5. Simon Frith, *Sound Effects: Youth, Leisure, and the Politics of Rock 'n' Roll* (New York: Pantheon Books, 1981), 47.
6. Anthony Seeger and Louise Spear, eds., *Early Field Recordings* (Bloomington: Indiana University Press, 1987), 2.
7. John Koegel, "Mexican-American Music in Nineteenth-Century Southern California: The Lummis Wax Cylinder Collection at the Southwest Museum, Los Angeles" (Ph.D. diss., The Claremont Graduate School, 1994); see also Koegel, "Mexican-American Music in Nineteenth-Century California" 26–41; and Koegel, "Preserving the Sounds of the 'Old' Southwest," 1–29.
8. Charles Lummis to Thomas Seymour, February 27, 1904, MS.1.1.3918A, Lummis Correspondence Series, Lummis Collection. On the issue of preservation, see Koegel, "Mexican-American Music in Nineteenth-Century California," 27–28; see also Koegel's dissertation, "Mexican-American Music in Nineteenth-Century Southern California," 21–23.
9. Charles Lummis, "Catching Our Archaeology Alive," *The Southwest Society of the Archaeological Institute of America: The Southwest Museum, Three Years of Success*, Third Bulletin (Los Angeles, CA, May 1, 1907), 51–62.
10. Lummis, "Catching Our Archaeology Alive," 53.
11. Lummis sent two checks to Manuela García to cover expenses: on Oct. 18, 1904, and on Oct. 13, 1920, MS.1.1.1598, Lummis Correspondence Series, Lummis Collection.
12. He described his recordings at the Sherman Institute in April 1904 to both Dr. Seymour and Arthur Farwell. Lummis to Seymour, April 12, 1904, MS.1.1.3918A; Lummis to Farwell, April 12, 1904, MS.1.1.1388B, Lummis

Correspondence Series, Lummis Collection. On the locations, see Koegel, "Mexican-American Music in Nineteenth-Century California," 27.

13. Koegel, "Preserving the Sounds of the 'Old' Southwest," 1; Koegel, "Mexican-American Music in Nineteenth-Century California," 26–27. Lummis claimed in a letter to Dr. Seymour in September 1904 that he had already recorded over 450 cylinders. Lummis to Seymour, September 19, 1904, MS.1.1.3918A, Lummis Correspondence Series, Lummis Collection.
14. Koegel, "Preserving the Sounds of the 'Old' Southwest," 3.
15. Koegel, "Preserving the Sounds of the 'Old' Southwest," 5. The article was titled "New Mexican Folk-Songs," *Cosmopolitan* (October 1892).
16. Amado Chaves was speaker of the House of Representatives of the Territory of New Mexico. Turbesé Lummis Fiske and Keith Lummis, *Charles F. Lummis: The Man and His West* (Norman: University of Oklahoma Press, 1975), 45. Also quoted in Koegel, "Preserving the Sounds of the 'Old' Southwest," 5.
17. Koegel, "Mexican-American Music in Nineteenth-Century California," 33.
18. Koegel, "*Canciones del país*," 162–63; Koegel, "Mexican-American Music in Nineteenth-Century Southern California," 58.
19. Because it is not known at what speed the wax cylinders were recorded, scholars are unsure of the speed the cylinders should be replayed, but Koegel estimates that García most likely sang in the mezzo soprano range, in his dissertation, "Mexican-American Music in Nineteenth-Century Southern California," 61 n. 157.
20. Lummis, "Catching Our Archaeology Alive," 61–62.
21. Koegel, "*Canciones del país*," 168.
22. Koegel, "*Canciones del país*," 170.
23. Koegel, "*Canciones del país*," 172–76.
24. On the founding of the school by Riverside businessman Frank Miller, see Nathan Gonzales, "Riverside, Tourism, and the Indian: Frank A. Miller and the Creation of Sherman Institute," *Southern California Quarterly* 84 (Fall/Winter 2002): 209–11.
25. Koegel, "Mexican-American Music in Nineteenth-Century Southern California," 23 n. 44, 25.
26. The collection is *Indian Melodies . . . Harmonized by Thomas Hastings* (New York, 1845); see Chase, *America's Music*, 144.
27. Tara Browner, " 'Breathing the Indian Spirit': Thoughts on Musical Borrowing and the 'Indianist' Movement in American Music," *American Music* 15 (Fall 1997): 265–84; Carol J. Oja, *Making Music Modern: New York in the 1920s* (New York: Oxford University Press, 2000), 167.
28. Arthur Farwell, "*Wanderjahre of a Revolutionist" and Other Essays on American Music*, ed. Thomas Stoner (Rochester, NY: University of Rochester Press, 1995), 104. The article is a reprint of Arthur Farwell, "1904: Charles F. Lummis," *Musical America* 9 (April 24, 1909): 11–12.
29. Evelyn Davis Culbertson, *He Heard America Singing: Arthur Farwell, Composer and Crusading Music Educator* (Metuchen, NJ: The Scarecrow Press, 1992), 115–16; Farwell, "*Wanderjahre of a Revolutionist*," 117; Arthur Farwell, "1904: Composers in San Francisco," *Musical America* 9 (May 1, 1909): 29.
30. Farwell, "*Wanderjahre of a Revolutionist*," 121. The article is a reprint of Arthur Farwell, "1904: Second Trip West," *Musical America* 9 (May 8, 1909): 23, 31.
31. *Folk Songs of the West and South* (Newton Centre, MA: Wa-Wan Press, 1905; reprint, *The Wa-Wan Press, 1901–1911*, ed. Vera Brodsky Lawrence [New York: Arno Press, 1970]); *Spanish Songs of Old California* (Los Angeles: Charles F. Lummis,

1923). See also Koegel, "Mexican-American Music in Nineteenth-Century California," 28–30.

32. Culbertson, *He Heard America Singing*, 203; the exact songs are not listed. The success of these Community Choruses persuaded Farwell to help found the Santa Barbara School of the Arts: ibid., 207.
33. Farwell, "*Wanderjahre of a Revolutionist*," 122. See also Koegel, "Preserving the Sounds of the 'Old' Southwest," 14.
34. Farwell, "*Wanderjahre of a Revolutionist*," 96.
35. Koegel, "Mexican-American Music in Nineteenth-Century California," 28–30.
36. Lummis to Thomas Seymour, February 27, 1904, Lummis Correspondence Series, Lummis Collection.
37. Lummis to Arthur Farwell, February 3, 1905; cited in Koegel's dissertation, "Mexican-American Music in Nineteenth-Century Southern California," 26.
38. U.K. Decca was founded in 1929; U.S. Decca was founded in 1934.
39. John Bentley, "Andrae (Arne) Nordskog" (unpublished manuscript, 1958), Fol. 21–37, Nordskog Collection.
40. Bentley, "Andrae (Arne) Nordskog," p. 2, Fol. 21–37, Nordskog Collection.
41. Nordskog described the concert in a letter to Bond, March 25, 1921, in Fol. 20–1. Nordskog's file on Roland Hayes is in Fol. 20–14, Nordskog Collection.
42. For example, Lynden E. Behymer to Nordskog, October 2, 1920, Fol. 19–36, Nordskog Collection.
43. Nordskog, "The Earliest Musical History," pp. 4–11, Fol. 20–12, Nordskog Collection.
44. Nordskog to Hartwell Webb, November 26, 1921, Fol. 21–29, Nordskog Collection.
45. Andrae Nordskog to Edmund Myer, April 14, 1921, Fol. 20–1, Nordskog Collection. See also Bentley, "Andrae (Arne) Nordskog," p. 2, Fol. 21–37, Nordskog Collection.
46. Nordskog to Los Angeles Chamber of Commerce, November 19, 1921, Fol. 21–29, Nordskog Collection.
47. Bentley, "Andrae (Arne) Nordskog," pp. 4–7, Fol. 21–37, Nordskog Collection.
48. Bentley, "Andrae (Arne) Nordskog," p. 3, Fol. 21–37, Nordskog Collection.
49. Mr. Thornbury, Mr. Newton, Mr. Macomber (of Fogel, Beeman & Macomber), and Mr. Booth. See Fol. 21–38, Nordskog Collection.
50. Mr. Laurance Lamber was president of the California Fruit Juice Company; the other three members were Mr. A. R. Giffin, Mr. E. F. Rybolt, and Mr. F. Bradley Cox. See Fol. 21–38, Nordskog Collection.
51. Santa Monica Chamber of Commerce to Nordskog Phonograph Record Co., Santa Monica, January 26, 1923, Fol. 21–31, Nordskog Collection.
52. Tanguay's signed contract of May 27, 1922 is in Fol. 21–26, Nordskog Collection. Nordskog Records reissued this song in 1951. Bentley, "Andrae (Arne) Nordskog," p. 6, Fol. 21–37, Nordskog Collection.
53. On this movement, see especially Michael B. Bakan, "Way out West on Central: Jazz in the African-American Community of Los Angeles before 1930," *California Soul: Music of African Americans in the West*, ed. Jacqueline Cogdell DjeDje and Eddie S. Meadows (Berkeley and Los Angeles: University of California Press, 1998), 23–78.
54. Lyle Griffin, "The Jazz Scene," *Dig Magazine* (February 1957), Fol. 21–36, Nordskog Collection.

55. Historians of recording technology tend to give Nordskog credit for the recordings: Pekka Gronow and Ilpo Saunio, *An International History of the Recording Industry*, trans. Christopher Moseley (London: Cassell, 1998), 29; and *Encyclopedia of Recorded Sound in the United States*, ed. Guy A. Marco (New York: Garland, 1993), 473. Jazz historians, however, tend to cite only Sunshine Records; see Burton Peretti, *The Creation of Jazz: Music, Race, and Culture in Urban America* (Urbana: University of Illinois Press, 1992), 42; Rick Kennedy and Randy McNutt, *Little Labels—Big Sound: Small Record Companies and the Rise of American Music* (Bloomington: Indiana University Press, 1990), xiv; Bryant, ed., *Central Avenue Sounds*, 11.
56. Bakan, "Way out West on Central," 41.
57. Charles Wakefield Cadman, "The 'Idealization' of Indian Music," *Musical Quarterly* 1 (July 1915): 387–96. See also Lance Bowling, "Charles Wakefield Cadman (1881–1946), Chamber Music," *Charles Wakefield Cadman*, American Classics, Naxos, LC 05537.
58. Nordskog Records List, Cambria.
59. Bentley, "Andrae (Arne) Nordskog," p. 7, Fol. 21–37, Nordskog Collection.
60. Nordskog details these problems in a letter to Santa Monica Branch, Security First National Bank, June 17, 1939, Fol. 21–34, Nordskog Collection.
61. John Ford's *The Iron Horse* was released in 1924; the Hollywood Record Company was located at 6725 Santa Monica Blvd. Lance Bowling, "Music and the Performing Arts in Southern California, 1900–1945: The Crucible of Mass Culture," paper presented at conference on Community and Culture in Los Angeles, La Verne, CA, October 5, 2002.
62. Russell Sanjek and David Sanjek, *Pennies from Heaven: The American Popular Music Business in the Twentieth Century* (New York: Da Capo Press, 1996).
63. Brian Rust, *Jazz Records 1897–1942*, 4th ed., 2 vols. (New Rochelle, NY: Arlington House, 1978).
64. On Stokowski's ventures into recording: Oliver Daniel, *Stokowski: A Counterpoint of View* (New York: Dodd, Mead & Co., 1982), chap. 33.
65. Ibid., 305.
66. Sanjek, *Pennies from Heaven*, 27–28; Lance Bowling, written communication with author, August 1, 2003.
67. On the music scene of Central Avenue, see Bakan, "Way out West on Central," 23–78; Cox, *Central Avenue*; Gary Marmorstein, "Central Avenue Jazz: Los Angeles Black Music of the Forties," *Southern California Quarterly* 70 (Winter 1988): 415–426; and the collection of interviews in Bryant, ed., *Central Avenue Sounds*.
68. Cox, *Central Avenue*, 23–24.
69. Reb's Legion Club Forty Fives, an 8-member group with Lionel Hampton and Les Hite, recorded "My Mammy's Blues" and "Sheffield Blues" on the Hollywood label in November 1924. Reb Spikes Majors and Minors, who numbered at least 11 members, recorded "My Mammy's Blues" and "Fight That Thing" on October 15, 1927 with Columbia. Rust, *Jazz Records*, 2:1485.
70. Bakan, "Way out West on Central," 47.
71. Bakan, "Way out West on Central," 47–48.
72. With the California Poppies Clay recorded "What a Wonderful Time" and "Lou"; a third song, "Mama Like to Do It," was probably rejected. Rust, *Jazz Records*, 1:218; Bakan, "Way out West on Central," 48–49.

73. In May 1925, the Stompin' Six recorded "Jimtown Blues," "Roamin' Around," "Down and Out Blues," and "Creole Blues" with Sunset before recording with Vocalion in 1925, 1926, and 1928. Some of his last recordings were with another group, the Dixie Serenaders, in 1931. See Bakan, "Way out West on Central," 49–50; Rust, *Jazz Records*, 2:1506.
74. Bakan, "Way out West on Central," 49.
75. This is an argument that Ted Gioia takes up in *West Coast Jazz: Modern Jazz in California, 1945–1960* (Berkeley and Los Angeles: University of California Press, 1992), esp. 14–15, 360–69.
76. Cox, *Central Avenue*, 30.
77. Rust, *Jazz Records*, 1:782.
78. Bakan, "Way Out West on Central," 62–63.
79. Cox, *Central Avenue*, 271.
80. Bakan, "Way out West on Central," 61.
81. Cox, *Central Avenue*, 123.
82. Cox, *Central Avenue*, 120.
83. Ralph Eastman, " 'Pitchin' up a Boogie': African-American Musicians, Nightlife, and Music Venues in Los Angeles, 1930–1945," *California Soul: Music of African Americans in the West*, ed. Jacqueline Cogdell DjeDje and Eddie S. Meadows (Berkeley and Los Angeles: University of California Press, 1998), 81.
84. Eastman, " 'Pitchin' up a Boogie,' " 81. Details on this amalgamation are on the Local 47 website, <http://www.promusic47.org/benefits/amalgame.asp>. Accessed on September 3, 2003.
85. Lance Bowling, "Local 47—Working Chronology," Cambria.
86. Lance Bowling, "Local 47—Working Chronology," Cambria.
87. "Our 'Do Patronize' List," *The Overture* [1935?], p. 24, Cambria.
88. Rust, *Jazz Records*, 2:1694 (Herb Wiedoeft's Cinderella Roof Orchestra on August 14, 1923, May 8, 14, 20, 1924, and October 21, 1924; Herb Wiedoeft and His Orchestra, around January 1928), 2:1051 (Vic Meyers and His Orchestra on August 21, 1923, and May 7, 8, 13, 1924). All of the recordings discussed here took place in Los Angeles. Bing Crosby's recording took place on October 18, 1926. Don Clark's Orchestra opened at the Biltmore Hotel on December 26, 1925; see C. L. Bagley, "History of the Band and Orchestra Business in Los Angeles," *The Overture* 6 (April 15, 1926): 4.
89. Rust, *Jazz Records*, 2:1223 (Jack Pettis and His Orchestra on April 21, 1937), 2:1236 (Ben Pollack and His Orchestra on December 18, 1936). A group called The Rhythm Wreckers recorded ten songs for the Vocalion label in 1937. Rust, *Jazz Records*, 2:1299 (March 27, 1937, and June 9, 16, 1937).
90. Rust, *Jazz Records*, 2:997 (Matty Malneck and His Orchestra on July 8, August 21, 1938, March 22, May 24, 1939); 2:1236–37 (Ben Pollack and His Orchestra on August 26, 1937, April 18, 1938; Ben Pollack also recorded with his Pick-A-Rib Boys on September 11, 21, 1937, and April 19, 1938).
91. Rust, *Jazz Records*, 2:1329 (Ginger Rogers with Victor Young and His Orchestra on November 27, 1935; Jimmy Dorsey and His Orchestra on April 13, 1936); 2:1330 (Jimmie Rodgers on June 30, July 10, and July 16, 1930).
92. The Palomar concert took place on August 21, 1935; see Lewis A. Erenberg, *Swingin' the Dream: Big Band Jazz and the Rebirth of American Culture* (Chicago: The University of Chicago Press, 1998), 3–4, 82–83.

93. John Chilton, "Bob Crosby," *The New Grove Dictionary of American Music*, ed. H. Wiley Hitchcock and Stanley Sadie, 4 vols. (London: Macmillan, 1986), 1:547.
94. The Bob Cats recorded six songs on November 13, 1937. The songs he recorded with his brother Bing were "Dolores" and "Pale Moon" on December 23, 1940; "Lazy," "Let's Start the New Year Right," and "I've Got Plenty To Be Thankful For" on May 25, 1942; and "I'll Capture Your Heart," "When My Dream Boat Comes Home," and "Walkin' The Floor Over You" on May 27, 1942. Rust, *Jazz Records*, 1:364–65.
95. Rust, *Jazz Records*, 1:598–99, 601–3, 612, 615–16. Recording dates were between August 13, 1936 and July 3, 1940.
96. On Goodman and Hampton, see Bakan, "Way Out West on Central," 43, 64.
97. Krin Gabbard, *Jammin' at the Margins: Jazz and the American Cinema* (Chicago: The University of Chicago Press, 1996), 19.
98. Bakan, "Way Out West on Central," 60–64.
99. Rust, *Jazz Records*, 1:491, 496, 498–500, 528. Recording dates were from December 21, 1936 to June 26, 1942.
100. Ralph Eastman, " 'Pitchin' up a Boogie,' " 83.
101. Some the films these artists appeared in were as follows: Duke Ellington and His Famous Orchestra: *Black and Tan* (1929), *Check and Double Check* (1930), *Symphony in Black* (1934), *Murder at the Vanities* (1934), *Belle of the Nineties* (1934), *Hit Parade* (1937), *Cabin in the Sky* (1943), *Duke Ellington and His Orchestra* (1943). Benny Goodman and His Orchestra: *Hollywood Hotel* (1937), *The Gang's All Here* (1943), *Sweet and Low Down* (1944). Bob Crosby and His Orchestra: *Holiday Inn* (1942), *Rookies on Parade* (1943), *Thousands Cheer* (1943).
102. Despite the Depression, the pace of building in 1935 was second only to New York, with $28,451,403 in building permits reported for the first eleven months of that year, compared to $127,176,234 in New York; in third place was the nation's capitol, Washington, D.C., with $19,685,603 in building permits reported. "City Second in Building," *Los Angeles Times*, Thursday, January 2, 1936, Part I, p. 1.
103. I have been unable to determine where these albums were recorded, but they were probably a compilation of the label's back catalog, and so would have been recorded at numerous locations.
104. Roland Gelatt, *The Fabulous Phonograph, 1877–1977*, 2nd ed. (New York: Macmillan, 1977), 273.

Chapter 6

1. In 1933, 26.9 percent of radio programming consisted of "classical and semi-classical music." Michele Hilmes, *Hollywood and Broadcasting: From Radio to Cable* (Urbana: University of Illinois Press, 1990), 52. See also Michele Hilmes, *Radio Voices: American Broadcasting, 1922–1952* (Minneapolis: University of Minnesota Press, 1997); Michele Hilmes and Jason Loviglio, eds., *Radio Reader: Essays in the Cultural History of Radio* (New York: Routledge, 2002).
2. Richard Butsch, *The Making of American Audiences: From Stage to Television, 1750–1990* (Cambridge: Cambridge University Press, 2000), 176.
3. Butsch, *The Making of American Audiences*, 175.

4. According to one source, the "Red" and "Blue" networks got their names from drawing on a map of the United States with red and blue pencils to designate planned networks. Erik Barnouw, *A History of Broadcasting in the United States*, 3 vols. (New York: Oxford University Press, 1966–70), 1:191 n. 5. The role of San Francisco I have drawn from Lance Bowling, "Music and the Performing Arts in Southern California, 1900–1945: The Crucible of Mass Culture," paper presented at conference on Community and Culture in Los Angeles, University of La Verne, CA, October 5, 2002.
5. De Forest's father, a Congregationalist minister, led Talladega College for Negroes in Alabama.
6. Barnouw, *History of Broadcasting*, 1:21–23; Alma Overholt, *The Catalina Story* (Catalina Island, CA: Catalina Island Museum Society, 1962), 38.
7. De Forest patented the Audion in 1906. Barnouw, *History of Broadcasting*, 1:25.
8. Quoted in Barnouw, *History of Broadcasting*, 1:25. Early in 1907 he formed the De Forest Radio Telephone Company in New York to develop the Audion further.
9. Bowling, "Music and the Performing Arts in Southern California, 1900–1945." On KDKA, see Barnouw, *History of Broadcasting*, 1:69–74; Oja, *Making Music Modern*, 61.
10. "The Radio Dial: Hour by Hour," *Los Angeles Times*, Monday, July 2, 1928, Part II, p. 10.
11. Nordskog, "The Earliest Musical History," pp. 1–2, Fol. 20–12, Nordskog Collection.
12. Nordskog claims to have received a letter from De Forest, dated June 1943, in which he described where he placed the microphones for this broadcast, in "The Earliest Musical History," pp. 1–2, Fol. 20–12, Nordskog Collection. See also Barnouw, *History of Broadcasting*, 1:25.
13. Nordskog, "The Earliest Musical History," p. 1, Fol. 20–12, Nordskog Collection.
14. Barnouw, *History of Broadcasting*, 2:170.
15. "KHJ Ends Year of Noble Work," *Los Angeles Times*, Saturday, April 14, 1923, Part II, p. 1.
16. "KHJ Ends Year of Noble Work," *Los Angeles Times*, Saturday, April 14, 1923, Part II, p. 1.
17. Butsch, *The Making of American Audiences*, 197.
18. "The Radio Dial: Hour by Hour," *Los Angeles Times*, Monday, December 5, 1927, Part II, p. 3; Monday, July 2, 1928, Part II, p. 10.
19. Philip Goff asserts that Fuller's program in October 1939 "ran on 152 stations, in every state, and across Southern Canada," in "Los Angeles Religious Radio and Modern American Religion: Charles E. Fuller's 'Old Fashioned Revival Hour,' 1933–1968," paper presented to the Los Angeles History Research Group, The Huntington Library, San Marino, CA, January 30, 1999.
20. "The Radio Dial: Hour by Hour," *Los Angeles Times*, Monday, July 2, 1928, Part II, p. 10.
21. Northcutt, *Symphony*, 39.
22. On the New York Philharmonic broadcasts, see John Erskine, *The Philharmonic—Symphony Society of New York* (New York: Macmillan, 1943), 37. For the Boston Symphony Orchestra, see M. A. DeWolfe Howe, *The Boston Symphony Orchestra, 1881–1931* (Boston: Houghton Mifflin, 1931), 166; for the New York Symphony, which began broadcasting on NBC on November 15, 1926, see Margaret Grant and Herman S. Hettinger, *American Symphony Orchestras and How They*

Are Supported (New York: W. W. Norton, 1940), 53. For the San Francisco Symphony and Chicago Symphony Orchestra, see <www.sfsymphony.org> and <www.cso.org>. Accessed on September 17, 2003. The Cleveland Orchestra first aired one-hour radio concerts on WJAX on November 16, 1922, whereas the Chicago Symphony Orchestra began broadcasting on WMAQ on December 10, 1925. On the Cleveland Orchestra, see Donald Rosenberg, *The Cleveland Orchestra Story: "Second to None"* (Cleveland, OH: Gray, 2000), 82.

23. Frances Anne Wister, *Twenty-five Years of the Philadelphia Orchestra, 1900–1925* (Philadelphia, PA: Edward Stern, 1925), 159.
24. Although the San Francisco Symphony went into artistic decline during the early 1930s, it began recording again with RCA-Victor when Pierre Monteux took over the orchestra in 1935, and it continued to record with RCA-Victor until 1958. David Schneider, *San Francisco Symphony: Music, Maestros, and Musicians*, rev. ed. (Novato, CA: Presidio Press, 1983), 34, Appendix M. See also <www.sfsymphony.org>. Accessed on September 17, 2003.
25. *Los Angeles Times*, Friday, December 31, 1937, Part I, p. 8.
26. Nancy Quam-Wickham, " 'Another World': Work, Home, and Autonomy in Blue-Collar Suburbs," in *Metropolis in the Making: Los Angeles in the 1920s*, ed. Tom Sitton and William Deverell (Berkeley and Los Angeles: University of California Press, 2001), 132.
27. The company even had a "Standard Oil float" for the Rose Bowl parade, such as the one in 1936 that featured "a fountain shooting white flower sprays in the air," for the benefit of an estimated crowd of 1,250,000 people. "Vast Throng Awed by Rose Parade's Miles of Color," *Los Angeles Times*, Thursday, January 2, 1936, Part I, pp. 1–2.
28. José Rodriguez, "Ears, Antennas and Sales," in *Music and Dance in California*, ed. José Rodriguez, 167.
29. Northcutt, *Symphony*, 39.
30. John S. Daggett, "Audition Rests in Public's Ear," *Los Angeles Times*, Thursday, October 17, 1929, Part II, p. 9.
31. "The Pacific Coast's Greatest Radio Feature," *Los Angeles Times*, Thursday, October 17, 1929, Part II, p. 9.
32. Horowitz, " 'Sermons in Tones,' " 328.
33. Grant and Hettinger, *American Symphony Orchestras*, 53–54.
34. Grant and Hettinger, *American Symphony Orchestras*, 55.
35. Horowitz, " 'Sermons in Tones,' " 328.
36. "The Pacific Coast's Greatest Radio Feature," *Los Angeles Times*, Thursday, October 17, 1929, Part II, p. 9.
37. The program had similarities to an educational program on CBS, called "The American School of the Air." John Dunning, *On the Air: The Encyclopedia of Old Time Radio* (New York: Oxford University Press, 1998), 634.
38. Radio Broadcast Programs, 1929–1935, LAPA.
39. Horowitz, " 'Sermons in Tones,' " 330. See also Horowitz, *Wagner Nights;* and Horowitz, *Understanding Toscanini*.
40. Horowitz, *Wagner Nights*, chap. 15.
41. Natalie Bowen Ritter, "The Los Angeles Philharmonic Orchestra: An Artistic Survey, 1919–1961" (master's thesis, The Claremont Graduate School, 1974), Appendix E. Percentages have been rounded to the nearest significant figure.
42. "Symphony Drive Open," *Los Angeles Times*, Friday, March 27, 1936, Part I, p. 6.

43. Percy Grainger, "Mock Morris Dance" (broadcast in 1929 and 1934), and "Shepherds Hey" (in 1930); George Chadwick, "Symphonic Sketches: Jubilee—Noel" (in 1929), Edward MacDowell, "Scottish War Poem" (in 1929), Charles Skilton, "War Dance" (in 1929), Charles Wakefield Cadman, "Oriental Rhapsody, Omar Khayyam" (in 1931). Although not an art music composer, Stephen Foster also had one work performed, "Old Folks at Home" (in 1934).
44. Ritter, "The Los Angeles Philharmonic Orchestra," Appendix F.
45. During his tenure from 1924 to 1946, Koussevitsky conducted over 150 American compositions. Hugo Leichtentritt, *Serge Koussevitzky: The Boston Symphony Orchestra and the New American Music* (Cambridge, MA: Harvard University Press, 1946), 151.
46. "The Dial," *Los Angeles Times*, Thursday, January 2, 1936, Part II, p. 12. Édouard Lalo, *Le Roi d'Ys* Overture; Franz Schubert, "Andante con moto" from Symphony No. 7; Georges Bizet, *L'Arlésienne* Suite No. 1; Johann Strauss Jr. "Where the Citrons Bloom" waltz; Victor Herbert, "Irish Rhapsody." Radio Broadcast Program, 1936, LAPA.
47. Deems Taylor, Three Movements from the Suite, *Through the Looking Glass*; Ferde Grofé, "Father of the Waters" from *Mississippi Suite*; Stephen Foster, "My Old Kentucky Home." The concert took place on April 23, 1936. Radio Broadcast Program, 1936, LAPA.
48. "The Dial," *Los Angeles Times*, Thursday, February 13, 1936, Part I, p. 7.
49. Edward MacDowell, Dirge from *Indian* Suite No. 2, Op. 48. Radio Broadcast Program, 1938, LAPA.
50. The manager of KFAC, Cal Smith, opted to go for an all-classical program because he saw it as profitable. Thomas Cassidy, telephone interview with author, Pasadena, CA, May 13, 2003.
51. KECA Concert Program, Vol. 1, No. 8 (May 1936), Cambria. I would like to thank Lance Bowling for bringing these programs to my attention.
52. KECA Concert Programs, 1935–36, Cambria.
53. *Who's Who in California* (Los Angeles: Who's Who Publications, 1941), 1:778–79.
54. Quoted in Starr, *Material Dreams*, 305.
55. KECA Concert Program, Vol. 1, No. 9 (June 1936), Cambria.
56. KECA Concert Program, Vol. 1, No. 9 (June 1936), Cambria. Emphasis in the original.
57. KECA Concert Program, Vol. 1, No. 8 (May 1936), Cambria.
58. *Los Angeles Times*, March 27, 1936, Part I, p. 10; March 13, 1936, Part I, p. 14; March 26, 1936, Part I, p. 18; March 12, 1937, Part I, p. 16; February 8, 1938, Part I, p. 9.
59. KECA Concert Program, Vol. 1, No. 8 (May 1936), Cambria.
60. The new transmitter was located on a ten-acre site at 82nd Street and Compton Avenue in Los Angeles. Concert Program, Vol. 1, No. 11 (August 1936), Cambria.
61. Still was one of six composers commissioned by CBS for works specifically for radio orchestra. Smith, *William Grant Still*, 82, 103, 164, 272 n. 53; Still et al, *William Grant Still*, 32–33.
62. *Los Angeles Times*, Friday, February 14, 1936, Part II, p. 22.
63. KECA Concert Program, Vol. 1, No. 5 (February 1936), Cambria.
64. KECA Concert Program, Vol. 1, No. 7 (April 1936), Cambria.
65. Grant and Hettinger, *American Symphony Orchestras*, 226–28.

66. Grant and Hettinger, *American Symphony Orchestras*, 229.
67. Grant and Hettinger, *American Symphony Orchestras*, 237.
68. Robert Leiter, *The Musicians and Petrillo* (New York: Bookman Associates, 1953), 55.
69. David Morton, *Off the Record: The Technology and Culture of Sound Recording in America* (New Brunswick, NJ: Rutgers University Press, 2000), 50–52. The eventual shift of the recording industry from 78 revolutions per minute (rpm) to 33 1/3 rpm had already taken place with radio broadcast transcriptions as well as synchronizing early sound recordings with talking pictures. Gelatt, *The Fabulous Phonograph*, 253.
70. Leiter, *Musicians and Petrillo*, 57.
71. Anders S. Lunde, "The American Federation of Musicians and the Recording Ban," *Public Opinion Quarterly* 12 (Spring 1948): 49. See also George Seltzer, *Music Matters: The Performer and the American Federation of Musicians* (Metuchen, NJ: The Scarecrow Press, 1989), 46.
72. Leiter, *Musicians and Petrillo*, 166.
73. Lunde points out that "over 400 radio stations are owned and operated by newspapers, which thus have an interest in maintaining the radio industry point of view." Lunde, "The American Federation of Musicians," 56.
74. Lunde, "The American Federation of Musicians," 55; Leiter, *Musicians and Petrillo*, 134; Seltzer, *Music Matters*, 48.
75. Jon Burlingame, *For the Record: The Struggle and Ultimate Political Rise of American Recording Musicians Within Their Labor Movement* (Hollywood: Recording Musicians Association, 1997), 7.
76. Seltzer, *Music Matters*, 48.
77. Seltzer, *Music Matters*, 49. John Anthony Mancini explores this issue further in "Musicians and Technology, 1920–1960s: A Brief History of the American Federation of Musicians" (Ph.D. diss., The Catholic University of America, 1996), 101–5.
78. Seltzer, *Music Matters*, 43; Mancini, "Musicians and Technology," 95–97.
79. Seltzer, *Music Matters*, 54.
80. In addition, the country's three largest locals, New York, Los Angeles, and Chicago, received even more from the fund: $10.43 for the first 5,000 members in good standing, and $2 for each additional member in good standing. Seltzer, *Music Matters*, 44–45.
81. Bowling, "The Evolution of the Recording Industry in Los Angeles, 1896–1950." See also Merrill-Mirsky, *Hollywood Bowl Souvenir Book*, 24.
82. José Rodriguez, "The Western Academic Problem," in *Music and Dance in California*, ed. José Rodriguez, 36.

Chapter 7

1. On the silent era, see Roy Prendergast, *Film Music: A Neglected Art*, 2nd ed. (New York: W. W. Norton, 1992), 6–8; Fred Karlin, *Listening to Movies: The Film Lover's Guide to Film Music* (New York: Schirmer, 1994), 156–60; Royal S. Brown, *Overtones and Undertones: Reading Film Music* (Berkeley and Los Angeles: University of California Press, 1994), 14. See also Kenneth Udy, "The California Years of American Organist Alexander Schreiner," in *Music in Performance and*

Society: Essays in Honor of Roland Jackson, ed. Malcolm Cole and John Koegel (Warren, MI: Harmonie Park Press, 1997), 534–44.

2. *Motion Picture Moods for Pianists and Organists*, arr. Erno Rapée (New York: Schirmer, 1924). Rapée also compiled a more detailed guide, *The Encyclopedia of Music for Pictures* (New York: Belwin, 1925), in which he outlined essential points in playing for motion pictures, such as choosing the musicians, maintaining a music library, and how to perform the music. Copies of both Rapée's *Motion Picture Moods for Pianists and Organists* and Zamecnik's *The Sam Fox Moving Picture Music Volumes* are in MHL.
3. Hazard's Pavilion was razed in 1904. Following the premiere of *The Birth of a Nation*, Temple Auditorium was renamed Clune's Auditorium, after the distributor of the film. It later became the auditorium of the Los Angeles Philharmonic Orchestra. John Northcutt, "Music Halls of Yesterday" (pamphlet, publisher unknown, 1931), California Historical Society Collection, Doheny.
4. Fred Karlin discusses orchestral music of silent films in chap. 8 of *Listening to Movies*; see also Kathryn Kalinak, *Settling the Score: Music and the Classical Hollywood Cinema* (Madison: University of Wisconsin Press, 1992), chap. 3. The final point on Mortimer Wilson I owe to a discussion with Lance Bowling, June 22, 1999.
5. Erno Rapée, *March of the Iron Horse* (New York: Belwin, 1925). Other folk songs in *Echoes From the Iron Horse* are "When Johnny Comes Marching Home Again" and "Old Black Joe." Lance Bowling discussed the film's prologue music in his paper, "Music and the Performing Arts in Southern California."
6. Robert Kimball and William Bolcom, *Reminiscing with Sissle and Blake* (New York: Viking Press, 1973), 138.
7. Warner Brothers produced *Don Juan*, which starred John Barrymore, Mary Astor, and Myrna Loy. William Axt wrote the score. Leslie Halliwell, *Halliwell's Film Guide*, 4th ed. (New York: Charles Scribner's Sons, 1985), 397.
8. William Darby and Jack DuBois, *American Film Music: Major Composers, Techniques, Trends, 1915–1990* (Jefferson, NC: McFarland, 1990), 8–9. See also Gabbard, *Jammin' at the Margins*, chap. 1.
9. Two such films were *The Barker* and *Divine Lady*, to which the orchestra performed works by Victor Herbert. "Carthay Circle Theater," *Pacific Coast Musician* 18 (January 5, 1929): 5; "At Circle Theater," *Pacific Coast Musician* 18 (January 19, 1929): 5; " 'Divine Lady' Premiere at the Circle Theater," *Pacific Coast Musician* 18 (January 26, 1929): 4. Elinor describes some of his personal experiences as arranger and conductor for silent films in "From Nickelodeon to Super-Colossal: The Evolution of Music to Pictures," *The Cue Sheet. The Journal of the Society for the Preservation of Film Music* 11 (October 1995): 5–15.
10. In 1929, theater musicians received a total of almost $1,000,000 per week in wages. Leiter, *Musicians and Petrillo*, 56–57.
11. Steven J. Ross, "How Hollywood Became Hollywood: Money, Politics, and Movies," in *Metropolis in the Making: Los Angeles in the 1920s*, ed. Tom Sitton and William Deverell (Berkeley and Los Angeles: University of California Press, 2001), 255.
12. Twentieth Century-Fox resulted from a merger between Twentieth Century Pictures and Fox Films on May 29, 1935. Aubrey Solomon, *Twentieth Century-Fox: A Corporate and Financial History* (Metuchen, NJ: The Scarecrow Press, 1988), 22.
13. Prendergast, *Film Music*, 35; Tony Thomas, *Music for the Movies*, 2nd ed. (Beverly Hills, CA: Silman-James Press, 1997), 50.

14. Nick Roddick, *A New Deal In Entertainment: Warner Brothers in the 1930s* (London: Nick Roddick, 1983, first published by the British Film Institute, 1983), 12. See also Steven J. Ross, *Working-Class Hollywood: Silent Film and the Shaping of Class in America* (Princeton, NJ: Princeton University Press, 1998).
15. Quoted in Karlin, *Listening to Movies*, 177. On Lange's career, see Lance Bowling, "Arthur Lange: A Biographical Sketch," *The Cue Sheet. The Journal of the Society for the Preservation of Film Music* 7 (December 1990): 128–39.
16. Karlin, *Listening to Movies*, 181, 183.
17. Crawford, *Evenings On and Off the Roof*, 24.
18. Darby and DuBois, *American Film Music*, 69–73.
19. Kalinak, *Settling the Score*, 113.
20. Gary Marmorstein, *Hollywood Rhapsody: Movie Music and Its Makers, 1900 to 1975* (New York: Schirmer Books, 1997), 68; Darby and DuBois, *American Film Music*, 15.
21. Thomas, *Music for the Movies*, 141–44; Marmorstein, *Hollywood Rhapsody*, 69
22. Christopher Palmer, *The Composer in Hollywood* (London: Marion Boyars, 1990), 25–27.
23. Kalinak, *Settling the Score*, 113.
24. Darby and DuBois, *American Film Music*, 18–20.
25. Darby and DuBois, *American Film Music*, 22.
26. Richard B. Jewell with Vernon Harbin, *The RKO Story* (New York: Arlington House, 1982), 56.
27. David Raksin, *David Raksin Remembers His Colleagues: Hollywood Composers* (Palo Alto, CA: The Stanford Theatre Foundation, 1995), 4.
28. Thomas, *Music for the Movies*, 148.
29. Steiner's own version is somewhat different: "I wrote the 3 hours and 45 minutes of original music for *Gone With the Wind* plus the score for another film that supervised the recording of both, all within the space of four weeks." Quoted in Karlin, *Listening to Movies*, 192.
30. Kalinak, *Settling the Score*, 123.
31. Laurence E. MacDonald, *The Invisible Art of Film Music: A Comprehensive History* (New York: Ardsley House, 1998), 53.
32. Darby and DuBois, *American Film Music*, 64.
33. Steiner won Academy Awards for *The Informer* (1935), *Now Voyager* (1942), and *Since You Went Away* (1944).
34. Program, Sundance Institute Concert, UCLA, March 22, 1988, Film Music Programs, MHL. A version on synthesizer of *Charge of the Light Brigade* was the first music viewers heard on the company's home video releases since the 1990s.
35. Frank Robert Ennis, "A Comparison of Style Between Selected Lieder and Film Songs of Erich Wolfgang Korngold" (Ph.D. diss., The University of Texas at Austin, 1999), 6–23.
36. Thomas, *Music for the Movies*, 164–66; Brendan G. Carroll, *The Last Prodigy: A Biography of Erich Wolfgang Korngold* (Portland, OR: Amadeus Press, 1997), 227–28.
37. Erich Wolfgang Korngold, "Some Experiences in Film Music," in *Music and Dance in California*, ed. José Rodriguez, 139; see also Carroll, *The Last Prodigy*, 299.
38. Gloria Ricci Lothrop, "Italians in Los Angeles: An Historical Overview," *Southern California Quarterly* 85 (Fall 2003): 276–77.

39. Friedhofer worked on 15 of the 16 original scores that Korngold wrote. Darby and DuBois, *American Film Music*, 159; Carroll, *The Last Prodigy*, 250–53; Thomas, *Music for the Movies*, 173.
40. Karlin, *Listening to Movies*, 96.
41. Karlin, *Listening to Movies*, 93.
42. Carroll, *The Last Prodigy*, 318–19; Thomas, *Music for the Movies*, 182.
43. Carroll, *The Last Prodigy*, 319.
44. Thomas, *Music for the Movies*, 69.
45. Teresa Chylinska, "Stojowski, Zygmunt [Sigismond] (Denis Antoni)," *Grove Music Online*, ed. L. Macy <http://www.grovemusic.com>. Accessed on December 16, 2003. Newman's piano scholarship was at the von Ende School of Music in New York.
46. Thomas, *Music for the Movies*, 67; Marmorstein, *Hollywood Rhapsody*, 211; Darby and DuBois, *American Film Music*, 76.
47. Darby and DuBois, *American Film Music*, 97–98.
48. Thomas, *Music for the Movies*, 70.
49. One of the animators, Wilfred Jackson, helped Disney with the music and developed an early version of the "click-track" to synchronize the music: "When the metronome was set at 120, there was one beat every 12 frames." David Tietyen, *The Musical World of Walt Disney* (Milwaukee, WI: Hal Leonard, 1990), 13–14.
50. Christopher Finch, *The Art of Walt Disney: From Mickey Mouse to the Magic Kingdom* (New York: Harry N. Abrams, 1995), 39.
51. Disney used a 17-piece orchestra, "and three of the best trap drummers and effect men in town." Carl Edouwarde, theater conductor at the Roxy chain, led the orchestra. Finch, *Art of Walt Disney*, 45.
52. Tietyen, *Musical World*, 15.
53. Finch, *Art of Walt Disney*, 56; Tietyen, *Musical World*, 11; Daniel Goldmark, "Happy Harmonies: Music and the Hollywood Animated Cartoon" (Ph.D. diss., University of California, Los Angeles, 2001), 66–69, 73–76.
54. Ross Care, "Cinesymphony: Music and Animation at the Disney Studio, 1928–42," *Sight and Sound* 46 (Winter 1976–77): 42. I would like to thank David Smith, Head of Walt Disney Archives, for bringing this article to my attention.
55. Finch, *Art of Walt Disney*, 57.
56. Quoted in Tietyen, *Musical World*, 25, from Mike Barrier, Milton Gray, and Bill Spicer, "An Interview with Carl Stalling," *Funnyworld* 13 (Spring 1971): 21–27. See also Care, "Cinesymphony," 42.
57. Tietyen, *Musical World*, 25. The manager of the Carthay Circle Theater was Fred Miller.
58. After *Flowers and Trees*, the pictures which received Academy Awards were *Three Little Pigs* (1933); *The Tortoise and the Hare* (1935); *Three Orphan Kittens* (1935); *Country Cousin* (1936); *The Old Mill* (1937); *Ferdinand the Bull* (1938); *The Ugly Duckling* (1939); *Lend a Paw* (1941); and *Der Fuehrer's Face* (1943). Tietyen, *Musical World*, 27–29.
59. Brown, *Overtones*, 39.
60. Not, as Steven Watts asserts, Tchaikovsky's *1812 Overture*, in *The Magic Kingdom: Walt Disney and the American Way of Life* (Boston: Houghton Mifflin, 1997), 112–13.

61. The composer had an opportunity to see the film in a special screening by Walt Disney in 1942. Merrill-Mirsky, *Exiles in Paradise*, 34.
62. Watts, *Magic Kingdom*, 34–35; Bob Thomas, *Walt Disney, The Art of Animation: The Story of the Disney Studio Contribution to a New Art* (New York: Simon and Schuster, 1958), 78.
63. Watts, *Magic Kingdom*, 65.
64. Finch, *Art of Walt Disney*, 179–80. Finch devotes an entire chapter of his book to this film alone (chap. 6), as does Tietyen, *Musical World*, chap. 4. A definitive account is John Culhane, *Walt Disney's Fantasia* (New York: Abradale Press/Harry N. Abrams, 1983).
65. Tietyen, *Musical World*, 45.
66. Finch, *Art of Walt Disney*, 181.
67. *100 Men and a Girl*, Music Scores Collection, MHL.
68. The plot of *The Big Broadcast of 1937* concerns a radio station manager who has difficulties with sponsors, and features Benny Goodman and His Swing Band among other artists, while Jack Benny, George Burns and Gracie Allen provide the comedy. Among the approximately fifteen popular songs, some are "Talking Through My Hat," "Here's Love In Your Eye," and "La Bomba." This picture formed part of a series of four movies; the earlier *Big Broadcast of 1936* featured the Vienna Boys Choir. *The Big Broadcast of 1937*, Mel Riddle Collection, MHL.
69. After Disney's death in 1966, this television series was renamed "The Wonderful World of Disney."
70. *Fantasia* was re-recorded in 1982 with digitized sound and with a new orchestra, although public outcry demanded a return to the original soundtrack. Culhane, *Walt Disney's Fantasia*, 31. Janet Wasko cites $1 million per year in profits in *Movies and Money: Financing the American Film Industry* (Norwood, NJ: Ablex, 1982), 173.
71. Quoted in Leonard Maltin, *Of Mice and Magic: A History of American Animated Cartoons* (New York: Plume, 1987), 63. See also Culhane, *Walt Disney's Fantasia*, 31–32; Oliver Daniel, *Stokowski: A Counterpoint of View* (New York: Dodd, Mead & Co., 1982), 379–91.
72. Finch, *Art of Walt Disney*, 60.
73. Finch, *Art of Walt Disney*, 85–86; Watts, *Magic Kingdom*, 122–23.
74. Richard Schickel, *The Disney Version: The Life, Times, Art and Commerce of Walt Disney*, 3rd ed. (Chicago: Elephant Paperbacks, 1997), 126–27.
75. Watts, *Magic Kingdom*, 229.
76. Barry Putterman, "A Short Critical History of Warner Bros. Cartoons," in *Reading the Rabbit: Explorations in Warner Bros. Animation*, ed. Kevin S. Sandler (New Brunswick, NJ: Rutgers University Press, 1998), 29.
77. Hank Sartin, "From Vaudeville to Hollywood, from Silence to Sound: Warner Bros. Cartoons of the Early Sound Era," in *Reading the Rabbit*, ed. Kevin S. Sandler, 69. While relying increasingly less on vaudeville as that form of entertainment declined, it still could be the focus of some features. As late as 1957, Warner Brothers released *Show Biz Bugs*, in which Bugs Bunny performs on a vaudeville stage, to the annoyance of his nemesis, Daffy Duck. It may have been "the last hurrah for the traditional Warner Brothers cartoons," but it represented a standard theme since the earliest days of animated films. Putterman, "A Short Critical History," 35.
78. Sartin, "From Vaudeville to Hollywood," 67.

79. Sartin, "From Vaudeville to Hollywood," 73.
80. Putterman, "A Short Critical History," 33, citing *Freleng Frame-By-Frame*, produced and directed by Greg Ford, written by Ronnie Scheib (Donovan Publishing, videocassette, 1994). See also Will Friedwald and Jerry Beck, *The Warner Brothers Cartoons* (Metuchen, NJ: The Scarecrow Press, 1981), 87. See also Goldmark, "Happy Harmonies," 190.
81. Putterman, "A Short Critical History," 33.
82. Kevin Sandler, "Introduction," in *Reading the Rabbit*, ed. Kevin S. Sandler, 7. Sandler cites in turn Joe Adamson, *Bugs Bunny: Fifty Years and Only One Grey Hare* (New York: Henry Holt, 1990), 64.
83. Sartin, "From Vaudeville to Hollywood," 67, quoting Steve Schneider, *That's All Folks! The Art of Warner Bros. Animation* (London: Aurum Press, 1988), 39. The first Merrie Melodie, *Lady, Play Your Mandolin* (1931), featured Latin music, in the setting of a Mexican saloon. In another one, *You Don't Know What You're Doin'*, a lion is conducting a theater orchestra. A pig, aptly named Piggy, picks up his girlfriend Fluffy and proceeds to disturb the performance, a common vaudeville technique. Sartin, "From Vaudeville to Hollywood," 75–77.
84. Friz (Isadore) Freleng supervised *Notes to You*, with animation by Manuel Perez and story by Michael Maltese. See also Friedwald and Beck, *The Warner Brothers Cartoons*, 85.
85. Quoted in Schneider, *That's All Folks!*, 18. See also Goldmark, "Happy Harmonies," 189.
86. *Long-Haired Hare* was released on June 25, 1949. I would like to thank Albert Miller for his comments on this cartoon.
87. On songwriters and Hollywood, see Sanjek, *Pennies From Heaven*, 107–8. On Stravinsky and Disney, see Finch, *Art of Walt Disney*, 189, 193.
88. Quoted in Karlin, *Listening to Movies*, 175.
89. See John Mauceri, "The Music Which Has No Name," *The Cue Sheet. Journal of the Society for the Preservation of Film Music* 12 (April 1996): 6–12.
90. Copland discusses his experiences writing scores for *Of Mice and Men* (1939) and *Our Town* (1940) in Aaron Copland with Vivian Perlis, *Copland, 1900 through 1942* (New York: St. Martin's/Marek, 1984), 297–304.
91. Karlin, *Listening to Movies*, 188.
92. Albert Goldberg, "The Sounding Board," *Los Angeles Times* [n.d.], 1954, Ernest Gold Collection, Scrapbook no. 2, Special Collections, MHL.
93. On Previn in Hollywood, see Helen Drees Ruttencutter, *Previn* (New York: St. Martin's/Marek, 1985), 37–57.
94. David Raksin, interview with author, tape recording, Sherman Oaks, CA, October 16, 1999.
95. The June 1945 concert was with the Los Angeles Philharmonic for the Russian War Relief Fund. Carroll, *The Last Prodigy*, 301.
96. For example, *The Blue Danube* (1939), *The Cat Concerto* (1947), and *Johann Mouse* (1953). MGM closed its animation division in 1958.

Epilogue

1. *The Federal Cylinder Project: A Guide to Field Cylinder Collections in Federal Agencies* (Washington, D.C.: Library of Congress, 1984), 5: v–vi.

2. Dudley C. Gordon, "Charles F. Lummis: Pioneer American Folklorist," *Western Folklore* 28 (July 1969): 181.
3. Levine, *Highbrow/Lowbrow*, 254, 240.
4. José Rodriguez, " 'Classic vs. Popular' a Futile Polemic," in *Music and Dance in California*, ed. José Rodriguez, 82.
5. José Rodriguez, "Music Mostly in the Air: Regarding Southland Broadcasting Activities," in *Who's Who in Music and Dance in Southern California*, ed. Bruno David Ussher, 121.

Bibliography

Archives and Collections

Arts File, Los Angeles, Southern California Library for Social Studies and Research, Los Angeles, Calif.

Lynden E. Behymer Collection, The Huntington Library, San Marino, Calif.

California Historical Society Collection, Doheny Memorial Library, Special Collections, University of Southern California.

George A. Dobinson Collection, Los Angeles Public Library, Los Angeles, Calif.

John Anson Ford Collection, The Huntington Library, San Marino, Calif.

T. Perceval Gerson Papers, The Huntington Library, San Marino, Calif.

T. Perceval Gerson Papers, Special Collections, Charles E. Young Research Library, University of California, Los Angeles.

Ernest Gold Collection, Special Collections, Margaret Herrick Library, Academy of Motion Picture Arts and Sciences, Beverly Hills, Calif.

Hollywood Bowl Collection, Music Center Archives, Los Angeles, Calif.

Hollywood Bowl File, Margaret Herrick Library, Academy of Motion Picture Arts and Sciences, Beverly Hills, Calif.

Hollywood Bowl Summer Popular Concerts Programs, Hollywood Bowl Archives, Calif.

Charles F. Lummis Collection, Southwest Museum Braun Research Library, Los Angeles, Calif.

Music Scores Collection, Margaret Herrick Library, Academy of Motion Picture Arts and Sciences, Beverly Hills, Calif.

Andrae B. Nordskog Collection, Urban Archives Center, California State University, Northridge.

Philharmonic Orchestra of Los Angeles Programs, Los Angeles Philharmonic Archives, Los Angeles, Calif.

Ramona Pageant Association Archives, Hemet, Calif.

Theater Collection, The Huntington Library, San Marino, Calif.

Theater Programs, Cambria Archives, private collection, Lance Bowling, San Pedro, Calif.

Theater Programs, Los Angeles, Seaver Center for Western History Research, Natural History Museum of Los Angeles County, Los Angeles, Calif.

Theater Programs, Special Collections, Honnold/Mudd Library, The Claremont Colleges, Claremont, Calif.

Interviews

Arias, José, Jr. Telephone interview with author. Pasadena, Calif., June 3, 2003. Interview with author. Pasadena, Calif., March 14, 2004.

Behymer, Glenarvon, Jr. Interview with author. Tape recording. Pasadena, Calif., May 25, 1999.

Boorstin, Leni. Interview with author. Tape recording. Los Angeles, Calif., June 21, 2000.

Cassidy, Thomas. Interview with author. Tape recording. Van Nuys, Calif., June 25, 1999. Telephone interview with author. Pasadena, Calif., May 13, 2003.

Kursinski, Robert. Interview with author. Boyle Heights, Calif., January 24, 2003.

Raksin, David. Interview with author. Tape recording. Sherman Oaks, Calif., October 16, 1999.

Papers

Bowling, Lance. "The Evolution of the Recording Industry in Los Angeles, 1896–1950." Paper presented at the Los Angeles Musical Heritage Conference, Biltmore Hotel, Los Angeles, Calif., October 31, 1987.

Bowling, Lance. "Music and the Performing Arts in Southern California, 1900–1945: The Crucible of Mass Culture." Paper presented at conference on Community and Culture in Los Angeles, University of La Verne, Calif., October 5, 2002.

Deverell, William. "Writing the History of Los Angeles." Paper presented at the Haynes Foundation Conference on the History of Los Angeles, The Huntington Library, San Marino, Calif., Fall 2001.

Goff, Philip. "Los Angeles Religious Radio and Modern American Religion: Charles E. Fuller's 'Old Fashioned Revival Hour,' 1933–1968." Paper presented to the Los Angeles History Research Group, The Huntington Library, San Marino, Calif., January 30, 1999.

Macías, Anthony. "From Progressivism to Policing: Youth Culture and Public Space in Postwar Los Angeles." Paper presented to the Los Angeles History Research Group, The Huntington Library, San Marino, Calif., September 21, 2002.

Smith, Catherine Parsons. " 'Our Awe Struck Vision': The Emergence of L.E. Behymer as an Impresario." Paper presented at the fiftieth anniversary of the Music Library Association, Pasadena Public Library, Pasadena, Calif., October 18, 1991.

Wanamaker, Marc. "Southern California Culture and Film, 1908–1930." Paper presented at conference on Community and Culture in Los Angeles, University of La Verne, Calif., October 5, 2002.

Discography

Cadman, Charles Wakefield. *Charles Wakefield Cadman*. Naxos compact disk LC 05537.

Clark, Don, dir., with Bing Crosby and Al Rinker. *I've Got the Girl*. Don Clark Orchestra. Columbia 824-D.

Goossens, Eugene, dir. *Carnival Overture*, by Antonín Dvorák. Los Angeles Philharmonic (Hollywood Bowl Orchestra). Victor 6868A/B.

Mauceri, John, dir. *Hollywood Dreams*. Hollywood Bowl Orchestra. Philips compact disk 432 109–2.

Morris, Margaret Messer and Charles Wakefield Cadman. *Land of the Sky Blue Water*. Nordskog 3028.

Kid Ory's Sunshine Orchestra. *Ory's Creole Trombone*. Nordskog 3009A/B.
Raksin, David, dir. *David Raksin Conducts His Great Film Scores*. BMG Classics 1976.
Slonimsky, Nicolas, dir. *Ionisation*, by Edgard Varèse. Columbia 4095M.
Steeb, Olga. *Rigaudon*, Op. 48/s, by Edward MacDowell. Edison 50980.
Steeb, Olga. *Mazurka in B-flat*, by Frederic Chopin. Edison 51315.
Villa, Rosa and Luisa. *La Serenata*. Lummis Wax Cylinder H26.

Other Published Sources

The Federal Cylinder Project: A Guide to Field Cylinder Collections in Federal Agencies. Washington, D.C.: Library of Congress, 1984.

Los Angeles County Culture and the Community. Los Angeles: Civic Bureau of Music and Art, 1929.

Las Posadas: The Songs of Christmas in Mexico As Sung Each Christmas at the Padua Hills Theatre. Padua Hills, CA: Bess Garner, 1935.

Music Education in the Elementary School. Sacramento: California State Department of Education, 1939.

Negro Who's Who in California. Los Angeles [?]: Negro Who's Who, 1948.

Notables of the Southwest, Being the Portraits and Biographies of Progressive Men of the Southwest. Los Angeles: The Los Angeles Examiner, 1912.

Occupations of the Twelfth Census. United States Bureau of the Census. Washington, D.C., 1904.

The Ramona Pageant: A Pictorial History, 1923–1998. Marceline, MO: Heritage House, 1997.

Southern California Musicians' Directory, 1916–1917, edited by Herman A. Horowitz. Los Angeles: The National Musicians Directory Company, 1916.

Who's Who in California. Los Angeles: Who's Who Publications Company, 1941.

Who's Who in Colored Los Angeles, 1930–31. Los Angeles: California Eagle Publishing, 1931.

Who's Who in Music in California. Los Angeles: Colby and Pryibil, 1920.

Who's Who in the Pacific Southwest: A Compilation of Authentic Biographical Sketches of Citizens of Southern California and Arizona. Los Angeles: The Times-Mirror Printing and Binding House, 1913.

Newspapers and Magazines

California Eagle
The Hemet News
Los Angeles Advertiser
Los Angeles Herald
Los Angeles Times
Los Angeles Times Illustrated Weekly
Musical Review
New York Times
Opinion
The Overture

Pacific Coast Musical Review
Pacific Coast Musician

Secondary Sources

Addams, Jane. *The Spirit of Youth and the City Streets.* New York: Macmillan, 1910.

Adorno, Theodor W. *Essays on Music*, edited by Richard Leppert. Berkeley and Los Angeles: University of California, 2002.

Ahlquist, Karen. *Democracy at the Opera: Music, Theater, and Culture in New York City, 1815–60.* Urbana: University of Illinois Press, 1997.

Allen, Robert C. *Horrible Prettiness: Burlesque and American Culture.* Chapel Hill: University of North Carolina Press, 1991.

Alper, Joshua. "The Cahuenga Pass Treasure." *Southern California Quarterly* 81 (Spring 1999): 89–116.

Arrízon, Alicia. "Contemporizing Performance: Mexican California and the Padua Hills Theater." *Mester* 22 and 23 (Special Double Issue, Chicana/o Discourse, Fall 1993/Spring 1994): 5–30.

Bagley, Charles L. "History of the Band and Orchestra Business in Los Angeles." *The Overture*, October 1, 1921–April 15, 1926.

Bakan, Michael B. "Way out West on Central: Jazz in the African-American Community of Los Angeles before 1930." In *California Soul: Music of African Americans in the West*, edited by Jacqueline Cogdell DjeDje and Eddie S. Meadows, 23–78. Berkeley and Los Angeles: University of California Press, 1998.

Barnouw, Erik. *A History of Broadcasting in the United States.* 3 vols. New York: Oxford University Press, 1966–70.

Barrier, Mike, Milton Gray, and Bill Spicer. "An Interview with Carl Stalling." *Funnyworld* 13 (Spring 1971): 21–27.

Bass, Charlotta. *Forty Years: Memoirs From the Pages of a Newspaper.* Los Angeles: Charlotta Bass, 1960.

Beasley, Delilah. *Negro Trail Blazers of California.* 1919. Reprint, New York: Negro Universities Press [1969].

Behymer, Lynden E. "The Manager's Lot in the Southland. The Eternal Triangle of Artist, Public and Impresario." In *Who's Who in Music and Dance in Southern California*, edited by Bruno David Ussher, 79–80. Hollywood: Bureau of Musical Research, 1933.

Behymer, Menetta S. *Starlit Trails: A Biography of L. E. Behymer, Impresario of the West, 1862–1947.* Oklahoma City, OK: Glen Behymer, 1998.

Blakeslee, Norma Hopland. "History of Padua Hills Theatre." *Pomona Valley Historian* 9 (Spring 1973): 47–68.

Blodgett, Peter J. and Sara Hodson. "Worlds of Leisure, Worlds of Grace: Recreation, Entertainment, and the Arts in the California Experience." *California History* 75 (Spring 1996): 68–83.

Bowie, Patricia Carr. "A Cultural History of Los Angeles, 1850–1967: From Rural Backwash to World Center." Ph.D. diss., University of Southern California, 1980.

Bowling, Lance. "Arthur Lange: A Biographical Sketch." *The Cue Sheet. The Journal of the Society for the Preservation of Film Music* 7 (December 1990): 128–39.

Brigandi, Phil. *Garnet Holme: California's Pageant Master.* Hemet, CA: Ramona Pageant Association, 1991.

——. "The Rancho and the Romance Rancho Camulos: The Home of Ramona." *Ventura County Historical Society Quarterly* 42, nos. 3 and 4 (1998): 5–45.

Brigandi, Phil and John W. Robinson. "The Killing of Juan Diego: From Murder to Mythology." *Journal of San Diego History* 5 (Winter/Spring 1994): 1–22.

Brown, Royal S. *Overtones and Undertones: Reading Film Music.* Berkeley and Los Angeles: University of California Press, 1994.

Browner, Tara. " 'Breathing the Indian Spirit': Thoughts on Musical Borrowing and the 'Indianist' Movement in American Music." *American Music* 15 (Fall 1997): 265–84.

Bryant, Clora, ed. *Central Avenue Sounds: Jazz in Los Angeles.* Berkeley and Los Angeles: University of California Press, 1998.

Buckland, Michael and John Henken, eds. *The Hollywood Bowl: Tales of Summer Nights.* Los Angeles: Balcony Press, 1996.

Burlingame, Jon. *For the Record: The Struggle and Ultimate Political Rise of American Recording Musicians Within Their Labor Movement.* Hollywood: Recording Musicians Association, 1997.

Butsch, Richard. *The Making of American Audiences: From Stage to Television, 1750–1990.* Cambridge, England: Cambridge University Press, 2000.

Cadman, Charles Wakefield. "The 'Idealization' of Indian Music." *Musical Quarterly* 1 (July 1915): 387–96.

Care, Ross. "Cinesymphony: Music and Animation at the Disney Studio, 1928–42." *Sight and Sound* 46 (Winter 1976–77): 40–44.

Carroll, Brendan G. *The Last Prodigy: A Biography of Erich Wolfgang Korngold.* Portland, OR: Amadeus Press, 1997.

Chalmers, Claudine. "Françoise, Lucienne, Rosalie: French Women-Adventurers in the Early Days of the California Gold Rush." *California History* 78 (Fall 1999): 138–53.

Chase, Gilbert. *America's Music: From the Pilgrims to the Present.* 3rd ed. Urbana: University of Illinois Press, 1987.

Copland, Aaron with Vivian Perlis. *Copland, 1900 through 1942.* New York: St. Martin's/Marek, 1984.

Cox, Bette Yarbrough. *Central Avenue—Its Rise and Fall (1890–c.1955), Including the Musical Renaissance of Black Los Angeles.* Los Angeles: BEEM, 1996.

Crawford, Dorothy Lamb. *Evenings On and Off the Roof: Pioneering Concerts in Los Angeles, 1939–1971.* Berkeley and Los Angeles: University of California Press, 1995.

Culbertson, Evelyn Davis. *He Heard America Singing: Arthur Farwell, Composer and Crusading Music Educator.* Metuchen, NJ: The Scarecrow Press, 1992.

Culhane, John. *Walt Disney's Fantasia.* New York: Abradale Press/Harry N. Abrams, 1983.

Damrosch, Walter. *My Musical Life.* New York: Charles Scribner's Sons, 1926.

Daniel, Oliver. *Stokowski: A Counterpoint of View.* New York: Dodd, Mead & Co., 1982.

Darby, William and Jack DuBois. *American Film Music: Major Composers, Techniques, Trends, 1915–1990.* Jefferson, NC: McFarland, 1990.

Davis, Mike. *City of Quartz: Excavating the Future in Los Angeles.* New York: Vintage Books, 1992.

Deuel, Pauline B. *Mexican Serenade: The Story of the Mexican Players and the Padua Hills Theatre.* Padua Hills, Claremont, CA: Padua Institute, 1961.

Deverell, William. "My America or Yours? Americanization and the Battle for the Youth of Los Angeles." In *Metropolis in the Making: Los Angeles in the 1920s*, edited by Tom Sitton and William Deverell, 277–301. Berkeley and Los Angeles: University of California Press, 2001.

——. *Railroad Crossing: Californians and the Railroad, 1850–1910.* Berkeley and Los Angeles: University of California Press, 1994.

——. *Whitewashed Adobe: The Rise of Los Angeles and the Remaking of its Mexican Past.* Berkeley and Los Angeles: University of California Press, 2004.

Deverell, William and Tom Sitton, ed. *California Progressivism Revisited.* Berkeley and Los Angeles: University of California Press, 1994.

DeWolfe Howe, M. A. *The Boston Symphony Orchestra, 1881–1931.* Boston: Houghton Mifflin, 1931.

Dickinson, Thomas H. *The Case of American Drama.* Boston: Houghton Mifflin, 1915.

Dumke, Glenn S. *The Boom of the Eighties in Southern California.* San Marino, CA: The Huntington Library, 1944.

Dunning, John. *On the Air: The Encyclopedia of Old Time Radio.* New York: Oxford University Press, 1998.

Earnest, Sue Wolfer. "An Historical Study of the Growth of the Theatre in Southern California, 1848–1894." 3 vols. Ph.D. diss., University of Southern California, 1947.

Eastman, Ralph. " 'Pitchin' up a Boogie': African-American Musicians, Nightlife, and Music Venues in Los Angeles, 1930–1945." In *California Soul: Music of African Americans in the West*, edited by Jacqueline Cogdell DjeDje and Eddie S. Meadows, 79–103. Berkeley and Los Angeles: University of California Press, 1998.

Elinor, Carli D. "From Nickelodeon to Super-Colossal: The Evolution of Music to Pictures." *The Cue Sheet. The Journal of the Society for the Preservation of Film Music* 11 (October 1995): 5–15.

Elliott-Scheinberg, Wendy. "Boyle Heights: Jewish Ambiance in a Multicultural Neighborhood." Ph.D. diss., Claremont Graduate University, 2001.

Elwood-Akers, Virginia. "George Henry Hewes and the Neighborhood Settlement in Los Angeles." *Southern California Quarterly* 83 (Winter 2001): 377–98.

Emerson, John A. "The Arrival of Edison's Tinfoil Phonograph in San Francisco and the Grand Musical Festival of May, 1878." *Inter-American Music Review* 11 (Spring-Summer 1991): 41–51.

——. "Madame Inez Fabbri, *Prima Donna Assoluta*, and the Performance of Opera in San Francisco during the 1870s." In *Music in Performance and Society: Essays in Honor of Roland Jackson*, edited by Malcolm Cole and John Koegel, 325–54. Warren, MI: Harmonie Park Press, 1997.

Engh, Michael E. "At Home in the Heteropolis: Understanding the Postmodern L.A." *American Historical Review* 105 (December 2000): 1676–82.

——. *Frontier Faiths: Church, Temple, and Synagogue in Los Angeles, 1846–1888.* Albuquerque: University of New Mexico Press, 1992.

Ennis, Frank Robert. "A Comparison of Style Between Selected Lieder and Film Songs of Erich Wolfgang Korngold." Ph.D. diss., The University of Texas at Austin, 1999.

Erenberg, Lewis A. *Swingin' the Dream: Big Band Jazz and the Rebirth of American Culture.* Chicago: The University of Chicago Press, 1998.

Erskine, John. *The Philharmonic—Symphony Society of New York.* New York: Macmillan, 1943.

Ethington, Philip J. "Waiting for the 'L.A. School': A Book Review Essay." *Southern California Quarterly* 80 (Fall 1998): 349–62.

Farwell, Arthur. *"Wanderjahre of a Revolutionist" and Other Essays on American Music*, edited by Thomas Stoner. Rochester, NY: University of Rochester Press, 1995.

Feldman, Eddy S. *The Art of Street Lighting in Los Angeles*. Los Angeles: Dawson's Book Shop, 1972.

Ferrier, William Warren. *Ninety Years of Education in California, 1846–1936: A Presentation of Educational Movements and Their Outcome in Education Today*. Berkeley, CA: Sather Gate Book Shop, 1937.

Finch, Christopher. *The Art of Walt Disney*. New York: Harry N. Abrams, 1995.

Fine, David. *Imagining Los Angeles: A City in Fiction*. Albuquerque: University of New Mexico Press, 2000.

Fiske, Turbesé Lummis and Keith Lummis. *Charles F. Lummis: The Man and His West*. Norman: University of Oklahoma Press, 1975.

Fogelson, Robert M. *The Fragmented Metropolis: Los Angeles, 1850–1930*, 1967. Reprint, with a foreword by Robert Fishman, Berkeley and Los Angeles: University of California Press, 1993.

Friedwald, Will and Jerry Beck. *The Warner Brothers Cartoons*. Metuchen, NJ: The Scarecrow Press, 1981.

Frith, Simon. *Sound Effects: Youth, Leisure, and the Politics of Rock 'n' Roll*. New York: Pantheon Books, 1981.

Gabbard, Krin. *Jammin' at the Margins: Jazz and the American Cinema*. Chicago: The University of Chicago Press, 1996.

Garcia, Matt. " 'Just Put On That Padua Hills Smile': The Mexican Players and the Padua Hills Theatre, 1931–1974." *California History* 74 (Fall 1995): 244–61.

——. *A World Of Its Own: Race, Labor, and Citrus in the Making of Greater Los Angeles, 1900–1970*. Chapel Hill: University of North Carolina Press, 2001.

Gelatt, Roland. *The Fabulous Phonograph, 1877–1977*. 2nd ed. New York: Macmillan, 1977.

Gidel, Henry. *Le vaudeville*. Paris: Presses universitaires de France, 1986.

Gilbert, Douglas. *American Vaudeville: Its Life and Times*. New York: Whittlesey House, 1940.

Gioia, Ted. *West Coast Jazz: Modern Jazz in California, 1945–1960*. Berkeley and Los Angeles: University of California Press, 1992.

Glass, Herbert. "A Home for Opera." In *The Hollywood Bowl: Tales of Summer Nights*, edited by Michael Buckland and John Henken, 60–73. Los Angeles: Balcony Press, 1996.

Glenn, Susan A. " 'Give an Imitation of Me': Vaudeville Mimics and the Play of the Self." *American Quarterly* 50 (March 1998): 47–76.

Goldmark, Daniel. "Happy Harmonies: Music and the Hollywood Animated Cartoon." Ph.D. diss., University of California, Los Angeles, 2001.

Gonzales, Nathan. "Riverside, Tourism, and the Indian: Frank A. Miller and the Creation of Sherman Institute." *Southern California Quarterly* 84 (Fall/Winter 2002): 193–222.

Gordon, Dudley C. "Charles F. Lummis: Pioneer American Folklorist." *Western Folklore* 28 (July 1969): 175–81.

Gottschild, Brenda Dixon. *Waltzing in the Dark: African American Vaudeville and Race Politics in the Swing Era*. New York: St. Martin's Press, 2000.

Grant, Margaret and Herman S. Hettinger. *American Symphony Orchestras and How They Are Supported*. New York: W. W. Norton, 1940.

Graves, J. A. *My Seventy Years in California, 1857–1927.* Los Angeles: Times-Mirror Press, 1927.

Hazen, Margaret Hindle and Robert M. Hazen. *The Music Men: An Illustrated History of Brass Bands in America, 1800–1920.* Washington, D.C.: Smithsonian Institution Press, 1987.

Henken, John. "A Bowl Resounding." In *The Hollywood Bowl: Tales of Summer Nights,* edited by Michael Buckland and John Henken, 8–27. Los Angeles: Balcony Press, 1996.

Heyworth, Peter, ed., *Conversations with Klemperer.* London: Victor Gollancz, 1973.

Hilmes, Michele. *Hollywood and Broadcasting: From Radio to Cable.* Urbana: University of Illinois Press, 1990.

——. *Radio Voices: American Broadcasting, 1922–1952.* Minneapolis: University of Minnesota Press, 1997.

Hilmes, Michele and Jason Loviglio, eds. *Radio Reader: Essays in the Cultural History of Radio.* New York: Routledge, 2002.

Hise, Greg, Michael J. Dear, and H. Eric Schockman. "Rethinking Los Angeles." In *Rethinking Los Angeles,* edited by Greg Hise, Michael J. Dear, and H. Eric Schockman, 1–14. Thousand Oaks, CA: Sage Publications, 1996.

Hise, Greg and William Deverell. *Eden By Design: The 1930 Olmsted-Bartholomew Plan for the Los Angeles Region.* Berkeley and Los Angeles: University of California Press, 2000.

Hoover, Mildred Brooke, Hero Eugene Rensch, and Ethel Grace Rensch. *Historic Spots in California.* Revised by Ruth Teiser with an introduction by Robert Glass Cleland. Stanford, CA: Stanford University Press, 1948.

Horowitz, Joseph. " 'Sermons in Tones': Sacralization as a Theme in American Classical Music," *American Music* 16 (Fall 1998): 311–39.

——. *Understanding Toscanini: A Social History of American Concert Life.* Berkeley and Los Angeles: University of California Press, 1994.

——. *Wagner Nights: An American History.* Berkeley and Los Angeles: University of California Press, 1994.

Jackson, Helen Hunt. *A Century of Dishonor.* Boston: Roberts Bros., 1881.

——. *Ramona: A Story.* Boston: Roberts Bros., 1884.

Jensen, Joan and Gloria Ricci Lothrop. *California Women: A History.* San Francisco: Boyd & Fraser, 1987.

Jewell, Richard B. with Vernon Harbin. *The RKO Story.* New York: Arlington House, 1982.

Jones, Isabel Morse. *Hollywood Bowl.* New York: Schirmer, 1936.

Jones, Jennie L. "Grade School Orchestras: What Los Angeles City Teachers are Doing." In *Who's Who in Music and Dance in Southern California,* edited by Bruno David Ussher, 85–89. Hollywood: Bureau of Musical Research, 1933.

Kalinak, Kathryn. *Settling the Score: Music and the Classical Hollywood Cinema.* Madison: University of Wisconsin Press, 1992.

Kammen, Michael. *Mystic Chords of Memory: The Transformation of Tradition in American Culture.* New York: Alfred A. Knopf, 1991.

Karlin, Fred. *Listening to Movies: The Film Lover's Guide to Film Music.* New York: Schirmer, 1994.

Katz, Mark. "Making America More Musical Through the Phonograph, 1900–1930." *American Music* 16 (Winter 1988): 448–75.

Kennedy, Rick and Randy McNutt. *Little Labels—Big Sound: Small Record Companies and the Rise of American Music.* Bloomington: Indiana University Press, 1990.

Kimball, Robert and William Bolcom. *Reminiscing with Sissle and Blake.* New York: Viking Press, 1973.

Koegel, John. "Calendar of Southern California Amusements 1852–1897 Designed for the Spanish-Speaking Public." *Inter-American Music Review* 13 (Spring-Summer 1993): 115–43.

——. "Mexican-American Music in Nineteenth-Century California: The Lummis Wax Cylinder Collection at the Southwest Museum, Los Angeles." *Revista de Musicología* 16, no. 4 (1993): 26–41.

——. "Mexican-American Music in Nineteenth-Century Southern California: The Lummis Wax Cylinder Collection at the Southwest Museum, Los Angeles." Ph.D. diss., The Claremont Graduate School, 1994.

——. "Preserving the Sounds of the 'Old' Southwest: Charles Lummis and his Cylinder Collection of Mexican-American and Indian Music." ARSC *Journal* 29 (Spring 1998): 1–29.

——. "*Canciones del país*: Mexican Musical Life in California after the Gold Rush." *California History* 78 (Fall 1999): 161–87.

Koopal, Grace. *Miracle of Music: The History of the Hollywood Bowl.* Los Angeles: Charles E. Toberman, 1972.

Korngold, Erich Wolfgang. "Some Experiences in Film Music." In *Music and Dance in California*, edited by José Rodriguez, 137–39. Hollywood: Bureau of Musical Research, 1940.

Kurashige, Lon. *Japanese American Celebration and Conflict: A History of Ethnic Identity and Festival, 1934–1990.* Berkeley and Los Angeles: University of California Press, 2002.

Laslett, John. "Historical Perspectives: Immigration and the Rise of a Distinctive Urban Region, 1900–1970." In *Ethnic Los Angeles*, edited by Robert Waldinger and Mehdi Bozorghmehr, 39–75. New York: Russell Sage Foundation, 1996.

Lavender, David. *Los Angeles Two Hundred: A Pictorial and Entertaining Commentary on the Growth and Development of Los Angeles, California.* Tulsa, OK: Continental Heritage Press, 1980.

Leichtentritt, Hugo. *Serge Koussevitzky: The Boston Symphony Orchestra and the New American Music.* Cambridge, MA: Harvard University Press, 1946.

Leiter, Robert D. *The Musicians and Petrillo.* New York: Bookman Associates, 1953.

Levant, Oscar. *A Smattering of Ignorance.* Garden City, NY: Garden City Publishing, 1942.

Levine, Lawrence. *Highbrow/Lowbrow: The Emergence of Cultural Hierarchy in America.* Cambridge, MA: Harvard University Press, 1988.

——. *Unpredictable Past: Explorations in American Cultural History.* New York: Oxford University Press, 1993.

Longstreth, Richard. *City Center to Regional Mall: Architecture, the Automobile, and Retailing in Los Angeles, 1920–1950.* Cambridge, MA: MIT Press, 1997.

Lothrop, Gloria Ricci. "The Boom of the '80s Revisited." *Southern California Quarterly* 75 (Fall/Winter 1993): 263–301.

——. "Italians in Los Angeles: An Historical Overview," *Southern California Quarterly* 85 (Fall 2003): 249–300.

——. "Nurturing Society's Children." *California History* 65 (December 1986): 274–83.

Lummis, Charles F. *The Home of Ramona: Photographs of Camulos, the fine old Spanish Estate described by Mrs. Helen Hunt Jackson, as the Home of "Ramona."* Los Angeles: Charles F. Lummis, 1888.

——. *The Southwest Society of the Archaeological Institute of America: The Southwest Museum, Three Years of Success*. Third Bulletin. Los Angeles, CA, May 1, 1907.

——. *Spanish Songs of Old California*. Collected and translated by Charles F. Lummis, with pianoforte accompaniments by Arthur Farwell. Los Angeles: Charles F. Lummis, 1923.

Lunde, Anders S. "The American Federation of Musicians and the Recording Ban." *Public Opinion Quarterly* 12 (Spring 1948): 45–56.

MacDonald, Laurence E. *The Invisible Art of Film Music: A Comprehensive History*. New York: Ardsley House, 1998.

MacKaye, Percy. *Caliban, by the Yellow Sands*. Garden City, NY: Doubleday, Page & Company, 1916.

——. *Community Drama: Its Motive and Method of Neighborliness*. Boston: Houghton Mifflin, 1917.

——. *The Playhouse and the Play*. New York: Macmillan, 1909.

Maltin, Leonard. *Of Mice and Magic: A History of American Animated Cartoons*. New York: Plume, 1987.

Mancini, John Anthony. "Musicians and Technology, 1920–1960s: A Brief History of the American Federation of Musicians." Ph.D. diss., The Catholic University of America, 1996.

Marchand, Bernard. *The Emergence of Los Angeles: Population and Housing in the City of Dreams, 1940–1970*. London: Pion, 1986.

Marmorstein, Gary. "Central Avenue Jazz: Los Angeles Black Music of the Forties." *Southern California Quarterly* 70 (Winter 1988): 415–26.

——. *Hollywood Rhapsody: Movie Music and Its Makers, 1900 to 1975*. New York: Schirmer Books, 1997.

McCalmon, George and Christian Moe. *Creating Historical Drama*. Carbondale: Southern Illinois University Press, 1965.

McCarthy, Kathleen D. *Women's Culture: American Philanthropy and Art, 1830–1930*. Chicago: The University of Chicago Press, 1991.

McGroarty, John Steven. *California—Its History and Romance*. Los Angeles: Grafton Publishing Co., 1911.

——. *History of Los Angeles County*. 3 vols. Chicago: American Historical Society, 1923.

——. *Los Angeles From the Mountains to the Sea*. 3 vols. Chicago: American Historical Society, 1921.

McWilliams, Carey. "Culture and the Community." *Opinion* 1 (October 1929): 9–10.

——. *Southern California Country: An Island on the Land*. Freeport, NY: Duell, Sloan & Pearce, 1946.

Merrill-Mirsky, Carol, ed. *Exiles in Paradise*. Los Angeles: Hollywood Bowl Museum, 1991.

——. *Hollywood Bowl Souvenir Book*. Los Angeles: Los Angeles Philharmonic Association, 2000.

Metzger, Alfred. "Symphony Orchestra is Leading Organization." *Musical Review* 9 (June 1906): 13–17.

Mitchell, Lisa. "Hollywood and the Bowl." In *The Hollywood Bowl: Tales of Summer Nights*, edited by Michael Buckland and John Henken, 74–89. Los Angeles: Balcony Press, 1996.

Morton, David. *Off the Record: The Technology and Culture of Sound Recording in America*. New Brunswick, NJ: Rutgers University Press, 2000.

Muir, Gladdys Esther. "The Founding of La Verne College." *Pomona Valley Historian* 6 (July 1970): 93–109.

Mussulman, Joseph A. *Music in the Cultured Generation: A Social History of Music in America, 1870–1900.* Evanston, IL: Northwestern University Press, 1971.

Nasaw, David. *Going Out: The Rise and Fall of Public Amusements.* Cambridge, MA: Harvard University Press, 1993.

Neumeyer, David. "Melodrama as a Compositional Resource in Early Hollywood Sound Cinema." *Current Musicology* 57 (1995): 61–94.

Newmark, Harris. *Sixty Years in Southern California, 1853–1913,* edited by Maurice H. Newmark and Mare R. Newmark, 3rd ed. Boston: Houghton Mifflin, 1930.

Northcutt, John Orlando. *The Hollywood Bowl Story.* Hollywood: Hollywood Bowl Association, 1962.

——. *Magic Valley: The Story of the Hollywood Bowl.* Los Angeles: Fashion Press, 1967.

——. *Symphony: The Story of the Los Angeles Philharmonic Orchestra.* Los Angeles: Southern California Symphony Association, 1963.

Oja, Carol J. *Making Music Modern: New York in the 1920s.* New York: Oxford University Press, 2000.

——. "Dane Rudhyar's Vision of American Dissonance." *American Music* 17 (Summer 1998): 129–37.

Overholt, Alma. *The Catalina Story.* Catalina Island, CA: Catalina Island Museum Society, 1962.

Peiss, Kathy. *Cheap Amusements: Working Women and Leisure in Turn-of-the Century New York.* Philadelphia: Temple University Press, 1986.

Peretti, Burton W. *The Creation of Jazz: Music, Race, and Culture in Urban America.* Urbana: University of Illinois Press, 1992.

Pomeroy, Earl. "From War Profits to Peace Profits." In *Los Angeles: Biography of a City,* edited by John and LaRee Caughey, 393–96. Berkeley and Los Angeles: University of California Press, 1977.

——. *The Pacific Slope: A History of California, Oregon, Washington, Idaho, Utah, and Nevada.* New York: Alfred A. Knopf, 1965.

Prendergast, Roy. *Film Music: A Neglected Art.* 2nd ed. New York: W. W. Norton, 1992. Also published as *A Neglected Art: A Critical Study of Music in Films.* New York: New York University Press, 1977.

Preston, Katherine K. *Opera on the Road: Traveling Opera Troupes in the United States, 1825–60.* Urbana: University of Illinois Press, 1993.

Prevots, Naima. *American Pageantry: A Movement for Art and Democracy.* Ann Arbor: University of Michigan Press, 1990.

——. "How the Bowl Danced: An Era of Exploration." In *The Hollywood Bowl: Tales of Summer Nights,* edited by Michael Buckland and John Henken, 46–59. Los Angeles: Balcony Press, 1996.

Price, Catherine. *The Oglala People, 1841–1879: A Political History.* Lincoln: University of Nebraska Press, 1996.

Pullen, William Augustus. "The Ramona Pageant: An Historical and Analytical Study." Master's thesis, University of Southern California, 1973.

Putnam, Robert. *Bowling Alone: The Collapse and Revival of American Community.* New York: Simon & Schuster, 2000.

Putterman, Barry. "A Short Critical History of Warner Bros. Cartoons." In *Reading the Rabbit: Explorations in Warner Bros. Animation,* edited by Kevin S. Sandler, 29–37. New Brunswick, NJ: Rutgers University Press, 1998.

Quam-Wickham, Nancy. " 'Another World': Work, Home, and Autonomy in Blue-Collar Suburbs." In *Metropolis in the Making: Los Angeles in the 1920s*, edited by Tom Sitton and William Deverell, 123–41. Berkeley and Los Angeles: University of California Press, 2001.

Raftery, Judith. *Land of Fair Promise: Politics and Reform in Los Angeles Schools, 1885–1941*. Stanford, CA: Stanford University Press, 1992.

——. "Los Angeles Clubwomen and Progressive Reform." In *California Progressivism Revisited*, edited by William Deverell and Tom Sitton, 144–74. Berkeley and Los Angeles: University of California Press, 1994.

Raksin, David. *David Raksin Remembers His Colleagues: Hollywood Composers*. Palo Alto, CA: The Stanford Theatre Foundation, 1995.

Rapée, Erno, ed. *The Encyclopedia of Music for Pictures*. New York: Belwin, 1925.

——, arr. *Motion Picture Moods for Pianists and Organists*. New York: Schirmer, 1924.

Rawls, James J. and Walton Bean. *California: An Interpretive History*. 12th ed. Boston: McGraw Hill, 1998.

Reese, Carol McMichael. "Architecture for Performance." In *The Hollywood Bowl: Tales of Summer Nights*, edited by Michael Buckland and John Henken, 28–45. Los Angeles: Balcony Press, 1996.

Ritter, Natalie Bowen. "The Los Angeles Philharmonic Orchestra: An Artistic Survey, 1919–1961." Master's thesis, The Claremont Graduate School, 1974.

Rodriguez, José. " 'Classic vs. Popular' a Futile Polemic." In *Music and Dance in California*, edited by José Rodriguez, 78–84. Hollywood: Bureau of Musical Research, 1940.

——. "Ears, Antennas and Sales." In *Music and Dance in California*, edited by José Rodriguez, 165–69. Hollywood: Bureau of Musical Research, 1940.

——. "Music Mostly in the Air: Regarding Southland Broadcasting Activities." In *Who's Who in Music and Dance in Southern California*, edited by Bruno David Ussher, 120–21. Hollywood: Bureau of Musical Research, 1933.

——. "The Western Academic Problem." In *Music and Dance in California*, edited by José Rodriguez, 29–37. Hollywood: Bureau of Musical Research, 1940.

Rolle, Andrew. *Los Angeles: From Pueblo to City of the Future*. 2nd ed. San Francisco: MTL, 1995.

Rosenberg, Donald. *The Cleveland Orchestra Story: "Second to None."* Cleveland, OH: Gray, 2000.

Ross, Joseph E. *Krotona of Old Hollywood, 1866–1913*. Montecito, CA: El Montecito Oaks Press, 1989.

Ross, Steven J. "How Hollywood Became Hollywood: Money, Politics, and Movies." In *Metropolis in the Making: Los Angeles in the 1920s*, edited by Tom Sitton and William Deverell, 255–76. Berkeley and Los Angeles: University of California Press, 2001.

——. *Working-Class Hollywood: Silent Film and the Shaping of Class in America*. Princeton, NJ: Princeton University Press, 1998.

Rubinstein, Anton. *My Many Years*. New York: Alfred A. Knopf, 1980.

Rust, Brian. *Jazz Records 1897–1942*. 4th ed. 2 vols. New Rochelle, NY: Arlington House, 1978.

Ruttencutter, Helen Drees. *Previn*. New York: St. Martin's/Marek, 1985.

Sanjek, Russell and David Sanjek. *Pennies from Heaven: The American Popular Music Business in the Twentieth Century*. New York: Da Capo Press, 1996.

Sartin, Hank. "From Vaudeville to Hollywood, from Silence to Sound: Warner Bros. Cartoons of the Early Sound Era." In *Reading the Rabbit: Explorations in Warner*

Bros. Animation, edited by Kevin S. Sandler, 67–85. New Brunswick, NJ: Rutgers University Press, 1998.

Schickel, Richard. *The Disney Version: The Life, Times, Art and Commerce of Walt Disney*. 3rd ed. Chicago: Elephant Paperbacks, 1997.

Schneider, David. *The San Francisco Symphony: Music, Maestros, and Musicians*. Rev. ed. Novato, CA: Presidio Press, 1987.

Schneider, Steve. *That's All Folks! The Art of Warner Bros. Animation*. London: Aurum Press, 1988.

Schockman, H. Eric. "Is Los Angeles Governable?" In *Rethinking Los Angeles*, edited by Greg Hise, Michael J. Dear, and H. Eric Schockman, 57–75. Thousand Oaks, CA: Sage Publications, 1996.

Seeger, Anthony and Louise Spear, eds. *Early Field Recordings*. Bloomington: Indiana University Press, 1987.

Seltzer, George. *Music Matters: The Performer and the American Federation of Musicians*. Metuchen, NJ: The Scarecrow Press, 1989.

Sitton, Tom. *John Randolph Haynes: California Progressive*. Stanford, CA: Stanford University Press, 1992.

Sitton, Tom and William Deverell, eds. *Metropolis in the Making: Los Angeles in the 1920s*. Berkeley and Los Angeles: University of California Press, 2001.

Slonimsky, Nicolas. *Baker's Biographical Dictionary of Musicians*. 8th ed. New York: Schirmer, 1992.

Smith, Caroline Estes. *The Philharmonic Orchestra of Los Angeles: "The First Decade" 1919–1929*. Los Angeles: Caroline Estes Smith, 1930.

Smith, Catherine Parsons. "Founding the Hollywood Bowl." *American Music* 11 (Summer 1993): 206–42.

——. "Inventing Tradition: Symphony and Opera in Progressive-Era Los Angeles." In *Music and Culture in America, 1861–1918*, edited by Michael Saffle, 299–321. New York: Garland, 1998.

——. "Of Pageantry and Politics." *American Quarterly* 44 (March 1992): 115–22.

——. " 'Popular Prices Will Prevail': Setting the Social Role of European-based Concert Music." In *Musical Aesthetics and Multiculturalism in Los Angeles*, edited by Steven Loza, 207–21. Selected Reports in Ethnomusicology, vol. 10. Los Angeles: Regents of the University of California, 1994.

——. " 'Something of Good for the Future': The People's Orchestra of Los Angeles." *Nineteenth-Century Music* 16 (Fall 1992): 146–60.

Smith, Catherine Parsons, with contributed essays by Gayle Murchison and Willard B. Gatewood. *William Grant Still: A Study in Contradictions*. Berkeley and Los Angeles: University of California Press, 2000.

Smith, Catherine Parsons and Cynthia S. Richardson. *Mary Carr Moore, American Composer*. Ann Arbor: University of Michigan Press, 1987.

Smith, Dave. *Disney A to Z: The Updated Official Encyclopedia*. New York: Hyperion, 1998.

Solomon, Aubrey. *Twentieth Century-Fox: A Corporate and Financial History*. Metuchen, NJ: The Scarecrow Press, 1988.

Sonenshein, Raphael. *Politics in Black and White: Race and Power in Los Angeles*. Princeton, NJ: Princeton University Press, 1993.

Southern, Eileen. *The Music of Black Americans: A History*. 2nd ed. New York: W. W. Norton, 1983.

Splitter, Henry Winfred. "Music in Los Angeles." *The Historical Society of Southern California Quarterly* 38 (December 1956): 307–44.

Splitter, Henry Winfred. "Education in Los Angeles, 1850 to 1900 (Part I)." *The Historical Society of Southern California Quarterly* 33 (June 1951): 101–18.

——. "Education in Los Angeles, 1850 to 1900 (Part II)." *The Historical Society of Southern California Quarterly* 33 (September 1951): 226–44.

Spottswood, Richard K. *Ethnic Music on Records: A Discography of Ethnic Recordings Produced in the United States, 1893 to 1942.* 7 vols. Urbana: University of Illinois Press, 1990.

Starr, Kevin. *Inventing the Dream: California Through the Progressive Era.* New York: Oxford University Press, 1985.

——. *Material Dreams: Southern California Through the 1920s.* New York: Oxford University Press, 1990.

Stevenson, Robert. "Carreño's 1875 California Appearances." *Inter-American Music Review* 10 (Spring-Summer 1983): 9–15.

——. "Local Music History Research in Los Angeles Area Libraries, Part I." *Inter-American Review* 10 (Fall-Winter 1988): 19–38.

——. "Music in Southern California: A Tale of Two Cities." *Inter-American Music Review* 10 (Fall-Winter 1988): 39–111.

——. "William Andrews Clark, Jr., Founder of the Los Angeles Philharmonic Orchestra." In *William Andrews Clark, Jr.: His Cultural Legacy. Papers read at a Clark Library Seminar, 7 November 1981, by William E. Conway, Robert Stevenson,* 31–52. UCLA: William Andrews Clark Memorial Library, 1985.

Still, Judith Anne, Michael J. Dabrishus, and Carolyn L. Quin. *William Grant Still: A Bio-Bibliography.* Westport, CT: Greenwood Press, 1996.

Stimson, Marshall. "History of Los Angeles High School." *Historical Society of Southern California Quarterly* 24 (September 1942): 98–109.

Stricker, Thomas Perry. *The Hollywood Bowl.* Los Angeles: Pepper Tree Press, 1939.

Swan, Howard. *Music in the Southwest, 1825–1950*, 1952. Reprint, Da Capo Press, 1977.

Taylor, John Russell. *Strangers in Paradise: The Hollywood Emigrés, 1933–1950.* New York: Faber and Faber, 1983.

Thomas, Bob. *Walt Disney, The Art of Animation: The Story of the Disney Studio Contribution to a New Art.* New York: Simon and Schuster, 1958.

Thomas, Tony. *Music for the Movies.* 2nd ed. Los Angeles: Silman-James Press, 1997.

Tietyen, David. *The Musical World of Walt Disney.* Milwaukee, WI: Hal Leonard, 1990.

Toll, Robert C. *On With the Show! The First Century of Show Business in America.* New York: Oxford University Press, 1976.

Traubner, Richard. *Operetta: A Theatrical History.* Garden City, NY: Doubleday, 1983.

Udy, Kenneth. "The California Years of American Organist Alexander Schreiner." In *Music in Performance and Society: Essays in Honor of Roland Jackson*, edited by Malcolm Cole and John Koegel, 531–87. Warren, MI: Harmonie Park Press, 1997.

Waldinger, Robert and Mehdi Bozorgmehr. *Ethnic Los Angeles.* New York: Russell Sage Foundation, 1996.

Wasko, Janet. *Movies and Money: Financing the American Film Industry.* Norwood, NJ: Ablex, 1982.

Watts, Steven. *The Magic Kingdom: Walt Disney and the American Way of Life.* Boston: Houghton Mifflin, 1997.

Weber, Francis J. *Memories of an Old Mission: San Fernando, Rey de España.* Mission Hills, CA: Saint Francis Historical Society, 1997.

Welch, Walter L. and Leah B. Stenzel Burt. *From Tinfoil to Stereo: The Acoustic Years of the Recording Industry, 1877–1929.* Gainesville: University of Florida, 1994.

Westphal, Ruth Lilly, ed. *Plein Air Painters of California: The Southland.* Irvine, CA: Westphal, 1982.

Wister, Frances Anne. *Twenty-five Years of the Philadelphia Orchestra, 1900–1925.* Philadelphia: Edward Stern, 1925.

Withington, Robert. *English Pageantry: An Historical Outline.* 2 vols. Cambridge, MA: Harvard University Press, 1918.

Woods, Gerald. "A Penchant for Probity: California Progressives and the Disreputable Pleasures." In *California Progressivism Revisited,* edited by William Deverell and Tom Sitton, 99–113. Berkeley and Los Angeles: University of California Press.

Yaari, Moshe. "The Merced Theater." *Historical Society of Southern California Quarterly* 37 (September 1955): 195–210.

Yu, Henry. *Thinking Orientals: Migration, Contact, and Exoticism in Modern America.* New York: Oxford University Press, 2001.

Appendix

Southern Californian Committees of the California-Western School Music Conference, 1935–37. Conference President: Mary E. Ireland, Supervisor of Music, Sacramento Public Schools

Committee on the Development of Vocal Music:
Chairperson: Louis Woodson Curtis, Supervisor of Music in Los Angeles Public Schools
Elsa B. Brenneman, Supervisor of Music, Glendale Public Schools
Jesse J. Coleman, Instructor in Public School Music, Pomona College
Helen Dill, Supervisor of Training, Department of Music, University of California at Los Angeles
Ruth M. Phillips, Supervisor of Music, Santa Barbara County
Paloma P. Prouty, Supervisor of Music, Riverside County
Helen Purcell, Hamilton Junior High School, Long Beach Public Schools
Alice Rogers, Supervisor of Music, Santa Monica Public Schools
Alfred H. Smith, Supervisor of Music, San Diego Public Schools
Julia E. Warren, Assistant Supervisor of Music, Los Angeles Public Schools
Frances Wright, Associate Professor of Music, University of California at Los Angeles

Committee on Music as an Integrative Experience:
Chairperson: Gertrude Fisher, Supervisor of Music, Long Beach Public Schools
Helen Baughton, Supervisor of Music, Burbank Public Schools
Lillian Mohr Fox, Supervisor of Elementary Music Education, Pasadena Public Schools
Laverna Lossing, Supervisor of Training, Department of Music, University of California at Los Angeles
Jessie Marker, Assistant Supervisor of Music, Los Angeles Public Schools
Amy McKee, Supervisor of Music, Ventura County
Lucille Ross, Supervisor of Music, San Diego County
Mae Knight Siddell, Special Music Teacher, Santa Monica Public Schools
Isobel Smith, Teacher of Music, Charles W. Eliot Junior High School, Pasadena Public Schools
Mabel S. Spizzy, Supervisor of Music, Orange County
Ernestine Spurgin, Supervisor of Music, San Bernardino County

Source: *Music Education in the Elementary School* (Sacramento: California State Department of Education, 1939), chaps. 2–3.

Abbreviations

Behymer Collection
Lynden E. Behymer Collection, The Huntington Library, San Marino, Calif.

Cambria
Cambria Archives, private collection, Lance Bowling, San Pedro, Calif.

Dobinson Collection
George A. Dobinson Collection, Los Angeles Public Library

Doheny
Special Collections, Doheny Memorial Library, University of Southern California

Ford Collection
John Anson Ford Collection, The Huntington Library, San Marino, Calif.

Gerson Papers/HL
T. Perceval Gerson Papers, The Huntington Library, San Marino, Calif.

Gerson Papers/YRL
T. Perceval Gerson Papers, Special Collections, Charles E. Young Research Library, University of California, Los Angeles

HBA
Hollywood Bowl Archives, Hollywood, Calif.

HL
The Huntington Library, San Marino Calif.

Honnold
Special Collections, Honnold/Mudd Library, The Claremont Colleges, Claremont, Calif.

LAPA
Los Angeles Philharmonic Archives, Los Angeles, Calif.

Lummis Collection
Charles F. Lummis Collection, Southwest Museum Braun Research Library, Los Angeles, Calif.

MCA
Music Center Archives, Los Angeles, Calif.

MHL
Margaret Herrick Library, Academy of Motion Picture Arts and Sciences, Beverly Hills, Calif.

Nordskog Collection
Andrae B. Nordskog Collection, Urban Archives Center, California State University, Northridge

PHC/PPL
Padua Hills Theatre Collection, Special Collections, Pomona Public Library, Pomona, Calif.

RPA
Ramona Pageant Association Archives, Hemet, Calif.

Seaver
Seaver Center for Western History Research, Natural History Museum of Los Angeles County, Los Angeles, Calif.

SCL
Southern California Library for Social Studies and Research, Los Angeles, Calif.

YRL
Charles E. Young Research Library, University of California, Los Angeles

Index